THE offers ... answers to those intimate questions we never have the nerve to ask.

Perversion, frigidity, incest, suicide— these and similar topics are treated with frankness and candor.

Here is a unique opportunity for the average person—in the privacy of his own living room—to share the wisdom and insights of America's leading authorities on subjects that are all too often taboo.

THE WHY REPORT
was originally published by
Arthur Bernhard, Inc.,
Purchase, N.Y. 10577, from whom the
hard-bound edition may be
purchased at $9.95.

Other books by Lucy Freeman

"Before I Kill More . . ."

Hope for the Troubled

The Story of Psychoanalysis (with Marvin H. Small)

Published by Pocket Books, Inc.

 Are there paperbound books you want but cannot find in your retail stores?

THE WHY REPORT

*Edited by Lucy Freeman
and Martin Theodores*

A BOOK OF 45 INTERVIEWS WITH
PSYCHIATRISTS, PSYCHOANALYSTS,
AND PSYCHOLOGISTS

A POCKET CARDINAL® EDITION published by
POCKET BOOKS, INC. • NEW YORK

THE WHY REPORT

Arthur Bernhard edition published July, 1964

A Pocket *Cardinal* edition

1st printing.............December, 1965

We Wish To Thank:

CHARLES H. BROWN
> for his painstaking and excellent editorial suggestions and copy-editing.

IRENE M. HADEISHI
> of Sansom Reporting, Inc., a court transcribing service, for her efficient and accurate reporting and transcribing of the interviews.

ROBERT INGRAM
> of Typing Pool, Inc., for his fine workmanship in transcribing from tape recordings of the interviews.

PHYLLIS SANDERS
> for her efficient stenographic services.

JOSEPHINE RUTHERFORD
> of Temporary Office Service, Inc., for supplying us with the following stenographers and typists:
>> ALICE BEINS
>> HELEN FEIL
>> SELMA FERBIN
>> DONALD MARLATT
>> MARY RICHARDS
>> MAXINE ROTH
>> ROSALINE STONE
>> GERTRUDE STONE

ESTHER TRAVERS
> for her valuable editorial suggestions and typing services.

LILLIAN LEWIS
> for her stenographic services.

JOAN BERNHARD
> for helping wherever needed, in all of the aspects of this work.

Come, come, and sit you down; You shall not budge;
You go not till I set you up a glass
Where you may see the inmost part of you.

—Shakespeare, *Hamlet*
Act III, Scene 4

Preface

IN THIS WORLD OF WAR, cold and hot, man today is faced with his very survival. At long last the time has come when, if nations fight each other, it is no longer jungle warfare, where the warriors kill only each other, but the very obliteration of civilization that is at stake. It does little good, ostrich-like, to minimize the terror of a situation where a push of a button can destroy us all.

But there is a way out, if we are able to take it. War is the sum total of the aggression of many men. If many men can face the aggression in their hearts, understand it, learn how to cope with it instead of ascribing it to other men, they may have peace.

When man understands his own aggression, he can then bestow some of his love of self on others. As Freud wrote to Romain Rolland: "I myself have always advocated the love for mankind not out of sentimentality or idealism . . . because in the face of our instinctual drives and the world as it is I was compelled to consider this love as indispensable for the preservation of the human species, as, say technology."

The wisdom of man is all we have today to combat annihilation. Our only weapon against war is the understanding of man and his warlike nature—not only nation against nation but person against person in the home. An attempt to further this understanding is presented in the pages of this

book which, I believe, strikes a blow for peace in the home,
peace in the world, peace in the soul of each one who reads
it.

GEORGE S. STEVENSON
President,
World Federation for Mental Health

Past President,
American Psychiatric Association

Past Medical Director,
National Association for Mental Health

Sectional Table of Contents

Table of Contents

Psychoanalyst

*"What Would You Say to a Man Who
Complains, 'Lately, I've Had the Strangest
Thoughts About Other Men . . . I Think I'm
Homosexual'?"*

"Can we be 'bi-sexual'?"
"Is homosexuality a reversion?"
"What is the true meaning of homosexuality?"
"Can homosexuality be used to 'hide' something
    else?"
"What is 'trade' in the lexicon of homosexuals?"
"Should homosexuals be legally punished?"
"What is a 'self-damaging' act?"
"Why is punishment attractive to the homo-
    sexual?"
"Underlying homosexuality, is there a more basic
    problem?"

PART FOUR

4. Family

Attending Psychiatrist, Chief, Adult Psychiatric
Outpatient Department, The Roosevelt Hospital

*"Can One Person Catch a Neurosis From
Another?"*

"Are there contagious patterns of behavior?"
"When do people most easily 'catch' a neurosis?"
"Can a family have an 'epidemic' of neurotic dis-
    orders?"
"Do parents complement each other in destruc-
    tive as well as constructive behavior?"

"How do we master our sexual and aggressive urges?"

"Can someone have both masculine and feminine feelings?"

"What are the biological urges of adolescence?"

"Who are the natural love objects of childhood?"

"What is a 'pseudo-hermaphrodite'?"

"When does the genital zone achieve primacy?"

"Can passivity be hiddenly 'active'?"

"What is the meaning of regression?"

"How significant to adolescents are the biological events of menstruation and seminal emission?"

Psychologist, specializing in the psychoanalytic treatment of children and adolescents

"What Forces Mold the Sex Life of the Teenager?"

"Why are the teenage years of sex life crucial to the development of the adult?"

"Why does a teenager have to become emancipated from his family?"

"Why is too much gratification or too little equally unhealthy for a child?"

"Why do some adolescent boys feel hostile toward girls?"

"How is friction between teenagers and their parents related to the sexual development of the teenager?"

"What relationship does the early struggle over training in cleanliness have to a feeling of revulsion about sex in the teenage years?"

"Should parents take children into bed with them?"

"How is the sex life of the teenager related to his childhood?"

"What effect does the divorce of parents have on the sex life of the teenager?"

        child when each parent tears the other down
        in front of the child?"
"What is promiscuity a sign of in the teenager?"
"Is masturbation during the teenage years normal
        and healthy?"
"Should a brother and sister ever share a bed-
        room?"
"What makes youngsters choose a partner who is
        unsuitable?"
"Should parents and children share off-color
        jokes?"

26. NORMAN V. LOURIE 268

    Deputy Secretary, Pennsylvania Department of
    Public Welfare

    "What Can the Parent of a Troubled Child
    Do for the Child and for Himself?"

    "What causes a child to feel troubled?"
    "Why do children want to please parents?"
    "Why do we blame others for our mistakes?"
    "How does a child learn from his parents?"
    "How can parents help a child to be himself?"
    "What is the meaning of 'juvenile delinquency'?"
    "Why is it important for the parent to look close-
            ly at himself?"

27. SAUL SCHEIDLINGER, PH.D. 273

    Consultant in Group Therapy, Community Service
    Society of New York City

    "What Do a Man's Children Need Most from
    Him?"

    "Can a father be a 'pal' to his children?"
    "Do fathers have to remain sexually 'good' to the
            child?"

"What does authority means to the child?"
"How many 'people' must a father be?"
"Why must a child learn to control himself?"
"How do children indentify with the parent of the same sex?"
"Do children imitate the destructive as well as the constructive in their parents?"

Honorary President of the Psychoanalytic Association of New York

"Should a Parent Appear Nude Before His Children?"

"Are children always curious about sex?"
"What are some of the sexual desires and needs of the child?"
"Is some frustration of sexual curiosity necessary to a child?"
"Why do some men exhibit themselves genitally?"
"Why do some women think of themselves as 'injured' people?"
"What do some men attempt to prove in looking at the naked female?"
"Can we defy conventions and not have guilt?"

Chief, Psychiatric Staff, Foster Care Division, Bureau of Child Welfare, City of New York

"Do Parents Have Mixed Feelings About Children? If so, to What Extent Are These Feelings Sexual?"

"Are mixed feelings about children natural?"
"Do children ever seduce adults?"
"What are some of the primitive feelings of

PART FIVE

5. Work

Founder and Honorary President, National Psychological Association for Psychoanalysis

"What Is the Meaning of Work to Man?"

Clinical Professor of Psychiatry, Department of Psychiatry, State University of New York, Downstate Medical Center

"Why Do Some People Want Something for Nothing?"

"Is there a hidden pleasure in stealing?"

"Do most people who steal, swindle and rob do so because they need what they take?"

"How does the conscience of man function?"

"Why won't many of us take something for nothing?"

"What does it mean if a man always allows others to pay his bill?"

"Is the taking of one pencil an act of stealing?"

"Is the Mann Act realistic?"

"Why are some only too willing to be 'suckers'?"

"What is an unconscious masochist?"

"What is the difference between guilt and remorse?"

"What function do our jails serve?"

"Why do many of us not separate aggressive from sexual pleasures?"

Chief, Department of Psychiatry and Neurology, The Hospital and Home for Aged and Infirm Hebrews

"What Makes for Successful Retirement?"

"Why are many afraid of retirement?"
"What is a 'Sunday neurosis'?"
"What are some of the real reasons for retirement?"
"Can you 'retire' into something?"
"Why do some elderly people complain a great deal?"
"Should the elderly try to act 'young'?"
"Can a man really prepare for retirement?"
"Do some people give retirement a bad name?"
"Is there a difference between the problems of men and women when they retire?"
"Why do the young tend to criticize the old?"
"What are the dangers of retirement to Florida or California?"
"What is the difference between the laborer and the professional man when they retire?"
"How is childhood experience related to adjustment in old age?"

PART SIX

6. Treatment

WILFRED HULSE, M.D.
HENRIETTE KLEIN, M.D.
PHILLIP POLATIN, M.D.
THEODOR, REIK, PH.D.
BERNARD F. RIESS, PH.D.
S. R. SLAVSON, PH.D.
OTTO E. SPERLING, M.D.

Associate Clinical Professor of Psychiatry, Department of Psychiatry, State University of New York, Downstate Medical Center

"What Is Freudian Psychoanalysis?"

"What is a Freudian psychoanalyst?"
"What is the meaning of psychoanalysis?"
"What is the drive, or instinct theory?"
"What is the meaning of sexuality?"
"Does aggression stem from frustrated love?"
"What is transference?"
"Why does a patient have to lie down to be psychoanalyzed?"
"Does the psychoanalyst 'influence' the patient?"
"How much does an average psychoanalysis cost?"
"Who is most suitable for psychoanalysis?"
"Can the average person benefit from psychoanalysis?"
"Where is the unconscious located?"

Clinical Professor of Psychiatry, College of Physicians and Surgeons, Columbia University

"What Are the Differences Between Freudian Psychoanalytic Treatment and Other Methods of Psychological Treatment?"

"Can everyone be helped by psychological treatment?"
"What is the theory of psychodynamics?"
"How is a method of treatment selected?"
"How can an individual get the type of help best suited to his needs?"
"Who is most eligible for psychoanalytic treatment?"

Introduction

BEFORE READING A NEW BOOK, just as before meeting a new person, it helps to have some background as to what it is like and what it is trying to do. In other words, what are its purposes and goals?

We are attempting to find answers to the many problems that haunt countless people. We want to find out what the world of science has learned about the emotional problems of people, that could be published with the feeling, "This is the best that we know. And, therefore, the most helpful information that can be presented."

We went to a number of America's leading psychoanalysts, psychiatrists and psychologists and asked questions that we felt were universal and important, questions many patients ask. Each psychoanalyst, psychiatrist and psychologist was interviewed individually. All questions and answers were either tape-recorded or taken down by a court stenotypist. Each interview was edited by the one who was interviewed and rechecked before it appeared. This work took approximately one year to complete.

All of those interviewed consider themselves "Freudian" in approach, in the sense that they subscribe to the philosophy of the founder of psychoanalysis, Sigmund Freud. But the reader will find some differing points of view, for not all of the contributors agree on some of the more peripheral points. It must be remembered, however, that psychoanalysis is a new applied science, scarcely fifty years old, and that to expect it to have all the final answers, is a demand for magic that comes out of childhood.

To all the contributors we are extremely grateful, not only for sharing with us their hard-earned wisdom (to become a psychoanalyst entails the longest training of any profession) but also because they cooperated with us in the belief that the public deserves to be informed by those best qualified to speak. Many have written books for popular consumption which are listed in the section, "About the Contributors." To our sorrow, Dr. Edmund Bergler, who had written many popular books, and Dr. Wilfred C. Hulse, who had just completed his first book, died before the publication of this book.

We feel the many insights revealed in these pages may do more than give momentary pleasure and release of anxiety. As Dr. Jan Ehrenwald, one of our contributors, said: "Above all, we must not forget that there is a margin of freedom in human behavior to which we may appeal, which we try to mobilize by good example, by persuasion and, if need be, by systematic psychotherapy. Psychoanalysis and psychotherapy presuppose the existence of this margin of freedom, this capacity to adjust to change through insight. It is this hope on which depend the insights that are the goods we analysts try to sell to the small consumer, trusting he will make good use of them."

This book, in a sense, brings the psychoanalyst to you to answer questions you might have asked. Although a wide variety of subjects is covered, perhaps in future volumes still more questions will be given answers by these authorities and others.

We hope this work offers some a start in the direction of self-understanding, the first step in mankind's march towards becoming truly civilized.

ARTHUR BERNHARD, *Publisher*

I. LOVE

Introduction

THE ONE QUESTION THAT PLAGUES most people, causing greater anguish than any other, probably goes, "Why doesn't love last?"

The exciting, glamorous feeling we call "love" all too often seems to vanish in a puff of smoke when we get to know the other person well. Achieving an intimate, enduring, harmonious relationship with a member of the opposite sex appears to be one of the most difficult of achievements.

"Love makes the world go 'round — but it also makes people go 'round in confusion as they face disillusionment and then despair. Some feel they are not getting all they should out of marriage. Others are unable ever to get married. Still others settle for unsatisfactory relationships.

In their search for the answer to why they fail to find enduring love, many turn to marriage manuals or books about sex. Although the Holy Bible is the most popular book of all time, the marriage-and-sex manual probably runs it a close second. These "Bibles of the bedroom" are sold in the hundreds of thousands each year.

There are few adults who have not, at one time or another, glanced through a book or magazine of this type. The publishing, distributing and selling of marital and sexual "How-to" information is an industry in itself. It is also only a small part of a greater industrial organization which indiscriminately grinds out, through movies, television, radio, magazines and advertising, the lure of sex, sex, and more sex.

People are apparently starved for something, even though satiated with sex information. For what, actually, are they starved? Could it be something else? Something elusive and intangible? Something related to sex but encompassing other parts of the personality, too?

3

For the answer to this, we sought out Theodor Reik, Ph.D., a pupil and friend of Freud's, who has written much about the psychology of sex. We thought this would offer a stimulating start to a discussion of the conflicts that interfere with love.

One of the blocks to the ability to love fully seems to be the idea many of us have that when we fall in love all our other problems will be solved. The average man and woman, to be sure, does not look for Cinderella or Prince Charming on a white horse in his marriage partner, but there are few who do not have romantic ideals. Some of these are realistic, others not. Some may be easily achieved, others must be worked for over a period of years and then, possibly, still not fall within reach.

But, whether real or unreal, possible or impossible, most of us want the so-called "ideal" relationship in marriage. We want it here and now, not in the distant future. We expect everything to be beautiful from the wedding night on, and if it is less than beautiful in all respects, we are disappointed and disillusioned.

We asked Peter Laderman, M.D., to answer the vital question, "Is there such a thing as an ideal relationship between a man and a woman?"

Another barrier to love seems to be the guilt many men and women feel about sexual desire. Sexual expression is the one area of human behavior which most lends itself to conflict, anxiety and guilt. A huge super-structure of fears, prejudices and ideals rests heavily upon our fundamental drive of sexuality.

This is particularly true for those young men and women not yet married but who expect to be. It is even truer for the hundreds of thousands of men and women who have essentially given up the idea of marriage.

Yet the unmarried, if normal, also possess the need to give expression to their sexual feelings. What price do they pay? Is the price necessary?

This we asked Solomon Machover, Ph.D., in the words, "Is it possible in our day and age for unmarried men and women to have sexual relations without guilt?"

America is a country in love with love. A popular song of some time ago was entitled, "Everybody Loves A Lover."

Everyone does seem to love lovers, and loves himself when he is in love.

But are we really talking about love? We all want to love and be loved in return. Then, why do so many of us fail in our avowed goal in life? Why is it that so many go on a long journey in search of the god of love, only to find a faker and a fraud at the end of a false rainbow?

We asked Preston G. McLean, M.D., "Why is there so much counterfeit love in our society?"

One of the greatest hardships in life appears to be the overcoming of the disillusionment that always sets in, to some degree, after a man and woman have known each other for a while and the first blush of love turns from rosy red to grey. Although the insurance statistics tell us that men and women can expect to live longer than ever, the divorce statistics reveal a high death rate to romance.

But divorce statistics do not disclose the full picture. Thousands of other couples live apart without being divorced, and there are countless marriages in which emotional separation occurs even though the man and woman still live together and "make love" mechanically.

We asked George Devereux, Ph.D., what he would say to a married man or woman who complained, "There's no fun, no excitement or discovery any more. We come at each other like machines turning over for the thousandth time."

In their effort to find a measure of excitement in life, a number of men and women engage in affairs outside of marriage, or never get married but reel from one affair to another. There is no way of getting statistics on the number of persons who, each year, engage in illicit romances, but there are undoubtedly more than we would like to admit.

We asked Otto E. Sperling, M.D., to talk about the fascination of the forbidden. We were thinking of a woman who confessed, "After five years of nothing with my husband, I finally went out and picked up a man. Any man would have done. It seemed he hardly touched me and I went off like a skyrocket. But I'm still cold with my husband and I love him."

We wanted to know from Dr. Sperling, "Why did this wife undertake a forbidden affair and find it far more exciting than her prosaic marriage?"

Many couples endure years of tortuous indecision, trying to make up their minds whether they should separate or stay together, wondering if they would be happier with someone else. Their tendency is to blame the other one for the unhappiness. This is a tendency we all have in childhood. But a child has to learn when he slams his finger with a toy hammer, that it is not the hammer's fault. Many children take a long time to absorb this simple lesson, hitting and punishing objects which hurt them for many a year.

Some of us never stop blaming other things and other people. It is always "their" fault, never our own. We are the innocent victim, they are the guilty villain.

Ask many a man or woman why he divorced his first mate and he will answer, "She (or he) was impossible!" This is supposed to explain everything. But it obviously does not explain anything. It raises more questions than it answers.

We asked Cornelia B. Wilbur, M.D., "Will a second marriage be any happier than a first?"

These seven interviews give answers, we hope, to many of the questions that trouble the sensitive man or woman who wants to live the richest possible life, who wants to enjoy the greatest of life's gifts — love.

I.

"Why do men and women read marriage manuals and sex magazines—are they starved for sex information or starved for something else?" we asked Dr. Reik.

XXXXXXXXXXXXXXXX!

THEODOR REIK, Ph.D.

Founder and Honorary President of the
National Psychological Association for Psychoanalysis

In this interview Dr. Reik also discusses:

"Is there a difference between the love life of a man and a woman?"

"Should a woman be active in the sexual relationship?"

"Is sexual technique important?"

"How is sexual inadequacy related to one's concept of the self?"

"Are there different arousal times sexually for men and women?"

"Is habitual masturbation destructive?"

"Are there different images of sexual satisfaction?"

"What are the special difficulties women are likely to have sexually?"

"Is there such a thing as 'hidden homosexuality'?"

I.

This is what Dr. Reik said when interviewed in his office:

Men and women who feel sexually inadequate are deceiving themselves if they hope, by reading sex and marriage manuals, to find out what they can do about it.

In the first place, they are likely to get much misinformation. Secondly, sexual inadequacy will not be helped by words in a book because it is related to one's feelings about himself as a human being. The barrier to a good sex life is not lack of knowledge about sexual technique—because satisfaction in sexual intercourse, paradoxical as it sounds, is not only sexual. It does not come only from the release of our sexual drives but is connected with our estimation of ourselves.

In other words, feelings of sexual inadequacy have to do with what we call our ego. The ego conveys reality to us. It is the middle agent, the arbiter, between our natural drives and our conscience. And that is why I say that sexual intercourse is connected with our estimation of ourselves for it is closely related to that part of our personality which is the middle agent between the self and the external world.

The ego enters into sexual intercourse in a number of ways. For instance, I would say that the woman needs not only to be desired but also to be admired, and to be assured that she's loved not only as a sex object but as a person. The same is true, with certain exceptions, for the man.

This is a change historically when you consider the Neanderthal man, who perhaps took a woman from behind in the manner of animals and who had not the slightest consideration about her feelings or his. Today, we consider equally important with satisfaction of our sex drive, the appreciation of the other as a person. Therefore, in addition to attaining general satisfaction in the release of sexual drive, the individual choice of the sex-or-love object is important.

This is one reason why many marriage manuals fail, for they cannot tell you which man or woman would give you the greatest pleasure as a person. You make the selection yourself, based on your own self-image.

Another way the manuals fail to take into consideration the ego is illustrated by the following extreme example. In a certain marriage the husband was a transvestite. That is, this man had to dress up as a woman, shoes and stockings and all, before he could have sexual intercourse. Then he received psychological help and gave up the perversion. But then the man had a very serious setback in his career and became deeply depressed. His ego, his opinion of himself, was lowered, and he returned to his former perversion.

Another man, a British aristocrat (who was in reality impotent), could have sexual intercourse only under the same bizarre circumstances of dressing as a woman. Then he would go to his wife and, so to speak, seduce her. He was playing two parts, himself and the woman. The deeper meaning of these roles became clear after he started analysis. He was very shy in his approach to women, so he played a scene in which a woman, impersonated by himself, encouraged him, made the first advance and invited him to have sexual intercourse. Then he was potent. You see here the decisive role the ego plays. He had to build up his self-confidence.

A POINT OF NO RETURN

Most sex and marriage manuals give a lot of wrong information to readers. For instance, one of the most recent books about female sexuality advises the woman to educate the man in sexual intercourse, to tell him to proceed at a slower pace so she can become aroused. It encourages her to consider herself first.

I think that is wrong. Such a verbal admonition would only hinder the man and prevent him from enjoying full, uninhibited sexual satisfaction. Only when he, after reaching a certain point of no return, acts selfishly without considering his partner, will he be able to satisfy the woman more fully. When he considers her primarily, he prevents himself, and her, from the fullest enjoyment.

There is, of course, a difference in the sexual arousal times. Freud calls this a difference of phases. This difference is due to the active role of the male and the more passive, receiving role of the woman. The man, in the beginning, has to wait a certain time until the woman is emotionally ready. But when this point, which I call the point of no return, is reached, the man has to go ahead without great consideration for his partner.

If he delays, he will not get full gratification for the simple reason that human nature is not made to carry sacrifices for a long time.

Sexual satisfaction is a mutual process. If it were not so, masturbation would lead to satisfaction. Actually, for the emotionally immature, sexual intercourse is a poor second best to masturbation because in masturbation, one's imagination has full range, while in sexual intercourse each person is restricted to one subject who cannot possibly fulfill all his daydreams.

Once I treated a man who had sexual intercourse with his wife, but instead of a full emission he had an incomplete and unsatisfactory one. He was restless afterwards and couldn't fall asleep, although he was stimulated. Then he had a fantasy in which he remembered a sexual intercourse he once had in the Vienna woods with the same woman before he was married to her. He became aroused, and masturbated with the fantasy that his partner was the same woman now sleeping by his side, only as a girl. Then he had a full orgasm. Thus you would conclude that sometimes in attaining full sexual satisfaction the real situation is not decisive but rather the fantasy.

Everybody has a certain personal image about sexual satisfaction which is partly the result of daydreams and partly, especially in the case of men, an echo of memories, of experiences he once had which he endeavors to regain.

For instance, a student of mine (Jules Nydes) once pointed out that the general opinion that masturbation is harmful when it becomes a habit, must have a certain justification psychologically. He explained it thus: Masturbation is a way of achieving sexual gratification which is very easily accessible and can be reached without overcoming great external or internal hindrances. Only the help of one's imagination is needed. He compared it, and very well, I think, with a situation in the Arabian Nights in which Aladdin rubs a certain, miraculous, magic lamp and the genie that appears bows down and says,

"What do you want? A kingdom? Beautiful women? Riches?" Whenever Aladdin rubs the lamp, his wish is fulfilled.

In the same manner, masturbation fulfills the immediate sexual needs of the individual. But it has many dangers. First of all, we know from Freud that the sexual behavior of a person forms a pattern for his behavior in other non-sexual directions. If a man is habitually masturbating, he will, in general, show a lack of drive in overcoming hindrances and obstacles in his career and in fulfilling the task which life puts before him.

The average male has to woo a woman and overcome her doubt and other inhibitions until she gives herself to him.

He has, in other words, to show that he has certain powers and energy which equip him with the ability to overcome obstacles. This is entirely lacking in men who habitually masturbate. They need consider no partner.

When this is so, the person probably needs some psychotherapeutic help in distinguishing between his fantasy and the reality so he can fully enjoy sexual intimacy.

Should Women Be Active Sexually?

Reading marriage manuals is an act of embarrassment arising from insecurity about one's own sexual role and one's self-image.

A woman has to like herself before she can hope to be liked by men. A girl who looks into a mirror and hates what she sees, who finds herself full of handicaps and shortcomings, has great difficulty in being admired and liked by men.

Men do not have quite that problem. Boys and girls develop different kinds of self-awareness. When a young man enters a room full of men and women, his self-awareness is not as great as that of a young woman who conceives of herself as the object of a great deal of attention, not only of men but of other women. She is, so to speak, in the crossfire of both sexes.

Furthermore, there is in general a difference in the love life of a man and woman. The man, when he is a boy, has his mother as his first object of love and sexual desire. She takes care of him, washes him, feeds him, powders him, and plays the role of the femme fatale, which means necessarily that she is the first seductress of the boy. Then he goes from his first love and sex choice to perhaps his sister then to friends of his sister then to girls outside the family circle.

The girl has an added difficulty. Her first love and sexual object is her mother but she now has the task of changing, from mother to a man, to father, to brother, to another man outside the family. Not all women succeed in making this transition, for there are still other emotional difficulties for the girl. They tell in the Austrian Alps of one girl, a kind of simpleton, who complained to her mother, "You had it easy. You married father. But I have to marry a total stranger."

Now, one of the misconceptions propagated by marriage manuals—and it is an increasing tendency throughout our society today—is to attribute to the woman a much more active role sexually. In Victorian times, women blushed or fainted if there was any mention of sex, real or implied. But today a woman rarely blushes, even when a risqué joke is told.

I would say the sexual aggressiveness of women should be restricted to certain situations in which a man is inhibited. For instance, if he is very shy. Or during certain times in his life when he is depressed and his self-confidence is low. Or when the woman is in the state of high pregnancy.

This aggressiveness should not be direct but subtle. A patient told me that his wife, just before she fell asleep, asked him casually, "Are you tired?"

He said, "Yes."

Then after a pause, she asked, "Are you too tired?"

He accepted her invitation with a smile. She was what I call subtle.

Women should also limit their aggressiveness to the beginning of sexual intimacy. If they are too aggressive, the man will not want her. A writer, a former patient of mine, was involved in a flirtation with an actress. One night she invited him to her apartment for a drink after the theater. He sat down and she went into her room, to return wearing a negligee.

She said to him, "Why should we make such a fuss? Let's go to bed."

He was not only astonished but indignant. He scolded her, saying in effect, "You deprive me in this way of the privilege not only of wooing you but of conquering you," and took his coat and hat and left.

Actually, her actions were not aggressive but hostile. When aggressiveness is very intense, it implies concealed hostility toward the male on the part of the woman. She wants to convince herself of her power to conquer the man sexually. Secretaries who flirt endlessly with their employers and women who have one lover after another, use the men merely as instruments by which they can show their sexual power. This is not love.

Another great danger in the sex manuals is that they do not take into consideration what Freud calls "the peaceful penetration" of analytic insights. For instance, they one-sidedly emphasize sexual technique, leaving out that very important part of intimacy which is based on feelings of tenderness and affection. The French differentiate between the need for lust and the need for tenderness very well in their phrases, "besoin de tendresse" and "besoin de volupté." For a good sexual relationship, there must be both, especially for the woman.

Sometimes women want to express tenderness without necessarily desiring sex. A wife may stroke her husband gently on the head, whereupon he may conceive this as an invitation to sex, which is actually far from her mind. She just wants to express her love and affection for him.

However, another misconception propagated by marriage manuals is that there is a traditional feeling on the part of women, perhaps even helped by the education of young girls, that if only the man feels satisfied, the woman should be content, that one-sided satisfaction is sufficient. In general this means the acceptance of a sadistic act rather than mutual sexual gratification, and although the marriage manuals indirectly recommend this sadism, it is obvious that one-sided satisfaction is far from sufficient.

Still another misconception propagated by sex magazines is the assumption that in general, during puberty, the boy develops a drive to conquer the outside world while the young girl resigns herself to a passive role. This is not true. The girl develops, in puberty, a very strong activity, but all of this activity is turned inward, so to speak. She develops the gift of fine feelings, delicacy of emotions and acts, tact, perceptions and empathy which we so highly appreciate in mature woman.

I shall never forget the sentence of a young girl whom I treated. She said, "When I am not well dressed, I hate everybody." She meant: "When I am not well dressed, I anticipate how people will look at me. Then I hate them." A woman's self-esteem is involved in her acceptance of all her surroundings, including the male partner.

Also, man's self-image plays a great role in the ability to woo a woman. For instance, a suppressed or disavowed hostility toward the other sex would prevent the man, or the woman, from reaching sexual satisfaction, often the case with homosexuals. My students speak of Reik's law, which I formulated, and which means the following: while we oscillate in general between two extremes in which we prefer the company of one sex or the other, too great a repressed hostility toward one sex is connected with a conscious or unconscious hostility toward the other sex.

In other words, rejection of sublimated homosexuality is connected with the outbreak of aggression against the other sex. I would assert that a girl who is not reconciled with her mother, who never thinks of her mother in terms of what she has endured or grants that her mother has done her best, that such a girl cannot get along with men.

It is not necessary that this woman "love" her mother, for not even the Bible demands that you should "love" your mother and father, only that you should "honor" them. This is a great difference. What is necessary is that a girl should sometimes feel sorry for her mother, understand that her mother also suffered and had great deprivation in her life. Otherwise, the girl will retain an unconscious fixation on her mother and will therefore be unable to really care for a man.

As with this type of woman who cannot make the transition of her affection to a man, so it is in general with the men and women who hope by reading sex and marriage manuals to find out what they can do about their sexual inadequacy.

It is like a ship in the harbor which is anchored with chains you cannot see. It cannot put out to sea because it is held fast by the invisible chains.

2.

"Is there such a thing as an 'ideal' relationship between a man and a woman?"
we asked Dr. Laderman.

XXXXXXXXXXXXXXXXXXX

PETER LADERMAN, M.D.
Member of the Association for Psychoanalytic Medicine

In this interview Dr. Laderman also discusses:

"What is the real romance in marriage?"
"Should there be equality between the sexes?"
"Do people go into marriage with unreal expectations?"
"Do most people get enough pleasure from a mate?"
"Are some men and women afraid of close relationships?"
"What is the difference in roles between a man and a woman?"
"How do the early and later years of marriage differ?"
"Why do men in particular feel the need to 'perform' in marriage?"
"Is it important to fully understand the other person?"
"What is a 'successful' relationship?"
"Are thoughts and words more meaningful than deeds?"

2.

This is what Dr. Laderman said when interviewed in his office:

A man and woman can reach a very satisfying relationship which may come close to the ideal if each brings certain qualities to it and recognizes that absolute perfection cannot be expected all the time.

Basic to all of these qualities is respect. There must be respect for the other person and a willingness to engage in cooperative effort to make life as good as it can be within the particular relationship.

Often what may seem to be a lack of respect may simply be lack of knowledge about the other's needs. Marriage manuals try to warn of this but are not always successful. The husband or wife finds they don't know what the partner is looking for. Consequently, feelings of anger often develop within a marriage and separate the couple either emotionally or in actuality.

I am not talking exclusively about sexual needs. Men and women often come into a marriage expecting the partner to understand automatically what is going on, without talking about it. Certainly such understanding cannot occur all the time. Sometimes a person may not understand what another feels unless he is told. Even then he may not immediately understand. A wife may feel, "My husband should know this if he loves me." He may love her very much but still not know what has made her angry, resentful or bitter. He will only know that they are further apart emotionally.

Many intelligent and sensitive people enter marriage without recognizing that for knowledge and understanding it takes more than just living together. Conversation, with respect for another's point of view, is very much a part of learning to sures of receiving as well as giving. Receiving does not com-

understand. One partner may find it necessary to explain what he thinks or feels about a problem or situation. To have to explain doesn't mean there is any lack of affection or understanding in either partner and it should not be thought of as such.

But the ideal relationship involves more than just words, more than an intellectual exercise. In addition to verbal communication, there is the non-verbal interchange of real feeling between two people. Each should not try to hide how he feels, hoping that somehow the other is going to "catch on." The feelings should come out, whether they are feelings of love or anger, of tenderness or resentment.

Some people feel that the expression of angry feelings means all is lost and the entire relationship will go down the drain. This is obviously not true. These people grow up with the false idea that if you love someone, you can't be angry with him. But to feel anger does not mean there is an absence of love. The expression of anger may help to relieve the pressure within the relationship, and often something can then be done to solve the immediate problem. There are angry feelings in the most idyllic of relationships. It is usually better to talk about them than to let them build up into coldness and emotional separation which can only lead to further difficulty.

SNOW WHITE AND PRINCE CHARMING

Maintaining the story-book concept of the perfect Prince Charming or the perfect Snow White becomes a way of protecting the individual from entering a meaningful relationship with another person. The search for the impossible ideal becomes a defense against the problems of real living and stands in the way of enjoying an experience that could bring with it mature happiness and satisfaction.

I think most men and women, if asked, would not admit to looking for a Snow White with all her virtues or a Prince Charming on a white horse. However, people do come to believe they should expect certain things to happen in marriage which just don't happen, or don't happen immediately. Then, experiencing less than what they unrealistically expected they may feel they have received inferior merchandise or they may develop doubts about their adequacy as men or women.

There are men, for example, who feel that they must satisfy women in every way all the time and that anything less than total satisfaction is not manly. Realistically, of course, no one can reach perfection every single time in every single way. We are not gods.

Many men and women are afraid of what will happen in close relationships. They can see only disaster to themselves or to their partners in such a situation. Because of this fear they protect themselves in every way possible. The reasons for this fear of close relationships can be found in the early childhood development of these people. Either cultural or family influences may play a part. If a person grew up in a family where there was little or no tenderness between its members, but where there was, on the contrary much tension and anger, he may consciously or unconsciously develop the idea that a close relationship can lead only to conflict. Consequently, as an adult, this individual may tend to avoid a close relationship because he conceives of it as dangerous. But, I repeat, his concept of danger does not necessarily have to be on a conscious level. It may be completely hidden from the individual himself.

In our culture today there is a rather strong pressure to marry at a young age, before we really possess the ability to establish a meaningful relationship. Tender feelings for others and the ability to love maturely develop over a long period of time. They do not come of themselves at some magic age of sixteen, or eighteen, or twenty-one. When the culture tends to push basically immature men and women into marriage, the tender feelings may not have strengthened sufficiently, In the face of even the ordinary resentments of marriage, further development of the affectionate feelings may be hampered and this, in turn, would increase the fears of a close relationship in the future.

The need to perform is another cultural factor that plays a role in creating difficulties within marriage. Men, in particular, are under much pressure to succeed in everything they attempt. The pressure is especially strong to perform well with a woman. The resulting tendency is to lose sight of the pleasures of love and tenderness in a close relationship with a woman. It may become a mechanical situation for a man if he measures only his performance and asks, "How good a job have I done here?" instead of "Have I felt any pleasure in love?"

Some men feel that it is not manly to receive in any way, that there is something feminine about "being on the receiving end" of any sensual experience. Some women also have this belief about men and their so-called passivity. But the man, as well as the woman, has every right to enjoy the pleasures of receiving as well as giving. Receiving does not compromise his masculinity. This misconception has developed in a culture which tries to categorize everything as either feminine or masculine, as either passive or active. There is a perfectly acceptable mixture of giving and receiving which is healthy, satisfying and necessary for the ideal relationship.

The drive for success is an additional cultural influence to be considered. Success should not mean how much money you earn, how big a house you own, or whether you give your wife an orgasm every time. Success is personal. It is not a competition to outdo someone. On the contrary, success comes from the deep satisfactions which arise from the sharing of adult experiences with someone you love.

In our world today there is a disturbing lack of "cooperativeness." A recent example involves the fallout shelter problem. "I will protect myself," some say, "and my neighbor can go to blazes." This attitude certainly does not make for cooperativeness. It indicates to me a deficit of love — love for neighbor, for fellow man. A culture which permits this kind of attitude is inhibiting tender relationships and is helping to destroy them.

Cooperativeness is essential to the development of the ideal relationship. Let us take the fairly common situation in a marriage where the wife is home all day taking care of the house and children. Comes the evening, she would quite naturally like to get away from it all, to go out. At that point the husband comes home. He has been out. What does he want? He wants to stay at home. He and she meet head-on and each feels the other lacks understanding. If they can never get together to explain their feelings and to work out some compromise, there is bound to be an explosion sooner or later. To reach a compromise there must be understanding and a willingness to make a cooperative effort.

Another difficult situation in marriage is created by the wife's demand that the husband play a large part in the raising of the children. Often men don't become very excited about tiny babies. Yet this is the time when a woman wants all the help she can get, especially if she is uncertain about herself as a mother. The husband, however, may feel incompetent and not see how he can be of any help to his wife. When she looks to him for help under these circumstances, but does not receive it, she feels resentful and begins to believe that he is not interested in her as a person or in the family. Although the husband usually does become more interested in the children as they grow and feels more competent in helping with them, the early resentments of the wife may linger on.

FROM EARLY CHILDHOOD

All of us carry some childish attitudes into adulthood. How much they influence our behavior depends upon their intensity. To a lesser or greater degree, many of us tend to ask, "How much has he done for me?" But this cannot be a measure of love because the doing alone does not mean there is love. Even when there is love, everything cannot always be done in such a way that all demands will be met all the time. This childish attitude of how-much-have-you-done-for-me-lately diminishes as it is superseded by an attitude of cooperative effort. A more mature measure of love comes in asking, "Has there been a sharing of the experiences of life?" The experience can be a concrete one, like a new car, or it can be a common feeling shared by two people.

A second childish way of reacting can be called "the report-card attitude." "You have done a good job, and now you will get an A," may be said consciously or unconsciously. In effect, it is an attitude of reward for being good. The husband says, "Now that you've been a good wife, I'll give you a mink coat." Naturally, women like mink coats, but they should not be given as a reward for so-called "good behavior." On the other hand, upon receiving the mink coat, the wife's response should not be, "Well, now we can go to bed together." Rewards and punishments in marriage can lead only to trouble.

The report-card attitude and the how-much-have-you-done-for-me-lately attitude are closely related to a third immature attitude, perfectionism. A striving for perfection may interfere with the development of a satisfactory sexual relationship especially if no allowance is made for the day-to-day living of the man and woman. There are normal variations in sexual interest. Sometimes the woman is tired, sometimes the man. Other factors may influence one partner or the other. The demand that sexual intercourse, or any other experience between two people, should always work out perfectly is completely unrealistic.

There are infantile wishes within us all. There is a part of us which wants to be treated as the helpless child we once were. Why this is a strong and important tendency in one person but fairly well submerged in another is a matter which we should consider for a moment.

As we grow up, we follow the paths that lead to gratifications. Thus, as adults, if we get satisfactions by acting as adults, we will keep on acting maturely. But if we do not succeed in this, we will tend to fall back upon infantile methods of trying to obtain satisfactions. These methods may have been adequate and appropriate as children, but they are certainly not desirable in the adult world in which we must live. There will probably be difficulty in the marriage of a dependent man who has won his wife by acting as a helpless boy in need of a mother. Similarly, the cute, coy woman who always plays the part of the siren may be too scared to find an adult role possible. In most people there is a mixture of the infantile and the adult. A certain amount of childish behavior is acceptable and tolerable as long as it is not the main approach to life.

NOT ON A PLATTER

I began by saying that respect is a basic factor in the ideal relationship. Respect comes from an awareness that the other person is a human being with needs, who deserves to have these needs met as much as possible in whatever ways are feasible. It means that neither is superior or inferior in the relationship. It means that each is willing to listen to what the other has to say and believes what the other says is important.

Marriages can be romantic, but the kind of romance I am talking about is hardly attainable in the first years. Tradition says that courtship and the honeymoon are the most romantic times, that romance leaves when the honeymoon is over. But I think that marriage can be more romantic and interesting in the tenth or twentieth year than in the first year. If one expects the romance too soon, or looks for it in ways in which it just can't be delivered, then there will be disappointment, and romance will not exist at all.

Marriages cannot be perfect at the start any more than people can know everything at birth. The early years of marriage are primarily for learning, not only sexual learning, but learning how to live with a close situation. The early years of marriage are crucial in the development of a close and tender relationship. The misconceptions that a person may have developed as he grew up will be tested in these early years. Either he gives up the infantile and the childish, or the marriage will begin to suffer.

It is not necessary to give up all romantic ideals about love, tenderness and marriage. It is only necessary to give up the unrealistic. People cannot realistically expect that life is going to be wonderful as soon as boy gets girl. Plays, movies or television stories may end there, but the work of marriage only begins there. This work is the learning of respect, cooperation, communication and understanding. Thus, after five or ten years of good, hard work, the marriage may indeed be romantic as the partners experience the thoughtfulness, tenderness and consideration they have learned. This is true for all aspects of life together, including the sexual. A sexual relationship can become more exciting as time goes on, rather than bog down in the early experiences of real or imagined failure. If a man and woman can overcome their expectations of immediate and constant perfection, sexual intercourse can become more exciting, more romantic, and less inhibited. As an added feature, it will probably be more successful as well.

People are not born knowing all there is to know. They cannot expect immediate success in every relationship. It requires time, and it requires work. The ideal relationship develops over a period of years. It is not presented to anyone on a "silver platter."

3.

*"Is it possible in our day and age for married
men and women to have sexual relations
without guilt?" we asked Dr. Machover.*

XXXXXXXXXXXXXXXXXXX

SOLOMON MACHOVER, Ph.D.

Chief Psychologist, Kings County Hospital

In this interview Dr. Machover also discusses:

*"Can we be free from anxiety about sex even though un-
married?"*
"What are some of the symptoms of guilt about sex?"
*"Can men and women accept guilt-free sex without
love?"*
"Who are the sexually irresponsible?"
"What is a 'sexual object'?"
"What are the special problems of unmarried women?"
*"What is the relationship in sex between guilt and the irra-
tional?"*
*"What is the meaning of the 'whore-customer' relation-
ship?"*
*"Is there a difference in the sexual relationship be-
tween those who expect to marry and those who do
not?"*
"Do childhood experiences have an effect on sexual life?"

3.

This is what Dr. Machover said when interviewed in his office:

In our society today unmarried adult men and women may, and often do, engage in heterosexual intercourse without guilt. Too often, however, sexual expression is prudishly avoided, obstructed by anxiety or attended by feelings of sinfulness and guilt. The frequent association between sex and guilt which hampers, degrades, or otherwise contaminates self-expression through sexual experience is the product of a learning process which begins in infancy. Unfortunately, the kind of learning likely to result in wholesome attitudes toward sex which, in turn, can make participation in unmarried sexual activity guilt-free, is difficult to come by in our society.

In the first place, sex is associated with socially determined general moral and aesthetic values whose violation generates guilt. These are values which are assimilated from the culture which surrounds us and, particularly, from our parents. In extreme instances, sexual expression under all circumstances is unfortunately viewed as somehow immoral, ugly, animalistic. More often, sex expression is expected to be reserved for special circumstances such as legal intimacy, procreative intent, a love relationship, mutual respect, romantic conditions. These are expectations which place a difficult burden on an insistent biological drive.

In the second place, parental conflicts concerning sex have a crucial bearing on the attitudes and conflicts regarding sex which people develop. Parents often surround the subject of sex with a seductive air of mystery that stimulates at the same time that it condemns. Whether by manifest behavior, or by all the subtle signals of emotional communication, they manage to transmit something of their own guilt feelings and sexual conflicts, or create the conditions which help to generate such feelings and conflicts in their children.

24

In the third place, the impact of parental personalities, in less direct ways, often sets the stage for the development of sexual problems in their children. It is all but inevitable that parents should relate to their children in ways largely determined by their own unresolved problems. They cannot easily set aside their conflicts, their covert feelings of guilt, their tensions and anxieties, their uncertainties about themselves, their own self-enhancing and defensive needs when they form their perceptions of their children and react to their children's behavior. As a result, parents may be possessive of their children, over-demanding, over-protective, subtly seductive and rejective, competitive, inconsistent.

The consequent effects on the personality development of children are virtually certain to include encumbered and conflicting sexual attitudes and feelings. The boy who loves and covertly, perhaps unconsciously, also hates his mother for her exploitative possessiveness, or who has failed to win his fathers respect, is all too likely fated for sexual self-doubt and guilt-burdened sex expression. The girl who never won the love of a cold and strait-laced father may find sexual expression as an adult to be obstructed and unrewarding because of unconscious guilt. The possibilities for the development of sexual conflict and guilt are myriad and, when their development is an intrinsic part of the process of personality development, they are not easily overcome.

Of course, there are many unmarried men and women in our society who do have sexual relations without excessively inhibiting, damaging and self-defeating guilt. And we can cite sex practices in primitive cultures, and in fact, in other civilized societies within our Western culture, where sexual expression has escaped the intense moral implications all too true of Anglo-Saxon society.

We know that there are irresponsible and highly egocentric individuals among us who have in one way or another managed to evade the currently strong moral values. I think, however, we are likely to find in such people that such evasions are not limited to sex. These are people who have a generalized freedom from conscience, and whether this irresponsible freedom is the kind of solution the rest of us would be ready to accept in order to gain unmarried sex without guilt is at least questionable. Also, it seems that men and women with less education, members of the lower socio-economic groups, may have a greater freedom from guilt in their unmarried sex activities. It appears to be true that unmarried sexual indulgence is more frequent in such groups and tends to occur with less consequent regret than is the case among individuals whose education is at a higher level, and who are members of the more complexly cultured levels of our society.

In addition to the above, many men and women who experience guilt in their first unmarried sex encounters learn they can survive, subsequent sexual experience having much less guilt, possibly none. These are people whose background of learning has not so intensely wedded them to moral attitudes and feelings of self-blame and self-censure.

And last, we should mention those blessed people who have been born to the right kind of parents and who have been fortunate beneficiaries of just the right kinds of circumstances in their development. In a very genuine sense, and without sacrificing the desirable values associated with sex, these men and women have been able to remain free from corrosive moral baggage.

THE SYMPTOMS OF GUILT

If you ask most people about feelings of guilt in relation to their unmarried sexual experiences they will probably deny that they have, or had, any guilt whatsoever. This denial of guilt would surely be true among self-styled sophisticates who consciously feel that they are emancipated from what they conceive to be the irrational moral baggage that most other people bear in relation to sex and sexual expression. But these people are expressing a "pseudo-emancipation," for they usually show some implicit experience of guilt. In other words it is what they do, not what they say, that is most revealing.

Before we continue, however, a distinction should be made between conscious guilt and denied or repressed guilt. An individual is aware of conscious guilt because he feels it. But guilt can be denied or repressed, and when this happens it is usually accompanied by a need for punishment which may be seen in the behavior of the individual but not consciously recognized.

In short, although the guilt is not consciously acknowledged by the person there are, nevertheless, symptomatic expressions which indicate the presence of guilt. For example, people who profess sophisticated and guilt-free feelings about themselves may have an "unaccountable" experience of impotence, or of frigidity. They may have an inability to really enjoy the sexual experience, or they may over-indulge in sex. In this latter example, the over-indulgence is a way of proving to themselves they have no guilt. But the tell-tale sign of repressed guilt is the fact they overdo sex.

There are other symptoms of guilt. In certain psychosomatic illnesses resulting from anxieties and tensions there may be deeply ingrained and internalized guilt with respect to sex, which has only been rationalized away, not actually resolved. Symptomatic expressions may include exaggerated feelings of responsibility for the sex partner, or marked feelings of gratitude and indebtedness, all of which, although easily rationalized, may be traced to a feeling of guilt associated with sexuality.

Then there are those curiously selective people who declare they do not indulge in sex because they "cannot find the right person." Too often, this is only another rationalization. Perhaps the most revealing are those men who are sexually adequate only with women of much lower social level, women for whom they have contempt. There are many men who are able to perform sexually only with prostitutes, respectable women of their own social level either leaving them completely cold or involving them in sexual relations in which they do not function satisfactorily, often without pleasure. The presence of guilt is shown most strikingly with these men in the fact that often they leave a prostitute not with conscious guilt but rather with disgust, not infrequently concluding the experience by beating up the girl.

I once treated a man who, though extremely successful in his profession had been sexually competent before marriage only with "sluts," as he puts it. He was actually married to a fine woman with whom he experienced no sexual difficulties. But, in an unguarded moment, he confessed he thought of his marital relationship as one between a potentate and his concubine. As far as he knew, he loved her. He received a great deal of pleasure out of lavishing expensive gifts on her. Yet, he could not bring himself to conventionalize his marriage by having children. He had not been aware that his aversion to having children arose from a need to defend himself from "respectable" sex. It was his rationalizing belief that men who consented to having children had been trapped by their wives' biological drives. Their bleak destiny was a life of bourgeois dullness in split-level suburbia.

It may seem strange that people can be warped, inhibited or guilt-ridden in one area of living, as in sex, yet outstandingly effective in another, as in business. Somehow we seem to think of the efficient executive in the competitive world of business as a man among men who should have no difficulty in the mature, masculine conduct of his sex life. Actually, the intricate patterns of human personality embrace innumerable apparent contradictions many of which, on analysis, prove to be dynamically interrelated. In another client it was possible to demonstrate that the same factors which underlay his sexual inhibition contributed substantially to his business success. Sexually, he was prudish, distant, cold, mechanically efficient, but emotionally uninvolved. As a child, he had harbored intense feelings of sinfulness because of his secret sexual fantasies stimulated, in part, by his mother who was at once artlessly seductive and unwittingly rejective. To protect himself from the risk of exposing his sinful secret self he built a wall of cynicism, of cold, logical objectivity between himself and others. He tried to view the problems of life with the dispassionate eye of a mathematician. These traits served him well in his management of a complex industrial enterprise. His decisions were unmarred by the ambiguities which emotional sensitivity so often imposes on objective logic. At the same time, these very traits, developed to conceal his vulnerability, made it impossible for him to become deeply involved in human relationships. He was incapable of the emotional intimacy, the trust, the emotional giving, the unreserved, self-exposing letting-go which can make sexual expression wholeheartedly self-fulfilling. There was, thus, a psychological consistency between his relative success in one area of life and his relative failure in another.

Some Distinctions Made

In a broad sense, a distinction may be made between sexual relations between men and women who have the expectation of future marriage (pre-marital sex), and sexual relations between men and women who have essentially given up the expectation they will ever be married to each other.

The expectation of marriage is very frequent, of course, and it is also true that many such pre-marital relationships do lead to marriage. Furthermore, it may well be doubted that the pre-marital experience would have been acceptable to many women without the expectation of marriage. In general, pre-marital sex in our society has been freed somewhat from its former moral onus. At the very least, the attitudes of society are flexible on this point, permitting a considerable diminution of guilt for pre-marital sex when marriage is the expected outcome. Altogether, it is highly probable that those people who are destined to have good sex relations in marriage can experience pre-marital sex without very much unnecessary guilt.

For those men and women who have essentially given up the expectation that they will ever be married a generalization may be made: with the sheer experience of living, there is a certain dilution of the irrational elements of moral involvement. The mature person who has repeated the experience of survival after transgressions, who has tested out religious and social values through his or her own personal experience, will tend to have some dilution of the guilt associated with moral values which would otherwise attend sexual indulgence. I think society in general tends to blame and censure less those people who are advanced in years but who have not yet married, or who have been divorced or widowed. Society can be more readily forgiving with such people who, consequently, have a tendency to be more readily forgiving of themselves.

A broad distinction may also be made between men and women in regard to guilt and unmarried sexual expression. Generally, there is more guilt among women. Sex outside the sanctified walls of marriage for the man is, in a sense an expression of his manliness, and although a segment of society may give lip service to male chastity, there is a strong tendency to turn the other way and not look at the actual behavior. This is much less true in the case of women, partially because society accords women a different sexual role in that they are forbidden to use men as sexual objects, whereas men can use women as sexual objects, perceiving them as little else than a transient means to the gratification of immediate appetite.

But physiologically there is no intrinsic reason why women can't use men as sex objects, and in fact, women have done so in other cultures and in other times in history. In addition, in our own culture today there is increasing evidence that women may have different attitudes towards themselves and sexual expression, and possibly the future may bring with it a real emancipation for women. I know there are those who decry this trend, who say that this is a violation of women's "intrinsic" nature. But by the word "intrinsic" I mean physiological, and there is nothing in woman's physiological make-up to prevent her from developing a different, entirely wholesome attitude toward sexual expression so that she may have less total personal involvement, not placing so many secondary, including religious, values upon sexuality.

Nevertheless, women today are in a more highly contradictory situation than men. For if they accept the seductions of the culture in the direction of complete emancipation, they are exposing themselves to greater conflicts and danger than men because society, and their own learned moral values, do not really allow them complete freedom. On the other hand, if the woman plays the sexual role which society says it demands, she is in constant conflict with her normal sexual impulses and with the ever present seductions of the culture.

NOT A PRESCRIPTION

It is always easier to say how men and women ought to feel, rather than to make a prescription for them which they can use with the aim of feeling that way. But for mature unmarried men and women who have unmanageable guilt in relation to sexual expression, it may help them to know there is a highly respectable segment of the community which believes that the guilts associated with this very human instinctual need are essentially irrational.

The guilts have been learned, and in a certain sense the individual has been victimized. Men and women have associated values to sex which are not necessary, for sex is not a sinful thing. The values have come from an unselective, undiscriminating persistence of archaic codes whose origin had a certain justification but which have no relevance whatsoever to the current state of affairs in our present-day culture.

Men and women who have unmanageable guilt in relation to unmarried—and married—sexual expression need to learn that today's representation of yesterday's codes of conduct have been imposed upon them. They have been victimized, and they themselves have assimilated these values of yesterday through the agency of their own parents. Furthermore, these men and women need to know that as adults they still see their parents as next to God, and a certain detachment from these infantile investments of authority in parental figures needs to be accomplished.

This means a readiness to confront one's self, to recognize the insidious ways in which this infantile perception of the parents still persists, despite a surface rational view of the parents as "just people." Men and women have to get at these more unconscious implicit attitudes toward authority. They need to recognize that when there is a discrepancy between their own beliefs with regard to sex and their actual helpless feelings about sex, these helpless feelings are symptomatic of an essentially unaltered infantile view of their parents as being next to God. They have to learn in depth that parents are people, that they are not gods.

In conclusion, the early influences in childhood are very much conditioned by the social values current at the time the parents were growing up. Consequently, there is an inevitable transmission of these values, if not in a literal sense, then certainly in some modified manner. But man is a finite being. He is the subject of conflict from many sources, and he is a whole person in whom it is virtually inevitable that difficulties arising in one area of life should, somehow, find their way into other areas. Thus, sex has to carry a great burden for most of us, for not only are social and individual moral values tied to it, but sex is also the battleground on which the person proves masculinity or femininity, and on which all prove their adequacy as people.

Yet there are men and women who wish to be completely devoid of guilt. This is the same as wishing to be devoid of conflict. Both wishes are completely hopeless, for only a dead thing has no conflict. But even if it were possible, I question whether it would be good for men and women not to have conflict and guilt. Having some feelings of guilt is not so disastrous. One can live with it. One can overcome it. This is how men and women grow. One does not grow by denying sensitivity and conflict, but rather by constructively using the former and resolving the latter. If conflict or guilt reaches a point where it is nonsensical and irrational, we must have the courage to face up to it, examining what is really involved in the situation so we can come to terms with the reality of our lives.

One does not have to be in love to enjoy wholesome sex relations. If you happen to be in love, so much the better. Ideally, one can still preserve those values associated with sex which view it as an intense and personal experience peculiarly suited to express a love relationship, while at the same time freeing it from associations and connotations of sin and other symbolic functions so that a more spontaneous and less burdened sexual expression may take place.

As adults we cannot change our childhood experiences of conflict, but we can have a sane, wholesome and constructive acceptance of unmarried sex if we will believe that sex is normal; that moral restraints have been learned and are legacies from archaic codes of conduct with limited relevance to present-day culture; that parents are not gods; that fear of the unknown gives way before the experience of survival; and that self is more than sex, and self-worth more than sexual expression.

For some men and women, these ideas will be difficult to accept, and if the burdens of guilt and conflict are too great in relation to unmarried, or married sexual expression then the individual may wish the help of some form of psychotherapy.

4.

*"Why is there so much counterfeit love
in our society?" we asked Dr. McLean.*

PRESTON G. McLEAN, M.D.

Teacher, American Foundation of
Religion and Psychiatry

In his interview Dr. McLean also discusses:

"What is the meaning of real love?"
 "What are some fantastic notions about love?"
  "Do men and women differ in their search for love?"
"What is counterfeit love?"
 "Is the magical thinking of childhood a detriment to love?"
  "What affects one's ability to love?"
"How important is it to give pleasure in love?"
 "Can people face the truth about themselves?"
  "How do 'ideals' interfere with being able to love?"
"Does vanity affect love?"
 "What part does jealousy play in love?"
 *"Can the desire to always tell the truth sometimes
  hide anger?"*

4.

This is what Dr. McLean said when interviewed in his office:

Trying to make illusion and magical thinking do the job of love is resorting to counterfeit love. You can test whether your love is genuine or counterfeit by asking how you would feel if you lost the person you think you love.

The reaction to the loss of someone who is really loved is grief and regret which, though painful, is never paralyzing. But, reactions to the loss of counterfeit love are depression and anger, often very paralyzing.

Here is a poem which offers a good example of what I mean by love. The Poet: Emperor Wu Ti (140 B.C.–86 B.C.) Hun Dynasty (202 B.C.–220 A.D.)

Remembering Li Fu-Jen

For your silken rustling my ear was quick.
For your lovely presence my heart is sick.
In your marble courtyard the dust lies thick.
  O my lady!
Your empty room is cold and still.
The fallen leaves are blown at will
And lie in heaps at your silent sill,
  My lady!
Gone never to come back again.
My restless heart is filled with pain.
I long for you, and my longing's vain,
  O lovely lady!

This is honest love. It was written by an Emperor for his concubine — the original beauty-contest winner, since from each district in China at this time the prettiest women competed for the favor of the Emperor. Here was a man who, when he lost his love, did not act out of despair, for he could easily find other women. He was obviously grief-stricken, although there was nothing paralyzing about his feelings.

Many people accept counterfeit love rather than the real thing. Why? For several reasons. One is the lack of knowledge about real love. You can only love what you know. Many adults have never had an example of the real thing in their early lives with their parents, from whom we learn what love is. Counterfeit love comes in part from making the best of a bad bargain, of trying to do well with what is available.

Another cause is the culture, which may be trying to palm off counterfeits as the real thing. This is particularly true in our culture insofar as it is materialistic, where to consume and to spend are important. People are taught to love expensive cars, expensive women, and other costly things.

A third cause of counterfeiting is a feeling of inability either to obtain the genuine or to keep it. Or a feeling that you will spoil the genuine out of a belief in your own inner badness.

Another cause is curiosity, the desire to know something, to gain experience. It is very hard, for example, to persuade a woman to go to bed with you because you are curious, or for the fun of it. It has to be for love. People train themselves to go through the act of loving, so they will not feel they are faking. They come to believe themselves that this is love, although their actual motive is curiosity and the acquisition of experience. You see this in adolescent loves.

Another cause of love of the counterfeit kind is that it may be a way of avoiding feeling depressed. You can't have a simple sexual relationship lift you out of a depression because sex is supposed to be for love. So again, people try to persuade themselves that they really love someone, whereas all they are hoping for is that the other person will cheer them up — through beauty, or talent, or sex.

Vanity is another great cause of love of counterfeits. Vanity is love of an elevated conception of oneself, based on illusions about oneself, expressed frequently in external embodiments. For instance, a man would like a wife who, in the eyes of the world is very desirable, either for her wealth or her beauty. A woman will express her own love of self, her vanity, by attaching herself to a man who is "somebody." Vanity is to be sharply distinguished, however, from the love of oneself as an honestly worthwhile person.

Another cause of counterfeit love is to improve one's opinion of the self. People feel good on two bases: either what others think about them or what is right and wrong. They will pretend to love someone or something because others think well of them for doing so, and thus they feel good. This is not to be confused with love. Or they will pretend to love something because they feel it's right to do so. They feel comfortable when they are doing what they think is "right."

We can illustrate further: a common problem in marriage is that basically women organize their opinions of themselves on what others think, and men, on what is right and wrong. Both of these ways of feeling at ease are important, but in a marriage, they may cause problems. For example, a wife may be very concerned because she does not have an adequate wardrobe, or that the furniture is old, because she cares about what people think. But her husband may become angry with her because he thinks it is wrong to be so materialistic at this stage of the marriage. There may ensue a bitter battle over who is going to be feeling good in the situation, and on what basis.

Love Is Not a Band-Aid

Another cause of counterfeit love is the need to repair damage, usually to self-esteem. This causes a lot of rebound loves. A man may feel he is unloved not because of himself, but that his marriage ended because on the surface he did not have enough money. Then he drives himself to find a woman who cares nothing whatsoever about money. This is to heal a wound. Love to him is a Band-Aid.

Then there are women who want their husbands to make up to them for everything they never got from their mothers (husbands, too, look to their wives for this). The husbands must treat them as the ideal mother would treat an ideal child, which is to be good to them, to understand everything, never to criticize, to give rather than to demand. There results much guilt as no one is as ideal as he wishes to be treated.

If people could only realize that they have settled for counterfeit love, instead of the real thing, there is a chance they will be able to find real love. I believe most people can face the truth about themselves. Their initial reaction may be one of not liking the truth, but there is something about facing the truth which is always very relieving and prepares for constructive change.

For instance, one patient of mine was very concerned that she was not a good mother. I said to her, "What other kind of mothers do they make?"

This woman could not tolerate staying for hours with her two children; they hurled spaghetti at each other. I asked, "Can you be a good mother for 1½ hours a day?" She said, "Yes." I said, "Well, that's tremendous." And she felt very reassured.

On the one hand, I think when you wake people up from a dream, they don't like it. But if you hand them a psychological road map at the same time, they feel they get something in exchange. They may not be able to take action after they find out where they are from looking at a road map, but at least they know where they are. This is something.

People kill themselves over ideals which are bigger than life-size, just dreams. Let's say, for example, that a woman keeps wondering why she doesn't love her husband more and do the things he wants. If she can realize that the reason she married him was to get away from home and to repair the damage she felt she suffered from her mother, perhaps she can stop expecting her husband to be the perfect mother. Even if you are not able to put the truth into practice, at least when you know the truth you don't feel too guilty. You realize there are some inner blocks, or that the situation itself doesn't allow for action.

The notion of love is already overly inflated. It is very hard to love, for one thing, because most people aren't that lovable. There are people whom everybody loves because they are lovable, but they are few. For instance, people to this day are proud to be related to anyone who served under Robert E. Lee, because he was such a lovable man. He was able to put an army into the field without paying the men. It was easy enough to desert for the Confederates. But who goes around saying how proud he is to have relatives who served with General Grant? Not many. It is not that Grant wasn't a good general or was a bad person, but that he wasn't so lovable a man as Lee.

In order to love, reality must be faced. When you stop dreaming, you stop sleepwalking. You can decide what you want to do. You see many of these moments of truth in analysis. I remember a patient many years ago who used to complain constantly about his wife. Finally he decided to leave her. Then he realized, as he put it, "You know, I'm always telling you what a crumb my wife is and she is. But I'm really a crumb, too." He added, "So I went back, and us two crumbs will keep this crumby marriage going."

This made sense under the circumstances. He woke up from his dream that he was entitled to Miss America. Thus, the cause of many problems in love is either that you are trying to love someone who is not that lovable, or you yourself are not that loving a person. Recognizing this, I think, can sometimes turn the tragedy into the comedy or practical joke that it is.

Some illustrations come to mind. One couple plays the following game with each other. The man comes home and notes that his spouse has been playing "hurt, crushed, and brave about it all" for several days. It is obvious to him that no one could be that crushed and hurt and live beyond three months of age, but he cannot end the emotional blackmail because he is very effective at getting the results he wants from his wife when it's his turn to be "hurt and brave about it all." Another couple plays the following game on occasion: the husband is seen as "the beast I married" by his wife who believes in her own mind that "someone as wonderful as I am deserves something better." The husband, at the same time, is casting himself as "a man any woman would be proud to have as a husband" and his wife as "a witch in angel's clothing."

LOVE DOES NOT HAVE TO BE TRAGEDY

The tragedy in love comes from the wishful and the magical thinking of childhood. The persistence of childhood ideals, in grown-up versions, leads people to counterfeit love.

The child thinks he is his mother's darling, whereas, to an outsider, he does not look quite so charming. There is a line in a poem called "The Boy Next Door" which goes, "The clabber-headed bastard with a head full of snot," which I'm sure is not the way his mother saw him. Children are fed unbelievably false notions of themselves, and of love, and how wonderful their parents are.

The personal myth by which the family usually lives goes to the effect "We are really, when you allow for this, that, and the other thing, much nicer than other people and consequently deserve more. If we don't get it, then we can feel we have been deprived and mistreated and not given our just desserts."

The reverse, "You are an awful child; there is no good in you whatsoever," is equally mythical. Brought up on these two extremes, I think it is very hard for people to be exactly as they are. They are always trying to pass themselves off as at least 25 to 100 per cent better than they are. There is also reverse vanity: one tries to pass himself as less than he knows himself to be, or than others know him to be.

Honesty is not necessarily real love, for it may be a form of counterfeit love. For example, there is the man who says, "Certainly I love my wife, but when she does something wrong, I tell her. No point in kidding her. This is an act of love."

It is rather an act of counterfeit love. It is primarily an aggressive move. So is jealousy. Jealousy is really the fear that something nice might happen to somebody you hate, although it is usually put in terms of loving the person so much you can't bear to be separated from him. A jealous husband can't stand the idea that his wife might be having fun away from him.

The test of whether a feeling is love or aggression is simply whether the other person is really wounding you, or only opening an abscess to drain the wound, then heal it. It's a difficult thing for a parent who really cares about his child to show him reality, to say, "John you will never be General MacArthur, but I think you will make a fine lieutenant colonel." If the parent does this, he is healing wounds, in advance you might say. But someone like the husband above, who claims he is frank with his wife, is being aggressive.

Aggression is often disguised as love, particularly in a show of possessiveness. People won't let another go if they think he is going on to something better. Parents may keep children from attempting anything self-fulfilling or good. A wealthy father may say, "Son, why don't you get up and do something on your own?" at the same time stamping on the son emotionally so he can't move at all. The father is pleased with himself that he sounds good, is saying the right words, urging the son to be independent and successful. But he isn't acting in a way that will allow the son to be on his own. I remember years ago a son who was seventeen years old and who lost two million dollars of his father's money on the New Orleans cotton exchange. His father's only comment was, "Well, he has to learn." This is a father.

With love, as with work, people often find they can perform but get no enjoyment from it. This is related to the fear of complete success. Some settle for partial success. They will succeed in marriage but not in work. Or in play, but not in work or marriage. A woman patient recently felt a failure because she was still a virgin. (She had the good sense not to translate this feeling into action and become promiscuous.) She comes from a staid New England background. I said, "Can you imagine your parents answering you if you asked 'What is sex like?' with, 'Sex is the most fun you can have without laughing, and if it isn't that, why do it'?"

She had never thought of this, that you took part in sexual intimacy for the pleasure and creativity of it. Very often many things which, on the surface, look like a lot of fun, are really the most driven things in the world. Many girl cheerleaders in high school or college, for example, appear to be having a great time. But a more frightened group it would be hard to find.

I think, for example, that the amount of fun that goes on in a night club is very little. On the surface, a night club is supposed to be a place to enjoy yourself, but attending one is largely a way of sharing a depression or avoiding depression by affecting an interest in sex and women.

All kinds of professional lives which really should be quite joyous are not. They are very driven. I would say there are relatively few doctors or lawyers who could answer, "Yes," if asked, "Do you really get fun out of your work?" They do a good job. But to enjoy it, is very difficult. This is one of the problems of psychoanalysts. They often feel guilty about the fun they get out of their work, or the money they make. They think they are not supposed to get pleasure from what they do.

It's hard to convince people you ought to be well paid for something you like to do. They feel that if you get pleasure out of it, this should be enough. Or if you get money out of it, that should be enough. For a teacher to ask for a lot of money, in addition to getting fulfillment from teaching, is thought to be too much. Or that a wife should be happy with her children, with nice clothes, with her husband — everyone objects to this as too much pleasure.

A patient missed a session the other day. When she arrived the next day, she said, "I bought six sweaters, the first clothes I have purchased in years." She also had been out on an enjoyable date. She also had told her mother off on a few things that had angered her. She said to me, "It's just too much success at once." So she had deprived herself of the analytic hour.

It is difficult for many to feel they are entitled to pleasure. Sometimes they hide the feeling by pretending not to be enjoying something. Or they may affect enjoying something they really do not enjoy. This is related to the inability to be completely successful. It may relate to an inability to love, or it may not.

Out of this inability to accept complete success comes counterfeit love and counterfeit pleasure, also, inflationary and deflationary people, those who inflate or deflate their own value. Let me conclude with a favorite observation of mine which goes: "Things are never as bad as they seem. They are always much worse, but you unconsciously keep from recognizing the full extent of the damage."

5.

*"What would you say to a married man or woman
who complains, 'There's no fun, no excitement,
or discovery any more — we come at each other like
machines turning over for the thousandth
time'?"* we asked Dr. Devereux.

**

GEORGE DEVEREUX, Ph.D.

Professor of Research in Ethnopsychiatry,
Temple University School of Medicine

In his interview Dr. Devereux also discusses:

"Why do some turn romance into 'Swedish gymnastics'?"
"Where do fairy-tale images of marriage start?"
*"Do most people ever achieve the depths of fulfill-
ment in love?"*
"Can one help the self to pleasure?"
*"What does it mean when we see our marriage partner
as only a device?"*
*"How are our infantile demands and cravings related
to happiness in sexual life?"*
"How does fantasy affect our sexuality?"
*"How does understanding someone else affect our own
happiness?"*
*"What must we do to see the other person in his full-
est measure?"*
"Why is it important for our sexual life that we be mature?"

5.

This is what Dr. Devereux said when interviewed in his office:

I would say that such a person had no romance to begin with. Instead, he had fantasies and delusions, a craving for the type of gratification that no adult should expect from another adult.

Many people very often demand from romance not the gratification of adult, mature love goals but the fulfillment of infantile, diffuse, and immature cravings. Let me put it this way. Someone who has been starved for milk in the early years of life cannot later on make it up by drinking nothing but milk all day long. He must learn to switch to steak, potatoes, vegetables and other adult foods, because that is what his adult body needs. Should he insist on sticking to a milk diet because he didn't get enough milk in childhood, he will get sick.

I think our society has failed to put across to many people just how much excitement, thrill, real romance and satisfaction is truly available to the adult.

Love-making is a good example. As is generally known, a child is neither physically nor emotionally capable of making love. In his early relationship to his mother he does not see her as a complete human being. She is not his mother in every sense nor even a real person; it is only the maternal breast as an object that he sees and loves.

It is the adult's privilege to enjoy the thrill and gratification of his capacity to see more and more in a person, to value more and more aspects of him.

Something else which belongs only to adults is the realization that a purely dependent, mutually parasitical relationship, in which the other person is not seen as an independent individual, but as a device, a mere means of gratification, is a very poor, very thin and very ungratifying relationship.

For instance, if a man loves a woman only because she cooks well and has the anatomical features needed to give him satisfaction, then she really is not a human being in his eyes. She has no independence, no autonomy, no color, no three-dimensionality. The relationship between his image of her and her real being, is comparable to the relationship between a blueprint and a house.

You cannot live in a blueprint, only in a house. You can fantasy what it would be like to live in the house which is to be built from the blueprint. But it's only in a real house in which you can live. In the same way, a menu can only titillate your appetite, but cannot satisfy your hunger.

The more you recognize the other person's independence and his value as an individual, the more you value and enrich your own life. At the same time you also enrich your partner, and the richer your partner is, the richer will be your mutual relationship and your own happiness.

Whenever romance disappears, I would therefore say that there was, to start with, only a figure out of a child's fairy tale, dressed up in adult clothes.

Let me give another example. Suppose that a single woman of twenty-five, with normally functioning glands and a natural sex impulse, comes to an analyst complaining about her fiancé. She describes what she thinks an ideal marriage should be. She tells about the wonderful meals she would cook, and how frilly and pretty her dresses would always be, and how he would never see her unkempt, and how well she would economize, and what a fine hostess she would be. She talks and talks and talks, but never once does she mention any hint of sexuality in this dreamed-of marital relationship.

Then, when the analyst asks her, "How about sex with him?" she might say, "Oh yes, of course, that would also be wonderful."

Such a woman has simply built up a fine fairy-tale image of a pseudo-marriage, which would not really be a marriage at all, but only a disguised gratification of an ideal father-daughter relationship, from which the mother has been successfully eliminated and where, because of the fear of incest, sex would naturally be taboo.

An Animated Vending Machine

A number of years ago I was traveling abroad in a relatively backward country and saw at a night club an eight-year-old girl, a dancer (a rather scrawny child, not very pretty, with a prematurely old face) made up as though she were a grown woman and taught to go through seductive dance motions as though she were a grown woman. This child did have a very good dance technique. But the impression she made on me was quite disagreeable. Her dance seemed obscene rather than sensual.

This is a good image of what many peoples' conception of married romance is, and it is this kind of "romance" — really a pseudo-romance — that dies.

When there is real romance, real emotion, real adult relationship, there is a love between husband and wife that is primarily a truly mature love. It is not a disguised father-daughter, mother-son type of relationship masquerading as a marriage, in which romance is doomed from the start, chiefly because there was no real romance in it to begin with.

Let me use a rather outlandish example. Hamburgers are good and chocolate fudge is good. But the chocolate fudge poured on the hamburger makes a mess. The pseudo-romance that dies is like a hamburger with chocolate fudge poured over it.

You cannot enter into and build a mature relationship with infantile expectations. You should not even seek to enter a mature relationship until you yourself are mature enough to handle it. If you are already in it, you can try to grow up quickly, preferably by consulting a good psychoanalyst.

Let me give you an example of how destructive it can be to engage in a relationship for which you do not possess the requisite maturity. Suppose that a little girl of seven, passionately fond of dolls, gets a little baby brother or sister and, trying to emulate her mother and show what a big girl she is, seeks to satisfy her future ambition to have a baby and therefore manages to persuade her mother to allow her to cart the new baby all over the place. Even if we suppose, for the sake of argument, that she really does this with devotion, it is a fact that she is simply not big enough to carry a ten-months old baby in her arms and is, therefore, likely to get a hernia or to drop the baby, which would be tragic if it were harmed.

People should not aim at things for which they are not ready. You don't start out, if you want to study music, by learning a Chopin concerto. You sit down and do finger exercises and study easy pieces until you are ready for the Chopin concerto.

Unfortunately, the law tells us that people can marry if they are X years old, the age varying from state to state, in other words, when they are physiologically capable of reproduction. Unfortunately, the state does not bother to ask if they are also emotionally mature enough to engage in a mature relationship. Yet, you can be fully formed physiologically, and still be terribly infantile emotionally.

The pseudo-romance, which I constantly compare to the fairy tale, is not the real romance — the kind of romance that requires the partners to be emotionally adult persons who can fully love and who truly enjoy being loved. That is the devil of it, that so many people cannot tolerate *being* loved. You can't imagine how often one hears patients say, "Anybody who falls in love with me immediately disqualifies himself (or herself), because he (or she) is a dope to care for somebody as immature, neurotic, contemptible, and sinful as I am."

When people enter a relationship in this frame of mind, the relationship gets destroyed and the partners get destroyed.

We are living in a very strange world. Let me tell you an anecdote. A distinguished anthropologist was visiting a rather primitive country and decided to send a Christmas present to a friend. Since, in that particular place, a certain kind of native textile was especially attractive, he went to the marketplace and chose such a textile. He started to bargain with the owner and after perhaps an hour they agreed on a price that seemed fair and square to both of them and concluded the deal.

Then it occurred to this anthropologist that it might be the simplest solution to send identical gifts to all of his friends for Christmas. So he said to the owner, "Look, since we have reached a fair price and you have more of these textiles, I'll buy them all for the same price."

"I have no intention of selling them all to you," replied the owner. "What fun would I have the rest of the day? I have dickered and gossiped with you part of the day and now I want to bargain and gossip with somebody else. I want to argue about the price and pass the time of day."

This kind of relationship is very rare in our society. You walk into a store, plunk down your thirty cents and say, "Pall Malls," then the man hands you your cigarettes, and you turn around and walk out. You never even said, "Good morning or good night"; you don't even know what the salesman looks like, or what he is called, or whether he's sad or gay. He's just an animated vending machine to you.

This highly prevalent kind of extremely schematized, streamlined, pared-down-to-essentials relationship, conditions us to think of all relationships as superficial, not intimate, not multi-valent — which means having many aspects. In a sense, in such pseudo-relationships we are back to Cicero's concept of the slave as a superior kind of machine, there for a particular purpose only, period. Everything else is incidental.

Far too often we simply transpose this approach even into our most important human relations. It is this conception of the marriage partner as a device which is the basis for the end of romance. You would not treat somebody as a device if there was real romance, instead of a childish fantasy of emotional parisitism. In romance, there is a great deal of realism. You may be aware of the fact that the movie actress you have just seen on the screen is more beautiful than your wife, or that some other woman is perhaps more skillful in bed, or that your wife does not cook as well as the chef at the Café Chauveron, and is not as erudite as Madame Curie. Yet you accept all this and still love her, if yours is a realistic, mature love.

You Push the Right Button

It is not mature to take a woman or a man and use them as a clothes-hanger, hanging onto it fairy-tale princess or prince clothing. One day the moths will get into the gossamer dress and then all that you will see will be what is underneath it: the clothes-hanger, the real person to whom you are married and whom you have never even known or tried to know. You have never for one moment concerned yourself with the real human being. She is imperfect, yes! She has her hair in curlers, yes. She does need, perhaps, a little extra makeup on certain days when she has pimples on her face. She does have menstrual cramps, she can get sick and hurt, yes. But if you love a human being and not a phantom, you can accept all this as a beloved part of her true and beloved self.

It is very important to be able to love. As you probably know, one of the basic psychoanalytic criteria of health, of recovery from emotional upsets, is the capacity to love.

Many people think the purpose of psychoanalysis is to turn you into an emotionally completely unmovable person. It is not the purpose of psychoanalysis to turn people into turnips. It is the purpose of psychoanalysis to turn turnips into human beings — to bring them to life, to give them the capacity to feel, to think. Of course, everybody feels, but often in contradictory ways that paralyze them. Let me give a parallel.

Suppose I spend my entire day pushing my two palms against each other. I would expend a tremendous amount of energy doing that while achieving nothing at all. That is what happens to most people's feelings.

They love and they hate. They love just enough to control their hate, they hate just enough to control their love, and the result is nothing except a futile exhaustion of the emotions.

The purpose of psychoanalysis and the purpose of the maturation which the analyst seeks to promote is delivery from this kind of self-defeating, self-cancelling struggle. Analysis tries to help people love freely and also to be able to put their aggressions to a constructive use. People should not use their aggressions to cancel their love nor their love to cancel their legitimate aggressions, and thus become frozen into immobility.

I am going to consider now the expression the interviewer suggested to me: "He comes at me like a machine turning over for the thousandth time."

The question is: Has this wife perhaps treated her husband like a machine? Of course, it is equally legitimate to ask whether the husband considers his wife a complicated machine, the kind where, if you turn the right knob and push the right button, certain mechanical, irreversible impulses and processes are mobilized which end up with intercourse and possibly an orgasm.

Such an approach to sex makes no allowances for fluctuations of mood, and, above all, for imagination.

They Dare Not Look Deeply

It seems to me the problem is very similar to that which confronts the literary critic who tries to distinguish between a superficial adventure novel and a very great and deep novel. There is often more imagination in a relatively plotless masterpiece than in the most hair-raising Western derring-do. So in marriage, the imagination, the originality, the excitement — the real excitement — comes from a partner whom you love, whom you have loved for a long time, and to whose subtlest clues and movements and emotions you are attuned.

I read somewhere that the hallmark of the great masterpiece in music is that, no matter how often you hear it, you discover new things in it. This is not true when you re-read the most exciting detective story, or a Western or a cloak-and-dagger, or a knights-in-armor romance. If you have read it once, you know all there is to know. Likewise, you get all there is to it the first time you listen to a superficial popular song. But if you listen to a Mozart String Quartet you can experience it time and again over a period of decades and each time it will seem newer and more exciting than ever before.

The mature human being has as much and more depth, as many and more values, and facets, as an artistic masterpiece. The thrill of discovery, the thrill of mature romance comes with greater frequency when you really love. But you must love a human being and not a phantom for it to be a real romance, not a fairy tale.

I think, quite naively perhaps, that those who get fun out of a man or woman once or twice, and then are through with that partner, are much like those who, as a rule, read nothing but murder mysteries, and try to read a masterpiece such as Stendhal's "The Red and the Black" only for the two or three pages of erotic scenes in it and, therefore, miss everything else in that great book. Such readers are afraid of depth of thought and feeling. They avoid the intensity of their emotions and the subtleties of insight.

They are unaware of other people because they dare not be aware of themselves. They dare not look deeply into other people because they dare not look deeply into themselves. The Bible says, "Love thy neighbor as thyself." However, as somebody once pointed out, you cannot love your neighbor if you cannot love yourself. I would add to this interesting comment the further statement that you cannot understand another human being unless you can — and are willing to — understand yourself first. You cannot tolerate another person's deeper emotions unless you can first tolerate your own.

A BLIND, DEAF READING OF LIFE

I think, on the whole, that all people are truly interesting and, on the whole, pretty nice. Therefore, if someone lives with another human being and is not able to form a deeper relationship with that person, he is missing the real story of life. He is very much like the primitive Indian tribe parked right on top of the Mesabi iron deposit: it never occurred to them that there was a very large fortune in iron ore. Some other Indians were sitting on top of gold placers in California. They didn't even know of the gold and were much more interested in catching jack rabbits and killing their enemies, than in mining the gold.

Essentially, I believe we must simply switch from a detective-novel "reading" of life to a Shakespeare "reading" of life. Look at Shakespeare's plots and the plots of the Greek dramatists. Frankly, what are they? Police court reports. Topics which today a tabloid newspaperman disposes of in a headline, thirty badly constructed sentences and some sensational photographs.

But along comes an Aeschylus or a Sophocles or a Euripides or a Shakespeare and humanizes the criminal court's shabby tragedy simply by going below the surface. The inspiration for the novel which I most admire and which to me is the best novel ever written, Stendhal's "The Red and the Black", was given to Stendhal by a newspaper clipping about a young man shooting his older ex-mistress in church.

Stendhal, being a genius, no doubt asked himself what made these people tick? What human emotions, what series of circumstances, led up to this criminal-court climax? He gave us his answer and we have "The Red and the Black". In the same way, you can take a very simple girl or a decent, ordinary fellow, and if you get to know her or him, you will see that there is a Shakespeare or a Euripides play or a Stendhal novel in them, too. This means that it is our unwillingness to seek the depths in our marriage partner that ends romance.

What comes to my mind here is the passage from the New Testament that there is no one as blind as he who does not want to see, nor as deaf as he who does not want to hear. What is appalling is that the destruction of romance results from a self-deafening and a self-blinding of one or both partners to the potentialities of the situation, and makes them turn what should be real romance into hygienic, indoor Swedish gymnastics.

There was a story that, at a certain Court, two fantastically noble and rich men vied with each other in the beauty and costliness of their attire. One day one of them came to Court loaded with diamonds and the other came loaded with rubies, one came in velvet, the other in silk, and so on, for quite a while. Finally, one day, one of them turned up in what looked like ordinary sackcloth and everybody was very much surprised.

They asked, "What's the big idea?"

The man opened his jacket and it turned out he had taken a great painting and had it cut down to make a suit out of it. That is how people deal far too often with their so-called "loved ones."

What can people do who feel that romance in marriage has died? The first thing they do is to blame the partner instead of looking hard at themselves. Consulting most textbooks on marriage seldom helps. Most of the time it's like presenting a starving explorer at the North Pole with a French cookbook. People who consult marriage manuals only remind me of a millionaire who has a fortune locked up in a safe whose lock he has allowed to rust and whose key he has bent. He is starved for a crust of bread even though he has a million dollars locked up in his safe.

I think a little "oil," of the variety known as "internal elbow grease," a little facing of yourself and a little aid tendered to the partner so that he or she too, may face himself or herself will help. I don't say it's a foolproof cure for everyone. Some will also want to find a good marriage counsellor. Others may seek out priests, ministers or rabbis who are insightful and kind people and use the Bible as they should use it, instead of beating people over the head with it. Still others will go to psychoanalysts.

There is one sentence in the Bible which I love very much: He who says he loves God and doesn't love his fellow man is a liar. I think if we abide by this view we can help others out a great deal.

Many people, if they did not spend most of their energy fighting themselves, or the phantoms they call "wife" or "husband," would very soon function much better if they tried to understand themselves. If I have both my hands busy pushing against each other, I don't have a hand free to greet a friend, or to embrace my wife. It's these inner knots in which people are tied, that keep them from fulfilling their potential. And, as they become more aware of what they really do, they learn to stop wasting so much energy fighting themselves and others — and learn to live.

Real romance is often born from the ashes of lost infantile illusions cremated in the test tube of reality.

6.

> "Why is the forbidden affair exciting?"
> we asked Dr. Sperling.

OTTO E. SPERLING, M.D.

Associate Clinical Professor of Psychiatry,
Department of Psychiatry, State University of
New York, Downstate Medical Center

In this interview Dr. Sperling also discusses:

*"Do men and women need a variety of partners for enjoy-
ment of sex?"*

"Is the feeling of the forbidden an added allure to sex?"

*"Must men and women feel safe in order to perform
sexually?"*

*"Should one concentrate on pleasure to achieve sexual satis-
faction?"*

"Does hate play a role in sex?"

"When is sex merely a release of anxiety?"

6.

This is what Dr. Sperling said when interviewed in his office:

It is often said that the forbidden affair is more pleasurable than the permitted. Is this true?

I would say no.

From observation of the sexual habits of human beings and of animals, it seems beyond doubt that people who wish to engage in sexual activity look for security. They look for a situation in which there is no danger.

People usually seek out a place of seclusion, a place where they cannot be surprised or attacked. They don't want to have witnesses. But above all, they want to be secure. That is one of the pre-conditions of sexual enjoyment.

The forbidden situation is dangerous, and the feeling of fear and the feeling of enjoyment are for a majority of people mutually exclusive. In order to achieve full pleasure, it is necessary to be able to concentrate on it.

This need to concentrate on pleasure applies not only to sexual matters but to any kind of pleasure. If one goes to the movies knowing he should be working, then the enjoyment of the movie will usually be lessened. It is not only tiredness or exhaustion which disturbs our full enjoyment of things, but much more, any kind of fear, anxiety, pain, jealousy or anger.

The fact remains that there are a number of people who do have to look for forbidden situations in order to enjoy themselves. But these people place themselves in situations where they can never have the full enjoyment they seek.

THE NEED FOR VARIETY

It is also said that the forbidden is pleasurable because there is a need for variety, particularly when men and women have been married for some time.

There is no doubt that human beings have a very strong need for variety. We need to hear the news every morning, see new shows, read new books, hear new jokes. In many respects, everything that is new is appreciated. But this is an intellectual, not an instinctual need.

In other words, we all have instinctual needs but in the gratification of the instinct, the element of the new is an intellectual addition, not an essential pre-condition for the gratification.

For instance, we all need a certain amount of water per day. If one is thirsty he wants water; variety in the taste of water or its chemical composition is unimportant. Or, if one is out of breath he doesn't have to get a different kind of air. He just wants to breathe.

There is no need for variety in these instinctual gratifications. And so it is with the sexual instinct, for in the narrow sense the sexual instinct is blind. There is a French expression, and some American ones also, which say in effect that one woman is just like another. This naturally assumes she is sexually able to behave in a normal way; thus there is no need for variety and there is no need for the forbidden. (There is, on the other hand, the need to meet new people and enjoy new friendships, but although this is sexual in a broad sense, it is not what is generally thought of as "sexual variety.")

In our civilization, monogamy restricts the gratification of the sexual instinct. This is necessary for society but leads to much personal unhappiness. However, unhappiness about monogamy seems to me to have as its main cause not the need for sexuality from new partners, but rather the accumulation of resentment and hatred toward the first marital partner; the desire for a new sexual partner is based on a wish to have a relationship based on love and not on hate, or at least one where the element of hate would not be so prominent.

FORBIDDEN IN CHILDHOOD

The fact that some people are able to enjoy sex only when it is within a forbidden situation is often encountered by psy-

chiatrists and psychoanalysts. It is a symptom like any other
symptom, and may have a variety of causes.

I remember, for example, a man who was having an affair
with a girl who had an apartment of her own. They had plenty of opportunity to meet there where there was no danger,
and occasionally they did so. But the man also felt a need to
have sexual relations on the staircase of a public building.

Although most employees use the elevator, some do use
the stairs, and so these two were often in a situation where
they could be surprised. In this man's case, the cause was
sadism. He wanted to see suffering and anxiety on the face
of the girl.

But you can't generalize. There may be all kinds of reasons
for seeking the forbidden. Frequently it is a sign of immaturity. In childhood, sexual activities are forbidden. Later on,
however, they are not forbidden in certain situations and under certain conditions.

A part of growing up consists in changing one's ideas and
feelings about what is right and what is wrong. For instance,
to sit in father's easy chair may be forbidden to the young
boy, but if, as a grown man he observes this prohibition and
cannot permit himself to sit in an easy chair, then this is a
sign of immaturity. He still carries with him the inhibition
of his childhood.

This carry-over of the forbidden is frequently true of sexual
matters. Sex was forbidden to the child; therefore, sex remains
for some people the forbidden thing — and is sought for
that reason. But, because of this same feeling, the man or
woman disturbs his sexual activity by anxiety.

In some people, incidentally, anxiety can be sexualized. Although it is rather rare, there are those who during a test,
or an interview for a job, or when cheating or stealing, or
riding on a roller coaster, will get a sexual discharge. For
them, the anxiety connected with these situations is enough
to bring on the discharge without any partner and without
any other kind of activity.

But the combination of sexual discharge and anxiety is
the exception; furthermore, such sexuality is without any real
happiness, without real feeling of fulfillment. These people
often feel very guilty because they realize that this is a perversion.

What Can Be Done

I would say that, in general, the more conditions attached to sexual enjoyment or any other pleasurable situation, the more difficult it is to achieve. If a man, for instance, says he wants to marry a girl who is not only a beauty queen but also very intelligent, who loves him and shares all of his interests, and who must also be a redhead because he wants red-headed children, the chances are very small he will ever marry.

In the same way the forbidden is one more condition. If, in addition to all of the other requirements of a sexual partner, the condition of being forbidden is also present, it makes so much more difficult, if not impossible, the achievement of full enjoyment.

Now, what can a man or woman do if they feel the forbidden *is* more exciting?

First of all, if they are married, they can look into their feelings about their marital partner. Is there resentment, anger and hate? In this respect I am reminded of a fable which Schopenhauer told of the many different types of animals which retreated to a cave during the winter. Each type of animal tried to survive the cold by huddling next to the others. This worked well until the porcupines got close and their long spikes hurt. Finally, the porcupines found the right distance where they could be near enough to be comforted but far enough not to hurt.

This story of Schopenhauer's is, I think, a very important description of human relationships. In the course of time, a too-close or too-distant relationship can often lead to hurt, resentment, anger and hate.

A man or woman, married or single, should realize that the attraction of the forbidden may be a problem of immaturity, for to look at sexuality as something forbidden is an adolescent way of feeling and thinking. They should be aware, too, that they are missing full enjoyment by putting the condition of the forbidden on sex. Those who have overcome this feeling enjoy themselves far more. In short, for many this is a problem of growing up.

7.

*"Will a second marriage be any happier
than a first?" we asked Dr. Wilbur.*

᚛᚛᚛᚛᚛᚛᚛᚛᚛᚛᚛᚛᚛᚛᚛᚛᚛᚛᚛᚛᚛!

CORNELIA B. WILBUR, M.D.
Clinical Director, Falkirk Hospital,
Central Valley, New York

As Told To
MELVIN HERMAN
Executive Director, National Association of
Private Psychiatric Hospitals

In this interview Dr. Wilbur also discusses:

"Do all of us bring to marriage unresolved problems?"
   "When are the first steps toward divorce often taken?"
      *"Can a marriage be saved if one partner is uncon-
      sciously sabotaging it?"*
*"What kinds of wishes, attitudes and feelings may be hidden
   in a marriage?"*
      "What is self-imposed guilt?"
         *"Can men and women be compatible in spite of their
         individual problems?"*
"Is there always a 'guilty party' in a divorce?"

CORNELIA B. WILBUR, M.D.

7.

This is what Dr. Wilbur said when interviewed in her office:

The woman who sat across the desk asked, "Do I have a right to a divorce?" Her story was not uncommon. Although she had lived with her husband for many years and their child was now a married adult, her husband throughout his life had been almost completely isolated from his wife and daughter.

He had been a detached person who had a few business and social acquaintances and no friends. She had married him when she was a young girl. Although she was unhappy from the beginning, when her daughter was born she felt she should stay with him. He had gone his own way, contributing to the upkeep of their home according to his own lights and she had worked most of their married life.

As the years wore on, he became quite hostile to her. After their daughter married, their home life was completely empty. The distance between husband and wife became so great that their association with each other was only for purposes of abuse. Was it reasonable to advise her to continue to live with him?

Divorce is sometimes as useful and necessary an institution as marriage itself. Not only is it often justifiable, but it may be the way to save a married couple and their children from lives of misery. However, divorce is often only an escape from facing up to the need of a real solution to a problem. Nevertheless, it may be a mature judgment.

The most normal of us bring to marriage our unresolved problems. The success of marriage depends on how the partners create a means of living happily together, in spite of their hidden neuroses. Paradoxically, they may succeed because of their neuroses or, if lucky, by working them out in the marriage partnership.

In most instances, the seeds of divorce are brought to the marriage. The boy who married the sexiest looking girl he knew, in order to be able to display her as his possession and conquest, regardless of whether or not she was going to make him a good wife, had at the outset a personal problem beyond that of his marriage.

This is also true of the girl who is an unwilling adult yet chooses to enter marriage unprepared to take on the responsibilities of a family or the rights and pleasures of an adult love life. This applies as well to the promiscuous husband who does not feel committed to marriage or as committed as he wishes his wife to be.

In short, the neurotic choice of a partner in marriage indicates unresolved conflicts in oneself which can be carried beyond a disastrous marriage, for we cannot arrange a legal separation from ourselves.

From Childhood On

Marriage usually means *more* rather than *fewer* demands. Marriage is a social institution involving children, the families of the married couple and their friends. It is quite different from a romance, or an affair, which usually remains a relationship between two people.

The evolution in marriage is more often towards satisfaction than towards destruction. Marriage doesn't stand still. For that matter, neither does the courtship which leads to marriage. A young woman, for example, currently in psychoanalysis, is about to be married. When she and her fiancé first met, in spite of an immense mutual attraction, they tended to irritate each other in their efforts to demonstrate their wit, intelligence and abilities. As their relationship developed, she recognized what they were doing to each other and, out of her affection, began to reassure him, thereby reducing his feeling of insecurity. In turn, he then was able to reassure her and the relationship became much closer and more satisfactory. These two people will marry with a good chance of success.

It is quite possible for a couple to be drawn together because of their individual neuroses. Such a marriage may be satisfactory in a way which other people consider incomprehensible. Yet, for the two people involved, it is an eminently satisfactory marriage, for their neurotic needs are satisfied.

There can be hidden provocations and clashes of emotional needs of which the individuals are unaware. The psychoanalytic approach to the question of marriage and divorce has shown that people unconsciously transfer from an important person in their lives a great many wishes, attitudes, feelings and convictions which do not fit the person to whom they are transferred. A man reaches adult life, for example, with unconscious needs and desires arising from a frustrating relationship with his mother. He chooses to marry a particular woman from whom he expects satisfaction of these unconscious needs. His marriage will be in difficulty from the beginning, because he cannot satisfactorily relate to his wife when he really looks upon her as the one whom he expects to fulfill the demands that were denied by his mother. His unconscious transference from his mother to his wife creates conflict in him and in the marriage. As he is unaware of this he is completely incapable of seeing the cause of the conflict.

In a similar way, the woman who screams at her husband, "You're just like my father," may be transferring, partially or wholly, her reactions to a significant figure of her childhood. Such can be a clue that she is projecting her difficulties with her father to her husband. A psychoanalyst might reveal to her the whole structure of transference, but her husband, too, may be projecting into the situation the need to be like his own father, or what he thinks a grown-up male in the image of his father should be. These irrational complications deepen the difficulties of the situation, for there is always the question of unconscious motivation. Understanding that no one operates with complete freedom of will helps to explain many surprising actions. When unconscious attitudes conflict, the marriage may be in difficulty.

People who do not relate satisfactorily to others in social, business or family situations, generally are the ones who have excessive difficulties in marriage. The fact that a marriage is not working, however, does not always mean a divorce is indicated. Many marriages can be saved if deterioration is not allowed to go on for too long a time.

Not only do people have a great capacity for adjustment but a divorce need not occur if both partners are motivated towards salvaging the marriage. If the basis for the marriage is highly neurotic, however, both partners may have to go through extreme personal readjustment. Yet, sometimes the reverberations of the clash are so severe that the marriage cannot be saved. But if along with the neurotic elements a sound basis for a reasonably good relationship exists, there is a chance of saving a marriage.

The steps that may lead to divorce are often first taken in childhood and adolescence. An example of this is a woman who was an arrogant beauty in her youth, the center of an admiring group of boys and girls. Her husband won her over other swains by sheer persistence. He idolized her for many years. All her life she had been self-centered. After years of marriage she became ill as the result of an accident and turned completely into herself. Her husband was forced to make his own social life. Soon he found solace with another woman and eventually asked for a divorce.

At this point she became realistically aware of her own shortcomings. She saw what she had done to their marriage and was willing to do anything to save it. They had children and considered it important that they try to stay together. Her husband agreed to a trial period of a year. During that time she tried to be a thoughtful wife. Yet what she could accomplish no longer depended on herself alone but also on her husband. At no point can a marriage be saved if one partner either consciously or unconsciously is committed to sabotaging it.

He had married an arrogant girl because he wanted one, and she had unconsciously understood this. His need to have a beautiful, arrogant wife to whom he could cater, at least for a period of time, suggests that this marriage started out on a false basis. Furthermore, he had found another woman towards whom he felt a genuine attraction. Regardless of whether this pull was neurotic or healthy, when a married man has found another woman the marriage is obviously in great difficulty. Where the husband sees other women but hasn't found a real attachment, it is easier to save the marriage.

In this case, where the husband agreed only to a limited period of trial, his motivation can be seriously questioned.

A situation such as the one just described may result in an emotional divorce, although the people remain in wedlock. Some people have a great capacity for managing their own lives independently and are able to live in a relatively peaceful state with a husband or wife and still be quite disassociated, in fact, almost unrelated emotionally. But such a marriage is apt to foster neuroses in the children, because there is no real warmth, affection or family relatedness. Beyond that, people who live in a state of emotional unrelatedness in marriage are people who by nature are neurotic and tend to be isolates.

Curiously, when two unhealthy people marry, their problems may be complementary. They satisfy neurotic needs in each other. Consider the complex situation of a man whose wife had always been dependent on him, thus satisfying his neurotic needs for superiority. He was working below his capacity and was dissatisfied with himself. He went into therapy and began to change. He came to the point where he no longer looked for dependency on the part of his wife. But this dependency was part of her neurotic needs; she always had been a dependent person. She then became disturbed about her own dependency. Feeling that her problems were a real threat to her marriage, she entered therapy herself. Eventually they were able to adjust on a healthier level. Where there are two neurotic partners and profound changes may occur in analysis, it is sometimes advisable for both husband and wife to enter therapy.

Although both husband and wife may emerge from a bad marriage with intense feelings of guilt, it is possible to recognize that the destructive force was in the interaction between the two people involved. Without this, they may not have responded as they did. Furthermore, it is possible for a husband or wife to feel guilty erroneously.

A young girl who had married a much older man is an example of self-imposed guilt. Once married they lived rather elegantly, for he introduced her to a world of graciousness and self-indulgence. As they always dined well and drank their share, it was quite a time before she realized that he had begun to drink to excess. His alcoholism dated from the time of her pregnancy, about a year after their marriage. He became worse as the time for the birth of their child approached, hitting her on several occasions.

She was confused by the change in him, only vaguely feeling it might have something to do with her pregnancy. She thought of herself as an enlightened person ready to help her husband whose alcoholism she realized was an illness. Furthermore, she felt that the situation would improve with the birth of their child whom, she thought, he would soon learn to love. After their daughter was born, however, the pattern continued, and she began to feel she had no place to turn with her young child, for her father was dead, her mother an incompetent woman, and she had no family upon whom she could rely.

A friend of her husband's tried to help at this point, and became deeply involved in their affairs. He was a gentle, amiable man who soon became the one pleasant person in her life. She had little idea how he felt about her for some time until he came to her and said, "You can't live through this abuse any longer. I've arranged a transfer to another town and I want to take you and the child with me." She turned to him with relief and love.

They lived together happily for twenty years until the day her daughter was married. Then, she did not return to him after the wedding. On that day, feeling that she had sinned against her daughter, she resolved to go back to her husband. But this she never did. She lived instead by herself. When she was found, she was in a severe depression and it was arranged for her to go into therapy. When she recovered, she obtained a divorce and married the man who loved her.

Blaming oneself and feeling guilty is never the answer. The partners must be willing to work out their problems together. A woman, for example, who at first felt her marriage was relatively happy, by the second year slowly came to realize that she was sexually unresponsive. As a matter of fact, her husband often said, "How can you expect me to live with a telephone pole?"

One day he announced he was leaving. She was completely defeated, feeling that she had destroyed her marriage. For the first time she challenged her puritanical upbringing and her acceptance of the dictum that men had all the sexual fun, women were only supposed to do their "duty." It simply hadn't occurred to her until her husband had actually walked out that she could do anything about her attitude.

She decided to enter therapy. But as her analysis progressed, she realized the fault wasn't hers alone. Her husband, a much more sophisticated person, had given her no assistance, although he could have helped her with her problems. If she had gone on carrying the burden of guilt, she may have used it as a defense against working out her problems herself.

There are more divorces than are really necessary. Everything isn't solved by breaking up a marriage, for the single state still has its problems. Making divorce difficult to obtain is not a solution, however, because no real marriage can be maintained by law. Actually under strict laws, divorce becomes easier as false evidence is employed and the true grounds are never considered.

People with children should do everything possible to resolve their problems. If they cannot, the children may be better off if there is a divorce rather than live with parents who bicker constantly and use the children as pawns in their quarrels. The damage to children may be done long before the divorce. Many patients have said, "If only my parents would have had the sense to get a divorce sooner I'd be better off today." Yet, every child would prefer to have his parents resolve their difficulties and assume their responsibilities to the family.

It is more difficult for children who are raised by one parent. But this plight also occurs in the family in which a parent has died. A marriage where one of the parents is literally a boarder in the home rather than a parent figure is many times more frustrating to the child than an absent parent. Most important, however, is the attitude of the parent who raises the child.

Most divorced people marry again, if they can. They are people who want to be married. Our social life is weighted against the unmarried. There is pressure on the single woman to marry again. Her friends are always match-making. A single woman is a nuisance to her married friends. She may even be a threat. So, too with men, who are looked upon as being on the prowl.

The person who has had an unhappy marriage and rushes into a second one does so because he or she really believes in marriage. However, a second unhappy marriage or a series of bad marriages may result due to a neurotic approach to marriage. There is a strong possibility that if the first marriage is a neurotic one, subsequent marriages will not be any better.

2. HATE

Introduction

There have been many gods of love, few gods of hate. But man has always lived as he lives today, in a two-faced world of love and hate.

Man talks peace, preparing for war. Man talks mercy, showing it only upon occasion. Man talks love, knowing full well he possesses deep anger and hatred.

We express anger and hatred at a political system different from ours, a political party different from ours, a religion or race different from ours. We express anger and hatred at our mates, even our defenseless children, and anger and hatred for ourselves.

To be sure, we also show love, tenderness and understanding. We are often kind, generous, considerate and respectful. But there are few of us who can honestly say that some anger and hatred does not get in the way of living a more satisfactory life.

We asked Hyman Spotnitz, M.D., "Do people have the right to hate as well as to love?"

Hatred wears many faces. It may wear the face of war, or of intolerance, or of not caring about others. When told to "Love thy neighbor," an angry man once replied, "But who is my neighbor?" There is spectacular evidence that man has long been in doubt as to who really is his neighbor.

Forty million died in the last great mass guillotine called the Second World War. Countless thousands have perished since from hunger and disease. In the last five hundred years there have been only a few periods of time when war was not man's bloody companion.

There is also "quiet" evidence that civilized man has great difficulty in handling his hatred and aggression. We asked Lewis L. Robbins, M.D., "Why do we have greater difficulty in dealing with our anger and hate than with our love?"

It has been said by some worried friends of the United States that our leaders and our people have "given up" hope

68

of peace. These critics point to the construction of bomb shelters as one example that we may be digging graves of our own making. Throughout the world, underdeveloped and neutral nations look with mounting concern at both American and Russian foreign policy.

What do we want — war or peace? Is it that we, as well as the Russians, really want the other just "to drop dead"? Can we admit and accept their anger, aggression and hatred, and then deal with it constructively? Can we admit our own anger, aggression and hatred, and deal with it constructively? It would appear that unless all mankind, American and Russian, Negro and White, Catholic and Atheist, can develop tolerance toward each other, peace on earth is impossible.

We asked S. R. Slavson, "What is the meaning of aggression?"

Another face behind which hatred hides is self-punishment. We would like to strike the other fellow, then feel guilty and instead, flagellate ourselves, and feel the victim, not the villain.

In the ever-popular Western, the so-called horse-opera, the "good guy" is always innocent of any wrongdoing. He doesn't smoke or drink or go to "houses of ill repute." His horse always stands as rival to both the "good" and the "bad" woman. In the typical mystery, the murderer is always "up to no good," the victim never deserving of that bullet or vat of lime.

In short, the "victim" is essentially the innocent, as seen in the hero of the Western, just as in the typical romance, he and the heroine must always be victim of some skullduggery before they find true and innocent love in each other's pure arms. There is innocence and its opposite, evil, almost every place we turn in popular entertainment. No hero or heroine is ever responsible for what they do; they are just mistreated and beaten unjustly by wicked forces.

Why? Why does the good sheriff allow himself to be continually slandered — why doesn't he move to another town? Why does the murder victim go down to the cellar in the first place, and bend over the vat of lime in the second? Why does the hero or heroine always allow himself to be discovered in a compromising (but innocent) situation in a motel room?

It doesn't make sense — or does it? In one way or another,

do we all not feel like innocent victims? All of us can point a finger, if we choose and claim, "They did it to me! I'm innocent."

But are we? We asked of Edmund Bergler, M.D., "What is a psychic masochist?"

Another mask behind which hatred lies disguised is that of humor. Rage, laughter and tears are no strangers to each other. For laughter is our secret weapon. A smile, a titter, a giggle, a hearty belly laugh directed at one's enemy or the self, is always more rewarding than a punch, a scream of hate or deep depression and tears.

We react with anger when we are laughed at. "But we're not laughing *at* you," people sometimes say in mock apology. "We're laughing *with* you." It does not help the hurt.

Suppose we have just made ourselves ridiculous in some way and know the laughter is rightly directed at us. We have given someone else pleasure, obviously, or he would not laugh. But what kind of pleasure is it? Why do we get angry at giving someone else a laugh?

We asked Martin Grotjahn, M.D., "Is there a hidden meaning to humor?"

One very popular way of hiding hatred is to be so ill and weak that you could not possibly hate anyone. The illness serves two purposes — it prevents the hatred from being put into action, and it punishes you because you dared to have such a wicked thought as hating someone.

Your sins are forgiven you, said Jesus of Nazareth to the four lepers. And the lepers were cured. Long before the time of Jesus, the vast majority of people believed that physical and emotional illness or injury were due to Fate, or God, punishing them for sinful behavior or thoughts.

Today, we are more sophisticated. We say we do not believe physical disease is punishment for real or imagined crimes. We may "catch" a virus, "fall ill" with some serious ailment or "have" an accident. We believe all of this has nothing to do with punishment of the self. But if this is true, why is it that the physically ill person, almost without exception, is forgiven everything, at least until he is well once again?

Even today, do we not atone for our real and imagined transgressions by punishing ourselves through the medium of illness?

We asked Paul Kay, M.D., "Can disease be a way of life?"

What we would like to do unto others, we sometimes do unto ourselves. We can even devour ourselves, turning inward the feeling we would like to eat up others whom we feel have threatened us. It is said by some that revenge is sweet, forgiveness sweeter, and understanding sweeter still. But it is hard to deny revenge is not attractive, at least in thought.

We still operate in some degree on one of the Old Testament's principles, "An eye for an eye, a tooth for a tooth." Revenge often takes the exact form of the injury suffered. It is death to the murderer, and not so long ago, the hand that stole was cut off.

But as we have become more civilized, we have given up the idea of revenge on the enemy. We feel it is not the wise way, that it achieves nothing. However, those who do not truly feel this but nonetheless hold back their anger for reasons of fear, are apt to turn it on themselves.

For instance, when man cannot "bite" the other fellow back, he tends to bite himself. Teeth are our first weapons in life, for the only way the baby can get revenge is to bite.

We asked Morton M. Golden, M.D., "Are toothaches and dental pathology related to hate, aggression and anger?"

Instead of attacking our teeth, there is another way we express anger through the mouth. Many people always seem to be doing something with their mouths, either eating or talking or smoking or drinking or chewing gum throughout every hour they are awake.

In one sense, they are still showing the superficial characteristics of the small baby as they pacify themselves continually. There is no doubt that far too many of us possess eating or drinking problems of one type or another which we cannot control even though we daily take the vow to lose twenty pounds or stop after two drinks.

We asked Leo L. Orenstein, M.D., "What lies behind compulsive eating and drinking?"

Hatred only harms us if there is too much of it and it is too repressed. A certain amount of aggression is necessary in order to survive. It is only when aggression becomes overwhelming in the ways described above, it may hurt us.

8.

"Do people have the right to hate as well as to love?" we asked Dr. Spotnitz.

XXXXXXXXXXXXXXXXXXXX

HYMAN SPOTNITZ, M.D.
Fellow, American Psychiatric Association

In this interview Dr. Spotnitz also discusses:

"Are aggression and sex related?"

> *"Is there a difference between aggression, anger and hate?"*

>> *"Does a 'good quarrel' have its advantages?"*

"What is mankind's real dilemma?"

> *"Can there be constructive uses of anger and hate in marriage?"*

>> *"Are homosexuals angrier than other men?"*

"Why do we punish ourselves — are we our own worst enemies?"

> *"What happens when anger is turned inwards?"*

>> *"Must we accept anger and hate in ourselves and others?"*

"Why is it difficult for parents to accept anger and hate in a child?"

> *"Why is it necessary that frustration and gratification be balanced?"*

>> *"What is the importance of communication in marriage?"*

"Are conflicts necessary between mother and child?"

> *"Do we need some anger and hatred in our lives?"*

HYMAN SPOTNITZ, M.D.

8.

This is what Dr. Spotnitz said when interviewed in his office:

A. First of all, the idea of people hating each other is not such a palatable subject because ordinarily we regard hatred as something undesirable. But hatred is really part of human nature, too, and in my work with patients for the past twenty-five years, I have found that hatred is a serious problem. That is, why people hate each other, how they come to hate, and how they deal with their hatred.

Furthermore, this is a much more serious concern than the sexual attraction they feel for each other or whether they love each other, although this, of course, is related to hate.

Q. *Why is hate such a problem?*

A. Let's take a person right from the beginning. A child is conceived and nine months later born into a world where, under ideal circumstances, the mother has a feeling of love for the child. She does what she can to help the child grow and mature. This experience is ordinarily pleasurable for both of them to the extent to which the mother loves the child.

But before the child came into the world, when it was inside her, the mother was able to take care of it without any effort at all on her part. She fed it, clothed it with her own body, and took complete care of it for nine months without any conscious voluntary effort beyond that of taking care of her own health.

At birth, the situation becomes dramatically and shockingly changed. Here is where you start to get a clash of personal interests. Consequently, from this clash of interests comes frustration and hatred between mother and child. Love and hate are in a sense related.

Q. Would you say this holds true for all mothers and children?

A. Yes. The mother always has the problem of meeting the child's needs. At birth a child has two types of needs. He has a need for satisfaction and for maturation. As he grows up he feels both frustration and gratification. To give the child everything it wants can be very harmful, and to give the same child too little satisfaction, too little pleasure, can also be damaging.

The proper balance of frustration — gratification is essential in helping a child grow up. The gratification induces positive feelings in the child for his mother and the frustration induces feelings of hatred and anger toward the mother. In order to become a healthy human being, a proper balance of love and affection, hatred and anger is necessary for a growing child.

Q. Are there other areas in life besides the mother-child relationship where there is aggression?

A. Aggression takes place in all areas of life. There's an aggressive problem in every human relationship. Aggression means one person putting more demands upon another person than that person is willing to meet.

Q. Would you elaborate?

A. Let us say that there's one piece of bread available for two children. As soon as one of them makes a grab for it, there is aggression. It is a process whereby one person makes a move to get something which the other person also needs or desires.

Q. But aggression doesn't necessarily mean anger?

A. Aggression is a concept which encompasses all types of feeling and action that could possibly lead to violating the rights of another person. Therefore, aggression does not always contain anger, but anger is always aggressive. Aggression is an all-encompassing term for any attempt to invade the area of another person.

Q. Then, that would mean there is aggression in all of our relationships with others?

A. Yes, we must be aggressive. If you are going to survive, aggression is necessary in all relationships.

Q. *So the problem is how to handle this aggression?*

A. Now you're hitting the mark. How do we handle it?

Q. *We can't deny it?*

A. You cannot only *not* deny it, you can't get away from it. If we try to deny it, we get into a lot more trouble than if we admit it and deal with it. For as soon as two people are in a room together, one person must start making demands upon the other, even if it's only the air they breathe.

Q. *At the beginning of the interview, Dr. Spotnitz, you said that man for centuries has stressed the importance of love. Were you also saying we do this so persistently to hide our aggression?*

A. Exactly. We've been told to love one another to keep us from hating each other so much. That's the main problem.

Q. *Why do you now use the word "hate?"*

A. I speak of hate rather than aggression because hate is the emotional component that often accompanies aggression. If you want something, set out to get it and are not stopped, you have engaged in an act of aggression that does not involve any anger, hatred or resentment. But the more desirable the object, and the more you are stopped, the more thwarted you will become. And from this thwarting will come anger, resentment and hatred which will then be involved in the continued act of aggression.

In my practice with very seriously ill patients, I have found that when they were frustrated in ordinary relationships, they did not know what to do with the anger and resentment they experienced. Usually, the anger and resentment were either buried inside or suppressed in some undesirable, unhealthful way in order not to offend others. When you can help such patients deal with their aggressions in a satisfactory way, they become healthy people.

But this is a very difficult task. From their earliest days, children are discouraged from going around hating their parents. Many parents raise their hands in horror if a child tells them, "I hate you." Furthermore, from a very early age children are taught continually to deny the feeling of hate.

But children have the right to hate as well as to love their parents. In adult relations it is the same. We all have the right to hate each other. But we have to learn not only to accept hate of each other at times but to express this hatred in a socially constructive form.

In other words, the problem is not *whether* we should hate each other. The problem is how we *use* the hatred in a constructive manner in society. Hatred has been so consistently denied, so consistently abhorred, because it has been used so often in socially destructive form. For hatred in socially constructive forms very rarely occurs. We have very few outlets for it.

Ordinarily, the only time hatred is advocated, encouraged, and used socially is in war. Then, we all hate each other, murder each other. But there's just as much need to hate other people when we are at peace, and the problems arises as to what a person does with his hatred when at peace? How does he use and express it then?

Let me give you an example of inability to handle hatred and anger. One of my patients resented and hated much that was unlikeable about her husband. She felt very guilty about her feelings. One night she dreamed she walked in front of a speeding automobile and was run over. She regarded the dream as punishment for these feelings. The next day, right in front of my office, she actually did walk in the path of an on-coming car and was hit. She was having guilty thoughts about her anger toward her husband at the time.

Q. *Is the turning inward of anger a common occurrence?*

A. Yes. It can take various forms besides automobile accidents. We can punish ourselves for anger and hate in the form of mental illness. We can literally "swallow" anger and develop a hole in the belly, an ulcer. Anger turned inward is a form of punishment because one believes he doesn't have the right to get angry. In our society, often the parent not only punishes the child for acts of anger but for feelings and words of anger. In learning from parents, the child will begin to punish himself. Frequently, I find that patients are not even able to get angry. Something or someone will provoke them in some way but instead of becoming angry they are only aware that they've suddenly cut their finger, or that they have burned themselves, or are involved in some kind of accident.

The point I am making is that anger here is expressed in an unconscious way in the form of a self-damaging, self-punishing act. You find this is true in homosexuality and certain sadistic sexual practices.

Q. Anger and sadistic sexuality seem to go together. But why homosexuality?

A. The homosexual is expressing his anger against the whole human race. For when a man chooses a man, or a woman chooses a woman as the sexual partner, he obviously cannot reproduce. Many homosexuals feel they are worthless. They feel they should never have been born. Many of them hate themselves and they are really saying, "My mother and father should never have had intercourse that night when they made me, and I am never going to have intercourse with a woman. I'm never going to make a child."

Q. Is there also aggression and anger in sex between a man and woman?

A. Yes, there's a great deal of aggression involved. We have recently discovered that if monkeys are raised with artificial mothers — dummies made of terry cloth which look like monkeys — these monkeys when grown cannot mate and reproduce. It was found they need a real mother in order to be frustrated and learn how to get angry. In other words, the absence of anger interferes with reproduction.

Many men and women know that a certain amount of aggression and anger is involved in the sexual act. Women feel they want to be possessed by the man, overpowered by him, and men feel they want to possess and overpower the woman. There's always some sort of battle going on between the sexes. You can see that in animals. The battle reaction in humans gets tempered by the love reaction but a certain amount of battling is always involved in the normal sexual relationship.

We need the emotions of anger, hatred and resentment in human relations. We need them for our own functioning and we need to be able to express them when we have a surplus of these feelings.

Q. How can anger be used in a marriage?

A. Anger can be used to improve relations between two people. But to do this requires an accurate channeling of these feelings. Let us take a wife who is angry at her husband. In the first place, this woman should know what she is angry about. This may sound simple, too simple. But frequently in marriage, the wife has expected the husband to be a father and the husband has expected the wife to be a mother. In effect, they both have expected that they're going to meet in their marital partners the ideal parents.

Now, as must happen sooner or later, the wife will find out she is not married to the good father (as will the husband find out he is not married to the good mother), she will become thwarted because of her unreal demands and grow angry. But it is not easy to face one's unreal demands. So, it may not always be a simple problem to know why you are angry.

However, let us say this wife knows she is angry about real and unreal things in relation to her husband. She then must use this anger to figure out ways of solving the problems.

One of the ways of solving a problem between two adults is to do a lot of talking so that feelings are expressed by both. The "talking out" of aggression and anger, as far as we know, is the best solution to this problem.

Sooner or later, in all marriages, there will be times when the wife will hate the husband and the husband will hate the wife. They both must recognize this is a normal feeling and they must learn how to deal with it in each other.

One of the best ways to handle anger and hate is to have a good quarrel once in a while. A husband and wife have the right to disagreement. It's a healthful way of "blowing off steam." It clears the atmosphere and it can help ease the situation by revealing the true feelings of a person.

But when one partner is angry, the other has to keep quiet and not respond in anger at that moment. In other words if they are a cooperative team, only one person is allowed to express his anger at any one time. This is possible when it is understood between man and wife that, every so often, one of them is going to blow up, and it is also understood that whatever is said will not be taken too seriously.

Let's say the husband explodes in anger. If the wife knows the marriage isn't threatened, that he is not going to ask for a divorce, or desert her, or stop loving her, she will be willing to let him express his anger. For, once he is through, his feelings of love toward her will return.

Furthermore, after anger has been given verbal expression by one, or by both at different times, they can sit down together and try to figure out a way of solving the particular problem.

Thus, we all have two ways to use the energy of anger. One is the release of anger in action. This is destructive and may prove tragic. But if husband and wife realize that no matter how much the other hates, he also loves, then the anger can be used to solve the normal problems of living together.

In summary, in a relationship where there is mutual love and understanding, hatred is entitled to expression along with the expression of love. If both partners can take it, then you have the basic foundation for a good marriage.

Q. What are the constructive uses of anger and hate with children?

A. With children anger is a much more serious matter. The parent can't blow up the way he might desire because it can be very damaging to the child. But it is well-known that some blowing up is better than no blowing up at all.

The parents have to show good judgment and proper consideration for the child in the extent to which they blow off. However, children are not disturbed by parents expressing their anger if they also feel the parents really love them and that this anger will not result in any destructive behavior.

Children themselves, in the process of growing up, have to learn how to accept the impulses of anger, rage and hate, and express them without physically attacking the objects of hate, such as parents and brothers and sisters.

In other words, instead of teaching a child he must not feel anger, rage and hate, he should be told that it is all right to have such feelings as long as they are expressed in action that is acceptable. But what is acceptable? On occasion, toys, dolls, and games may receive the child's anger in action. And, when he is angry he should be allowed and encouraged to talk it out.

"I hate you!" can be accepted from the child if the parent will realize this is normal, and that love is there also.

Anger is never a dangerous force. It is only the act that may be committed in anger of which people are afraid. Because of this fear, what they usually do is to check the angry feeling so it won't lead to the angry action. The angry action is undesirable, but the angry feeling is healthy. What we have to develop in people is the ability to be angry and say so without acting out of anger.

That is the art of dealing with aggression: to be able to be aggressive, to be able to feel anger, to be able to express the anger in words, to be able to use it constructively in a social relationship, but not to act out of anger in a way damaging to another person.

Q. But what can we do about the guilt and self-punishment that we all feel about our anger?

A. That's the problem. This is mankind's dilemma and the only way to really solve it is to start with the children from the day they are born. Children have to be educated that they have a right to have feelings of love and feelings of hatred. They have to learn to operate and function with both these feelings.

I can tell you, frankly, years ago I wouldn't have accepted this point of view myself. But I have seen the havoc in human relations and the wasted lives of men and women in mental hospitals when anger was not felt to be rightful. These people feel that anger must be kept in and they act as though they've been intoxicated by their own anger.

Human health requires that we function with the emotions we have to start out with. The child at birth has a capacity to love and a capacity to hate. Human engineering requires that we work with the machinery we possess.

But we have to make a distinction between acting out of anger and feeling anger and using it constructively. For centuries we have been told to love one another. That is correct. But we also should feel we can hate one another and use this hatred for mutual benefit. In other words, act out of love. Use the energy of hatred to act out of love, too.

Thank you, Dr. Spotnitz.

9.

*"Why do we seem to have greater difficulty
dealing with our anger and hate than
with our love?" we asked Dr. Robbins.*

∞∞∞∞∞∞∞∞∞∞∞∞∞∞∞∞∞∞

LEWIS L. ROBBINS, M.D.
Medical Director, Hillside Hospital

In this interview Dr. Robbins also discusses:

"How are love and hate related?"

"Why do we fear the intense feelings of hate and love?"

"What are man's two strongest urges?"

"Why do we feel guilty about hating?"

"What is the meaning of guilt?"

*"How does society provide for the control of
aggression?"*

"Is hostility important in our lives?"

*"What disturbs us about the sexual pervert, such as the
rapist?"*

*"What do men get out of the business world other
than money?"*

*"Why do men and women enjoy sports such as hunting and
fishing?"*

Is the Don Juan type of man a true lover?"

What does the phrase 'man against himself mean?"

"Does gambling serve a purpose?"

"Are children basically more aggressive than adults?"

9.

This is what Dr. Robbins said when interviewed in his office:

When I first went into psychiatry and was in training at the Menninger Clinic in Topeka, Kansas, I was, naturally, unsure about many psychoanalytic ideas, among them this problem of aggression. Although Dr. Karl Menninger, the director of the Clinic, had written the very fascinating and stimulating book "Man Against Himself," which is essentially about man's aggressive urges, after three months at the clinic I asked him the following question:

"When I first started training in psychoanalysis I thought that the major psychiatric illnesses were due to disturbances in the erotic drive. But you keep talking about disturbances in the aggressive drive. Why?"

Dr. Menninger answered that he felt people suffered more trouble in their lives because of their inability to handle their aggression than because of their inability to handle love. He further said that many of the love problems of people existed because hate was there also, and that if we could help people to deal with their hostility successfully, their ability to give love and receive love would almost take care of itself.

In short, as a practical therapeutic task, if we could help people resolve their conflicts about hating, this in itself would often be enough. We would not need to go into love. It could flower by itself.

In the early years of psychoanalysis the main belief was that most neurotic disturbances were due to some inhibition or distortion of the love impulses. Since this was the first theme, the public to a large extent has not caught up with the fact that there is another theme — the problem of aggression. People tend to ignore the problem of aggression for a number of reasons, one of which is that they are tremendously preoccupied with only a part of love — sex. Secondly, when

Freud first began to suspect that, besides Eros, there was another equally potent instinctual drive, it was quite late in the development of psychoanalytic theory, and for both doctors and laymen alike, it was less easy to understand than the concept of the love drive.

THE TWO URGES

Even today among psychoanalysts there are debates as to whether we should operate from a single-instinct theory or a dual-instinct theory. In other words, is aggression a basic and inborn quality of man, or is it merely the inevitable and constant partner to frustration of love? I would personally say that to a certain degree this theoretical question, while very important, is a little like arguing about how many angels can dance on the point of a pin. For aggression, no matter how it gets there, is nevertheless present in man. It exists within us all.

There are certain implications, however, in the belief that aggression is not a basic and inborn quality of man. One of these is that if a person can find adequate fulfillment of his erotic needs — erotic in the sense of a need for love, closeness, companionship and the like, which also includes the sexual — then his aggression will disappear. This is, in fact, one of the hypotheses of the theory of communism (not the current Russian system) in which there is the belief that if economic struggle and frustration are abolished, people will live together in harmony. In effect, the theory of communism says that if the frustrations and insecurities of life are handled adequately in an Utopian economic system, the people themselves will not have any aggression.

Whether this belief is hypothetically true is not the question, in my opinion. I believe that this state of affairs has never been a reality, and will not likely ever be a reality, because man has two basic instinctual urges. He has the urge to preserve the species, and he has the urge to preserve himself as an individual.

There is a constant desire on the part of man for close and positive relationships with other men and women. Biologically, this brings one organism together with another, with the result that there are created new organisms. But there is also the destructive energy which is purely that of personal self-preservation. In order to eat, one must kill. We have to eat to survive, and we cannot survive without destroying something, whether it be beef, fish or vegetables.

Man is a unique herd animal. Although some other animals travel and live in groups, man's society imposes much greater restrictions on the extent to which the destructive energy of the individual can be expressed. These restrictions may be related to the high degree of social organization of the "herd" in which man lives, or may be related to the fact that man is the only animal who has a real awareness of death as a consequence of destructive behavior.

Primarily, a man cannot kill another man without provoking the danger of being killed himself by society. Secondly, because of his unique intellectual functions man is able to transform instinctual energy into ideas and abstractions, and very often much of our instinctual energy goes through tremendous transformations before there is ultimate action.

In this sense, most of our basic instinctual impulses can hardly be recognized in terms of their primitive origins. Going fishing, for example, is called play and sport. Even further removed from primitive aggression is the champion of a political position, or the scientist who is out to destroy bacteria in order to save life.

Let us first look at man as an infant. We are all cute, sweet, little and helpless. But if we as adults can objectively stand off and look at a baby, we certainly know that rage is no stranger to him. If he has cried more than a minute or so, the cry is not merely a plea for help, or an expression of hunger. It is one of rage, and although it may be difficult for some parents, and others, to attribute rage to a cute little baby, it is nevertheless there within him.

One of the major problems of bringing up a child is not teaching it how to love but teaching it how to control its aggressiveness. Society in general, and parents in particular, are constantly working to impose and teach a system of values that constitute "Don'ts" directed against the aggressive impulses of a child. On the other hand, if a child goes over and kisses the mother, or even a comparative stranger, no one says, "Don't." The desire to give and receive love is perfectly acceptable, provided it does not become genitally sexualized too soon.

But when a child is angry, he is naughty. "Don't" say the parents. "You're not supposed to hit. You can't strike out. You can't destroy."

We also say, "Even when you just feel like hitting, biting and kicking you are naughty. You are bad. You are no good." Thus, the thought, as well as the deed, begins to carry with it a sense of guilt.

"This is the way I feel, and this is what I would like to do," the child unconsciously says. "But that means I am a bad person. I'm naughty. I'm no good. I'm unlovable because I hate."

There has been much written and said about guilt in our society, especially in relation to sexuality which most certainly has an aggressive component. There is an element of hating in loving, and I believe that the people who have a great deal of guilt about sexuality are not so much guilty for the love side of it, but rather for the hate concealed within it. A Don Juan type man, for example, does not love women. There is a strong element of aggression in his sexual behavior because he seduces and then disappoints them.

Inherent in the sexual act, however, is a certain amount of sadism on the male part and masochism on the female part. One penetrates the other. I do not mean to imply here that the sexual act need be for the purposes of sadism and masochism. But it may easily be used for those purposes because the possibilities are built into the act itself.

WHAT IS THE EVIDENCE

The evidence that man has a problem in dealing with his aggressiveness may be observed in many spectacular ways. Mankind's history is one long story of war and murder, which still continues today throughout most of the world. But there is also very "quiet" evidence.

Since man cannot escape his biological nature, he must build social institutions which provide some legitimate way to express his biological needs while, at the very same time, not destroying the structure of society. Although he is not very good at maintaining this balance as yet, the idea is one of the basic elements of any social organization from the most primitive to the most complex.

We are all aware, for example, that business and making a

living in our complex society has much more to it than merely providing food, clothing and shelter for ourselves and our families. Most of us do quite a bit more than is necessary in order just to live. We are hunting for other things besides the basic essentials of life, and we all know that one of the things we are hunting for in business is so-called fun. In other words in our society business is highly competitive and we enjoy the battle. In addition, many rewards fall to the winner which are, in a sense, similar to the reward of life to the victorious Roman gladiator, while death is the lot of the vanquished.

We can see, therefore, that by the very way in which man conducts his daily affairs in order to meet his basic needs, he has added an outlet for his aggressive needs. He engages in aggressive interchange, if he can. There are some who cannot. But for the rest of us it is — "All is fair in love, war and business."

Let us now look at some of the other evidence which may indicate that man has a problem of aggressiveness which, possibly without recognizing, he has attempted to handle within the structure of society. With more leisure time than ever before, what are the forms of play commonly used by man? A vast part of our play is hitting something or someone in some type of competitive game. Baseball, football, golf, ping-pong and badminton are only a few of the sports which involve something being hit, and in most of them the player has some type of instrument in his hand with which he can deal a blow. Another feature of our games is that we usually have an opponent, someone we are trying to beat. Beat means "hit," not just "win."

Some people, however, don't like to play games. They hunt and fish, instead. But what is a better illustration of undisguised aggression? After all, the fundamental element of hunting and fishing is killing. A one hundred and eighty pound man goes out and fights an eight-ounce trout, and fishing is no fun unless the fish puts up a good fight. To make it more of a struggle, however, the fisherman gives the fish some odds by using thin line, and the like. But in the long run, a stupid thing called a fish, weighing all of eight ounces, and a brilliant thing called a man, weighing hundreds of times more, spend hours having a war with each other. There are many fishermen who don't like to eat fish but the eating is not the point at all. The fighting, killing and winning are the satisfactions.

But there are a number of people who do not hunt or fish, nor do they actively engage in sports. Instead they sit passively and watch while somebody else does something. This could be called lazy-aggressive. We hire somebody to be aggressive for us, such as the prizefighter. All we have to do is watch the audience at a prizefight, or a baseball game for that matter, and we see that they are vicariously participating in the fight with their yelling, cheering, booing and screaming, "Kill the bum!"

The prizefighter is the modified modern day gladiator, a not-so highly civilized version of aggression. What do we see in motion pictures and on television if not murder, gruesome mystery and robbery, in all of which someone is killing or being killed? When one of my boys was only six years old he could look at a Western for a moment and say, "There's the bad guy."

"How do you know?" I asked.

"He's got a mustache," he may have answered. Or, "He's wearing the dark suit" might have been the clue.

In all of these types of dramas the villain and the hero are clearly seen, and half the fun for the audience (of whatever age) is in the booing of the villian. The grim fairy tales which children so love are also filled with villains. There are witches and goblins and bad stepmothers and all kinds of other evil people lurking about doing nasty things, and eventually dying horrible deaths.

I do not mean to imply that sports, games, television and fairy tales are bad because of the obvious aggressiveness and hostility evidenced within them. On the contrary, society has unconsciously been aware of the need of man to have outlets for his aggression. We need these safe outlets in order to discharge the aggression in non-destructive ways. Let us examine the evidence for a moment more.

A reader may say at this point, "I don't happen to like those kinds of things you've mentioned. I don't watch television. I don't go to prizefights or baseball games. I play bridge." But all we would have to do is to make a tape recording of a bridge game and play it in a country where people didn't know the language. They would surely think a riot was in progress. Why is it that in bridge or poker a monetary stake is put upon the score? In football, for example, the team with the highest score is the winner. But in most card games people say, "Let's play for a little something to make it interesting."

In my opinion, we put money on games of this type because there is no other way of hurting or being hurt. Although I am not positive of this, I think that in those sports and games in which the expression of aggression is direct, where there is bodily contact or the hitting of something, we don't need the extra stake of money. But in those games where the aggressiveness has become more abstracted and attenuated, money makes up for the difference.

In tennis, for example, people swat at each other for hours on end, and no player ever bets on the outcome of a tennis game. They don't need to bet because they have had a direct outlet for their aggression, not as in bridge, poker, pinochle or cribbage. Chess is an exception. Players seldom, if ever, bet on the outcome of a chess game. But it is essentially a game of war, and thus we are right back where we started.

Although I have largely been talking about adults, if we look at children at play we can see the aggressive element in a much more direct and undisguised form. Children wrestle, fight, trip, hit, kick and scuffle with each other like bear cubs, and in part, these actions help to discharge their aggressive energy in safe and appropriate ways. But what we do with children is the same thing we do in our games. We set up rules and limits of behavior, telling them and ourselves, "You may be aggressive in this way but not in that way. When the whistle blows, or the bell rings, (or when Mommy says 'Stop') then that is the end of the fight, temporarily. You stop being aggressive and you rest for a moment. Afterwards, you can go back to pounding at each other."

We tell adults as well as children that they can't hit a man below the belt, nor in the kidneys. They can't kick him in the shins, they can't bite each other, and if they abide by all of these rules then everything is all right. There is no guilt about the aggression because it falls within the rules. In effect, the rules and limits take care of the conscience of both adult and child alike. If either one does not play fair and breaks the rules, there is immediate punishment. The adult is thrown out of the game, or he loses a point, and the child is spanked by Mommy.

Within the controlled framework, therefore, we are permitted to be directly hostile in almost as rough a manner as we wish. We sometimes become worried, however, if we see someone playing too rough. We, as well as children, recognize there can be too much aggressiveness, and we don't want to play with a particular fellow. He is not sublimating well enough, and part of our discomfort comes not from the fact that he is going to hit us too hard, but from the fact he threatens our own restraint. In other words, all of us at one time or another have a difficult time in not playing too rough, and when someone else does lose his controls, we become concerned lest we will lose ours.

Many adults hobbies also have the element of aggression in them. I enjoy gardening, for example, but most of my time is not spent in growing something. It is spent in killing something — the weeds which get in the way of everything else. In a sense, this is a parable of love and hate. If I can kill the weeds successfully, the flowers will grow, and this was Karl Menninger's thesis many years ago in dealing with patients.

MAN AGAINST HIMSELF

From what I have briefly said, it is now possible to conclude there is overwhelming evidence that the problem of handling aggression is in front of us constantly. We can see this in our society as in our mental hospitals. I wish to add here that in spite of all the safe outlets for aggression we have in our society, there still obviously remains an excess of aggression which spills over in crime and war. As a world society, we still cannot sit down and talk intelligently to each other in a place like the United Nations unless we have a great big gun that forces the other fellow to listen, and consequently, war and destruction are still part of our lives.

Nevertheless, I would say that the most difficult thing for a patient in a mental hospital to face and express, or even at times to allow himself to feel, is hate. A depressed patient is probably one of the best examples. He comes into the hospital and says, "I have no right to be here. I am a terrible person, and I have no right to take the food out of the mouths of my wife and children to even pay for the trip here."

But the fact of the matter is that he *has* come to the hospital, and we know that his feelings conceal a wish to take something from his wife and children, At the same time, he is feeling very guilty. Many schizophrenic patients, for example have what we call world-destructive fantasies. The new world which they create in fantasy follows the destruction of the world of reality, and they are afraid, not of loving, but that in the process of loving they will destroy the object they love. To love means to consume, and to consume means to destroy and ultimately to lose. It is as if the loved object were a piece of cake — they can't have it unless they eat it.

They are afraid of loving and they stay away from people because of the destructiveness they feel in their loving process. They want to eat you up. But at the same time, there is a terrific sense of shame and guilt, and this, incidentally, is one of the reasons a neurotic patient has great difficulty in freely speaking to a psychiatrist. He is afraid that the psychiatrist will hate him if he really reveals himself, and if the psychiatrist hates him, then he is lost to the patient.

Many patients express another fear. "If I really would let loose my feelings," they say, "I'm afraid I'll lose my mind and go crazy." When we attempt to find out just precisely what they are afraid of in "going crazy," we find it is not a fear of doing something erotically unacceptable. On the contrary, it is a fear of doing something destructive, primitive and full of rage. The patient is afraid of not maintaining what inner controls he might possess, if he "really would let loose his feelings."

He is afraid even to express feelings verbally lest he be carried away, just as a person might get too involved in a football game and hit the other fellow harder than necessary in order to block him. We handle this clinical problem at Hillside Hospital all the time by providing multiple activities for the patients in which hitting, tearing, pulling and the like, are done on an individual basis. At the present time, one of the most exciting activities, which the patients have a lot of fun doing, is tearing down a fence they don't like. It was separating one group of patients from another, and although the activity of tearing down is destructive, it is nevertheless constructive work because it will beautify the grounds and make for a better life within the hospital.

In general, we find in the treatment of patients in a mental hospital that we have to afford them opportunities to learn how to enjoyably deal with their hostility in a safe and sublimated fashion. In this sense, genital sexuality and direct aggression have something in common: the presence of undischarged erotic and aggressive impulses are both experienced by the individual as a kind of tension which when discharged, as in an orgasm, creates a following sense of relief and pleasure.

Many of the sexual perversions, for example, are considered dangerous and unsavory because of the too undisguised elements of aggression in them. Rape is aggressive also. A rapist is never thought of as a man so attracted to a woman he could not restrain himself and just had to make love to her because he loved her so intensely. On the contrary, rape is seen as a hostile act which, of course, it is because the rapist is imposing his own aggressive feelings upon the woman without any consideration of her feelings.

One of the most unfortunate characteristics of man is expressed through psychological and physical illnesses. Because of external or internal reasons, if man cannot give expression to his aggression in some safe and sublimated fashion, he will turn it against himself. He becomes the object of his own rage, and becomes self-destructive. Psychoses, suicide, alcoholism and drug addiction are among the many forms which self-destruction may take, and a high percentage of the physical illnesses from which neurotic patients suffer are the result of rage turned against the self.

But it is not only the individual who suffers when there is self-destruction. Here more often than not, the illness is also directed against society. For this reason we are all concerned with drug addiction, crime, delinquency, homosexuality and the like. We are concerned about the neurotic because he disturbs his environment even though he may disturb himself much more. In fact, one of the reasons why man has consciously always taken a negative attitude towards the psychologically ill is because mankind has unconsciously understood that psychiatric illness is in part an expression by the patient of his aggression against the rest of us.

There is the completely untrue belief, for example, that psychotic people are dangerous. Generally speaking, that idea is nonsense. In over twenty years of practice in psychiatry I have been struck twice by patients. It is much safer to walk around Hillside Hospital than it is to drive along the Long Island Expressway. We kill each other off on our American highways at the rate of about 40,000 people per year. If that is not hostility, then nothing is hostile. In our mental hospitals, on the other hand, we deal with people who have turned their hostility against themselves. This fact is evidenced, in part, by their lowered self-esteem.

"I'm no good," they say. "I'm worthless, nobody loves me."

Or, they say, "I don't think I have anything to offer other people. They will reject me."

It is guilt which makes a person say, "I am no good," and although it is imaginary guilt for the most part, the patient feels it just the same. He feels worthless because somewhere within himself he is aware that he has certain thoughts, feeling and impulses which he has always been taught were wrong and bad. Yet, he can't help himself, he has them just the same. This feeling is similar to that of the woman who has been raised in a very strict family where she has been taught that to have sexual feelings is wrong. But when she gets married and begins to find herself sexually aroused, she then feels guilty because sex is wrong and nasty and only naughty and bad people have those feelings.

Although all of us are not taught that sex is nasty and wrong, all of us are taught that aggressiveness and hostility are bad and nasty, and the treatment of many psychologically ill people is essentially helping them to recognize the quality of aggressiveness, guilt and anxiety within themselves. Treatment is aimed at helping them to understand that the guilt and anxieties come from the infantile past where these feelings may have once been appropriate and necessary but which are no longer so in adulthood. It is an acceptance of the self as it is, with feelings of anger and aggressiveness as well as tenderness and love.

The nature of all men has within it both aggressiveness and love. The aggressive part cannot be rejected and thrown out. There must be a joining of hands between the constructive and destructive. In this sense, we can all take a hammer and chisel to cut, slice, break and smash at a piece of marble and thus make a beautiful statue. When we, as human beings, find useful ways of getting our constructive and destructive parts to work sufficiently together, then we will not need to invent superbombs, nerve gases and bacterias to wipe out civilization. We will then have caught up with ourselves as men.

10.

"What is the meaning of aggression?"
we asked Mr. Slavson.

§§§§§§§§§§§§§§§§§§§§

S. R. SLAVSON
Consultant In Group Therapy

In this interview Mr. Slavson also discusses:

"What is man's essential tragedy?"
   "What is the basic nature of mankind?"
      "What is the difference between a thought and an act?"
"Are there different kinds of aggression?"
   "What is the difference between aggression and hostility?"
      "How are tension, anxiety and guilt created?"
"What is passive hostility?"
   "Why are there murderous feelings between parents and children?"
"What are some of the aggressive fantasies of children?"
   "Why must we develop tolerance towards our own and other people's aggressions?"

S. R. SLAVSON

10.

This is what Mr. Slavson said when interviewed in his office:

The term "aggression" is grossly misunderstood because it is frequently confused with assertiveness, enterprise and hostility.

Aggression is inherent to nature and life. It is a law of nature without which nothing on this earth would survive. The seeds of plants must push their way through the soil. Unless it is aggressive, and forces its way through the bud, the flower would never make an appearance. The farmer, by tilling the soil, is committing an aggressive act against it, and the wind is aggressive against trees and plants as it sows the seeds for new life.

The very nature of life is derived from aggression for without it there would be no life. A major difference between living and non-living matter is aggression. Chemical action is the foundation of life, and in its process of dissolving, combining and separating elements in an organism, chemical action is essentially aggressive against existing matter and non-matter.

This is true of plant life, lower animals, and for the so-called "higher" forms of life, including man. Man's very survival is derived from aggression. In attaining sustenance and shelter and in the act of procreation, aggression is the basis. Assertiveness, achievement, and creativity involve aggression to varying degrees.

The greatest misunderstanding arises, however, from the synonymous use of the terms aggression and hostility. An act of aggression becomes hostile when its intent is to hurt or destroy. Normally, aggression is part of constructive behavior, whereas the aim of hostility is to hurt or destroy. Aggression is ordinarily not accompanied by hatred against an object, while hostility always has an element of hatred. Constructive aggression has been the boon of mankind, hostility its greatest bane. The motives of aggression are achievement; that of hostility is discharging hate and anger and relieving fear.

Biologically, what we call aggression in lower animals derived its motivation from rage and fear, both of which involve the exact same chemical process in the body. A male animal fighting for the possession of a female, experiences both fear and rage which propel him to achieve his end, the elimination of his adversary. Similarly, in the process of obtaining food, rage and fear are involved during the combat between the aggressor and the victim. Thus anger, rage and killing have become organically associated with the aggressive act.

This neuronic relation between aggression and hostility has been passed on in the evolutionary process also to man and thus hostility and aggression have become linguistically associated. But man can be aggressive without being hostile as he can be hostile without being aggressive. Enterprise and assertiveness are forms of aggression that do not involve hostility, while a person can be seething with hostility without expressing it in action. Strictly speaking, the term aggression is an abstraction or a concept. What we observe are acts which we, due to our own reactions, call aggressive.

In psychotherapy, for example, the therapist has to deal with *passive* aggression on the part of patients. Passive aggression is manifested by non-participation, by avoidance and even by compliance, the conscious or unconscious aim of which is to defeat or frustrate the therapist or other persons. This type of so-called "aggression," though manifestly unrevealed, is actually strongly charged with hostility.

In everyday life, too, hostility can be expressed in withdrawal, non-cooperation and in detachment as well as in openly hostile actions. In human relations, the passive kind of hostility is very frequently more difficult to deal with than the active. Actively hostile acts can be dealt with, and not infrequently the emotional barriers may be broken down by placation or explanation. But in the absence of overt manifestation of hostile feelings, it is very difficult to reach a person and dissolve his feelings.

FOUR TYPES OF AGGRESSION

Much of human nature is similar to, and derived from, the lower animal, which has been carried along by man up the evolutionary ladder as urges, impulses, cravings, needs and feelings. Humans behave aggressively toward one another with considerable accompanying hostility, not because it is efficient or in their best interests, but rather because of neuronic structure, engrams, within the human anatomy. These cause them to react automatically to certain stimuli without exercising judgment and restraining faculties of which they are capable but which appeared much later in the ladder of evolution. Thus, the sudden anger due to a trivial irritant or provocation, such as being brushed up against inadvertently, may throw a person into a rage and lead to a fight. This automatic, uncontrolled reaction without calling in the faculties of deliberation and choice we consider as *atavistic* aggression.

The sources of atavistic aggression lie in the neuronic and glandular systems of the body, both of which, being much older in biologic service, take precedence over reasoning, understanding and conscious purpose which appeared much later in the evolutionary scale.

The second type of aggression is that derived from the totality of the historic experiences of mankind. This is the accumulation of the racial responses to the demands and pressures of life to which man had to accommodate himself in order to survive. Because of this source, we term such aggression *phylogenic*. This aggression is sanctioned and rewarded by society. Killing in war, for example, is accepted by society, an acceptability integrated in the mores of the group and imprinted in the personality of the individual through education, attitude conditioning and mass communication — through codes, laws, systems of values, school, religion, customs, literature and the arts.

Aggression is not only a biological and psychological concept but also a cultural one. In one culture, an act of aggression may be proscribed, while the same act in another culture is acceptable and may be even rewarded.

In addition, behavior assumes different values in the same culture at different times. What is prohibited at one period of history is acceptable in another. One of the most blatant examples of this is war. Killing, plundering and torturing are punished in ordinary circumstances but become heroic acts and a virtue in wartime. Although in war, one must kill and hurt the right person, the enemy.

A third type is *ontogenic* aggression. This is the pattern of aggressive acts, both hostile and benign, acquired through the particular set of experiences of an individual in his early environment and the values of his particular culture. These influences are total; they include the immediate family, the sub-culture, the social groups to which he belongs and the social world in which he has lived. A child excessively frustrated in his family, treated brutally, his ego starved and his self-esteem debased, will inevitably store up a great quantum of resentment and hostility. Or, a child forced to fight for status in his family and in his neighborhood in order not to be considered a "sissy," will become excessively aggressive as well as hostile.

Many experiences may be added to the hostile reservoir of the individual which is passed on to him both by his biological (atavistic) background and the over-all cultural, educational (phylogenic) forces from which no one can escape. The accumulated mass of feeling from the necessary training, discipline and punishment to which every child has to be subjected during various stages in his development, forms the background for later resentments and hostile aggression. These can be acted out against others or transformed into neurotic symptoms such as conversions and depression. This type of aggression, whether turned against one's self or toward others is a resolution of inner struggle and forms the basis for many cases of delinquency and crime.

The healthy, outgoing, assertive activity which has a constructive purpose and aim and is socially beneficial, we consider *instrumental* aggression. The chief aim of education, the systems of morals and ethics, and the law, is to find ways to moderate, repress, suppress or sublimate the other three types of aggression and encourage instrumental aggression. This is the basic purpose of culture and education.

USES OF AGGRESSION

Man's dualistic nature is the source of his tragedy. He cannot escape his biologic heritage and is impelled by his atavistic animal nature on the one hand, and the culturally implanted values and guilts on the other. Therefore, the conflict between what is considered to be socially and morally good, and his original nature create man's unendurable tensions, anxieties and guilts. These can be viewed as existential anxiety. Society could not have survived nor achieved its high levels of scientific and spiritual development unless man's primitivism was either repressed, controlled or transformed into instrumental aggression.

To obtain a clearer picture of aggression, however, requires further classification. Aggression can be also *compensative*. An individual can compensate for various feelings of inferiority by boisterousness and overassertiveness. Some of these feelings of inferiority may stem from physical size, from inadequately developed personality, sexual inadequacies, sense of failure, low status in one's family, exposure to overdominating parents or siblings, and similar experiences and relationships. The anxieties these generate in man can be termed *neurotic* anxieties.

Aggression can also be *defensive*. One can defend himself by aggression against the expectation of attack from others which may be realistic or a result of neurotic or psychotic feelings. To prevent such an attack, an individual may act aggressively to save himself from possible unpleasantness or pain.

Aggression can also stem from organic states. Some have more active constitutional dispositions than others. Many are essentially passive. Aggression also serves as an important release from tension, and a form of canalizing energy which establishes a balance in the body, or homeostasis.

Another type of aggression we first observed in group psychotherapy sessions is *deflective* aggression which can be frequently observed in the play of children as well as in the affairs of adults and whole nations. Persons or groups afraid of the aggression of another person or group, may engage the potential enemy in cooperating with them against a third party. Internationally, this is a common pattern. Defensive alliances among nations are, in effect, methods of deflective aggression as was the case in the alliance between Nazi Germany and Communist Russia. It is not inconceivable, for example, that in the future, Russia and the United States may join against a third power, Communist China. This would be an example of deflective aggression par excellence.

A widespread understanding of hostility and aggression, their place in nature and their biological sources, is essential to human relations. Individuals would then become more tolerant of each other and able to accept each other's aggressions and mild hostilities.

Above all, it is essential to mental health that each one reconcile himself to his own feelings of hostility and be free of over-burdening guilt. Comparative freedom from guilt in relation to one's acts favors self-improvement and personality growth, since anxiety that results from guilt leads to further hostile and aggressive acts. Freedom from neurotic anxiety, on the other hand, makes possible contemplation and objective self-confrontation, and the ability to re-orient one's values and conduct. Self-acceptance is the basis of acceptance of others.

PARENT-CHILD RELATIONS

We have said that in the case of a severe neurosis, the unconscious, and sometimes the conscious aim of an individual's aggression is to hurt, destroy and even kill. These urges, however, need not find fulfillment in actual murder. In fact, under certain conditions and in certain relationships, they may be transformed into acts associated with intense love. The underlying relationship in some instances between children and parents and husbands and wives, is frequently of this type.

While most people have learned to suppress or sublimate hostility and unconscious wishes to hurt or destroy, many have developed reaction-formations to these urges. Nevertheless, there is considerable truth to the adage, "Every birth is a potential murder." This rather extreme assertion can be supported by anthropological evidence. Infanticide, a widespread practice among some primitive tribes, was abandoned both because of rising ethical and religious precepts, and increasingly adequate food supplies. However, ritualistic sacrifices of children to propitiate gods persisted for many centuries after the abandonment of wholesale infanticidal practices, which to the modern mind are almost inconceivable. But viewing the matter objectively, we cannot escape the fact that, potentially, man is capable of these practices, as witness reports in newspapers of fathers and mothers who Medea-like destroy their children in episodes of stress, rage or revenge. During the famine in Russia after the Revolution, parents resorted to consuming children to sustain themselves.

The hostility of the child toward his parents is equally intense, and it, too, is borne out in anthropological facts. When parents in the South Sea Islands reached an advanced age, the children, with the participation of other members of the community, would ceremoniously bury them alive. This was a ritual accompanied by great jollification. The intended "victim" would march at the head of the procession to a grave to the accompaniment of music, screeching and dance. The victim was able to accept his destiny, however, because the prevalent belief among these primitives was that death was merely a journey to the playground of ancestors. The murders of parents by resentful children occasionally reported in our contemporary press leave no doubt as to the persistence of this savage survival, though it is deeply lodged in the unconscious and breaks through only on occasion. During psychotherapeutic interviews, wishes for the death of parents are more or less common, as also are the death wishes of parents toward their children. This is atavistic hostile aggression which tradition and mores hold in repression.

Some of the sources of the basic antagonism between parents and children are obvious and of common experience. In order for a child to become an acceptable member of society it is necessary to discipline and train him. Because the child cannot understand either the parents' intent or the necessity for the training and the frustrations involved, he perceives them as acts of hostility and rejection. Even such acts as substituting a spoon for the nipple, a pottie for the diaper, and protecting the child against danger and disaster are perceived by him as hostile acts. This misunderstanding generates resentment and hostility toward parents.

As the child grows older, it is necessary to set further limits on his physical movement within the environment, and the child develops a fantasy of the parent as a brutal, hostile, destructive person. In too many instances, children come to dread parents and in some instances they are even afraid of being poisoned or killed by them. Such magnified feelings are always found in psychotic individuals, but they exist in psychoneurotics, and are also potentially present in so-called normal persons.

Adolescents, particularly, reveal in therapy their fantasies and wishes for the death of one or both parents. One youngster, told by his mother that his father had bought a new car, suddenly found himself wishing his father would have an accident. "The thought came through my mind very quickly," he told the therapy group, " 'I hope he gets into an accident.' I hoped he would be killed. But then I stopped myself and changed my thought. I said to myself, 'I don't want him to get into an accident.' I had the two ideas at the same time."

Other boys in the group spoke of fleeting wishes for the death of mothers who treated them unkindly. They would lie in bed at night, they said, and "kind of wish my mother would die." These wishes can be viewed as a resurgence of infantile resentments directed toward parents, though the Oedipal struggle is also involved here. To a child, lines of demarcation between wish and act are less sharply drawn than in adults. Children, as do psychoneurotic adults, think in terms of magic and miracle.

Possibly, it is more difficult to understand the parents' basic, though repressed hostility toward children. This is, in part, due to the fact that the mother views the child as an extension of herself. The child, having been a part of herself and sustained by her body, cannot but represent in the mother's unconscious the feeling that he is part of herself. When the child is born, the birth is an act of castration. Something was taken away from her which was a part of her. With few extraordinary exceptions, mothers are much kinder to their offspring when they are infants and small babies than when they grow up and become self-assertive individuals. This is partly inspired by the weakness and helplessness of babies but, in part, it is also a result of their feelings of physical oneness. Mutual hostility between parents and children is particularly increased during the so-called "negativistic period" between the ages of two and four years when the child begins to display assertiveness and rudiments of an independent self.

In other words, when the child begins to become a person

in his own right and is no longer a part of the mother and an extension of her personality, her hostilities are intensified. If these are intense and the child becomes disobedient, stubborn and negativistic, death wishes arise in some mothers, but these negative feelings may even be aroused before the negativistic period. For all babies cry, all become ill at some time or another, and all demand attention twenty-four hours a day. Thus, there is bound to be an accumulated mass of resentment, irritation and hostility toward the child and consequent guilt feelings — all of which serve only to further intensify hostility.

A Dog Chasing His Own Tail

We have seen how great is man's task to harmonize his dualistic nature. He is aggressive and hostile, yet he is taught that to be angry and to hurt is bad. As a result, all feelings of hostility generate guilt since they run counter to the moral code. In turn, this very guilt produces hostile acts. These acts may be direct punishment of oneself for real and imaginary transgressions against moral codes either in action or thought, a self-punishment that may take many forms, among which are psychoses, neuroses, physical illnesses, suicides, alcoholism and drug addiction.

On the other hand, guilt may be father to the wish to destroy the object which is the source of the guilt. Anti-Semitism, for example, is a wish to destroy such an object of guilt. According to the teachings of Christ, all of us should love all people. But we cannot love everybody because love is a selective process. We can love some people but we find it impossible to love others. And when we do not love, we feel guilty and sinful.

Hence, in the absence of a solution we become antagonistic to the cause of our guilt. We are outraged because of it and persecute and seek to liquidate the source of our discomfort, Hostility and guilt cannot always end in either self-destruction or in the destruction of the object which produce them in our culture, so we continue being guilty and hostile. (The immense difference between love and hate is that the former can be fulfilled, but hate cannot, since its aim is murder.) Thus we are in a situation akin to that of a dog chasing his own tail. For when, as a result of hostility, guilt is engendered which begets further hostility, the vicious circle continues on and on

In psychotherapy, we try to break the vicious circle of hostility-anxiety-guilt-anxiety-hostility, although some individuals can undercut this complex by acquiring wisdom through self-understanding. Each must face his own aggressive feelings and either suppress them, sublimate them, or allow himself a moderate amount of hostility without guilt, which he should spread thinly, instead of concentrating it on one object. In this very important step toward mental health and inner peace, it is essential to have the ability to accept the inevitability of the irrational urges of aggression and hostility in oneself and in others. For unless we develop tolerance toward ourselves and others, a harmonious social life is impossible to envisage. There is no solution to the problems of mankind, or to the problems of the individual, unless man begins to understand himself and accepts his unconscious.

One of the first steps in this direction is to know and accept the function of emotions in life and survival, and their indestructibility. Only then will individuals and nations be more tolerant of each other and give themselves a chance.

II.

*"Why must men and women punish
themselves?" we asked Dr. Bergler.*

XXXXXXXXXXXXXXXXXXXX

EDMUND BERGLER, M.D. (1900-1962)

Psychoanalyst

In this interview Dr. Bergler also discusses:

"What is a sexual masochist?"
  *"Why must people always believe themselves the 'inno-
    cent victim'?"*
    "Does neurosis grow worse over the years?"
"Is a masochist falsely aggressive?"
  "Can anger be expressed in humor?"
    "What is the meaning of 'pseudo-moral connotation'?"
"Are childish expectations carried into adult life?"
  "Why is there anger and hate in children?"

II.

This is what Dr. Bergler said when interviewed in his office:

There is the old joke about the Jewish man who stuttered and who wanted to be a radio announcer. He studied for five years at various dramatic schools, and finally went for an audition at one of the large networks.

Afterwards, a friend asked him what happened.

"T-t-terri-b-ble," the would-be announcer stuttered.

"You didn't get the job?" his friend asked, not too surprised.

"N-n-no-o-o," was the agonized answer.

"But how c-c-could I?" he added scornfully. "They're all anti-S-S-Semites."

This man, as with all neurotic psychic masochists, imagined himself a genius always in the same situation — behind the eight-ball. Somebody was always unjust, unfair, didn't treat him right, slighted him, and he never got what he deserved. In other words, he was always jinxed.

Many people think of a "masochist" as a man who goes to a prostitute, pays her a double fee and wants to be whipped or beaten. Or a woman who seeks a beating from a man. But this is a comparatively rare sexual perversion, where the desire to be hurt is completely conscious; with psychic masochism we are confronted with an unconscious way of acting and feeling and thinking. Psychic masochists are unconscious injustice collectors.

Everybody has psychic masochistic tendencies. In certain people, however, these trends are increased to a point where we can speak of "neurotic masochism."

If you ask this type of person, "How come? Why is it that you always end up behind the eight ball?" he will have a ready answer.

"People are malicious," he will say. "I don't have the

right connections. I have no luck. Fate is against me. Everybody is against me!"

Thus, we now have the first of a series of six member processes that the psychic masochist must perform, which he does in a split second.

First, he maneuvers himself into a situation where he pretends to be the innocent victim.

Secondly, the psychic masochist has to convince himself that he is a very aggressive type. It is not that if you go to a psychic masochist and kick him in the pants, he will say, "Thank you." He will fight like hell. But he will always inwardly choose an enemy who is stronger than he, who he knows will defeat him.

But if you say to him, "You're just looking for a kick in the pants," he will laugh.

"Ask my wife, ask my boss," he will answer. "They'll tell you what a fantastic fighter I am."

What he does not understand is that there are two types of fights, and two types of aggression: true and phony (pseudo-aggression). You can fight to win, and you can fight to lose. Psychic masochists will always provoke a fight in which they lose—such as the case of the man who stuttered, yet wanted to be a radio announcer, who provoked a situation where he could not win, then had a ready explanation and indignantly retired into the lachrymal corner, whining over the injustice done him.

Let us look closely at his own "explanation." As is generally known, the child thinks on a completely different level than the adult. The child lives on the premise that everything good comes from himself and everything bad comes from the outer world.

This is very nice psychic bookkeeping because it absolves you completely of any responsibility. But how is the child able to feel this way?

The child doesn't make a distinction between himself and the outer world. The outer world is simply non-existing; other people are treated as some kind of slave. Only gradually does the child find out that the "slave" has a life of his own. The "slave" is not always available, and cannot be always relied upon to carry out the peculiar ideas of the child.

We call this childish way of seeing the world "infantile megalomania." A patient of mine told me a wonderful story about this. She and her son took a walk on Fifth Ave. on Washington's Birthday. The three-year old boy looked at all the flags, then asked his mother, "Why are the flags out? My birthday was yesterday."

In most of us this childish megalomania is knocked out by growing up. We concede that the world is not our slave. The psychic masochist unconsciously fails to make that concession. However, he now must reconcile two things which, from the standpoint of logic, are completely irreconcilable. This is his third task.

On the one hand, the masochist wants to be the center of the universe, to be all-powerful. But on the other hand, he has an aim which only a very passive person can have: he wants to be kicked in the pants. He wants humiliation which is the opposite of infantile megalomania.

How does he reconcile these two opposites? Well, he's a genius. Under the conditions of provocation that he unconsciously creates (the Jewish stutterer who wants to be a radio announcer), he demotes the other person to an executive organ of himself. He makes the other powerless. Thus, he performs his *third* inner task.

A gambler patient of mine illustrates this quite well. He told me that he was watching on television a horse race in which he had bet heavily. When the horses left the post he started to cross and recross his legs. In his fantasy, this shifting of his legs was a signal to the jockey of the horse on which he had bet. He was, in effect, directing the race from his armchair. This is very similar to those people who place bets at roulette or at the dice tables, and who believe that the wheel or dice will deliver riches to them because they can "talk to" (control) the little ball or ivory cubes.

HIGH CLASS IRONY

Mind you, all these things go on in his mind within a split second, before the psychic masochist acts. Unconsciously, at one and the same time he has maneuvered himself into the position of the innocent victim, he is fighting a prearranged lost battle, and he is all-powerful, the center of the universe.

But that is not all. There is the story told by a woman who owned a brothel in Miami Beach, Florida, for thirty-some years and who is now retired and has written her memoirs. She tells about one of the prostitutes who had a peculiar habit. If she was not occupied in bed, she was sitting before her mirror brushing her hair. Everybody knew about this peculiarity and one day the other girls asked her why she did it.

She answered, "My mother told me that every time I went to bed I should brush my hair one hundred times. Now, I'm going to bed so frequently I can't keep it up as much as I'd like — But I try."

This is some kind of high class irony. It is also what we call "pseudo-moral connotation"—the *fourth* labor of the psychic masochist. It means that you take an educational precept actually communicated during childhood, and apply it in such a manner that you are right but at the wrong time, in the wrong place, and with the wrong meaning. You use something your mother and father once told you as a prop, even though it no longer applies.

I had an Englishman as a patient who had originally planned to be a pastor. His father was a churchman himself and a very severe man. My patient had gone to a theological seminary but had later quit. At the time he was nineteen, he started an affair with a neighbor's wife and felt terrible guilt.

One day, as he was going upstairs to the bedroom of this woman he found himself saying, "Love thy neighbor!"

Now, undoubtedly his father had told him always to love thy neighbor, but we can be sure that the father didn't mean it in quite this literal manner.

The *fifth* quality that the psychic masochist possesses is that he must be a sharpshooter—and he aims low.

For example, a patient of mine told me the following story. He was a professional man who was a voluntary chairman of one of the committees of a charitable organization. One year he was chairman of the publicity committee, the next year he was rotated to the finance committee. He did a wonderful job on the publicity committee, but the man who followed him did a poor job. Everyone knew the latter had failed, but everyone was polite. Not my patient. How did he act?

Well, at the end of every year there was a dinner where

each chairman made his report. My patient followed his successor to the speaker's stand, after the latter had glossed over all of his failures and misrepresented facts. Everyone had been polite and applauded except my patient.

He stood up at the speaker's stand and started his report by saying he would like first to tell a little joke. Now, no one tells jokes in this organization. It is a very serious group. But my patient was going to tell a joke anyway.

Here was his joke. A counterfeiter and his partner print a large number of twenty-dollar bills. The counterfeiter looks at the finished product and says, "It's wonderful."

"No!" says the partner. "There's a mistake. Where it should be marked $20, it's marked $18."

So, who's going to take an eighteen-dollar bill? They have to do the best they can and decide to go to a hick town where they think no one will know the difference. They find the town, and head for a bar. "Two martinis," they said, handing over an eighteen-dollar bill.

"Sure," says the bartender. "How do you want your change, two nines or three sixes?"

Now look at the amazing cleverness of my patient. I asked him if he prepared the joke before-hand?

"Oh, no," my patient said. "I thought of it as I walked up to the speaker's stand."

I asked, "Do you know what you said?"

"Sure," he answered. "It made an excellent joke."

"Yes, you make an excellent joke," I answered, "But you are calling the other man a 'phony,' and you are saying to the audience that he considers them hicktown people but that they are as smart as the bartender, hence they see through this phoniness."

"Oh, no!" my patient said. "I didn't mean it that way at all."

"How did this 'phony' take the joke?" I asked.

"He didn't want to talk to me afterwards," said my patient. "I don't know why."

Remember, a masochist has to think quickly, otherwise tension develops. Tension can be defined psychologically as an uncomfortable feeling arising at moments when your inner conscience accuses you of being a psychic masochist and your unconscious ego does not have a defense ready immediately. To avoid this tension, is the psychic masochist's *sixth* inner necessity.

For example, a patient of mine had a peculiar way of choosing his girl friends. He picked up a chorus girl, put her into a very nice apartment, and supported her. He also engaged a detective agency to report her movements from day to day.

This man was frequently absent from town on business trips. But the first thing he would do upon his return would be to read the dossier from the detective agency.

One day, he came to me. "Look!" he said, waving the reports "It's reported that she saw Mr. X at 1:15 A.M. in *my* apartment and he stayed until 4:20 A.M."

"Yes?" I said.

"Well," he demanded, "what do you believe they were doing?"

"I give you three guesses," I answered.

He didn't want to hear the other two. "Don't you see it is my money?" he said.

"No, I don't see that it's your money," I replied. "I only see that this is sheer foolishness. What do you want? Why did you pick a half-prostitute?"

He had no answer.

I said, "Look, you are provoking all of this. You know that she will be unfaithful. You want her to be unfaithful because unconsciously you like the conflict you now have."

Then I asked him, "What would happen if after reading this report and once more coming to your favorite conclusion that women are whores, you didn't get mad and start to fight with her? Suppose instead, you said to yourself 'You fool! *You* created the situation.' "

Obviously, he would have tension. Instead he has a rationalization. He fights with her and proves to himself that he is a very aggressive fellow.

If a genius or a poet or a writer tried to figure out a life situation as clever as the psychic masochist, he would fail. It is absolutely foolproof.

Now you could ask, "What happens to these people when things go right? After all, we cannot always direct the actions of others. And sometimes things turn out for the best."

True. However, the neurotic psychic masochist is prepared

for this also. We all know the story of the man who asked a woman why she was crying? "Because I am so happy," she answered. This is completely idiotic from a rational viewpoint.

But this crying, happy woman is neither an idiot or crazy. Because if you expect in advance the worst, and the masochist does expect the worst, if you have imagined all of the negative possibilities, and then all goes well, you can cry about all the terrible things you suffered before the act.

An old joke explains this situation. Two passengers sit next to each other on a train, one reading and the other groaning and holding his stomach.

"What's the matter?" asks the reader.

"Intestinal cramps," is the reply.

"Here," the reader says, handing the groaner some pills. "My doctor gave them to me for my intestinal cramps."

The man takes the pills and all is quiet for five minutes. Then he starts groaning and moaning and rubbing his stomach again.

"What's the matter now?" asks the reader. "Didn't the pills work?"

"Yes," replies the groaner. "But I'm thinking of how horrible the pain was while it lasted."

Too Much Too Soon

At this point, you may ask how all of this began. Where does it come from?

Imagine what would happen if there were a great river and men put up a dam in all directions with little or no outlet for the water. Soon, the river would start backing up, reversing itself.

Now, let us talk about a child. Potentially, all the anger, fury and aggression that an adult has, the child has also. But the fact that the child is physically helpless does not allow him to do anything effective in the outside world with his anger, fury and aggression.

The inner conscience ("superego") becomes the beneficiary of this rebounding (internalized) baby aggression. The result is that the unconscious conscience is a torture institution, constantly reproaching the ego. What differentiates neurotics from not-too-neurotic people (euphemistically called "normal") is not the structure of the superego, but the different techniques the ego uses to cope with this avalanche of inner reproaches. The more normal person inwardly says, "Not guilty," and "that's that." The psychic masochist does not fight back, accepts all the punishment meted out by the inner conscience, but surreptitiously makes a pleasure out of it. And *the only pleasure one can derive from displeasure, is to make that displeasure—a pleasure*. All this is, of course, going on unconsciously.

In other words, the child has a capacity for too much aggression too early. Unable to attack the world, he attacks himself. This is what the psychic masochist does as an adult. He makes out of a transitory phase a permanent station in life.

But you may now say, "This doesn't make sense. Why should a person hurt himself?"

The most obvious answer is that this type of person must get something out of it. But what?

Pleasure.

In other words, masochism is anger, fury and aggression turned inward but, instead of pain, the person manages to outsmart a part of himself. One part is saying, "Hurt," the other part, "Hurt is fun."

Imagine, for instance, a situation during the Nazi tyranny in Europe. A guard in a jail starts each day by going down to the cell of Mr. X and beating him until the blood flows. One day he is late and when he arrives at the cell he finds that Mr. X hasn't waited for him, but is frantically beating his head up against the wall.

The Nazi watches, and sure enough, blood begins to flow. "Well, he's saved me my work for today," says the guard happily.

But supposing another guard said to this happy Nazi, "Maybe Mr. X is enjoying it." Although the Nazi is stupid he might understand this seemingly fantastic but true statement. And what will happen? If he is a true sadist he will devise other tortures or kill Mr. X so as to be one step ahead of him, the masochist.

Now, this is exactly what happens with the psychic masochist. He must always increase the masochistic provocation and his own self-damage to prove to his inner conscience, "No, I couldn't enjoy that."

In effect, psychic masochism is not self-limiting but progressive. Look at acquaintances whom you have known for ten or twenty years, and you will see that, with one exception, which I will mention, if they fit into this pattern of self-damage they have become better and better at it.

The best example of the one exception to this progressiveness is a patient whom I saw in New York once. This man was from San Francisco and he had fifty or so symptoms of neurosis troubling him. But he had to live in California, so I offered him the names of a few psychiatrists in his area.

He returned to San Francisco. Two weeks later he wrote saying he had misplaced the piece of paper and could I give him the names of the analysts again?

I sent him the information. Two weeks later he again wrote for the same information. Again I sent it to him.

Two years went by without a word. One day I met him by accident in Central Park. "Doctor!" he said. "You know, I never went into treatment but I don't need it now. All the things that were wrong, stopped."

I didn't say anything. I did not want to say what I normally would. That is, I would have asked, "For what did you exchange all your symptoms?"

Instead I asked what he was doing in New York. "Are you on business here?"

"Oh no," he said. "I married an absolutely horrible creature and I've just come from Reno to get over the divorce."

I said nothing, now knowing for what he had exchanged his symptoms.

"Do you still believe I should go into treatment?" he asked.

"Well," I replied, "should the fifty symptoms come back, you may want to think about it."

A few weeks later I received a letter asking for the name of a psychiatrist.

For the psychic masochist must keep on beating himself, unless he obtains help in understanding and therapeutically working out why he does so.

12.

"Is there a hidden meaning in humor?"
we asked Dr. Grotjahn.

∿∿∿∿∿∿∿∿∿∿∿∿∿∿∿

MARTIN GROTJAHN, M.D.

Clinical Professor of Psychiatry,
University of Southern California

In this interview Dr. Grotjahn also discusses:

"Why do we laugh at the sexual and obscene joke?"
    "What does it mean when a man or woman laughs during sexual play?"
        "Is the witty man or woman sexually dangerous?"
"What can be fearful about the joke?"
    "Are there things about which we cannot laugh?"
        "How do we learn to laugh?"
"Does laughter ease our anxiety?"
    "What is the artistry of great comedians?"
        "How is repression of our aggression involved in humor?"
"Does the psychotic have a sense of humor?"
    "Why do adolescents laugh at 'sick' jokes?"
        "What is the meaning of the 'reverse Oedipus'?"

12.

This is what Dr. Grotjahn said when interviewed:

Q. *Will you analyze why the following joke is funny? A patient was having trouble talking freely on the couch, so his analyst suggested that he would go out of the room but leave his tape recorder behind, and the patient could talk into it. The patient agreed. A few weeks later, the analyst was having a drink at a nearby bar, during the time of the patient's session, when who should walk in but the patient. "What are you doing here?" asked the analyst in surprise. "I got tired talking into your tape recorder, so I went out and bought one of my own, and now your tape recorder is talking to my tape recorder," explained the patient. Dr. Grotjahn why do we laugh at this joke?*

A. It is not the best joke of the season, but it is funny in two respects: There is a two-fold aggression, first against the analyst and then against modern technology which is so dehumanizing. The analyst's behavior is questioned since he retreats from his duty, leaving the electronic recorder in charge. The aggression against technology is directed at the idea of gadgets talking to each other. Thus, we see a double attack.

I have a joke for you. Two homosexual men stand on a street corner. They see a beautiful girl wiggle by. The young men stare at her. Then one says to the other, "These are the moments when I would like to be a lesbian." You laugh? It's a very serious story. As Bobby Clark would complain, "Here I tell all these wonderful jokes and what do people do? They laugh."

This story is also an aggressive joke. The sexual or obscene joke is always an aggressive one. There is the hidden aggression against "all the fuss about sex between boys and girls." It is aggression against all sex by denying normal sex, by denying such interest in the girl as a man might show.

Q. Is the basis of laughter at that joke one of laughing at the aggression?

A. Yes. The first part of the joke probably activated your aggression against homosexuals. The direct aggressive insult would have been, "All homosexuals are fools who cannot appreciate a beautiful girl." But that is not a joke. Only when disguised skillfully does it become a joke. According to Freud, we laugh because of the energy we save when we do not need to repress aggression any more. We save a lot of energy; we laugh in relief from repression no longer needed.

Q. Could you explain a little more fully what you mean by "repression of aggression?"

A. Let's take a line I heard in the play, *Mary, Mary.* The husband says to his wife while they get ready to go to bed, "Are you interested, or shall I take a sleeping pill?" The direct aggression would be an obscene remark. Here, the direct sexual attack is repressed, then disguised in the indifferent, but still insulting, remark.

In the joke about the two homosexuals who stared at the pretty girl, these two men use aggression to wipe out all normal heterosexual sex. "Boys have no interest in girls; girls have no interest in boys." This is aggression. "Sex is nonsense. Boys stick together and girls stick together. If I see a girl, I want to become a girl. I want to be a girl to enjoy a girl like that."

Freud explained it this way: I have an aggressive intent. This I do not allow myself to express. I repress it. The aggressive thought, then forbidden, gets into the unconscious, is censored and disguised. This Freud called the dream work or the wit work. The aggression is well disguised and can be expressed.

Freud was very fond of the Jewish joke. It is difficult to visualize Freud laughing. Freud was a witty person who could make very sharp, biting remarks. And he could laugh, where otherwise he was a tragic figure.

Q. Does man have a "need" to laugh?

A. Yes. Laughter is very important for us. People are the only living beings who can laugh. Animals do not laugh. By the way, any analysis destroys laughter and talking about jokes is usually a sad affair.

Q. Is it true that the psychotic has little or no humor?

A. No, that is not entirely true. He has a psychotic humor. For a psychotic schizophrenic, for instance, something can seem funny. It is a mad laughter, the laughter of the madman.

Humor may become pathological humor. Take all the "sick" jokes that go the rounds. In my book, "Beyond Laughter," I discuss the pathology of humor in detail.

There is a lot of talk about the fact that our time no longer produces real comedians or real comedy. In the first place, our era is not very creative; we are caught in a time where religion doesn't stimulate art any longer because we are not religious. Most of our creativity goes into science and technique. So real artistic creativity, whether it be tragedy or comedy, does not exist.

There is another point, too. We are very aware of aggressive behavior; we try to control it. And the sublimation of aggression into comedy is very difficult in our time because we are so suspicious of all aggression that we become more and more careful and self-censoring. We do not allow ourselves to be aggressive.

In the American scene until recently, aggression was thought very bad. Under President Kennedy, it was coming out a little bit more, in the person of the young man who was successful, for he had the privilege of being aggressive. You see it, too, in the birth of a whole generation of young comedians. Take for example, people I admire especially, Elaine May and Mike Nichols. I think of a scene where she plays a mother and he plays her son, a famous scientist caught in an atomic experiment and unable to call his mother. Finally he does phone her. She says, "Here three weeks, I don't even dare eat because I don't want to have food in my mouth when my son calls and my son doesn't call." Thus it starts — these hidden aggressions of the Jewish mother and her only son. Finally, the mother succeeds in reducing her son, the famous scientist, to a babbling idiot. It is beautifully done. You see the aggressive, domineering, powerful mother, whom we all fear, whom we try to love, and who finally establishes herself as a mother, not of a big man, but of a little baby. For her, every man remains a baby.

Such aggression is what you find in all great comedians. It is a perversion of the comedian when he does not attack or when he apologizes for it. Mort Sahl, whether you believe what he says or not, is a most skillful aggressor.

A second reason why our time is so estranged from comedy occurred to me when I was living in Germany and Hitler rose to power. We all made jokes about him; it was easy at first. I remember one evening when we sat in a café and things looked gloomy. In came Hans Fallada, the man who wrote the wonderful novel, "Little Man, What Now?" He raised his arm in salute and said: "Heil—hem—ahem. Heil—what was the name?" At that time, it was very funny. But after a while, when Hitler became overwhelmingly horrible, it was no longer possible to make a joke about him.

Similarly, today it is impossible to make a joke about a nuclear war or an atomic explosion. It is too dangerous. It activates too much anxiety. When many of us who lived in Germany escaped to America, we could not tolerate slapstick because we were too close to the anxiety where slapstick was no joke, but torture and cruelty.

Q. *A recent* New Yorker *cartoon showed a man walking up to a sign that said, "Do not Push." He pushes and the whole world explodes. This was a joke about atomic war, wasn't it?*
A. Yes. This one was very well done. It was not tactless. It had something I call "the adult discount." We know it cannot happen this way. It was too grotesque to be true. The idea was bearable — because it was so grotesque.

The aggressive idea, which was well disguised, was expressed as, "If there is such a button, are we sure that the man who has access to this button will not push it just because he can't resist?" There is another story going the rounds: The President has a secret telephone which only he can answer and which will be used only in extreme emergency. It is supposed to be absolutely foolproof. Suddenly the telephone rings. Kennedy answers. An angry man says, "Is this the gas company? I have a leak in my house."

Such are the stories just easing through on the thin line between tactless, terrible danger, and relief by laughter. Wit

gives freedom; freedom gives wit. When you are on the end
of that telephone call between mother and son as done by
May and Nichols, you have enjoyed great freedom. You have
enjoyed the strength of your aggression in a form which does
not hurt, but which gives insight and is, therefore, one powerful tool in becoming mature.

*Q. When do children start to have a sense of humor? Is
there any specific time?*

A. Yes. A first forerunner of humor is the child's smile. Did
you ever think what it means in our development that only
the human baby can nurse on the mother and look in her
face? No other animal can. Nursing animals don't see anything. They are just satisfied. But the baby sucks on the
breast, looks up at the mother and they smile at each other.

This is the forerunner of humor. This happy union we
try to establish again in humorous situations later in life. The
next step takes place with toilet training. There comes a time
when children think there is nothing funnier than anal
noises. In a nursery school of children between two and
four, the laughter over such noises breaks up the house. The
interest in anality still carries on in jokes in adult life.

Every new joke is built on the grave of anxiety overcome.
Out of that mastery grows the freedom to make a joke.
When the child begins to master language, he tells those horrible moron, idiotic jokes that go: "Little Paul jumped out
of the window on the tenth floor to make a splash on Broadway." Adults don't laugh at this, they just groan.

The smile of the baby, the anal joke of toilet training and
the pun of the child who has just learned to master language,
are all steps in the direction of maturation — the finest form
is humor which is quite different from wit. In between stands
comedy, which I consider the reverse tragedy.

The tragic hero, Oedipus, rebels, wants to kill his father
and possess his mother. In the comedy, the young man has
won, even casts his father in the role of Oedipus. This happens in the life of every man whose son is growing up, and
it can be quite educational. In my book, "Beyond Laughter,"
I describe "The Reverse Oedipus" in a scene where I play
with my son on the beach. Suddenly my wife says, "Can't
you pick on a person of your size?" But for the first time,

she did not mean me, but my son! She didn't protect him any longer, because he was now five inches taller than I.

Q. Is it the things that frighten us the most about which we have the greatest difficulty joking?

A. Yes. Anxiety must be overcome to a certain extent. Not completely, but we must feel we are the master. We cannot joke about the gallows when we are too frightened by it. The Roman who is condemned to die, stumbles on the way to the gallows and says, "This week begins badly." This is funny to us. But not a joke about Eichmann. That's too dangerous to handle. So, when a child has not mastered a certain amount of toilet training, he will be frightened of anal jokes, rather than delighted by them, because he is afraid of an accident; afraid of loosing his mastery. Children may get frightened in a circus, where adults have a good time.

Q. Why do so many of us tell obscene jokes? Is it that we have anxiety about sex?

A. Yes. Sometimes it also seems that a man with great inner anxiety tells these jokes so that a woman will believe he has overcome his anxiety about sex. Most women know the witty man is not the dangerous man. The witty man makes his joke — and that's all.

Women are less fond of jokes than men. Comedies are made for men. The movie industry knows this. The woman wants, not comedies, but sentimental love stories.

Q. You mean telling jokes takes away the power of the woman? Takes away her femininity?

A. Yes. A witty woman is a masculine woman. She can be wonderful — some of our wittiest women are, but they are also frightening and dangerous to most men. Some of us, however, love frightening and dangerous women.

Q. Didn't Henry Miller say this, when he wrote that there is nothing that will make an erection go down faster than laughter from a woman in bed?

A. Yes. And I have heard that the Japanese prostitute giggles, which is the same thing. Most unnerving for the G. I.'s who tell about it. The women do it to be polite; they aren't laughing at the men, but rather giving the polite kind of giggle you find at a cocktail party. But it proves very un-nerving to some men.

Even the sexual joke is an aggressive joke. Sexuality is used only secondarily — to disguise an aggression. This is very important because when it is primary it then becomes something else and is no longer a joke. It is the disguise of an aggression which makes an obscene joke really good.

Q. Although you are saying it is disguised aggression, is there a moral orientation to our jokes? Are jokes an attack on our morality?

A. I do not know a good joke which is truly immoral — I mean, truly bad, truly inviting to something wicked and hurtful. There is a difference between laughter of today and yesterday. Once people could laugh when eyes were gouged out or hands cut off. This we can no longer do. It is one of the few signs of human progress.

Q. Why is it that apparently the "sick" jokes are most appreciated by adolescents?

A. There is no better term for those awful jokes than to call them "sick" for that's what they are. I have the answer, I think. At first it worried me very much. Here is my guess: I have heard about some Indian tribes where people have beautiful hands — they have one hand with which they only receive, one hand with which they only give. They manicure their hands, oil them and doll them up. Their hands are sacred. But when somebody dies, the mourners use their sensitive hands to tear the corpse apart, to bury it, and two weeks later they unbury, then bury it again. Finally, they wash the bones in brandy and put them in the temple. They show they can use their hands for something awful.

I think adolescents of today have to go through an episode where they must deny their love, their tenderness, their decency and show they can do the awful. After that, they get "unsick." They do the forbidden, the unspeakable, as a way to liberate themselves. Of course, there are those who never liberate themselves, who get stuck in adolescent struggle about their own decency, their feelings of love and tenderness. They feel that to be appreciative of anyone means to be small and meek and soft, and a victim for any tough guy.

But the real hero does not deny his weakness, just as the mature man does not deny a certain need for dependency and passivity, his tenderness and love.

The main instrument of the joke is the word. The main instrument of the comic is action. A very comical thing I have seen was a fantastic dancer in the Mosieyev ballet who played two boys wrestling. It was absolutely hilarious. Why? Because in all of us are always two boys struggling, a good boy and a bad boy. Here we really could see the struggle — one person who was two.

James Thurber, in his story of Walter Mitty, gave us the courage not to deny the Walter Mitty in us, not to fight it, not to trample with the dirty feet of repression on the Walter Mitty in us, but to enjoy him, to let him live in us. That's what we are after in our analytic way. Thurber does it in an artistic way. If you read his fantastic description of how Mitty fixes the operation machine with his fountain pen, that's what we dream about. Let's have the courage to accept ourselves as little people and big dreamers. Somewhere in between lies the answer.

Q. Could you describe what "repression" is?

A. Repression is anti-freedom. Repression is pushing something down into the unconscious which should come out, should be integrated. There in the unconscious it will grow and become a cancer. Any repression is pathological. This does not mean I am against control or discipline — it is not a sign of being analyzed that you allow yourself to belch in public. Repression means not allowing yourself to look at things and handle things but to declare them as forbidden and push them back into the unconscious, keep them away from consciousness. Only in consciousness can you deal with things. The mature person does not repress, he is not an impulsive, instinctive-driven person. He has found better methods than repression. And this is integration.

If you really allow yourself to think about what you repress, you have a much better chance to deal with it, to see whether it is true. If it is, you can then understand and live with it.

Q. What purpose does repression serve?

A. To keep dangerous thoughts from our conscious, to keep them forgotten, in the unconscious. When they come out, it does not mean that we have to obey our instincts, but rather we have to learn how to deal with our thoughts.

Q. Does humor relieve aggression?

A. It does. It is always testing the rigidity of the repression. It can lift the repression. For instance, the compulsive neurotic who always has to keep guard over his repressions makes sarcastic and cynical remarks but cannot become that really relieving clown, the jokester. The man who can create freely with his unconscious loses his repressions. He will become free — not bad.

Don't think of aggression and hostility as the same thing. Aggression is different from hostility. You can be aggressive while feeling great love. That is what we experience when we laugh. What is learned with laughter is learned well. Laughter gives freedom, and freedom gives laughter. He who understands the comic begins to understand the struggle for freedom and happiness. He will understand what it means to be human.

Thank you, Dr. Grotjahn.

13.

*"Can physical disease be a way of
life?" we asked Dr. Kay.*

xxxxxxxxxxxxxxxxxxxx

PAUL KAY, M.D.
Assistant Clinical Professor, Department of Psychiatry,
State University of New York, Downstate Medical Center

In this interview Dr. Kay also discusses:

"How real are the psychological factors in physical illness?"
"Do our emotions affect our body?"
"What causes love and hate to become confused?"
"Can the unconscious cause physical illness?"
"Is self-punishment related to physical illness?"
"Why do we pay the high price of illness?"
"Can talking to somebody ease physical distress?"
*"What are some of the emotional needs taken care of by
physical illnesses?"*
"What is 'constitutional weakness'?"
"Is repression of anger related to physical illness?"
"What is the connection between guilt and illness?"
"What is a child's idea of death?"

13.

This is what Dr. Kay said when interviewed in his office:

One of the professional incidents that led me into psychiatry happened a number of years ago when I was a general practitioner in a midwestern state. I lived in a village of about nine hundred people, a community which barely interrupted the magnificent, desolate prairie country stretching out to meet the sky in every direction. Out there, living meant farming for almost everyone. Both the men and women worked hard. But the men had time off. They could hunt, drink and smoke. The women could pray in their spare time. When a woman wanted to smoke and drink she first drew the curtains. The women did everything from making clothing for their children out of potato sacks to hard, physical labor in the fields. Aside from this, they had to be mothers, wives, and active in church. Whatever inner satisfactions they derived from their labors, they got little from their busy or tired husbands.

One of these women came to me for help with a rich array of symptoms most of which pointed to gall-bladder and joint disease. Being an excessively conscientious young man and also because I was only two years out of medical school with all sorts of charming illusions about being a great doctor, I took a very careful history and gave her a thorough physical examination. But this was not enough. In my tiny laboratory, I analyzed her urine chemically, examined it under a microscope and did a blood count. I came up with nothing on which I could base a diagnosis. I had to see her several times but she did not mind in the least. Finally, I sent her to a consultant, a "big man," in a large town about a hundred miles away, for additional investigation. The big man, in effect, slapped me on the back and reassured me that there was nothing "really wrong" with my patient: nothing "physical" to account for her symptoms.

These investigations extended over a period of several months. During this time, I slowly came to realize that an interesting development had taken place. I noticed that this woman liked to come in to me and talk about her symptoms. While she talked about what bothered her physically, she would also talk with considerable feeling about her farm life and what she did, thought and felt in relation to herself, her husband and other people. She felt better after these talks. I began to give her less and less medication, eventually stopping it completely. Finally, her symptoms had almost entirely disappeared and she felt fine. She continued to see me from time to time subsequently with occasional minor complaints. I left the village for specialty training soon after this experience and had no further contact with her. But she had opened my eyes.

Certainly, I had attended lectures on psychiatry in medical school, read books on the relationship between people's emotions and their physical and mental health, and had already seen examples of this relationship in my internship and Navy experience. But neither intellectual knowledge nor the passing, hurried, clinical experiences had impressed me. Lack of experience and emotional immaturity had helped me to develop a strong talent for denying the fact that people could suffer emotionally and that such suffering could be beautifully and destructively hidden behind physical symptoms. Fortunately, I had begun to give up this talent by the time I was confronted with this challenging clinical experience so that at least on an intuitive level I could help her by letting her talk.

I perceived at the time that the "talking out" was connected with the relief of her physical symptoms, but little more than that. Now, in retrospect, it is clear that in her "talking" she was releasing disturbing ideas and feelings which if held back or shoved aside got themselves translated into bodily symptoms. This expression was only part of the therapeutic process that she experienced. The other part consisted of something more positive. She "got" some-

thing from the energy I had invested in her which she had
sorely needed. Her reaction to this lack had consisted of the
disturbing ideas and feelings she was finally able to release
in words, rather than in tension which led to a bodily reaction.

In my patient, of course, these mental processes and, in
particular, the connection between her mental suffering and
her physical symptoms was and remained essentially unconscious. We have all had the experience some time in our
lives of getting a mysterious, whacking sore throat or diarrhea just as we were about to face a situation we dreaded.
Only later, if at all, (after overcoming the natural repug-
nance to discovering anything imperfect in ourselves) could
we dare to realize how much we had craved some respectable way of avoiding or minimizing the dreaded experience.

The idea that my patient, an intelligent, conscientious,
hard-working woman devoted to her family, could feel so
dissatisfied with her life, so angry at how much she was giving to her family and how little she was getting or felt she
was getting and that therefore she had developed disturbing
bodily symptoms, was totally unacceptable to her. Her
symptoms permitted her to get away from an intolerable
situation and into one in which she was given something
precious to her, namely, serious, undivided attention. She
could feel important and cared for not only by me but by
her husband, who now had to attend to her. At the same
time and in a perfectly acceptable way, she could revenge
herself on her husband whom she unconsciously considered
the sole source of her frustration. Her illness had almost reversed the previous family situation. Husband and children
were relatively neglected while her illness forced them to
give her their concern and time: nor was the money used up
in her medical care inconsequential. Further, the guilt she
experienced from satisfying her consciously condemned
wishes was conveniently soaked up by her suffering. Who
could possibly suspect a victim of being a satisfied avenger,
a sufferer, of making or trying to make others suffer?

This type of medical problem is and always has been
quite common. Many people, for shorter or longer periods
of time, wrap their lives around this or that physical symptom which may be severely disabling or even threatening to

life because of emotional conflicts which they cannot solve in any other way.

In a certain real sense this situation is no different than that of the child who tries to solve the difficulties which going to school creates within him by truancy, or the man who reacts to the normal demands of a wife and children by getting only jobs which keep him far away from home. These reactions are also "diseases." Only they occur on a different level: that of attitude and action rather than on the level of bodily reactions. In this talk, I want to explore with you in some detail why and how emotional difficulties may reveal themselves in physical "disease" with the hope that the information may be of interest and possibly even of practical value.

We can begin our discussion with the definition of "disease." It breaks down easily into "dis" and "ease": lack of ease. When an organ such as the stomach or a system, for example the respiratory system, is not working smoothly, it is "diseased." A variety of factors singly or in combination may produce such a state: injury, infection, tumors, certain chemicals (those produced by the body as well as those introduced externally such as drugs or "poisons") and emotions. The symptoms produced by these varied causes may be so alike as to be indistinguishable. Fatigue, for example, may be brought about by hard work, an upper respiratory infection, insufficient food, a drug used for sleeping or an emotional state such as fear or depression, to mention just a few possibilities. Similarly, a common symptom like backache, usually harmless in its origin, may be caused by anything from a kidney infection or muscular injury to anxiety. The anxiety may lead to actual muscular tension or stiffness which then causes the "ache."

An emotional conflict may disturb physical health in several ways. A depressed person feels hopeless. He loses his appetite and as a result may enter a state of semi-starvation. The resulting malnutrition will most likely lead to an actual anemia which in turn may set the stage for a variety of infections. Such a person may not necessarily be aware of the depression. Or, a young woman is guilty and fearful that her affairs will be discovered. She wishes she were ill so that her parents would love her instead of punishing her. Unconsciously, she also wants the illness as a punishment for her "sin." An insect bites her. Absent-mindedly she scratches it excessively. The bacteria from under her finger nails and around the bite gain entry into the wound and bring about an infection. A few days of "unwitting neglect" and suddenly she is in the throes of a severe infection already spread to the local lymph glands and threatening to invade the blood stream. She is now surrounded by concerned, loving parents and a soothing physician. A wonderful commotion fills her home and silently absorbs her guilty fears.

Fear and anger themselves may more directly (through stimulation of certain areas of the brain) lead ultimately to the production of various chemical substances which can produce a great variety of temporary bodily changes and symptoms which look disturbingly like those caused by actual damage to organs or systems. These body chemicals, for example, can lead to episodes of palpitation, indigestion, diarrhea, an asthmatic type of breathing, or frequency of urination. A very proper, conscientious woman I once treated was afraid of her anger, especially toward people who were important to her. One of her main ways of getting rid of her anger which lay buried beneath the surface was to have severe abdominal cramps and diarrhea. As she began to be less fearful of her anger and could acknowledge it, she put it into words instead of into bowel movements.

Just as kicking and biting are universal and common modes of expressing rage in the infant, defecation is similarly resorted to by the toddler. The child talks of "making a duty" on the object of his anger and, indeed, the adult has at his verbal command several colorful variations on the same theme. When a person like my patient cannot express his anger for certain specific reasons in a mature way, he then returns to a more primitive pathway. In these instances, the conflicts giving rise to the disturbing emotions as well as the physiological changes to which they lead are usually entirely unconscious.

Clinical and laboratory studies have already strongly indicated, if not clearly demonstrated, that as a result of emotional stimulation, the various hormone-producing glands of the body may be sufficiently affected by way of the central nervous system so that the functions associated with reproduction in both men and women, the healing of wounds, the resistance to infection and the tendency to react with an allergic response are unfavorably influenced.

I once treated a woman who had been desperately trying to conceive for several years. She was anatomically normal. First she and I discovered that she hated men, including her husband. Second, she was afraid that if she gave birth, she might have a boy. Third, she therefore did not want to conceive at all. On the other side of the ledger was the fact that she herself had not outgrown her childhood wish to be a man and her condemnation of femininity. Eventually, these psychological problems were found to be related to old, powerful buried feelings toward her parents: for mother, contempt and for her father, a deep hatred borne out of envy and despair as a result of his lack of interest in her. Through treatment and her own fine courage, she developed sufficient recognition and understanding of her difficulties so she could begin to take some pride in her womanliness and could accept men with much less fear and hatred. She stopped treatment. About a year later she informed me that she had given birth and that mother and son were doing well.

Daily observation teaches us that our emotional state can, and often does, influence our physical functioning in many ways and in varying degrees. If our physical functioning is already impaired, our emotions may increase the impairment and precipitate an attack. Birthdays, anniversaries, graduation ceremonies, funerals, examinations, job interviews, marriage, the birth of a baby, holidays — indeed, for some people who are work addicts, even week-ends — can be emotionally disturbing and bring about distressing bodily reactions of all kinds.

Except for a few investigators, most psychoanalysts and psychiatrists do not think that a particular emotional conflict necessarily brings about, or contributes to particular physical symptoms or for that matter, any physical symptoms. Disease processes commonly regarded as being either determined or influenced to a significant degree by emotional factors — such as asthma, ulcerative colitis, rheumatoid arthritis, peptic ulcer, migraine, some forms of hypertension, hyperthyroidism, baldness, diabetes and coronary artery disease — have been found to be associated with emotional conflicts which also occur in people without such conditions. Fear and anger themselves may increase the blood pressure in some people drastically and in others elevate it only slightly or even depress it. Frustration of an unconscious wish for love may in time bring on or aggravate a peptic ulcer in one person, an attack of asthma in another, depression in a third or sexual promiscuity in a fourth. One man may react to an unconscious wish to be a woman by developing an attack of asthma, another by behaving as a super virile man. To make matters more complex, what is usually found is a constellation or interrelated series of underlying psychological conflicts in connection with a physical symptom or set of symptoms. Further, those who have physical symptoms in connection with emotional factors also often turn out to have a variety of mental symptoms. The boy with asthma may also be unable to concentrate, have fears of women and be unable to sleep. The woman who suffers from severe attacks of anxiety when alone may also develop a chronic, stubborn skin condition which defies all medication. The rapidly growing knowledge in the science of heredity adds still another complex set of causative factors to the problem.

Features which indicate that a physical condition is due to, or significantly influenced by emotional factors are the occurrence or aggravation of symptoms when the individual has been emotionally distressed; when he is in a situation which is painful to him or threatens to be; when the suffering is out of proportion to the actual degree of physical disturbance; or when the patient cannot or will not cooperate with the physician's recommendations or may even do the opposite.

Suspecting or detecting that emotional factors are at work in one way or another in a physical condition is easy enough but it is only the first step in understanding how the two are related. No one certainly knows exactly where and how in the brain ideas and feelings get translated into bodily reactions. Certainly, physicians know in a broad way that certain parts of the brain are instrumental in our talking, hearing, seeing, memorizing, performing various skilled and unskilled actions and understanding. But no study in the field has as yet been sufficiently precise or conclusive to give all or even many of the answers as to what happens between the occurrence of specific ideas and feelings in a particular individual and the bodily reactions or disease with which they are more or less clearly connected. Nor is there any indisputable proof that the most powerful emotional disturbances over a long period can alone bring about significant damage to the body. Indeed, isn't it annoying at times to see the person who is always upset, always complaining and always burdened with all sorts of diseases living a long and healthy life?

In an analogous fashion, the complete psychological answer is still far away. Why in a particular person his or her emotions or emotional conflicts choose to express themselves not only in specific physical symptoms but even, at times, in different physical symptoms although the emotions and conflicts appear to be the same, is at best incompletely understood. But there is considerable knowledge available on this aspect as a result of the increasing number of careful studies of individual patients extending over months and years by psychiatrists, especially psychoanalysts, internists and physiologists, plus the ever-present recorded experiences by physicians from all the fields of medicine.

A prominent psychological mechanism by means of which emotional conflicts may be expressed physically is called "identification." The individual, without realizing it, takes over one or more features of another. I have in mind a boy of twelve who suffered from severe attacks of asthma. They occurred in connection with upper respiratory infections and also in connection with certain holidays. These holidays, it turned out, were distressing to him because of the attention and admiration his older sister received, especially from his father. His sister was considered beautiful, brilliant and eminently personable. She suffered from asthma. As a result of an asthmatic attack, my young patient could solve many unbearable problems. For one thing he was a very proud and sensitive boy and condemned his jealousy toward his sister. He found intolerable the pain at seeing his sister get the love he craved from his parents, especially father. Most unacceptable to him was his wish to be his sister or as much like her as possible. The attacks of asthma absorbed, as it were, his unacceptable painful feelings and ideas. They forced parents, sister and others to give him all the attention he wanted whereas then his sister got none. They also represented an excellent revenge against the frustrations (only some of which were factual) he experienced from his father, a revenge he was otherwise powerless to obtain directly because he felt terrorized by his father. The asthmatic attacks enabled him to avoid much conscious mental suffering. He sought treatment, for example, only because of his difficulty in attending to his studies. He considered "laziness" as his problem.

The upper respiratory infections which often led to asthmatic symptoms tended to occur when he had failed in school or felt threatened with failure. These situations stirred up the same feelings and ideas toward sister and father which the holidays did.

Since allergic tendencies existed in mother and father, there is little doubt that hereditary factors were at work in the boy's asthma. The occurrence of attacks under specific types of circumstances and their almost complete disappearance (over a four year period) as the boy was able to express his buried problems in words and feelings and gradually make peace with himself, testify to the presence and importance of the psychological factor.

A second frequent type of psychological mechanism by which emotional problems are expressed through the body is that of symbolic representation. Our language mirrors this mechanism so aptly. Who had not had the experience of someone literally giving him a "headache?" I once came across an extraordinarily energetic and ambitious young man in his early twenties, gifted in many directions. Since birth he had been affected by a rare disease of his spinal cord which left him crippled in one leg and with a bladder over which he had but slight control. The dread of an "accident" left him self-conscious and ashamed. Wherever he went he stationed himself as close as possible to the nearest toilet. At night he was even worse off. A "dry-night" was a blessing and special occasion. Nor did the warm sympathy of his wife significantly diminish the humiliation he suffered on arising.

But there were times when he did not wet the bed or

have an "accident" during the day. Gradually a pattern emerged showing a suspiciously close correlation between certain types of events during or after which he showed loss of bladder control. When someone whom he regarded as important criticized him or made him feel as if he were being criticized, he felt hurt and angry and sooner or later urinated uncontrollably. When someone complimented him, he felt elated and could exercise normal control over his bladder.

In the unconscious part of his personality, criticism made him feel that he was not only a "baby" but a big burden. This idea led to the desire to get even with the critic by angrily urinating uncontrollably as if he were a baby. Thus, when his uncle, for whom he worked and whom he regarded as his worst persecutor, was away or agreeable, he was "dry." This pattern had its onset in childhood when he became extremely sensitive and rebellious towards his parents who had left him with the feeling that he was too much trouble and would be better off in an institution. Because of his tormenting fear of being abandoned by his parents, he buried his hurts and vengeful wishes as best he could and expressed them physically. The fact that there was a basis for his bladder condition in his spinal cord damage, according to most of the doctors who examined and treated him, made it possible for him easily to deceive himself as well as others for many years.

As a result of psychotherapy, he achieved considerable, although not complete control over his bladder. This only partial result was most likely due to the physical condition itself as well as the incomplete resolution of his psychological problems.

There are several other psychological mechanisms by means of which emotional difficulties are expressed physically. I will bring up just one more in a general way. This one is most easily observed in children. The child carries out unwittingly what it senses mother or father really wants it to do regardless of what the parent actually says. A mother, for example, with an unconscious desire to overeat and become heavy, constantly confronts her child with mounds of tempting food or candy. Sooner or later, unless the child is inwardly restrained by some stronger counter desire, he begins to eat excessively and put on weight. The same mother may, in words, be constantly imploring the child to reduce.

Another common example is the mother who is overly solicitous about her son's health partly as a result of unconsciously wanting him to be sick and suffer. This wish, in turn, may be based on the unfortunate circumstance that the child happens to remind the mother, without her ever being aware of it, of a hated person in the past, a brother or father, for example. Every time her son shows the slightest indisposition, she calls the doctor. Anxiously, she feeds him vitamins and tonics and special foods. She lets him know that dangerous germs are all about and must be kept away by any and all means. The boy is kept at a high pitch of anxiety which itself may actually lower his resistance to infection in time. He may overeat or eat too little. He learns to exaggerate slight physical discomforts or illnesses and then use his illness to his advantage. He usually will rebel sooner or later against such excessive solicitude and actually get himself into situations in which he can get sick or be hurt by being genuinely reckless and flouting elementary rules of self-protection.

In no way are any of the problems of the patients whom I have presented uniquely set apart from those met in every-day life. Everyone at some time or other is reckless, overly sensitive, rebellious, jealous and hateful. Everyone at some time or other suffers from feelings of deprivation. There is no adult who at some time or other hasn't wanted to be a baby or fancied deep inside his mind that the other sex has all the triumphs. But where the conflict gets too strong or lasts too long, it may in some people, along with other factors such as heredity, lead to disabling or persistent physical symptoms. In many instances, these symptoms and the emotional troubles which produced them can be relieved by the understanding general practitioner. In other instances, the psychiatrist's services may be needed. Fortunately, people are tough and resilient and tend to recover from their "diseases" more often than not. Fortunately, medicine has long since reached such a stage of effectiveness that where natural toughness has not spontaneously healed the "lack of ease," medicine often can.

14.

"How are dental pain and pathology related to aggression, anger and hate?" we asked Dr. Golden.

MORTON M. GOLDEN, M.D.

Psychoanalyst

In this interview Dr. Golden also discusses:

"What may be the psychological meaning of oral decay?"

"Why do adolescents show more oral decay than any other group?"

"Why do we sometimes have an unconscious wish to bite others?"

"How may aggressive feelings affect our teeth?"

"Why do some believe physical illness a punishment for sins?"

"Are there physiological predispositions to tooth decay?"

"What is the meaning of hysterical pain?"

"What is the 'ego ideal' of man?"

"What may be the psychological meaning of teeth to children?"

"What should parents teach their children about teeth?"

"How are teeth related to the body image of man?"

14.

This is what Dr. Golden said when interviewed in his office:

In speaking of disease as a way of life and, in particular, of dental disease, a number of points should be made clear. First of all, I assume the reader accepts the fact that the unconscious exists in all individuals. Secondly, I assume the reader not only accepts the existence of the unconscious but also believes it is extremely powerful, as it works either for love or hate.

The basic theory and premise of psychosomatic medicine is that pain, injury and pathology, including dental pain and pathology, can serve as a mask for emotional distress. Human beings often would rather camouflage painful, subjective feelings under the disguise of somatic pain or injury. In other words, it is far better to have a dentist treat a pain in a tooth or the jaw than to recognize certain emotional difficulties with which one cannot fully cope. This is the basic theory of conversion of emotional problems into bodily disease.

Allow me to explain more fully. Man has always driven for a certain "ego ideal" of himself. Man has an image of himself both as he is and as he wants and desires to be. But this image can easily be threatened by pressures and forces outside and inside of himself. If a man finds himself in a situation that makes him feel helpless and overburdened, because he cannot adequately deal with the situation, in self-defense — and on an unconscious level — he may channel this conflict into some physiological disturbance. When this happens, he can then center his energy and preoccupation on the bodily disease.

Remember that this procedure takes place unconsciously, as the individual sincerely and righteously reaches out for

medical or dental attention. The pain of the bodily afflic-
tion is evidently easier to accept than the pain of the emotional frustration. In addition, the organ which is afflicted, or
the part of the body which develops a somatic conversion,
is usually the part of the body that will also gain by the
conflict. If a man develops hysterical paralysis of his hand,
for example, he may unconsciously wish to attack someone
with that hand, and he punishes that part of the body that
would inflict too much guilt upon himself.

MAN'S FIRST WEAPON

By the time a child is one year old — if not sooner — he has
already learned that teeth can hurt. He has learned this
through his own teething, the pain of his own teeth coming
out often being severe. The child also knows at an early age
that by biting and grasping objects, he possesses a weapon.
Young children will bite in self-defense as though this were
their only weapon. Through training and education we try
to teach the children that teeth are a dangerous weapon,
and that we, as civilized people, avoid the use of biting.

However, aggression is a normal response to painful physical or psychological stimuli. Aggression is a normal defensive
maneuver when we are attacked or threatened with attack
by outside forces. The instinctual release of aggression is a
way of achieving emotional equilibrium and producing a
harmonious condition in our environment. But in our society,
educational and cultural mores teach us to hide our aggression and not display it too openly. Consequently, the person
who tends to fear his own aggression, or fear retaliation from
others because of his aggression, may become quite submissive, and by this maneuver hide a normal display that
would ordinarily give him a sense of bodily comfort.

Teeth are vested with the primitive aggressive desires and
needs of biting, tearing and chewing into food — and supposedly into our enemies. If a man has repressed most of his
aggression, very often the unconscious guilt of this aggression may make him fear retaliation. We all know the old
Talmudic law, "An eye for an eye, a tooth for a tooth."

In other words, we will be punished for all our misdeeds,
and often the fear of punishment is felt at the source of the
weapon. I mean, if a man has unconscious wishes to bite

and to attack other individuals, and has guilt because of this tendency, he may develop pain in his teeth as if, unconsciously, he is trying to remove the source of his own aggression.

But let this be very clear. The wish to show aggression, hostility, anger or hate may be conscious or unconscious. The wish to bite, however, is most always unconscious. In fact, in our language today we speak of the "biting person," or "biting criticism" and "crushing denunciation," as if we are unconsciously aware that in our verbal attack we are regressing to our earliest form of aggression — the direct use of our teeth. Many psychoanalysts, for example, feel that the weaning process takes place when the child may accidentally bite the mother's breast. The child may unconsciously realize that punishment will occur at the display of undue aggression.

As I have said, the teeth are basically an organ of destruction used to help man with mastication. Teeth are used for grinding, tearing, chopping and cutting, and their prime purpose to a child is as an aggressive weapon. It stands to reason that if the child knows he has this aggressive weapon, there will be a fixed representation within his mind of the use of the teeth as an aggressive defense when attacked or threatened with attack. We see this in the animal kingdom. We know animals survive by the use of their teeth.

In early childhood development, particularly in the first six years of life, the child knows that the more teeth he has the harder he can bite and the more difficult objects he can devour. Physiologically and psychologically the teeth always represent to the child a biting and aggressive instrument, and therefore, for example, when the child loses his first tooth at around the age of six, he may misinterpret this loss as a punishment for the aggressive tendencies within himself.

Parents sometimes encourage this misinterpretation by threatening the child with the dentist as if the dentist were a punishing agent. "If you bite again," says the mother. "I'll take you to the dentist and have him yank out all of your teeth." Some parents actually say to their children, "I'll knock your teeth out!"

Although I am fully aware that many uninformed people scoff at psychoanalytic theory and insights, I would like to mention that when the first tooth is lost at about six years of age, there ensues a great deal of anxiety for the child because this loss represents a destruction of his image of himself, both physiologically and psychologically. The child is losing a portion of the body, a portion of himself, and this is a great threat to both boys and girls, especially at this age. Parents seem to be unconsciously aware of the child's anxiety, however, and even today we have magical customs where wishes are made on lost teeth, coins are put under the pillow, and wonderful gifts are promised to the child as restitution.

But as I said at the beginning of our talk, dental pain and pathology, as well as other bodily disfunctions, can serve as a mask for emotional distress. In addition, I have stressed the fact that the damming up of the adequate expression of aggression can lead to self-punishing behavior because of the unconscious guilts which are created. I have seen a number of individuals who had previously gone from dentist to dentist with excruciating pain in the jawbone. They had been sincerely looking for help but there had been no dental pathology, and the only real help they could find was through psychotherapy and the relief of unconscious aggression. Unconsciously they needed to suffer and atone for their aggressive feelings. Again, we can say that it is as though the teeth represented a weapon of attack.

At the same time, however, I have seen individuals who because of extreme pathology have had all of their teeth removed but refused to wear dental plates. They wish to be edentalized. They unconsciously wish to be passive, submissive, and to be nursed and to regress to a childhood state. We see this commonly in older people who are afraid of the forces of life, the competition of life, and want their children to take care of them. Thereby they reverse the original parent-child relationship with their own offspring and imitate their first relationship with their own parents.

Some people often have a symbolic dream in which there is a loss or crumbling of teeth. Individuals who fear punishment, or some bodily injury, will often project this in the form of a dream. Also, men who fear a waning of sexual powers in middle age may have these dreams and women who fear the menopause and the loss of their femininity will often dream of the loss of teeth as a destruction of their body image. As a rule, this is a very frightening dream, causing many people to wake in agony and terror.

In addition, women at the menopause will often refuse to have diseased teeth extracted, holding on to the last residue of their youth as if the menopause were a destructive force to their body image. The menopause represents the loss of their youth, the fear of death, and the holding on to each tooth then becomes an act of survival. In these instances, the dentist may symbolize an agent who will either destroy or demolish certain bodily functions. In effect, this is often a displacement to the teeth of certain guilts and fears; the dentist then becomes the retaliatory agent. Common sense and intellectual explanations may never remove the fear of going to the dentist unless the individual has some insight as to the displacement of her inner fears and tensions.

A PRIMITIVE DISPLAY

With this brief background in which I have attempted to relate inadequately expressed aggression, guilt, and the primitive and unconscious use of the teeth, I can now talk specifically about dental decay (caries). First of all, although at the present time no one knows the actual cause of caries, there is good reason to believe that oral decay is one of the most primitive areas of aggressive display found in the human being.

As I have implied previously, although mankind has evolved from a primitive and savage past, man still has the same amount of aggression within himself. In effect, we have substituted speech for the gnashing of teeth. For example, malicious gossip is a much more deadly weapon than the bite of teeth. Therefore, at the present time some psychoanalysts, psychiatrists and dentists feel that the suppression of this basically primitive aggression can often lead to certain emotional states that, in turn, could interfere with the normal health of teeth.

Since dental caries occur most frequently in adolescents, it is thought that the decay may be due to the damming up of the aggressive needs of the adolescent. This phenomenon, which can be explained physiologically, is similar to a widely held belief as to the cause of the common cold. It is thought by many researchers that the common cold is brought about by a lowering of resistance which, in turn, is brought about by the individual being under emotional tension. When resistance is lowered, the normal virus inhabitants of the mouth and throat are then enabled to grow profusely and cause the condition called the common cold.

In the same sense, it may be true that the mouth normally contains the enamel-destroying bacteria and that, under stress and strain, there is a change in the acid-base values of the saliva, thereby allowing the bacteria to become activated and thus produce decay. We know that people who are under emotional stress have a tendency to eat carbohydrates such as candy and other sweets excessively. It is as if those foods were a replacement for the affection they seek in life but cannot find. This eating behavior is very prevalent in adolescents and in those adults who feel they have lost the love of family or children. One of the most common theories of caries development, in fact, is that excessive carbohydrate intake, plus significant chemical changes of the saliva, hasten bacterial growth and enamel destruction.

We know that less saliva is produced in the mouth when the individual is under tension, and we know that the reduction of salivary secretion can definitely change the acid-base potentials within the mouth and lead to a condition which may enhance decay. Thus, if adolescent youngsters are subjected to severe tension and have disturbed salivary production, this may be another strong factor in the production of caries.

Allow me to point out here that there are hundreds of explanations as to the cause of caries. I am just mentioning some of the psychological concepts which may play an important part, and may be revealed to an even greater extent by future researchers. At the present, fluoride is being used on the basis that it is deposited on the enamel of the teeth and thereby prevents the attack by acids and bacteria. This does not interfere with our basic psychosomatic theory.

It is true that psychosomatic dentistry is comparatively new. For in large measure, teeth have been thought of as inanimate objects. We cannot forget, however, that the tooth is not an inert substance and can play a host to psychosomatic problems just as much as the stomach and heart.

In other words, we have known for some time from psychosomatic medicine that the damming up of aggression is one of the important factors in the production of ulcers, coronary attacks and gastro-intestinal disease. We are now beginning to feel it can also play a vital role in the production of caries. I have said that, although there are many theories about the cause of dental decay, one is that acid production due to the decomposition of carbohydrates, plus salivary changes, can help the *bacillus acidophilus* work to greater degree in the destruction of enamel. We think that caries may be the eating up of oneself by the solution of one's enamel.

It must be remembered that, in the theories of psychosomatic medicine, which includes dentistry, although we say that disease can be activated and precipitated by psychological factors, we also say that the specific disease occurs in a part of the body where there has been a physiological predisposition. In the same sense, we know that numerous individuals develop hysterical pain in healthy teeth. The pain may come directly from constant grinding and clenching of the teeth, possibly while asleep. If grinding and clenching are produced by the pain in an attempt to ease it, the individual may wear away the cusps of his teeth. This may interfere with the proper nourishment of the soft tissues around the teeth, which, in turn, will cause loose teeth, and eventually, loss of teeth.

In particular reference to the grinding and gnashing of teeth while asleep, it is interesting to note that this behavior occurs as if the person were repressing all of his aggressive tendencies during waking hours, only able to release his unconscious hostility and bitterness in this primitive and infantile fashion while asleep. If continued to a great extent, gnashing and grinding of teeth will lead to dental pathology by weakening the underlying tissue. We do know that from about the age of thirty-five onwards, loss of teeth is primarily due to faulty dental tissue rather than to cavities.

Faulty dental tissue may also be caused by vasospasm, or circulatory disturbance of individuals who suffer from tension and cannot show their aggression. Many individuals constantly walk about with their jaws clenched and fixed as if they are in a state of perpetual anger, aggression and tension. These individuals may also develop dental pain and dental disease through interference of the blood circulation in the soft tissues of the jaw.

Although I have emphasized that the actual formation of dental caries is still unknown, the psychosomatic approach is becoming much more important. Many dentists are beginning to believe aggression may play a part in a manner similar to that which I have described. We know, for example, that under emotional duress many individuals suffer from a rampant attack of dental decay. Often from six to eight teeth suddenly develop caries as if a change in the physiological conditions in the mouth — caused by emotional tension and stress — had brought about conditions which led to decay.

A Tooth For a Tooth

Since we know the teeth are closely related to aggressive desires, it should now be quite obvious that guilt arising from those aggressive desires would physiologically return to the weapon (the teeth) which would be used in attack. Thus, the guilt that follows unconscious aggression is alleviated by pain and punishment to the organ involved — according to one of the oldest laws formulated in the Mosaic pattern — a tooth for a tooth.

Even today in our modern culture, society still feels relief when a criminal is punished in a way related to his own crime. In other words, we either pay the attacker back in exactly the same way as he attacked, or we make him pay in some other manner which comes close to it. The killer dies in the electric chair, the robber is robbed of his freedom.

If a man has unconscious wishes to bite, attack and destroy, he may unconsciously set in motion the same punitive factors against himself. We have a common expression that explains this phenomenon. If a man wants to destroy a rival and is somehow prevented from doing so, we often say, "He eats himself up in anger." This eating up of oneself is not only a discharge of a frustrated wish, it is also an unconscious punishment for the guilt of his attack — the punishment fits the crime. In effect, an individual who is so constituted that his teeth have become a fixed point of aggression, may develop pain in his teeth and/or develop acute dental disease.

At this point we can ask what effect psychoanalytic insights have had on practical dentistry. For one thing, the dentist is using analytic insights when he attempts to educate parents to bring the child to him prophylactically at an early age, so he can develop a close relationship with the child, and not represent a threatening authoritative figure. Also, the dentist is using analytical concepts in trying to avoid the unnecessary display of instruments to the child. Many dentists are now aware that when careful examination reveals no true pathology, they must try to look at the patient as a whole human being to find out if the dental problem may not be a symptomatic expression of some underlying emotional disturbance.

It is high time that the general population recognizes the dentist as an important specialist in the field of general medicine. The dentist is beginning to recognize the human being as a whole and is not treating a tooth by itself but treating the tooth of a specific person.

We have heard the old adage, "A sound mind in a sound body." We can also say, "A calm person, a healthy person, has a healthy mouth." There is research going on to obtain statistics relating the type of personality to the type of dental problem. This research may prove to be of extreme value in showing that certain personality patterns are significantly related to specific dental disease.

The psychoanalyst can only look at the dental symptom as a sign flashing some emotional distress — if caused by psychological reasons. Then he treats the person as a whole. Unfortunately, dentistry has been purely curative until recently. In time to come, however, we hope it will be prophylactic and preventive. Through the understanding of human beings and the application of psychoanalytic insights to dentistry, we think dentistry will achieve an even greater force in helping people realize their problems.

15.

"What is compulsive eating and drinking?"
we asked Dr. Orenstein.

LEO L. ORENSTEIN, M.D.

Associate Clinical Professor, Department of
Psychiatry and Neurology, New York University
School of Medicine

In this interview Dr. Orenstein also discusses:

"Who is the compulsive eater?"

"What are the special problems of the alcoholic?"

"What purpose does cigarette smoking serve?"

"What is the significance of food to the child?"

"What causes tension while eating?"

"Why is the compulsive eater and drinker a lonely person?"

"How can hostility be turned inward toward the self?"

LEO L. ORENSTEIN, M.D.

15.

This is what Dr. Orenstein said when interviewed in his office:

In discussing the compulsive eater or drinker, we do not include the person who, on occasion, eats more than he consciously knows he should, or even wants to. In a state of conviviality, for example, an otherwise perfectly sober individual may take a few drinks too many and, by the end of the evening even be drunk and argue vociferously that he is not.

For that short period of time he is denying reality in the same way as does the compulsive drinker. But we do not consider his behavior as compulsive or abnormal, because it is rather normal for a person to be able to deviate, within bounds, from the ordinary requirements of everyday life. We do not consider it abnormal, or a problem, or a symptom, if someone goes to a birthday party and eats a great deal of food or gets drunk. I think getting drunk on occasion is no more abnormal than going to the beach on a sunny day and daring to stay out a little too long, even sometimes at the risk of getting too much sun. However, if a person felt he had to go to the beach every day and thereby suffer severe disabling sunburn, I would then want to raise some questions about his behavior.

Since eating, and the habits of eating, are not only physiologically determined but also psychologically, it follows that what may be true in the compulsive eater may to some degree be true in everybody else.

Everyone remembers some foods which were his favorites in early life. While this may seem like a very individual experience in development of taste and understanding of the quality of food as such, nonetheless, I believe it involves the early relationship with the mother, because it is the mother who prepared the child's food.

Sometimes, again without becoming a compulsion, eating may be a fairly significant characteristic of one's behavior — as his wish that if only his wife cooked as well as his mother he would be very happy. It has been shown in some instances that the food his mother cooked was rather unsavory. Yet, to the person yearning for it, his mother's cooking was good. What he remembered was not only the taste of the dish before him but those intangible qualities added by his mother's presence.

Before we go further into the compulsive eater and drinker, let's discuss the smoker, who also fits into this concept of compulsion. Smoking, like eating, drinking and drug addiction, is, in itself, an addiction. It has the components of a physical addiction in that after a period of smoking, one may find it difficult (for some people it is impossible) to give it up. Some doctors who advise their patients to stop smoking, are themselves not capable of stopping.

While I agree that smoking can be harmful to some individuals, I would not rush in to say that to prohibit smoking on the grounds of its physical harm is the only consideration. If smoking is resorted to as a way of toning down inner tensions and frustrations, which it does, then one should consider the total personality of the patient.

We do know there is a very close relationship between physical and psychological functioning. I am not convinced one can make a blanket rule, therefore, that everyone should give up smoking. For someone to be compelled abruptly to give up all the psychological advantages of smoking may not be the wisest thing for him to do. Every smoker knows there are periods in a day or in his life where he needs to smoke. If one were to make statistical studies, I believe it could be demonstrated that, when there is increased tension, the smoker will smoke more heavily. Thus, there is a compulsive component to the way such an individual deals with his inner tensions.

To return to compulsive eating and drinking, the very fact that we use the word "compulsive" should indicate that we are talking about something other than normal patterns of behavior. By "compulsive," I do not mean the relative overeating that is common in our culture, for we do have many obese people. I am not implying that anyone who is overweight, and significantly overweight, is necessarily a compulsive eater. Compulsive eating, in itself, is a rather well-defined pattern of behavior, which poses many questions concerning its origin as well as its management or cure.

Fairly frequently — and this is particularly true of the compulsive drinker — the compulsion leads to complications in the life of the individual. When such people come for psychiatric help, careful investigation usually leads to the discovery that the compulsion has its roots in early life.

This does not mean the symptom appears early in life. In fact, symptoms may appear at any time from early childhood to old age. But the compulsive eater usually has shown some evidence of his problem at a reasonably early age. The compulsive drinker, on the other hand, most often will not appear as such until the early adult years. By this I mean, seventeen, eighteen and more often in the twenties.

Compulsive eating is a state of behavior in which the person is rather helpless against intense appetites; it may occur periodically or even become chronic. The behavior consists of a need to eat and eat and eat some more. Some people even need to train themselves to get rid of the food rapidly, in order to be able to eat some more. And, while they are striving, will eat a great deal of food, then vomit it up in order to be able to eat again.

The compulsive drinker very frequently, even more than the eater, will rationalize his behavior. He may claim that what he does is only an "average" amount of drinking. But very soon even he may be able to discern that he is not at all the master of his fate. Rather he is helpless before an inner tension which can only be relieved by drinking.

We are talking here primarily about the drinker of alcoholic beverages. While there may be rare persons whose compulsion is limited to the drinking of milk, let us say, they would be classified more in the category of the compulsive eater. We are not concerned here, either, with the drug addict. Although we might say in passing that the compulsions or inner forces that make a person experience a severe need for taking in a lot of food, or alcoholic drink, may manifest themselves not in either of these two reactions but rather in the discovery that the taking of one or another of the many available drugs will satisfy the tensions. The compulsion is shown, then, through the addiction that follows.

What brings about a compulsion to eat or drink? From what we know today, it definitely stems from disturbances in early relationships between the child and his mother. In a general way, the unsatisfactory relationship that prevails early in life apparently stimulates in the youngster feelings of anxiety which develop directly from his relationship with the mother. This includes, frequently, the mother's attitude towards food and feeding habits, and the way the child reacts to these.

A child may develop an attitude that Mother is not happy with him unless he eats as much as Mother requires. This understandably could happen with a mother who has and shows excessive concern about the child's state of nutrition. There are mothers who are never satisfied unless their child is plump or even a little bit fat. This, I believe, is a reflection of the mother's own anxieties, about which the child very soon learns through the mother's behavior. If the goal of the child is to be pleasing only to the mother, he may begin to overeat and become chronically overweight.

But ordinarily, a pattern of behavior in a child which is the result of some particular relationship with the mother, does not run so smooth a course. While on the one hand, the child may be eager to please his mother, he may at the same time experience tense, angry and hostile reactions to the demanding and oversolicitous mother. Then her interest in his eating is no longer felt as an evidence of love and concern but rather as evidence of demand for obedience and self-subjugation. To this, the youngster sometimes reacts with extreme hostility: "I could eat you up, I'm so angry!" or "I could kill you."

Overeating often occurs at the time of some critical life situation. For instance, on the surface, leaving home and going away to college may appear to be a very happy occasion, but to a large number of young people it proves, unconsciously, to be most disastrous. The removal from home to a distant part of the country may be the crisis which sets in motion deep anxieties.

Instead of the student being able to dedicate and mobilize

his energies towards the creative work college requires, he may begin to feel great tension, discover that drinking relieves the tension, and before long actually experience a yearning for drink with so much intensity as to fall into the category of what we call the compulsive drinker. On occasion, he may also react with compulsive eating.

Perhaps at this point we might introduce, without developing it too fully, a wider comcept of what I mean by compulsive eating. Ordinarily we mean the person who eats compulsively and too much. But this, I believe, should also include the individual who, for similar psychological reasons, may stop eating periodically, who is not able to eat at all.

In a sense, the drinker does both. He is a compulsive drinker and thereby becomes at the same time a rejector of food. In the well-established drinker (the chronic alcoholic) nutritional deficiencies of all varieties have been observed. Alcohol actually is a great source of energy, so a person who drinks may, through the alcohol, take in enough calories to permit him to go about his daily work. But, having omitted the essential food requirements, he may develop deficiencies of one or another of the many required vitamins and other important nutrients. It has been a frequent experience in different parts of the United States to find in hospitalized alcoholics varying degrees of vitamin deficiency. At times it is of such severity as to endanger the life of the patient.

Compulsive eating and drinking, like any emotional symptoms, invariably interfere with satisfactory functioning and adjustment. Why, then, do people indulge in them? Because they help solve early and unresolved problems in which hostile feelings are turned upon one's self. Also, in a less technical sense, it is a way the victim has found "to get even." He behaves as if his anger, appearing very early in life towards his mother or her substitute, has persisted and caused him to do things for which he unwittingly arranges to make her sorry. The compulsive eater invariably, once he has established his pattern, proves to be a great source of consternation to the mother.

This is seen not infrequently in teenagers who are chronically at odds with their mothers. The same mothers who, very early in their children's life, may have shown tremendous anxiety and concern over Johnny's failing to have enough breakfast or forgetting his glass of milk, will now make dramatic arrangements in their home to avoid bringing food into the house except in raw form. It requires preparation, so the youngster will not find it easy to rush into the icebox and raid it, a favorite occupation of the compulsive eater.

A compulsive eater attempts to deal with his problem of frustration and anger by resorting to large quantities of food. Occasionally one encounters a patient who knows this: that he eats too much at times because he has no other way of dealing with his inner rage.

The compulsive eaters and drinkers are very lonely people. They struggle to keep their loneliness secret. Sometimes, in the act of overeating or overdrinking they are gratifying a need for contact which a more normal human being would seek to gratify in one of many other ways. It is not abnormal to experience loneliness sometimes, and everyone suffers from it on occasion. A reasonably healthy human being discovers he can deal with such states of tension by seeking out a friend, or finding something constructive and creative to do, or engaging in a temporary activity that proves both entertaining and energy-consuming, such as a good game of tennis or a round of golf, which brings him into contact with other persons and also helps get rid of some pent-up energy.

But the compulsive drinker or eater will not even find himself thinking of these possibilities. Somehow, he doesn't conceive of the world as that friendly. Rather, he rushes in his lonely state to the food compartment, or the nearest bar, or his own liquor cabinet or, even more secretly, to a place where he can obtain and use drugs.

Another prominent characteristic of people in this group is that, not only are they lonely in the sense of failing to relate to others, but they feel very insecure and inadequate—and are quite aware of these feelings. They are constantly seeking to assure themselves. The drinker, after a reasonable quantity of alcohol has been consumed, feels less lonely, less tense, more able to talk to others and even, at times, more competent in the execution of his daily duties.

These people require a constant need for identification with others, thereby documenting their own sense of insecurity as well as a sense of diminished self-esteem. For example, a compulsive eater who may become excessively obese, will rationalize his behavior by pointing to people about whom he knows very little other than they too are obese, but who have accomplished something worthwhile.

This is seen even more commonly in the drinker, who readily rationalizes that he drinks for no other reason than that his profession requires increased sociability, and increased sociability leads to increased drinking. Many drinkers take great pains to convince their listeners, whether doctors or anyone else, that there is nothing unusual about their drinking, even though they may have reached a point of recognizing that the amount of drinking in which they engage seriously interferes with their growth and maturation.

If it is true, as it appears to be, that as a nation we are overweight, I think this reflects broader aspects of the total picture, specifically, cultural influences and affluence. Because we live in a state of plenty, we inevitably eat more than is physiologically necessary. When one sits down to a banquet dinner — which the average dinner in an American home is, particularly in the middle and upper classes — one is prone to eat more than is physiologically required. I do not consider this compulsive eating. I consider it, rather, reflective of broader cultural phenomena.

I think it is a little tragic to walk into a very fine and inevitably expensive restaurant and enjoy a good meal but also discover that the portions served are too large and that a significant quantity of food is wasted. It would be better if we could arrange our pattern of serving food so that we waste less and perhaps offer it free to those who never get enough.

It goes without saying that, in countries or parts of a country where economics preclude lavish living, the number of overweight people will be remarkably small. But this is more of a cultural than purely psychological problem in the sense of a symptom formation about which I have just talked.

3. SEXUAL PROBLEMS

Introduction

One of the many problems created by man's effort to become civilized arises in the realm of sex. We must learn to manage wisely our sexual feelings so they will not harm ourselves and others. Most of us are able to do so. But there are a number of men and women who find they are unable to live a happy life sexually, even though they try as hard as they can.

Some cannot settle for one sexual partner. They find they are unhappy in marriage. Or they never marry. They go from one affair to another in ceaseless search of "the" magical man or woman who will make them the perfect partner. Promiscuity is their escape.

The promiscuous person is an unhappy person. In spite of his endless affairs, he feels empty and lonely. Why does he keep up his purposeless quest? We asked Smiley Blanton, M.D., to explain, "What is the cause of promiscuity?"

Some solve their sexual confusion through perversion. Most of us look with horror and disgust on the sexual pervert. We condemn him to prison in many instances. We do not understand the agony in which he lives, nor the reason for his perversion.

Yet, normal sexual foreplay is composed of many so-called "perverse acts." Freud pointed to the similarity of the pervert's means of sexual expression and the pleasure of normal sex before the culmination in orgasm. He also compared the pervert's sexual expression to that of the child's. He described a pervert as one who was "fixated" at a childish level of sexual expression.

We asked Harold Greenwald, Ph.D., "What is the meaning of 'perversion,' and how does it differ from normal sex?"

A number of American women complain they are never sexually satisfied, that they can never reach a satisfactory climax. They live in a state of unfilled sexuality, never feeling fully feminine and always reaching to fill an emptiness, psychologically and physically.

They blame their husbands, or the puritanical way they were brought up by their parents which intensified their fear of sex to such a degree they now get little pleasure from the sexual act. Some fail to get any pleasure at all, but merely endure it as a task, or refuse their husbands much of the time.

"What causes frigidity?" we asked Ludwig Eidelberg, M.D., "Is it something a woman can cure or must she endure it?"

Although most men are not troubled by impotence, a number suffer from premature ejaculation. This, in a way, is a form of impotence in that it leaves the woman unsatisfied and in a state of aroused sexual desire. Such men do not deliberately inflict this torture but their partners go through the same frustration as though the quick ejaculation were a deliberate act.

"What are the causes of premature ejaculation?" we asked Ralph Manning Crowley, M.D. "Can a man do something to prevent it?"

Everyone has feelings for members of the same sex. Such feelings are natural, for they permit one to form friendships which are necessary for the fullest of living. It is only when these feelings become intensified and distorted that people feel troubled by them.

Some cannot control these feelings, which become so strong they must engage in sexual activity with members of the same sex. This is regarded in our society as criminal, especially when men do it. Somehow the same stigma does not apply to women, towards whom society seems more tolerant.

We asked Lewis L. Robbins, M.D., "What is the cause of homosexuality?" And of Edmund Bergler, M.D., we wanted to know, "What do you say to a patient who tells you, 'Lately I've had the strongest thoughts about other men — I think I'm homosexual. Can you help me?'"

16.

"What are the causes of promiscuity?"
we asked Dr. Blanton.

XXXXXXXXXXXXXXXXXX

SMILEY BLANTON, M.D.
Associate Founder and Director,
American Foundation of Religion and Psychiatry

In this interview Dr. Blanton also discussess:

"Why do we separate tenderness and sensuality?"
   "Why is sex a sacred act?"
      "Why do some men and women reject sex?"
"Is it destructive to act out natural feelings?"
   "Why are there incest taboos?"
      "Is the promiscuous person childish?"
"Must there always be antagonism between men and women?"
   "What are the tender feelings of childhood?"
      "Is it necessary to understand our own behavior and desires in order to love?"
"Are childhood relationships related to promiscuity?"

16.

This is what Dr. Blanton said when interviewed in his office:

"We all have feelings that would shame hell," said Robert Louis Stevenson. A large part of our unconscious is infantile, amoral, bigamous, promiscuous and savage. We cannot afford to feel offended when told we are often dominated by these motives hidden in the deeper mind. If we reject this fact, we pay the penalty of illness and unhappiness.

A more mature person is more apt to be faithful to one wife or husband than one who is dominated by immature, infantile impulses. We must ask ourselves what we want out of life. Is it our desire to love one person and remain true forever? Do we wish to marry and live with someone in sickness and in health, for richer or poorer, for better or for worse until death do us part? Or do we wish to allow the immature, bigamous, promiscuous, selfish and savage impulses inside of us to govern our lives?

Everyone is potentially promiscuous and it requires a certain maturity to remain true to one person. Also, a fundamental principle of life is that if we do certain things we get certain results and God-Almighty cannot change it. (I remember speaking like this to a woman one time and she said I was being sacrilegious. I pointed out to her that in New York we have a credit bureau with records of people's credit. If I do not pay my bills, I have a poor credit rating and I don't think the Lord could change that.)

In general, promiscuity on the part of a man is an effort to find a loving mother. He must seek a mother substitute because what he demands of a woman is what no woman can give him. Such a man cultivates a veneer of being really self-contained, but in the deep unconscious he is quite otherwise, a passive, dependent, mama's boy.

There was a case of a man who was married for twenty years who had to have another woman besides his wife. It was an obsession with him. The result, of course, was that his marriage broke up.

Another man, a very successful business man, has to have affairs once or twice a week. There is no pleasure in this for him, no happiness; it only creates anxiety for him.

Still another case was that of a man who, whenever he came to town, had to go to a house of prostitution or to a call girl. After sex relations he would go in a panic of fear over the possibility he might have contracted a venereal disease. His behavior caused him more pain than pleasure.

Another man had been married three times, the marriages lasting only a matter of weeks, and had been engaged a half dozen times. A psychological test revealed he possessed a morbid dependence on his mother and was constantly looking for a woman on whom he could be completely dependent. To him sex was a physical act; there was no tenderness or love involved. There was a strict division between tenderness and sensuality. When such a man loves he cannot have sex feelings and when he has sex feelings there can be no love, as Freud pointed out.

HERE AND NOW'ERS

What caused the split in this man's love pattern? Many people have grown tired of hearing about the importance of early-childhood relationships in determining adult behavior. Theologians as well as laymen would like to emphasize the "here and now" — but what you put in a hot oven ten hours ago has very much to do with the smoke pouring out of the kitchen now. The "here and now" comes from the past, and promiscuity comes from the all-important relationships of childhood. In short, the promiscuous man is one who has never broken the childhood relationship with his mother, and the promiscuous woman has never broken with her father.

The dependence of an infant upon his mother is complete. If a mother goes out of sight for an instant, tears may appear in the baby's eyes. For the baby may very well feel that "going away," even if just for a moment, is really for ever and ever. To a baby "going away" is death, and death to the mother, in her baby's eyes, is death to itself, for it depends on her to take care of all needs.

The child's first love for his parents contains mostly tenderness. However, as the months go by sensuous elements enter into it. He likes to be handled during his bath, wants to get into bed with his parents, wants to be kissed and petted. He receives sensual stimulation through his skin, mostly.

By the time he is four or five years old, he must give up some of these tendencies. At that age he does not want his mother, and turns to his father and boy companions. Then at puberty he feels the sex urge, and a few years later wants to marry and have a home and children of his own.

In general, this is how we all grow up. But let us go back for a moment. Although it is true that the child must give up his complete dependence upon his mother, this dependence is never completely broken in the subconscious. It remains there from childhood to the grave. The manner in which the adult handles this ever-present dependence determines how well the child will get on in an adult relationship with another.

For many people, divorce is caused by the fact that they cannot adjust to marriage, so great is their dependence on parents. The man is looking for a woman who will be the good mother; the woman wants a loving daddy. They cannot accept anything less than the perfect parent.

In the case of a man, if he holds on to his attraction to his mother, if he still grasps the image of her he held as a child, his sex feelings will remain at the earlier childish stage where they were blocked by the barriers against incest. He will be unable to love a woman in a mature sense.

Anthropologists tell us that about six hundred thousand years ago some animal took his nose off the ground, got up on his hind legs, lost his seasonal mating urge, and good and evil came into his life — he became a man. As soon as he became a man he had to put up barriers in his mind: one was against having sex relations inside the family (incest). Without this barrier people could not live together in tribes. The other barrier man had to erect was against murder. Both of these taboos are clearly expressed in the Bible in the story of Lot's daughters, who had incestuous relations with him, and in the story of Cain, who killed his brother Abel.

If the man has never given up the image of his mother, and the woman that of her father, a severe conflict will result when they try to know each other. With such men and women a division between tenderness and sensuality must take place, because of their repressed love for the "forbidden" parent. Such a man treats his wife in stand-offish fashion. She receives the idealized-mother treatment. He gives her sex without sex play, usually clumsily and without much pleasure.

Let me give you an example. A woman patient of mine married a man a number of years ago who made her swear on her wedding night that she would never have children. He never kissed her, never had sex play with her, although they had genital sex. In the course of time she bore him two children — she fooled him! But he left her each time she became pregnant. He was horrified and called her a liar, cheat and deceiver because she refused to have an abortion. He would leave her on business trips and only return to have more sex relations, leaving immediately on another trip.

Such a man never realizes the importance and sacredness of sex. As Seward Hiltner in his book, "Sex Ethics and the Kinsey Reports," says, "Through sex, one discovers something he can explore in no other way. He is a physical being; and through sex he discovers something of another being, and thus also of himself, that he had not, from the inside, 'known' before. The riddle of his existence does not lie in the stars. Through his physical existence he has received a gift that transcends the physical existence he shares with animals. How this happens is a mystery. Sex is in some basic sense sacramental, in that a spiritual gift has emerged through a physical act. Sex is not apart from God. It is a part of God's creation."

A mother of three, whom we saw in our American Foundation of Religion and Psychiatry, had no idea of what a passionate kiss could be, or what sex play could be between two people who love each other, because she had never had that experience with her husband. He was a man who could find a defense against his incestuous feelings — all unconscious, mind you; he was not aware of them — only in a relationship with a woman who did not represent the mother to him, a woman with whom he could be crude, a woman far removed from his "holy wife," a woman low in his estimation. This man was unable to have sex play with a woman because he was afraid. He had to have someone like a prostitute with whom he could be crude and vulgar. With such a person he would have potency and pleasure.

Anthropologists and psychologists have clearly shown there is very definite antagonism between men and women. The reason seems to be that men feel that women are inferior because they do not have the male sex organ. Indeed, among primitive men we find tremendous antagonism toward women because they not only do not have the male organ but they have a place from which blood issues from time to time. The horror primitive man had, and many civilized men as well, of the menstruating woman is well known, studied by Daly, Frazer and others.

It is also a fact that women are biologically superior to men and this is very disturbing to men. Biologically, it is not necessary to have a man for every woman in order to carry on the race. In animals such as sheep and cattle we find only a few males to the herd or flock. Man realizes this superiority in women — quite unconsciously — and, therefore, he is full of antagonism toward them. It is only when he recognizes his feelings and is able to give love and tenderness as well as sensuality at the proper time, that he can ever feel comfortable.

To Halt Promiscuity

The promiscuous man or woman is usually sick and tired of his own situation and unhappy with himself. His conscience says, "This is not right. Why are you doing it? It's not getting you anywhere. It's not much fun. Why, why, why are you doing it?"

It is good to ask the "why's." Why do you want new experiences? How much will it cost you to have them? For instance, you might want to take a three months' cruise. But if you're a businessman and perhaps a cruise will mean the ruin of your business, you will forego the cruise. But, the promiscuous cannot control themselves that way. So, what is to be done? How can the person help himself?

First of all let us make some distinctions. I have had many a patient come in and say in effect, "Oh, Doctor, I'm a dirty dog. I've lusted after a woman and the Bible says that it's a sin . . . to lust after a woman is to commit adultery with her in your heart . . . I saw a girl on the street and I thought wouldn't it be nice to go to bed with her . . ."

Everyone has these thoughts and feelings. As Stevenson said, everyone has feelings that would "shame hell." But everyone doesn't *keep thinking* about that pretty girl or handsome man, mentally carrying out the act in detail. Nor does everyone *act it out* in real life.

Therefore, you must start by accepting your feelings and your thoughts. These primitive feelings are a part of everyone. But the way you manage your life and actually live it depends upon how strong are the controls from within.

Secondly, you must have self-understanding to help build toward a strong emotional mechanism that permits you to make a transference to a particular person. Even wishing this, people often weary of the same sex partner. However, you must either make the sacrifice required to hold the home together and preserve love and affection, or pay a great emotional price for philandering.

I recently reviewed a book called "*The Listening Heart*," by Jane Mayer. It's about a promiscuous young widow. Why did she become promiscuous after her husband died? It was a reaction directed against her dead husband who had been a father figure — authoritative and demanding. She was, in effect, saying, "To hell with you. I'll do anything I damn please now that you are dead."

Also, she wanted to prove she was a woman, for she still unconsciously identified herself with her father and wished for the coveted penis, as does every little girl. The promiscuous woman is trying to prove she is feminine by protesting too much.

The same problems that give rise to promiscuity in men and women sometimes result in frigidity and rejection of sex. We recently saw a couple who were having such problems. The man was 45 and the woman 40 years old and they had three grown children. The wife had decided there was no point in having sex relations any more because they were too old. Obviously, a healthy married couple of this age would regard sex as a pleasure and a "sacrament of unity," as Dean Pike says. Infrequently young married couples come to us because the wife rejects sex altogether and feels they should wait to have sex until they wish a child. Obviously such an attitude makes a happy marriage impossible.

This is the opposite of promiscuity although the feelings are the same in that tenderness and sensuality are not combined, as they must be if one is to be happy.

A man or woman who cannot settle down with one person, who can't transfer the tender and the sensual feelings which began in the child-parent relationship to another adult of the opposite sex with enough force and power so that it remains fixed in the present, rather than the past, is a person whose love is like light pouring through a prism. It is diffused. He becomes involved with one person for a while and then must find someone else. Or he has to have four or five lovers at a time.

In other words, there are many who cannot fuse their sensual and tender feelings of childhood into adult love. They are constantly fighting a battle in the unconscious which tells them that their relationship with wife or husband represents a forbidden act.

We have all had to deal with immature, childish feelings toward our parents. These feelings are personified in the great play by Sophocles, "Oedipus Rex." How have you dealt with them? As a man, are you still looking for Mother? As a woman, is it a loving Daddy you want? These are questions you must ask yourself. For only you can start to change the way you are if you are troubled by promiscuity.

17.

"What is the meaning of perversion?"
we asked Dr. Greenwald.

XXXXXXXXXXXXXXXXXXXX

HAROLD GREENWALD, Ph.D.

Faculty Member, Training Institute, National
Psychological Association of Psychoanalysis

In this interview Dr. Greenwald also discusses:

"What are the varieties of love play between men and women?"

   "Is love play between a man and woman 'normal'?"

      "Can talking increase sexual pleasure?"

"What is the one meaningful definition of perversion?"

   "What causes men and women to take part in sexual orgies?"

      "How may guilt be related to perversion?"

"Is the pervert essentially a shy person?"

   "What is a sadist and a masochist?"

      "Is guilt ever justified?"

17.

This is what Dr. Greenwald said when interviewed in his office:

The words "pervert" and "perversion" have been used as a verbal playground by newspaper headline writers and sensational magazines for years. In particular, the word "pervert" brings to many minds the image of a distorted, maddened figure skulking in some alleyway ready to pounce upon an innocent child. But when used technically, a "perversion" is any kind of sex play other than actual sexual intercourse between a man and a woman.

Consequently, if used in this technical sense, almost every human being who engages in sexual relations engages in "perversion" also. Kissing, petting, even hand holding, could then be considered a "perversion" because in none of these activities is there direct genital contact. Yet, this is obviously not what most people mean when they think of "pervert," or "perversion."

Secondly, many of the things which are considered "perversions" in one culture or one society are not considered "perversions" in a whole variety of other cultures and societies. In our culture, for example, there are many people who consider the only normal and non-perverted position to assume in sexual intercourse is for the female to be prone and the male over her. However, some authorities believe that in Roman society the "normal" position was for the male to be on the bottom and the female on top, and the Roman might have looked just as much askance at our particular position as many of us do at his.

There are a whole variety of sexual methods employed by men and women in love play to stimulate each other, which are not accepted by society today. For example, it is on the books of most, if not all, state statutes, that oral contact is "perverse." That is, contact between the mouth and lips of one and the genital, or the sexual area of the other, is considered criminal behavior. Yet anyone who has watched animals at play knows that oral contact is natural. (I here use the term "natural" as meaning "found in nature.") Furthermore, in many other cultures and societies oral contact is acceptable love play. It is an impulse which many lovers who feel close to each other frequently feel and sometimes enjoy without psychological damage.

The Important Issue

The one definition of "perversion" which seems important to observe is that sex must not be painful, injurious or shameful to the partner. Extreme forms of sadism in which the other person is humiliated, degraded, or made to feel great pain, is "perversion," because if a person can only get sexual gratification from hurting the other partner seriously, then there is little or no respect for the integrity, personality and bodily well-being of the other.

But before we continue, I want to distinguish between hurting seriously and the "normal" kind of sadistic-masochistic love play between lovers such as biting, pulling hair and the like. For in love these things are done with a certain amount of tenderness and control, and the other person does not feel any great physical pain or danger.

The difficulty with sexual activities in which one of the partners is injured, degraded or forced to submit against his or her will, is that not only is it injurious to the individual who is subjugated but it is also injurious to the one who does the subjugating. The man who finds it necessary to inflict serious bodily damage with whips and hot irons, let us say, frequently sets up within himself such severe guilt reactions and such an attitude of responsibility for the pain that he has inflicted, that the very act which he perhaps fantasied for so long becomes unpleasurable.

Not only is it unpleasurable because of the guilt reactions engendered by hurting another individual but it is unpleasurable even during the act because, in order to be able to inflict pain on another human being, one has to destroy understanding, feeling and sympathy. One almost has to look upon the other person as being not quite human because it is very difficult for us as social animals to seriously injure another person, or destroy completely, except perhaps in great anger or in a state of self-defense.

My experience has been that most individuals who have indulged in such sadistic activities for sensual gratification report that during the act they are seized with a compulsion in which they do not even consider the other person as a human being. He or she is merely an object on which they can vent their particular form of brutality.

Usually the man or woman who requires some form of extreme stimulation to achieve sexual discharge is a person who feels very guilty about his sexual feelings. Some serious inhibition is operating.

Let me give an example. Some years ago I saw a young man who had made a series of abortive rape attempts. Far from being the monster that one usually associates with this kind of activity, he was, in fact, an extremely polite and outwardly very decent young man, with his anger carefully repressed. Upon examination it was quite clear that he felt so guilty about his own sexual impulses that he projected his guilt onto all women.

In other words, he himself felt that sex was nasty, brutal, rotten, and undesirable; and therefore, he was sure that all women felt the same way. Also, he was extremely fearful of approaching women, and so inhibited that he had no sexual outlet whatsoever, not even the outlet that he could have provided for himself through masturbation. Thus, his sexual feelings were carefully dammed up. But when they finally exploded into expression he could only attempt forcibly to overcome what he considered the resistance that would have to be present in any woman towards an act so vile as sexual intercourse seemed to him. But fortunately for him and his would-be victims, his rape attempts were always unsuccessful.

In the examination of other perverts it has been observed that many of them are similarly inhibited and fearful of impotence. So, rather than the oversexed monster that such people are usually thought of as being, we find in those who can have sex only under the most brutal and degrading circumstances people who are suffering from severe inhibitions and who need extreme stimulants to overcome them.

A similar situation is found in the people who indulge in orgies where sex is acted out on a mass basis. A typical example of such an orgy would be a group of people of both sexes getting together at a party. Stimulated by alcohol or some drug such as marijuana, both of which have uninhibiting reactions, they then engage in promiscuous helter-skelter sexual contact of both a homosexual and heterosexual nature with all of the members of the group simultaneously involved.

Despite their own self-descriptions, these men and women are not necessarily strongly sexed or really uninhibited. On the contrary, they are usually people in which the inhibitions against sexual expression are so great that they need this extreme stimulant to have any kind of sexual activity whatsoever. It is no accident that activities such as orgies arose in primitive societies where primitive man, due to inadequate nutritional intake, had comparatively little sexual appetite. He needed the orgy in order to build himself up to a physical and mental pitch where he was able to muster strong sexual feelings, and thus overcome his fears and bodily weaknesses.

A VARIETY OF IMPULSES

With this brief background we can now talk about the more normal person. First of all, at one time or another, most of us have had a variety of thoughts, feelings and impulses about sex. They may have ranged from what we would consider the normal, non-hurtful perverse activities such as oral-genital contact to extremely sadistic acts. As I said, these impulses arise in most of us and if a person is not consciously aware of them they are nevertheless expressed in dreams and in a variety of other ways. But the individual who is functioning well finds no difficulty in resisting the acting-out of such impulses.

Many of us, however, have guilt about our thoughts, and it is often helpful for such a person to realize that perverse impulses, feelings and thoughts are common to most of humanity. But just because we have such a thought or desire does not mean we have to act upon it, nor is a thought the same as an act. In addition, men and women do not have to repress the *idea*, for you can even get some pleasure from contemplating the particular act. It may be true that only those who can't fantasize about such things have to act upon them. This is one case where fantasy does not necessarily lead to action.

Yet most mature people find that love play and sexual intercourse are more pleasurable without the use of fantasy. They concentrate on what they are actually doing because those things are pretty good, too, and they can be far more aware of the other person if they are not buried in fantasy.

In connection with this point, a married young man came to me because of a severe problem of impotence. He could have sexual relations with his wife only on rare occasions and then only if he simultaneously had certain fantasies about beating her up. After two years of treatment he didn't need those fantasies any more and could have sexual intercourse just by concentrating on what was going on.

Before treatment he felt that the fantasies themselves were wrong, and he may have never solved the problem of impotence because the nature of the fantasies helped him work through the problem itself. His impotence arose in part from his fear that he would act out what was in his fantasy. However, in the therapeutic situation he could allow himself the luxury of discussing his brutality and sadism, knowing it was unnecessary to ever act upon it. As time went by, and he realized he need not be afraid of his controls over himself, he found he did not need the fantasies any longer.

There is another problem. Many of us have been miseducated to believe that something which freely happens between two adults, each of whom is capable of making decisions, may be wrong because it violates some moral code. But that moral code may be outworn. Obviously, each person has a right to his or her own moral beliefs and actions; and I might add, parenthetically, that if a man or woman's own moral code coincides with that of society's, they need not necessarily act otherwise just because so-called experts say that "X" behavior is within the "normal range." For example, the Kinsey investigators, who had the opportunity of interviewing thousands of people, reported that mouth-genital contact was habitually engaged in by large numbers of men and women in certain socio-economic groups. Thus, one can come to the tentative conclusion that this type of sexual behavior is within the "normal range" for the general population but one cannot therefore say that *all* people should behave this way because it is considered "normal." I repeat, each person has a right to his or her own moral beliefs and actions.

I don't want to imply here that guilt is never justified, however. Guilt is justified when the sexual activities of one partner are harmful and destructive to the other person. But very often the feelings of guilt about a so-called perverse activity are in reality feelings of guilt about sex, or even about pleasure in general.

A person who feels guilty about enjoying himself sexually is one who frequently feels guilty about enjoying a good meal, or anything devoted to pleasure. Such people often feel that life must be hard, earnest, devoted to toil and to good works, and perhaps to prayer and religious observances. Yet the function of their guilt may very well be to maintain control. That is, individuals who are afraid that they cannot control themselves need the guilt in order to support what controls they do possess.

In addition, the guilt feelings which have been built in about sex in general are often transferred to a part of the act rather than attached to the whole act. There are not many people today who intellectually consider sexual intercourse between a husband and wife immoral; yet there are still great numbers of men and women who have been so indoctrinated in sexual guilt that emotionally they have sexual difficulties with their mate, because the whole act is shrouded in a guilt which even the sanctions of God and State cannot remove.

I would say, therefore, that a person who feels guilty about his or her sexual desires and actions that are not destructive to the partner or to himself, would do well to examine whether the guilt is actually about the so-called perverse act or about sexuality and pleasure in general. It might be helpful for such a person to get professional consultation if he feels excessively guilty because life is too short to rob ourselves of pleasure, and guilt can be one of the greatest despoilers and rapists of pleasure.

The Bridge of Intimacy

Communication is the important thing between partners. For example, if the wife finds that a little biting by her husband on the shoulder is pleasurable and enjoyable and she doesn't find it particularly painful, there is no harm done. I knew a widower whose second wife found such activities as biting and being held tightly in a bear-like embrace quite pleasurable, comfortable and enjoyable. His first wife, however, had found such activities repulsive and painful.

For the first few months of his first marriage he didn't understand why she tended to shy away from relations with him and evidently found his advances obnoxious. However, they were eventually able to discuss this problem and after she explained how she felt, he found that it was no great sacrifice to his pleasure to give up biting and crushing.

The important thing here is how the activity affects the other person. Some activities which may feel degrading to you may not be considered so by another individual. There are some men, for example, who think it extremely degrading to have their wives apply their mouths to their penises. But there are many women who do not think of oral contact as an act of degradation. For if an act is one of acceptance, love, and an expression of intimacy and warmth, it could hardly be degrading.

In dealing with this problem of discovering what is considered degrading and painful to the other person, one merely increases sexual pleasure because experience indicates that sexual pleasure is heightened by intimacy. Having such a discussion, explaining your feelings about the various acts involved in the full activity of sexual relations, often helps to build the bridge of intimacy and closeness between individuals.

18.

"What are the causes of frigidity?"
we asked Dr. Eidelberg.

XXXXXXXXXXXXXXXXXXXXX

LUDWIG EIDELBERG, M.D.

Clinical Professor of Psychiatry, Department of
Psychiatry, State University of New York,
Downstate Medical Center

In this interview Dr. Eidelberg also discusses:

"What is the meaning of 'normal'?"
  "What is a genital orgasm?"
    *"Is it possible for a man to have an orgasm and still
    be impotent?"*
"Why is sexual pleasure so important?"
  "Are there different degrees of frigidity?"
    "Do we all wish to gratify the forbidden?"
"Is there a 'moral innuendo' in neurotic acts?"
  *"Do some adult men and women retain their infantile
  wishes?"*
    "Are childhood experiences related to frigidity?"
"What is a 'screen memory'?"

18.

This is what Dr. Eidelberg said when interviewed in his office:

A married woman with four children came to me because, whenever she tried to drive an automobile, she was overcome by terrible fear and anxiety. After some discussion, I asked her if she had any other fears. She had none, she answered. I then asked her if her sexual relations were normal, and she answered that they were quite normal and satisfactory.

However, after the start of treatment it became obvious that she was completely anesthetic sexually. I asked her why she didn't mention this fact in the first interview. She replied that she thought her frigidity was "normal." Furthermore, she believed that most women "exaggerated" their pleasure in sexual intercourse, or they invented descriptions of "marvelous excitement."

The treatment continued, and it wasn't until some months more had passed before another bit of information was brought into the open. Some two years before, soon after her first child was born, she had experienced full vaginal climax for about three weeks. But this was a fact she had completely "forgotten," eliminating it entirely from her conscious memory.

In this case history are illustrated two points which must be clearly understood. First, when interviewing a woman about her sexual life, or when studying statistics about women, it is necessary to be most careful in accepting statements as true even if they are expressed in the best of faith; a woman may not be lying but what she says is not the truth, either. Secondly, there is the question of what is "normal?"

Most psychoanalysts today assume that about 60% of American women are frigid. But in medicine, what is average should not be called "normal." As a matter of fact, the average human being is not normal. In Egypt, for example, most of the population suffers from a blinding eye disease, trachoma; and after the First World War in Vienna, 80% of the population had tuberculosis in one form or another. Yet, nobody suggested that tuberculosis was normal. So, the "average" woman in the United States may be considered frigid, but still pathological.

The word "frigid" is used by most authors to describe the reaction of a woman who does not respond in a healthy manner while having sexual intercourse. Broadly speaking, there are four groups of these women. There are women who feel absolutely nothing while having sexual intercourse — they might very well be thinking of what to have for dinner the next day. There are women who feel some degree of disgust, revulsion, or anger during intercourse. There are women who feel a certain genital pleasure at the beginning of the sexual act but who do not have a continuation of tension, nor do they have a release of that tension, and their pleasure may be characterized as "forepleasure," or "anticipated" pleasure. Finally, there are women who have a clitoral climax but not a full vaginal climax. These, too, are considered neurotic.

But I should add that, if a woman is very happy with her clitoral orgasm, we, being doctors and not preachers or reformers, should certainly not interfere with her happiness. If, however, such a woman resorts to analysis because of some other symptoms, we will try to find out why she uses only her clitoris as a source of pleasure. It obviously represents an underdeveloped penis, and we would want to know why she refuses to use her vagina and concentrates on her clitoris for the climax.

As I have illustrated, the diagnosis of frigidity is quite difficult for a number of reasons, and it must also be remembered that the normal woman is not supposed to have a genital reaction to every or any man. Consequently, the diagnosis of frigidity can only be made if the woman has sexual intercourse with a man to whom she is attracted.

About this woman I would want to know, first, whether she has feeling of pleasure, and if so, is this pleasure projected to the genital region? I would want to know if she is overwhelmed by this pleasure, and does she arrive at a state of high tension, then experience a pleasant relief of this tension? I would also want to know if her vagina becomes wet and moist before the act of sexual intercourse and while she is becoming excited. Finally, I would want to know whether or not certain muscles in the depths of the vagina contract as she starts to have the climax. For all of these are signs of a full vaginal climax.

THE INFANTILE WISH

Contrary to popular concept, Freud never believed that "every neurosis is due to sex." But what he did believe, and what I have found to be true in my practice, is that all neuroses are caused by repressed infantile wishes and their defenses. For instance, a certain woman is frigid because as a little girl she had the desire to take her father away from her mother. Let this be very clear — most, if not all, little girls have such a wish. However, the frigid woman is not a little girl any longer; she is a grown-up woman who still has the *unconscious* infantile wish to take her father from her mother.

I should also explain that when I say the child wants to "take the father from the mother," I do not mean that she wants to have sexual intercourse with him. The child does not understand, feel or know adult sexuality but nevertheless, all children have sexual (not genital) feelings. Therefore, when we talk about the repressed infantile wishes of the frigid woman we are speaking of childhood sexuality which has been unconsciously carried over into adulthood.

In other words, every time a frigid woman has sexual intercourse, she may unconsciously take the man to represent her father. Thus, the grown-up woman is unconsciously gratifying the forbidden wish to take her father away from her mother. But this cannot be allowed.

Consequently, as this is an unconscious wish, it has to be stopped in an unconscious manner; and it is stopped by having sexual intercourse without feeling or pleasure. In this way, the woman's frigidity may represent a partial gratification of the infantile wish to take the father. It may also represent frustration and punishment because, by the lack of excitement, she is unable to enjoy the forbidden. And, one can add, without pleasure sexual intercourse becomes boring.

I should point out here that every neurotic act, including that of frigidity, has a "moral innuendo." The frigid woman is unconsciously saying, in effect: "I am a chaste woman. I don't enjoy sex. I am chaste because this man is my father — the infantile object."

But frigidity serves the woman in many ways. The woman is also saying unconsciously, "By being frigid I am able to be aggressive to a man without actually hitting him over the head. Why? Simply, because I don't need him!" She is saying to the man: "I am self-sufficient because I don't need this dirty sex. I am omnipotent because I never have a desire. I am self-contained, and I am completely different from other women. For other women depend on you while I always remain cool, and consequently, I remain dominating."

The completely frigid woman is never in a situation where she is in love, or desires someone, or where she has to renounce a part of herself and wait for the man.

THE SCREEN MEMORY

As an example of how infantile wishes and defenses may operate and how they may be screened and hidden from consciousness, let me tell you of a frigid patient, who after months of analysis, one day told me, "I feel funny."

She was lying on the couch and she asked, "Do you have electrical currents on the couch?"

"No, it is just an ordinary couch," I replied.

"I'm frightened," she said.

"Of what?" I asked

"I'm afraid that I'm getting sexually excited."

"But you are here because of frigidity," I replied. "What are you afraid of?"

"You can seduce me," was the answer.

Using this fear of seduction as a lead, we finally obtained a memory which, although not the original memory but a "screen memory," helped to explain her frigidity. When this patient was thirteen years old and had started to menstruate, her aunt told her that she was now a young lady and thus had to be "most careful" when she played with boys.

"Don't let them touch you there," the aunt said indicating the girl's genitals. "If you do, you'll get pregnant."

A few weeks later the girl was in the garden with her male cousin, a few years older, and he wanted to play sexually with her. When he started to touch her genitals she developed great fear of pregnancy and, with the help of this fear, she was able to stop the pleasurable sensations which might possibly have made her unable to resist his advances. She had unconsciously continued to use this defensive fear, appropriate at thirteen, but now, in adulthood, self-defeating and self-punishing.

But what do we mean by saying that the experience in the garden was a "screen memory?" By itself, this experience would not have produced a neurosis if she had not suffered as a child what we call a traumatic experience; this is an experience that the child cannot assimilate and which, therefore, represses the wishes involved that remain unconscious. Very often, however, a screen memory is remembered even without analysis because it is used to hide something which is even more unpleasant.

In this case, the real memory was that as a girl of six she had looked at a motion picture of a woman passionately kissing a man. Later, she had tried to imitate the woman with her uncle, and everybody laughed uproariously. "Look at the little siren," they had said. "See how she seduces him," they had teased, and of course, they had said many other things which made the little girl feel ashamed. She was completely humiliated, and this experience was repressed.

In all adult neuroses there are infantile wishes which have been repressed — for example, a married man, who every time he meets his mistress at a particular hotel, has a terrible fear that his wife is going to walk into the room. How could she know? It doesn't make sense unless we understand that the wife is not a wife but the omniscient mother. Or, let us think of another man who drinks only black coffee for breakfast. His wife, however, continuously nags at him to "have something more." So eventually he starts to prepare his own breakfast and he pretends that he has two eggs and toast. But he really throws them away. Again, this behavior only makes sense if we realize that he wants to be a child and be treated like a child.

A person, whoever he is, will not actually insist on wearing the shoes he had when he was three years old. That would be crazy. But figuratively the neurotic still wishes to wear the shoes.

Sometimes the infantile wish may be disguised. For instance, a man may be interested in female breasts, but we have to find out whether he is interested in caressing the breasts to increase his genital desires and have sexual intercourse, or, whether he is interested in sucking and devouring the breasts as an end in itself. In short, an interest in breasts, may represent forepleasure and be quite adult. On the other hand, it may actually be closely related to infantile wishes. Only a detailed study of the individual would reveal which of the two is the case.

The same infantile wish that can be related to frigidity in one woman can also be responsible for a different hysterical symptom in another woman, for example, paralysis, hysterical blindness, or any of the phobias. In one individual the germ responsible for tuberculosis may cause an illness of the lungs. But another person may be affected in the brain, kidney, joints or bones. Therefore, after we discover the cause of an illness we still try to find out why in one case it appears in this form, or, in another one. However, it must be admitted that we still don't fully understand the choice of neuroses.

I say this because so many people would like psychoanalysis to be an exact science. They would like us not only to say why something happens, but why something also does not happen. I, too, would like to know this. But it will not be possible for many years. At this stage, I am glad if I am able to explain why a certain woman developed the hysterical symptoms of frigidity.

I am still unable to explain why she did not develop a paralysis instead, because a paralysis of the leg would also have protected her. Why is one man afraid to go near an open window, another afraid of fire? At this time I can only say that something happened when each man was growing up that caused him to make this selection of symptoms. It is part of an individual pattern which fits the unconscious experience of childhood.

Even without exact statistics, one can say that there are more cases of frigidity than of other neuroses. However, it is not true that frigidity is the only frequent form of neurosis. For example, no one knows how many women suffer from what is called "character neurosis" in which they seldom recognize their personality traits as self-defeating, self-punishing and neurotic.

On the other hand, frigidity, phobia, obsession, melan-

cholia, and other symptoms which appear as a result of repressed infantile wishes and their defenses, are most always
at least recognized as existing, if not always recognized as
self-defeating and self-punishing.

As an example of character neurosis, as compared to
"symptom neurosis" (frigidity and the like), a patient of
mine refused to take a taxi when the light was red but instead
always waited until the light was green because he considered himself a thrifty man who wanted to save the one-
and-a-half minutes on the taxi meter, thus saving perhaps five
cents. It was most difficult to get him to realize he was not
thrifty but pathologically stingy. It was hard for him to see
how his stinginess interfered with his success in all areas of
life, not just taxicab rides.

To Feel and to Act

Although no neurosis can suitably gratify the adult wish, it
is also true that some immediate function may be served by
the neurosis. For example, a patient who suffers from a
phobia which does not allow him to cross the street by himself may get a certain gratification from the fact that his wife
must accompany him whenever he wishes. Or, if the husband has a bad cold, he may enjoy having a great deal of
attention paid to him by his wife. But in both these cases,
the gratification the husband gets from the attention is not
the reason for his phobia on the one hand, or the bad cold,
on the other.

In the same sense, it is possible that a frigid woman who
has some hostile feelings toward her husband may get a certain gratification out of making him see that she is not responding in the way he would like her to respond. She is a
woman unable to enjoy a part of life — sexuality. That is her
real problem.

Incidentally, when speaking of man's sexual role many
people use the word "emission" as meaning the same thing
as "climax." But scientifically speaking, "climax" is an emotional reaction which, under normal conditions, accompanies
the emission. A man may have an emission and be, in effect,
impotent. Freud called this "orgastic impotence." And like
the frigid woman, the man with orgastic impotence can
perform sexually but does not enjoy it.

You can swallow food but it doesn't mean that you enjoy it. This is why man is superior to all the machines so far invented, for even the greatest of computers and atomic reactors cannot enjoy the sensation of pleasure.

19.

"What are the causes of premature ejaculation?" we asked Dr. Crowley.

XXXXXXXXXXXXXXXXXX

RALPH M. CROWLEY, M.D.

Fellow, William Alanson White Institute
of Psychiatry, Psychoanalysis and Psychology

In this interview Dr. Crowley also discusses:

"Do some men separate performance and pleasure?"
"Must neurotics always prove themselves right?"
"How does a man feel adequate as a man?"
"Why do some men and women have conflict during sexual intercourse?"
"What is the difference between the situational and chronic premature ejaculation?"
"Can the wife help her husband in sexual intercourse?"
"What are the 'unreal' fights between men and women?"

19.

This is what Dr. Crowley said when interviewed in his office:

A. First of all, premature ejaculation is not the problem. It is a symptom of a problem, maybe many problems. Secondly, it is never a matter of dealing with the symptom alone, or its causes and background. There is the important matter of the reaction of the person to the symptom. And the reactions depend on the structure of the entire personality.

Q. *Do you mean that there is no such thing as this problem?*

A. No, for there most certainly is. But what I'm emphasizing here is that a person who has this "problem" may conspire with himself not to do anything about it and to continue with it.

Q. *Why would he do that? It doesn't make sense.*

A. It does make sense if you will consider that usually there are feelings of embarrassment, disgrace and guilt involved. He may feel it's something that shouldn't be, that he should be in control of. It must be his "fault" in some way, and he should, he thinks, be able to take care of it himself.

Q. *Can he cure it himself?*

A. Not always. He may help himself somewhat. But if we are talking about a "cure" we must make some distinctions.

First of all, let's separate the situational premature ejaculation and the chronic. By the situational, I mean those times when a man who's generally all right has an orgasm before he enters the woman or immediately afterwards. This may be due to a number of reasons. There may be some current emotional reaction going on with the person involved. That is, something has disturbed the personal relationship in some way that has not been dealt with by the two people. Possibly the woman has said something that made the man angry or apprehensive.

Then again, this might be a young man who is frightened in a new situation. I don't know if there are any statistics, but I would guess that more often than not the first intercourse for the man is frequently a premature ejaculation. There is tremendous excitement in the newness of it all, so one could almost say that premature ejaculation is to be expected in this situation and not to worry about it as anything pathological.

Another source is simply in the technical handling of love. The man and woman may indulge in so much foreplay that they misjudge it in terms of the time for intercourse.

Yet, because some people don't realize that premature ejaculation may come from a purely current mishandling, they will get terribly disturbed by it, possibly feeling that something has gone wrong with their sexual apparatus.

Q. *Is there a sense of failure about it? A sense of incompetence?*

A. This is a good transition point to the more chronic situation. It would be hard to imagine a man being really disturbed about premature ejaculation unless it was in terms of the sexual failure. For, to many men the carrying out of the successful sexual act is a prop to their feeling of being adequate men. And to need this kind of prop means that there is some feeling of inadequacy about their masculinity although they may be very adequate males. But to them, it's a question of how good they are.

Therefore, when such a man has sexual failure it can be like any other kind of failure in life, as in athletics, or an examination, or failing at a business venture. The feelings may go back to an earlier time in life.

Q. *Except that this is a failure to please a woman. Would the same man come to see you about a business failure?*

A. Yes, sometimes the same man would come about a business failure. But the question is whether or not there is special significance to a man in failing in his sexual performance, a significance that is different from other kinds of failure, such as that in business or athletics.

Although in some instances it is not different; in those

cases, the meaning of sex for a man is that of competing with other men.

In many instances, however, premature ejaculation does have a different significance. The problem of one's relationship to women is involved, either primarily, or in addition to a problem with men. A man may need to prove himself to a woman, to be someone in her eyes. Or, it may not be a status problem; it may be that he is compelled to give pleasure, to give an orgasm to a woman, in order not to feel a failure.

Let us go into this latter problem a bit more. The man thinks he should not be concerned with his own satisfaction. He gets caught in a false dichotomy, which can be expressed as, "If sex is for my pleasure, it is not for the woman's pleasure." He doesn't think in terms of the pleasure being mutual. He is secretly saying, "I am not selfish in sex, because this is for you and not for myself."

But this "giving unselfishness," does not come from a strong self, but from a weak one. The self is weak because it is being denied. And when there is denial of self involved in a self-imposed obligation such as having to give the woman pleasure, a person cannot help resenting the activity, and also his partner.

Yet, he isn't aware of his own resentment, so that he unwittingly engages in sex in such a way as to defeat the woman's getting the very pleasure he feels obligated to give her, even at the cost of his own satisfaction.

One last point about this: In a sense it is not entirely at the cost of his own satisfaction. In not getting pleasure himself he is satisfying the need to deny himself, the need to be selfless as he sees it.

Q. *Why is it these men can't see themselves and what they are doing?*

A. I think the inability to see themselves in this particular situation is part of a general inability to see themselves in relationship to other people, especially in close relationships. In fact, they usually want to destroy emotional closeness because closeness means to them that one must win and the other must lose. They see close human relationships as a battle.

Q. *But in this case, no one is the winner. As you've said, they both lose.*

A. Yes, this is important to remember — especially for the man's wife if she persists in berating him for it.

They both must realize that his is not a need to defeat this particular, real wife. It is a need to defeat the wife he imagines her to be, how he pictures her. For, if unconsciously he sees her only as somebody powerful who is going to "get" him, then what else can he do but attempt to defeat her?

Now, if he sees the relationship as a battle, or of her battling him, and she puts on the pressure and blames him, it confirms what he unconsciously thinks.

The important thing is that this is a symbolic fight, not something that has to be, or something that they act out unless their mutual angers get into it and then it becomes something which seems real.

Q. *In other words, the man's not fighting reality but a phantom?*

A. That's right. But one of the things about a neurosis is that it tends to confirm itself. It tends to structure life in terms of the phantoms and fantasies. In this way, the person proves over and over again that the neurosis is justified. And if the wife berates the husband, it just proves to him that he is in battle.

Q. *Who is this man really battling?*

A. Himself. No one, in reality. To say a man is fighting a phantom means that he is fighting a phantom in himself. The phantom is his own. Naturally, his experiences with significant people in the past enter into various aspects of his fantasies. However, it is his images of these people that matter here, not what they were in reality when he was a child, and certainly not what they are today.

That is why no one kind of family background makes for the development of premature ejaculation. What counts is the meaning and significance of the family background for the child; it is crucial how he experiences and perceives his parents and other people close to him, not only how they are in reality.

Premature ejaculation can be an outlet for various kinds of tensions and conflicts that have to do with childhood experiences in the family. There is no one kind of family constellation responsible.

Q. Could you give some examples of experiences which do not necessarily cause premature ejaculation, but might be found in the background of someone who has this symptom?

A. Yes. Indoctrination of certain attitudes might well play a part. For example, it is not at all infrequent that a child grows up hearing over and over again, "Give that toy to your brother; don't be selfish." This kind of thing, if uncorrected by other experiences, may lead a child to conclude that for him to enjoy himself is selfish, and to give enjoyment to others is unselfish. It may lead to the attitude I quoted previously, "If it is for myself, it is not for you."

In another family, sex is regarded not as good but as bad and the child finds he is regarded with disapproval insofar as he manifests any connection with, or enjoyment of sex. He observes that it is all right for other people, including his parents. This may continue into adulthood in the form of a feeling that he is a worthwhile human being as long as he is not interested in sexual pleasure for himself, but is interested in giving his wife that pleasure.

Q. Is this what is called "repetition of childhood experiences?"

A. In a sense, but there is never direct repetition. As with other adult problems, so with premature ejaculation: there is a close tie to the emotional relationships with the significant people in childhood. For example, I had a patient who had a great deal of trouble with premature ejaculation. He felt that this was a problem with his wife but he was actually extremely scared and quite certain that if he had intercourse with somebody else the same thing would happen and he would again be proved a failure.

In this particular case, the man's wife wished only that he would forget about her, not worry and not blame himself every time it happened. However, he couldn't help but always attack himself, although she was not particularly interested in having an orgasm every time, and did not feel unfulfilled when it wasn't forthcoming. Certainly, this man's tremendous concern about his failure bothered her more than the lack of orgasm itself. Thus, what was he concerned about? You asked me, "Who is the man battling?" And the man could ask himself the same question.

Q. *You have said that a man can ask himself some questions. But what else can this man do for himself if therapy is not available?*

A. First of all, if he is berating himself about this problem, blaming himself, he should realize that the cases are unconscious and his only responsibility is to become more aware of the reasons. He is not any less of a man because of it, in effect.

Secondly, this problem should be discussed openly with his wife. They can talk about it without anger or shame or guilt. Possibly together they can get at the conditions that make it worse and conditions that make it better so that she can try to set up those conditions that favor his being able to last a longer time.

For both the man and the woman, there is defeat of a kind. But the man is the most defeated. If the wife can understand this and not think that he is doing something wrong to her it might be the first step towards a happier situation. However, it may be hard for her not to feel resentment and anger, and difficult for her not to put sexual pressure on him. Yet, many wives are able to place anger and resentment someplace else, not apply any pressures, and then together the pair can try to solve this as a problem and not a crime.

Also, they might both look into their attitudes to the whole sexual experience. Is it all concerned with the orgastic experience, or are there other aspects that can bring pleasure? The orgasm doesn't have to be the end-all and be-all of the sexual experience. Then, they can both try not to let the lack of it spoil all the other parts of their relationship, which may be fine.

Q. *What about psychological help from an expert? Can you cure a man who has a premature ejaculation?*

A. It is sometimes curable, sometimes not, and sometimes to a degree. I know a patient who, after therapy, sometimes didn't have a premature ejaculation. But if anything went wrong it would tend to come back. He never got over the possibility of it happening, in other words, but he was much less afraid of it and took it much more in stride, and as a consequence it happened much less often. The very fear of it can help make it occur again.

In my experience, there have been cases where there was a great improvement. However, one may have to settle with what positives there are. But the earlier the problem is dealt with, the much less crystallized it becomes in the whole pattern of life, and the easier it is to deal with therapeutically.

Thank you, Dr. Crowley.

20.

"What are the causes of homosexuality?"
we asked Dr. Robbins.

XXXXXXXXXXXXXXXXXXX

LEWIS L. ROBBINS, M.D.

Medical Director, Hillside Hospital

In this interview Dr. Robbins also discusses:

"What is the meaning of 'erotic'?"
"Do all of us have homosexual feelings?"
"What do we mean by perversion?"
"Is the Oedipus complex universal among men?"
"Are men who use prostitutes fighting homosexuality?"
"What is the dream of the 'dentate vagina'?"
"Why is the child so dependent upon the mother?"
"What are a boy's conflicts with his father?"
"Do young children have sexual feelings?"
"What is the difference between the active and passive homosexual?"
"What purpose does repression serve?"
"Can homosexuals be helped by psychological therapy?"

20.

This is what Dr. Robbins said when interviewed in his office:

Before discussing homosexuality I wish to speak briefly about two psychoanalytic concepts which have been largely misunderstood and rejected by a great many people. Freud used the words "erotic" and "sexual" to include all forms and varieties of human behavior which bring people close together for a constructive goal. I could even say that what I am doing now, being interviewed, and what the reader will be doing when he reads these words, is a derivative of the erotic urge.

Our respective acts, of course, have obviously been de-sexualized in a genital sense, but they are still erotic in the broad sense of the word. We want to get together, we communicate in a way, and maybe we even want to love one another. Although we do not have to hug and kiss, there is something which brings us together towards some common goal or mutual pleasure and satisfaction.

The most exquisite and intense form of the erotic, however, is in a genital sexual relationship between two people who love one another. The sexual act of copulation is the ultimate and most intimate expression of love between two people, and normally, this expression takes place between a man and a woman. But the point to remember is simply that the meaning of "erotic" is that of a total constructive life force of which genital sexuality is a part.

One of the major reasons why there is so much rejection of psychoanalysis by the lay public is related to this broad meaning of eroticism or love. I am speaking of the universality of the Oedipus complex. But Freud and psychoanalysis did not invent children's feelings towards their parents. The story of Oedipus is a Greek myth thousands of years old, and in the Old Testament and Shakespeare, just to name two other sources, there is ample evidence that the struggles and conflicts of mankind in relationship to the mother and father were well known and recognized.

Many people today, however, completely reject this very old concept which Freud clarified, and I think it would be best first to discuss the parent-child relationship before continuing with the Oedipal complex and homosexuality.

NOT A PSYCHIATRIC SOAP OPERA

The poor modern-day mother has been indicted for almost every psychiatric illness known to man, including homosexuality. This is not without some justification, for it is true that the mother-child relationship is the first key relationship in any person's life. Before birth, there is the close biological relationship, and it must be remembered that after birth the human infant, more than any other animal, is still an embryo. All other animals become semi-independent or completely independent comparatively quickly, the time required taking anywhere from a few seconds or minutes (in the lower animals) to a few years (in the higher animals). But the human infant, although outside the mother's uterus is embryonic for almost ten years, certainly for five or six.

In other words, all other animals reach maturity in a comparatively short amount of time. We have a much longer postnatal development ahead of us at birth, and this is the basis for man's biological dependence, and consequently, his psychological dependence, upon the mother. Furthermore, if a child's earliest and most important initial human relationship is disturbed, the chance of that child's development being disturbed is greater.

Because of this intense biological-psychological inter-relationship, the mother thereby becomes a tremendously, but not exclusively, significant figure in the psychological growth of the child. Yet, if we only think of the mother, to the exclusion of the father, we will have a psychiatric soap opera in talking about the problem of homosexuality.

We have to recognize several important normal factors in the growth of any individual, male or female. But we cannot discuss male and female homosexuality at the same time, and thus all my remarks here will be directed towards male homosexuality.

Keeping in mind what I have said about eroticism (love) being a total constructive life force, including genital sexuality, the mother is the first object of love of any child. She is the first object of anything, love or hate. For the purposes of our discussion, it does not matter whether or not the hate is instinctive, as is love, or if it develops from frustration and anger. Hate is nevertheless there, and it is directed, along with love, toward the mother because she is the first human object in a child's life, establishing the first pattern-setting relationship.

Thus, much of the child's capacity to love — and the nature and form of his love—will be built upon this earliest relationship which will, in turn, tremendously influence his potential adult love relationships to other people. As an example of what can happen, let us take two extremes. If a mother is warm and really loves the child, anticipating most of his needs as a growing person, the child will tend to grow up with a sense of inner security and optimism, and will seek out and enjoy new relationships. On the other hand, if a child experiences only pain and frustration at the hands of the mother, whom he needs to love, then his way of approaching a new love object will tend to be modified. He may be afraid and inhibited in his ability to form new relationships.

When I was a child, for example, there was the current expression, "He's got a face only a mother could love — and she died when she saw it." This is an extremely unfunny and inane joke, but if a person did feel that he had a face only a mother could love — and she died when she saw it — he might be hesitant to show his face to anyone else. He would be afraid he would automatically lose anyone he loved. The point here is simply that the first pattern-setting relationship tends strongly to influence later relationships.

The form and nature of the mother-child relationship can take on varied characteristics. There has been much talk, for example, of the over-rejecting but seductive mother, especially in relation to homosexuality. But what has been found to be even more common than the grossly seductive mother is the woman who keeps the child dependent upon her for some reasons of her own. She does not allow the child to grow up, never cutting the umbilical cord, and thus increases the child's sense of insecurity that he cannot survive without her. She has, in a sense, taught him thoroughly — but badly.

Then there is the "smother-love" mother who over-protects and smothers the child, feeling he cannot possibly become free and independent; if he does, then he is made to feel it is an act of aggression against her. With the feeling of aggression would go guilt, and the guilt will not allow him to revolt and wrest himself free. Once again, the child is tied to the infantile apron strings which he may never break.

With this very brief description of the early mother-child relationship, we can now talk about what seems to disturb so many people about psychoanalysis. At around the age of five or six in the normal growth of every child, there develops a very intense erotic interest in the parent of the opposite sex. The dependent little boy has as the legitimate object of his love and affection his mother, and the little girl, her father. The little boy wants to have Mommy in every way and, of course, this means taking her away from Daddy. He becomes jealous and antagonistic toward his father, as well as his brothers and sisters or anyone with whom he has to share Mommy. But it is the father who has the most exclusive and intimate relationship with her, and it is the father who is the prime object of his rivalry.

The little boy has various ways open to him to solve this Oedipal rivalry. In the first place, if he wants mother to want him and he sees that she prefers Dad, then the more he can be like Dad the more likely she is to want him. I do not mean to imply here that the little boy sits down one day and figures this all out. On the contrary, it is an inner and, for the most part, unconscious process which takes place in which he identifies with his father, wanting to be as much like him as possible in order to be attractive to mother.

But a little boy is not stupid. He easily sees that father is bigger and stronger and that he is weak and helpless in comparison. This fact of life presents a problem to the little boy. "Suppose Daddy finds out that I want to get rid of him and take his place?" the little boy unconsciously says to himself. "If he finds out, he'll kill me. He won't let it happen.

And he can kill me because every time I've been naughty he's turned me over his knee and beat me, and such little naughtiness as I've done is nowhere nearly as forbidden as this. I won't even dare admit it to myself that I want to take his place."

The father, therefore, is often the feared and dangerous rival because, "If he knew that I wanted to kill him, then he would kill me." But what is this "killing" to the little boy? On an entirely unconscious level, the killing takes the form of castration. "Daddy will cut off my penis," the little boy says, with complete unawareness that he is saying it. "He will take my sexuality away because it is my sexuality that makes me dangerous to him, and because that is what impels me towards my mother."

Is there any reality to the little boy's fear that people do get castrated if they are bad? Yes, there are castrated people in the world. As a matter of fact, half of the people are castrated — Women. You may now say to yourself that children are not really aware of the anatomical differences between the sexes. However, you do not have to read Sigmund Freud and believe, or not believe, what he has to say. Just listen to children three or four years of age and hear what they have to say and you will find that to children of this age little girls either had a penis and lost it, or they have not grown one yet.

Thus, the lack of a penis is not just a fantasy without reality to a little boy. Added to this reality is what may be called a conspiracy of loud silence. A little boy can proudly and excitedly discover, manipulate and exhibit any part of his body. But when he finds out that he has a penis also, and he goes ahead and manipulates and exhibits it, the world crashes about his ears. He suddenly finds out that what he does with great approval with all of the other parts of his body is absolutely forbidden with this particular part. "Don't touch yourself there!" he is told. "I'll slap your hands," or other threats.

This is one reason the penis becomes tremendously important to the little boy, for it is loaded with all of the prejudices and special conflicts of sexuality which are in the culture. But irrespective of its forbidden quality is the fact that the penis happens to be a place where the little boy receives the most pleasurable sensations, even at the age of four and five. Stroking the genitals for a little boy or little girl produces a sense of comfort. You may see that this is true in any hospital where children are confined for some illness. The sick child will touch his genitals to comfort himself and reassure himself that his body can feel good as well as hurt. Every pediatrician and nurse knows this fact and does nothing about it. It is transient behavior when a child is lonely and in pain.

As I have said, Freud did not invent the Oedipus complex, nor did he invent the fact that infants and children are genitally sexualized human beings. All mothers, for example, know that little boy babies have erections. Many of these women will deny that they know it, and deny that babies do have erections. But it is not only mothers who do not talk or think about the genital sensations of the children. The general conspiracy of loud silence throughout society increases the sense of mystery, taboo and anxiety for the child.

A WOMAN WITH A PENIS

We all know the old but still rather popular song, "I Want A Girl Just Like The Girl Who Married Dear Old Dad." This is the normal solution to the Oedipal rivalry. In other words, first there is the identification with the father because of a mixture of jealousy, fear and admiration, and then in young adulthood the interest in the mother is shifted to another woman. The major problem in homosexuality is that this shift goes awry.

I should first add, however, that the intensity of the Oedipal conflict at around five or six years of age results in a massive repression and covering up of most sexuality in children. For the next few years they exist in a relative state of quiescence called "latency." This is the grade-school period where they are busy learning how to be little men and growing up. In a sense, it is postponement period under the threat of the Oedipal danger. But with the resurgence of sexual feelings on a physiological basis in adolescence, this conflict comes back.

There occurs the beginning of adolescent masturbation, and until the heterosexual solution has occurred in the form of getting interested in somebody other than mother, there is an intermediate phase of homosexuality. I do not necessarily mean homosexuality in a literal sense. I just mean preferring one's own sex. It is an aggressive preference of boys for boys. Girls are "no good, awful and terrible," and there is a sense of revulsion and even disgust towards them.

But what is really wrong with the girls? Simply, they are castrated. There are all kinds of silly rationalizations during this period. The boy thinks his mother and all woman are stupid, weak, incapable of doing anything, and in general, completely unnecessary. In other words, the adolescent boy's way of getting rid of something is to say, "The grapes are sour." He helps himself detach himself from his mother by thinking. "Well, she's not so hot after all. Mabel down the street is cuter — but still awful dumb."

If all is well, the boy becomes masculine. He detaches himself from his mother, he ceases to be afraid of his father, and he grows up and becomes a man who marries another woman. That is the very best. He has gone through a normal phase of transient homosexuality in a more or less sublimated way, and what is still left of it in adulthood takes the form of joining men's clubs, going out with the boys on Friday night for a game of poker, or any number of other activities because society provides legitimate opportunities for us to have fun together as "the boys" or as "the girls."

We all know what often happens when "the fellows" get together at conventions away from home, or are in the Army and separated from women. They tell smutty stories about women which is, in a very hidden way, a sexualized act. Or they may go with prostitutes who are themselves homosexual objects. A prostitute is a woman with the aura of other men around her. The man shares her with other men, and in a sense, she really becomes an erotic relationship with other men. A man does not possess a prostitute. He does not love a prostitute. She is a masturbatory substitute, for there is no interest in her as a person and as a female. One of the unconscious attractions of prostitutes to a man is, "I'm doing what other men do."

Although homosexuality is not one simple thing, we can now discuss what may go wrong in the normal growth towards masculinity. Possibly one of the most common problems is that the father is such a fearfully authoritarian figure that the boy never resolves the fear of the father and thus never fully overcomes his castration anxiety. Therefore, the sight of the castrated genitals of the woman arouses such anxiety that he cannot go near them. He will seek out a feminine object with a penis. This object, let us say, would be a person with a number of feminine characteristics but who would also have a penis, a young boy, for example. With a young boy who is not manly and masculine, the homosexual can engage in sexual relations without the arousal of tremendous castration anxiety. The male object, you might say, is a woman with a penis.

On the other hand, the father may be weak and ineffectual and the mother's relationship to the father may be dominant and aggressive. The young boy, therefore, may view the mother as the person possessing the penis. In our language today we use the expression, "She wears the pants in the family." In other words, she has taken the pants from the father and put them on. This is a nice and polite way of the young man saying, "She has taken father's penis and acquired it for herself. And if I love her, she will do the same thing to me. So that there is danger in my loving her because she is the castrating object. She's the dangerous one. She will make me weak and dependent and thus I must avoid her."

In this case, the boy runs from women and keeps on running, seeking other men as his love partners because they will not do what he fears the woman will most certainly do, castrate him. In effect, he keeps the fact that he has a penis hidden from women. It is a secret he shares only with other men lest the woman grab it. Thus, in one instance it is the mother who is the feared object, in the other instance, the father. But in either case, "woman" must be avoided.

Before continuing, I should point out that the unconscious is timeless. Once conflicts of the type that I have described come into being and are repressed, they are no longer subject to changes as a result of real experience. They are permanent because they are out of reach of the higher mental processes. I might add, this is the most difficult thing for people to understand about psychoanalysis.

In the treatment of these persistent infantile conflicts, the aim is to bring them into consciousness by undoing the process of repression. In the light of day, the individual's ego can take hold of these conflicts and help him understand that they serve no useful function in the adult world in which we must live and survive.

The third major psychological reason for homosexuality is that the boy may turn his competitive rivalry with his father into excessive love. It is a reversing of the Oedipal conflict. Instead of the mother being the prime target of his erotic interest, the father becomes it. This may be simply a way of handling the fear of his father by turning it into love and saying, in effect, to the father, "Look, dear father, I'm no threat to you. I will not love women, I will not love your wife. I will always be a boy and only want you to love me. I don't hate you. I don't want to get rid of you. Oh, no, I want to be with you forever, and I want you to love me."

This type of man then tries to become close to the kind of person his father loves, a woman. Thus, in this case, the male's wish to be loved by the father results in his effort to become feminine rather than masculine. It should be remembered that not all homosexuals are effeminate. On the contrary, some are quite masculine (the Muscle Beach type) and they tend to seek out these effeminate homosexual counterparts of whom I am speaking.

Curiously enough, effeminate homosexuals behave like no real women. They are but a caricature of femininity in the way they walk, talk and dress. Possibly, this simpering picture, with which many of us are familiar, is a not too subtle degradation of women. "Even if I act feminine," the man may be saying, "I don't love women, I really despise them and make fun of them." In addition, this exaggerated imitation of femininity may be an unconscious hiding of masculinity (the genitals) so that it is safe for the homosexual to engage in sexual relations with the feared man.

The passive feminine homosexual unconsciously says to the father, "I won't compete with you. I give up, see? You win. Go ahead, kill me!" Here, I must become somewhat literal. This man wants to be attacked by the male because he is the "female." He not only feels revulsion towards the castrated woman, which drives him towards the woman with the penis, but he also wants to be attacked, often willing to undergo other perversions of a masochistic type in which he is penetrated by the strong and all-powerful father. He seeks out the "Muscle Beach" man, who himself wants a woman with a penis, because he wants to be treated like a woman. Very often, in fact, homosexual "marriages" are of this combination. One stays at home, keeps house and acts the wife while the other goes to work and earns a living. There are some very stable relationships of exactly this kind.

In addition, I should point out that when one man wishes to be dominated and penetrated, and another man wishes to have the woman with the penis, there are only two choices open to them while having sexual relations. They must use the mouth or the rectum, both symbolic vaginas. In this sense, therefore, there is no special significance to the perverse activity. Furthermore, if a woman wants to act as a man towards another woman, she can only use her fingers, her mouth and tongue, and/or an object which symbolically replaces the missing penis.

One of the most frightening dreams a young boy or man can have is the dream of the dentate vagina — a vagina with teeth. This anxiety and fear comes from the fear of the castrating woman who has hidden in the vagina something that will snap off the penis.

Allow me to use a very simple illustration. A child, let us say, goes to a doctor and gets stuck with a hypodermic needle, and comes home and plays doctor, thereby mastering his anxiety because that which was done to him he now does himself. Instead of being the passive victim, he now becomes the aggressor.

This is similar to a daredevil who is afraid of high places but who, nevertheless, earns his living by walking a tightrope high in the air, defying his fear and reassuring himself of his safety. Thus, if a man has a fear of the castrating vagina and has oral relationships with either women or other men in which he puts his penis into an orifice with teeth and pulls it out safely, he is doing the same thing as the child who plays doctor or the daredevil. He is unconsciously saying, "I can put it in and it doesn't hurt at all."

It is very dangerous to generalize. We cannot say, "All homosexuals who experience oral play must have had a castrating mother and they are reassuring themselves that their penises won't be bitten off." All we can truthfully say is that this may or may not be so for this person. It would take individual investigation to find out.

The Treatment of Homosexuals

Although I have briefly covered the three most common psychological patterns which lead to homosexuality, it is nevertheless not the whole story. Freud always suspected that homosexuality had a strong constitutional, or biological, component in it — an unknown factor aside from the matter of life experience. At this point in our knowledge of mankind we still have no clear answer to this suspicion.

For years we have been studying the parts of man that we can see, his actual life experience and his behavior, and there is a remarkable correlation between the two. At the present time, therefore, although inborn constitutional factors may play a role in the development of homosexuality, we must stay with what we know.

Homosexuality is a perversion, and Freud referred to perversions as the inverse of neuroses. In other words, the same conflict which leads to disguised symptoms and anxiety in most people, leads to perverse behavior in others. I would like to add here that one of the reasons society is so disturbed about so-called perverse activity, including homosexuality, is because much of it is part of normal sexual foreplay. All of us play with each other, kiss, hug, feel, touch, do all kinds of things. But ultimately they all lead to normal sexual intercourse.

Perversion is simply an interruption in which some part of the foreplay becomes the goal and copulation is avoided. Anything which interferes with the survival of the species, whether it be homosexual perversion or any other kind, society tends to fight. I have emphasized, for example, that the infantile and child relationship to the mother is often the first and most important source of disturbance. In the first six years, however, the psycho-sexual development of the individual goes through an oral and anal stage, and even if there has not been severe disturbance, the more immature oral and anal wishes are still preserved to some extent.

In effect, all of us to some degree in our normal sexual relationships tend to repeat our sexual development. Oversimplifying it, perhaps a husband and wife start by kissing each other on the mouth, then the man slaps his wife's back-side, and after even more foreplay they end up by having sexual intercourse. The point is simply that they do have sexual intercourse. They do not block mankind's survival as does the pervert and homosexual by swerving from the main goal.

I have intimated above that many homosexuals do not have neurotic conflicts. Their problem is society, because if society would leave them alone there would be no problem. Many of these men do not want to change, and they do not need to change because their behavior is a solution to conflict which is not necessarily disabling. On the other hand, a compulsion, or schizophrenia, or severe psychoneurosis, is either a completely disabling or limiting solution. In other words, homosexuality need not impose any limitation on life whatsoever. A man may have another man as a sexual partner, enjoy a permanent relationship, and live without anxiety.

This is one of the problems in treating the homosexual. Many of them do not necessarily need or want to change themselves. It is society's persecution and scorn which makes them unhappy. Many of these men, for example, find the solution by moving to a community where homosexuality is accepted. They feel more at home with people like themselves who uncritically accept their pattern of living. In this type of situation, they typically do not seek psychological help and they do not suffer.

Professionally, I did not see homosexuals at all until I went into the United States Army. There, the very nature of Army life — the danger of exposure, of being beaten up, the constant temptations and the like — brought them to me for help. But the great majority did not want help to change from being homosexual. On the contrary, they wanted to get out of the impossible, painful and difficult situation. The homosexual man in the Army is similar to the heterosexual man forced to live in a WAC barracks. "Don't get an erection," he would be told. "Because if you do, we are going to beat you and humiliate you. But you have to dress and undress, go to the toilet, bathe and do everything in front of and with all these girls."

This is exactly the homosexual's problem in the Army. He is not vicious and mean. He is like the normal man in a WAC barracks. These men would come to me and say, "Dr. Robbins, I have to get up at five o'clock in the morning and get out of the barracks before anybody else gets up. And at night I wander around the camp until everybody has gone to bed." These men were decent in every respect. They were simply in an intolerable situation. They did not want to cause trouble, or be the object of trouble. They wanted to do their jobs, and in my experience, they were good soldiers in every other respect but this one.

At the same time, however, they were a terrible threat to the rest of the men. The men's own latent homosexuality was stimulated by being herded together with other men. They were without women, and they could not stand being near the overt homosexual. In large part, this is why there is always the danger of violence. For if a homosexual makes a sexual proposition to a man, why should he be struck and beaten if not because the proposition is some kind of threat to the non-homosexual?

In each of us there is a certain amount of latent homosexuality, and in the Army situation, for example, we struggle against it by pseudo-masculinity and excessive masculinity, and we do not want anyone to threaten this adjustment. The homosexual is dangerous, tempting and seductive, and consequently, we strike out, hit him, beat him, and thus destroy the enemy which really lies within ourselves.

Nevertheless, as I have said, many homosexuals are most difficult to treat because they have found a satisfactory and psychologically inexpensive solution to their unconscious sexual problems. It is only because of society's inability to accept them as "just another fellow" that they may be under pressure. I do not mean to imply the homosexual is immune to neurosis. He may have other neurotic qualities which can be successfully treated psychologically. But the fundamental character disorder lends itself to no real solution, and if he does not want to change of himself then we cannot fundamentally help him.

On the other hand, there are many homosexuals whose compromise solution is still short of what they want for themselves. Their homosexual adjustment is not acceptable. They want to change, and if their homosexuality is not too deeprooted, they can respond to psychoanalytic investigation and treatment. I have seen homosexuals in treatment who have become well, married and had children. We must remember that homosexuality is not a "thing," any more than fever is a "thing." There are multiple causes and multiple degrees and intensities of homosexuality.

To me, this is one of the reasons why most of our laws in regard to homosexuality are quite stupid. They simply do not make sense because they cut much too wide, and since society condemns homosexuality, the homosexual is apt to be easily victimized and blackmailed. The private sexual life of two adult males should be their own business, and the law of the land, in my opinion, should so state.

Society is much more condemnatory of men than of women. As a matter of fact, unless there is a minor involved, homosexuality between women is not usually considered a criminal act and is seldom prosecuted in the courts. Women can kiss each other, hold hands, and even share an apartment and sleep in the same bed without anyone thinking anything strange about it. Two men, on the other hand, cannot even kiss in our society without suspicious whisperings from the rest of us. But women do not suffer from castration anxiety, and although they may suffer from penis envy, they do not have the same problems as men.

Let us not forget one very important point. To grow up as an adequate man or woman, all individuals must primarily have a healthy relationship with the parent of the same sex in order to identify and model themselves in that image. In addition, all individuals also need the parent of the opposite sex from whom to differentiate. It is not enough for a man to have had a father who can be the model for the masculine part of himself. He needs also to have had a mother in order to learn how to relate to women as a man, to be a man, and to differentiate himself.

But personality characteristics and much of the behavior which we call masculine and feminine in our society are purely artificial distinctions. We take these distinctions for granted, although Margaret Mead in her book, "Male and Female," has pointed out quite clearly that what is labeled masculine and feminine in one culture may be modified or completely reversed in another culture. To be sure, no man has ever given birth to a baby, but that is about the only difference between male and female which is not otherwise completely cultural.

I began this discussion by attempting to explain the broad concept of sexuality. Everything and anything which tends to bring an individual into constructive contact with other individuals, whether they be men or women, comes from man's basic erotic urge. It does not matter whether the close, affectionate relationship contains a direct genital component—in this sense, therefore, all of us are more or less both homosexual and heterosexual.

21.

"What would you say to a man who complains, 'Lately, I've had the strangest thoughts about other men ... I think I'm homosexual'?"
we asked Dr. Bergler.

×××××××××××××××××××××

EDMUND BERGLER, M.D. (1900-1962)

Psychoanalyst

In this interview Dr. Bergler also discusses:

"Can we be 'bi-sexual'?"
   "Is homosexuality a reversion?"
     "What is the true meaning of homosexuality?"
"Can homosexuality be used to 'hide' something else?"
    "What is 'trade' in the lexicon of homosexuals?"
     "Should homosexuals be legally punished?"
"What is a 'self-damaging' act?"
    "Why is punishment attractive to the homosexual?"
     "Underlying homosexuality, is there a more basic problem?"

21.

This is what Dr. Bergler said when interviewed in his office:

The first difficulty is that many people do not know the meaning of the term "homosexuality." A homosexual is a man or woman who is sexually attracted to the same sex.

A thirty-year-old married man, father of two children, comes for psychiatric help saying that he has recently been seized by some "strange" thoughts about men.

I ask him what he means by "strange thoughts about men?" What kind of strange thoughts?

He is vague in his answer.

"Are you sexually attracted to these men?" I then ask, because this is the only criterion that exists. In other words, if a man is heterosexual and attracted to a woman, he doesn't necessarily have to have an erection but he can imagine he could have an erection with this woman. The same thing is true with the male homosexual. He can either get an erection if he sees a man, or he can imagine that under certain specific circumstances he would have one.

Thus, if our young married man says that he would or could get an erection, that he wants to be together with men, or a certain man, or if he imagines being with men in bed, then he is obviously a homosexual. This is true regardless of whether he has had sexual contact with men. But if he says "no," he doesn't have an erection and does not imagine himself being in bed with men, and if he is repelled by the idea, then there are certain other possibilities.

First of all, this man may be on the verge of becoming a practicing homosexual and not admitting this to himself—yet. Or, he is not a homosexual at all but uses this alleged homosexuality to cover up something else. The inner conscience works on the following principle: Your inner conscience accuses you of the crime X, but your inner (unconscious) ego says, "I cannot be guilty of such an awful crime but I am guilty of crime 'Y'." Now you have produced a substitute crime to help protect yourself from crime X, the more serious one. Consequently, even if a man says that he has ideas about homosexuality, it doesn't always mean that he is already a homosexual.

But we have to face the realistic situation as it occurs in the consultation room. In the majority of cases, men and women do not come for help because of "strange thoughts." Rather, they come with very specific situations.

They may say, "From the time I was thirteen or fourteen I have been a homosexual. I am completely uninterested in women. I tried once or twice to go to a prostitute but I was completely impotent."

When this is said, there is no doubt that he is a homosexual. Then I ask, "What kind of fellow do you prefer. What is your type?"

Or a man may come and tell me, "I am married and have two children. The marriage is a good one but recently I had a few homosexual experiences."

"What do you mean by 'recently'?" I ask. "Does it mean, in fact, that you have always been a homosexual? Does it mean that you believed you could rescue yourself from it by marriage and that now, 'recently,' you have become impotent with your wife and you are reverting to homosexuality?"

"Yes, that is the truth," ninety percent of these men will answer, for the typical homosexual is not another Oscar Wilde who was heterosexual until the age of thirty-eight and then "at once" became a homosexual. This does exist but it is not typical.

More typical are those people who call themselves, in complete misnomer, "bi-sexual." Bi-sexuality is a biological term, meaning the possession of male and female tendencies by one and the same person. Yet, those who use the term about themselves do not mean that. They mean, simply, that they can have sex with either a man or a woman.

Furthermore, according to many homosexuals, biology ("more femininity") explains homosexuality. But this theory is wrong because to every passive homosexual belongs an active one, and the latter cannot be explained by that theory. Moreover, since homosexuality is curable, the biological theory is erroneous.

No one, however, can dance at two weddings at the same time. It does not work even though some believe it can and they keep trying it. Take a man who is homosexual but unhappy because he is not attracted to women, who possesses a great deal of guilty feelings because of his homosexuality. One day he finds a woman who is nice to him for some reason, gets married, then believes for a while that he is now heterosexual. But within a short length of time he becomes impotent and eventually goes back to men.

THE REAL PROBLEM

Homosexuals have perhaps fooled more psychiatrists than any other group of men and women in the world. Until a few years ago homosexuality was believed to be a completely incurable disease. In the past, the homosexual came to the psychiatrist who acted in one of three ways.

He might say, "Psychiatrists have nothing to offer homosexuals. Goodby."

Or, he might say, "We can do nothing for you. We cannot change your homosexuality but we can adjust you to the specific situation."

A third psychiatrist would say nothing. He would put the patient on the couch, let him talk for a few years, and after these years the patient was just as homosexual as before.

The reason for this was that the psychiatrist as well as the man-in-the-street, was fascinated by the word "*homosexual.*" He looked at homosexuality as a sexual problem, such as promiscuity. But it is not a sexual problem. It has little or nothing to do with sex, at best with counterfeit-sex. It has a great deal to do with a completely different problem — "the self-damaging act."

Before talking about this "self-damaging" behavior, we want to talk about the commonly accepted belief that homosexuals have mothers who were domineering and controlling, on the one hand, and/or who were extremely seductive at the same time.

It is a good excuse to blame the parent. But reality is only the raw material from which each individual works. Let me give a typical example. A young man came in and said he was a homosexual and he knew exactly why he became one. If I would visit his parental home in the Middle West, he said, in less than an hour I would see what a "bitch" his mother was and what terrible things she had done to his "poor" father. It was "bitch, bitch, bitch mother" in his conversation, and he gave many examples which were very likely true. Even if only one-tenth of what he said was true, the mother nevertheless would appear to be a very aggressive and irrational woman.

This young man told me that, at the age of seven, he and his twin brother began to play homosexually. They continued this behavior through the age of seventeen. Then they were separated when some wealthy relatives sent them to different colleges. Came the war, and he didn't see his brother for many years. As he himself continued his homosexual life he assumed his twin brother did so as well. Consequently, he was shocked when he found out that his brother had married.

He figured the whole thing out immediately. His brother, he thought, must have married a "bitch" like mother. However he had to prove this to himself. He took a 2000 mile trip just to make the investigation. After a week, he found not a "bitch" but, on the contrary, a very nice girl.

"How do you explain this?" I asked. "You say you know why you are a homosexual, mother's 'bitchiness' being responsible. But the fact is that your twin brother is not one. Do you have the answer to that also?"

He didn't know the answer.

Obviously, he had possessed three choices. He could have married a kind, loving and devoted wife as his brother had evidently done, hence correcting the infantile disappointments; or, he could have perpetuated his mother and father's relationship and married a "bitch" himself; or he could have acted in exactly the way he did — flight to man. In effect, he could keep on running away from the "bitch" woman as he did when he first became a homosexual, also acting the "bitch woman" in his homosexual relationships, for there is nothing more "bitchy" than homosexuals towards each other.

In this sense, therefore, what the mother and father were or were not is relatively immaterial, for, as I said, reality is only the raw stuff we mold ourselves for our own inner purposes. It is not true that all domineering and seductive mothers produce homosexuals. Homosexuality is an inner defense, which may become powerful, from harmless, or relatively harmless, infantile fears. These fears are only projections of the infant's way of looking at the world and have nothing to do with the reality of the adult world.

I said previously that homosexuality has little or nothing to do with sex proper but does have a great deal to do with "self-damaging" behavior. Imagine a man who, for unconscious reasons which go back to childhood, is at first scared to death of a woman (mother). Instead of overcoming these fears, he inwardly elaborates on them masochistically, and wants to be mistreated by a woman, though consciously unaware of this wish. Imagine, further, that this person inwardly fears his own wish, but instead of giving up the wish itself he gives up its alleged or imagined central figure, woman. Since there are only two sexes, this leaves him only one alternative in his frantic flight — man. As a defense against his real inner wish, he turns to man in order to find peace, quiet, love, understanding and safety. But underneath these outward aims, his real, compelling need remains the need to be mistreated. This retreat to "another continent" does not alter the old conflict. Sooner or later (and sooner rather than later) he will feel that the man with whom he has sought refuge mistreats him, misunderstands him, fails to do him justice, and tortures him by arousing his jealousy. Moreover, his flight in no way altered his sex glands. Since they are still working, it is inevitable that man, his antidote against the feared sex, woman, will secondarily be elevated to the status of sexual attraction.

This fact is of great practical importance. Don't forget, in many parts of the United States homosexuality is prosecuted. You can go to jail for two years, if not longer. I recently received a series of letters from a minister in the West who had been thrown out of the church, jailed, and in general placed in intolerable circumstances. He got into trouble with the law by approaching a man from the vice squad, but it could just as well have been somebody else blackmailing him, or writing destructive letters to his parishioners.

But if you ask a man like this why he didn't avoid getting into trouble by sharing an apartment with another man, he will probably tell you that he tried it but it doesn't work.

The basic problem is the personality structure of the homosexual who is what we call a "psychic masochist." Although every homosexual is a psychic masochist, plus, not every psychic masochist is a homosexual.

The "plus" means that if you give him a whip, figuratively speaking, with which he wants to be hit, he will not allow a woman to use it but gives it to a man instead. This is a shift of the masochistic relationship, and as a result of this shift, there is a great deal more trouble for the homosexual than for the average psychic masochist.

THE BI-SEXUAL AND "TRADE"

I mentioned previously the men who incorrectly label themselves "bi-sexual." When they come for psychological help, I ask, "Why do you come at this moment?"

"My wife found out," they may answer.

"How did she find out?"

The answers to this question, although somewhat different, always amount to the same thing. One man may say that his potency deteriorated. His wife, not knowing that he is a homosexual, believes there is another woman involved. She presses and presses him about the other woman, and finally, to prove to her how wrong she is, he tells her that he is a homosexual. You can imagine he will never hear the end of this.

Or, the man may say that his wife received an anonymous telephone call, which means that he chooses his masculine friends in such a manner that, when he gives them up, they take revenge by informing his wife. Or, the wife unexpectedly comes home and finds him in bed with a young man.

"You couldn't go somewhere else to get into bed?" I ask.

"How was I to know she would come home at three o'clock?" says he. "She always comes home at five-thirty."

All of this sounds completely idiotic, for they are confessing and getting into deeper trouble without any apparent reason. It does not seem logical for the homosexual to take such extreme chances of being caught when he could just as well live with another man in complete privacy. But it takes time to figure out just what these people are talking about — they are running after troubles.

This leads to the strange problem of "trade." In homosexual language, there are three types of "trade." First, there is the homosexual whore who is not "officially" a homosexual himself. "Officially," a homosexual whore is a young heterosexual boy who sells himself to men as a prostitute. A patient once told me that he picked up a young man, slept with him, and in the morning the young man asked for ten dollars. Since the boy was well dressed and didn't give the impression he needed the money, my patient asked why he wanted money.

"I wouldn't feel right if I didn't take money," was the answer. In other words, if he does not take money, he is a homosexual, but if he is paid he is only "trade."

The second type is called "rough trade." This means that the homosexual picks up a man, takes him to his apartment, and in the morning finds himself beaten, tied up, and robbed.

The third type of "trade" is most illustrative of what we are talking about. You frequently hear from homosexuals that they hate homosexuals.

"You are a homosexual?"

"Yes."

"Yet, you say you hate homosexuals?"

"Yes."

"Well, what do you want?"

"Trade," is the answer.

At first, you think he is talking about the official whore, or "rough trade," but that is not the case. This man wants the following situation:

He wants a man who is seven feet tall, 220 pounds, an athlete, married, and he wants him to be a heterosexual who he seduces into homosexuality. But not only does he have to seduce this man, the man has to respond, to want him, the homosexual!

This is fantastic. Why?

Suppose, a truly tragic situation, that in a drunken state the 220 pound heterosexual is seduced into bed. This seven-footer will be so guilt-ridden, so uncomfortable, that at best he will be completely passive and probably impotent. This will be a complete defeat for the homosexual because the athletic giant is supposed to love him and yet cannot.

Thus, this type of homosexual gives himself a set of conditions which are so fantastic that only a psychic masochist could figure them out. Unconsciously he wants to be constantly rejected, psychically beaten and punished. One wealthy young homosexual was traveling in Italy and one night as he was returning to his hotel he was approached by a teenage homosexual whore who asked in broken English if he wanted to have a good time.

The wealthy American, however, found the boy repulsive and said no. But instead of walking away after the "no," he turned to the young prostitute and asked him a question.

"What made you a male whore?" he wanted to know.

The Italian youngster didn't understand the question. At that moment the American saw two sinister men in the shadows watching them. He immediately figured out in his mind that the two men were using the young boy as bait for robbery or blackmail. He instantly walked away, returned to his hotel and checked out.

That was all there was to it. But this particular scene became the young man's masturbation fantasy for an entire year. Now, why is it that, although he found the prostitute repulsive, he became nevertheless, sexually excited for a year? What atracted him was not the boy — he found him repulsive — but rather the situation of danger. Once more, psychic masochism is decisive. In fantasy he saw headlines in the paper — AMERICAN MILLIONAIRE ARRESTED ON MORALS CHARGE.

With the exception of psychic masochism, everything else in homosexuality is window dressing. For example, the feminine attitudes some homosexuals display are camouflage; they are acting out an imitation of the woman-man relationship. At bottom, homosexuals act the mistreated baby-mistreating mother relationship.

To sum up, the basic problem in homosexuality is the personality structure. Although not every psychic masochist is a homosexual, every homosexual is a psychic masochist—plus. Splitting off in treatment the superficial sexual camouflage from the basic masochistic structure makes homosexuality a curable disease. "Sexual tension" turns out to be "masochistic tension."

NOTE: Dr. Bergler discusses psychic masochism in detail in Part II.

4. FAMILY

Introduction

We are all familiar with the "catching" of contagious diseases. Children can catch measles or mumps from other children. Men and women can contract venereal disease from each other. Is neurosis, or emotional illness, also "catching?"

This we asked Jan Ehrenwald, M.D., in the words, "Can one person catch a neurosis from another, particularly children from their parents?"

How early does neurosis start? Some psychoanalysts believe it starts in the cradle, some even think that the mother's physical and emotional state while the embryo is growing in her body may affect the child's later emotional development.

At least we know that the way a baby is fed proves important to his entire growth. We asked Rhoda Lorand, Ph.D., to discuss, "What is the significance of food and eating to the child?"

Within a family, one of the most difficult times for a parent occurs when the child enters adolescence. Some parents scarcely recognize their son or daughter, so bizarre does behavior become at this time.

Yet it is important for the parent to know what his child is going through. Adolescence may be a very hard time for a child; he behaves as he does out of his need to survive, to achieve independence. If he is ever going to stand on his own, this is the time he will start to do so.

"How does a boy become a man, and a girl become a woman?" we asked Henry I. Schneer, M.D. He explained what takes place in the development of the child that often causes adolescent conflicts with parents.

No doubt the issue that most disturbs both adolescent and parent is that of the adolescent's increasing preoccupation with sexual feelings. Parents become concerned lest the son or daughter engage too prematurely in sexual activity. Adolescents must grapple with the control of strong sexual desire in themselves and also with the standards set in their particular society as to sexual behavior.

We returned to Rhoda Lorand, Ph.D., to ask, "What is the sex life of the teenager in present-day America?" We also wanted to know if she thought sex instruction and education would be valuable to the boy and girl in high school.

It is astounding how many parents know little about their children, especially about the child who is in trouble. They are not aware of what the child feels. They judge him only by what he does, not taking into account that he may be going through a deep torment.

"How can a parent better understand his troubled child?" we asked Norman Lourie.

No one would deny the importance of the father's role in the family. There seems to be confusion, however, as to what it actually involves. We asked Saul Scheidlinger, Ph.D., to tell us, "What do a man's children need most from him?"

Nudist magazines on our news stands, bikinis on our beaches and sequences in foreign and domestic films often show the human figure in its barest form.

Times are changing. Standards of morality and ethics are in transition, as they usually are. But the great majority of us still wear some form of clothing in most situations. The nudists, however, if they had their way, would have us all appearing naked. There are also many adults who, although they do not belong to nudist organizations, appear in the nude before each other and their children, who allow the children to "see" and who are themselves "seen."

Is this disturbing to the child? What are people doing when they appear naked before children, each other or complete strangers? Are the mysteries of sexuality better explained to the child if he can "see" the nude body? Can the absence of ten square inches of a bathing suit make the sun's rays and the open air more beneficial to us, as the nudists claim?

We received the answers to these provocative questions from Sandor Lorand, M.D. The interview was based on an article, "The Psychology of Nudism," that appeared in his book, "Clinical Studies in Psychoanalysis", published by International Universities Press, Inc., 1950.

It is impossible for a parent to feel one hundred percent love for his child, for he is a human being and human beings all possess feelings of hate as well as love. It is only, however, when the hate overwhelms the love that the feelings become destructive to the child.

"What are the mixed feelings parents have about children?" we asked the late Wilfred C. Hulse, M.D. "To what extent are these feelings sexual?"

It is a cliché by now that children need love and security. In the United States today, more children are killed and permanently injured by accidents than all other causes combined. Accidents of a minor nature are the constant worry and concern of millions of parents. Do they have any relation to a child's feelings, his need to be secure?

We asked Hyman Spotnitz, M.D., "Do accidents just happen to children?"

As a result of accidents, many children are crippled or otherwise handicapped. Other children are handicapped from birth. It would seem that life is difficult enough without the added disadvantage of suffering a handicap.

"Is it true that a handicap must be a disability to a child?" we asked H. Robert Blank, M.D. We believe his answer will interest not only the parent of the handicapped child but everyone, for he discusses feelings that exist in all of us, both towards ourselves and towards the handicapped.

22.

"Can one person catch a neurosis from another?" we asked Dr. Ehrenwald.

JAN EHRENWALD, M.D.

Attending Psychiatrist, Chief, Adult Psychiatric
Outpatient Department, The Roosevelt Hospital

In this interview Dr. Ehrenwald also discusses:

"Are there contagious patterns of behavior?"

"When do people most easily 'catch' a neurosis?"

"Can a family have an 'epidemic' of neurotic disorders?"

"Do parents complement each other in destructive as well as constructive behavior?"

"What is an 'obsessive-compulsive' neurosis?"

"Do all of us have healthy potentialities?"

JAN EHRENWALD, M.D.

22.

This is what Dr. Ehrenwald said when interviewed in his office:

If you ever happen to be in Austria, you may wish to drop in for a visit with a man who, when he takes a walk on his farm, is followed by a group of ducklings who consider him an over-sized mother duck.

The man's name is Dr. Conrad Lorenz, and he is a noted zoologist. He has shown that if he hatches the eggs of ducks in an incubator and then makes sure to be the first object of which the little ducklings catch sight, those ducklings will follow him rather than the mother duck through thick and thin, considering him the "mother figure."

Animal psychologists call this "imprinting" (a strong, early and lasting impression upon the animal). Imprinting in the animal kingdom is somewhat similar to what we shall talk about here.

Can you "catch" a personality? Well, not really. But what is catching, or contagious, are certain fixed attitudes characteristic of a personality.

I have seen four generations of a family where we could say there was a minor epidemic of neurotic disorder. Each pair of parents showed a specific set of disturbed attitudes. In turn, each generation of children tended to be "infected" with the same attitudes. Of course, they could have rebelled but they did not. So, they found themselves between the devil and the deep blue sea: rebellion or compliance. They complied. They all chose the same way out, each one becoming a carbon copy of the generation before. Each member of every generation was under a steady compulsion to do certain things, to carry out certain actions. He was preoccupied with all sorts of obsessive thoughts and rituals which, if not carried out, made him restless, unhappy or depressed.

In human psychology we call this "obsessive compulsive neurosis." It is fairly frequent in our society today. Now, how did this veritable family epidemic come about? This leads to the question: "Has the neurosis been 'home grown' in every member, or is it something like an infectious disease?"

We answer with both "Yes" and "No."

To understand this apparent contradiction we must first do away with a few misconceptions and popular ideas held not only by people at large but even by some in the psychological professions.

First of all, mental disorder (neurosis or psychosis) is not like syphilis, tuberculosis, or the common measles and mumps. It does not lie in the blood system, in the lungs, or erupt on the skin. Therefore, it is impossible to "give" or "catch" mental disorders as we do physical illness. Nor is it a well defined illness like one of the bacterial infections.

In this sense we can say that neurosis as such is not an infectious disease. It is not due to contagion. What is infectious is something else. It is a set of sick interpersonal attitudes, a certain fixed pattern of undesirable attitudes held by a person which may ultimately lead to various maladjustments — for instance, to obsessive-compulsive neurosis. If we focus on the attitudes underlying such a neurosis, then we can answer our question with a "Yes." Fixed attitudes and actions can be transmitted and can be caught. But to what degree they can be caught is dependent upon two things, as with Professor Lorenz' ducklings — the age in life that the exposure to sick attitudes began, and the length of time the person was exposed to such attitudes.

But let us pause at this point and clarify what we mean by "fixed attitudes." An attitude has been defined as the tendency of a person to act in a certain way. For instance, a mother may be in the habit of being bossy, controlling, or manipulative in relation to her son or daughter. Furthermore, this may be a persistent tendency; she is not bossy today and permissive tomorrow. Similarly, we may come across a father who is weak and over-permissive with the children and other members of the family.

Observing such attitudes requires no scientific sophistication. You just watch how one member of the family behaves with the other members. You may find certain enduring patterns that are quite characteristic of the relationship between, let us say husband and wife, mother and son, father and daughter, and brother and sister.

It is these patterns or "fixed attitudes" we are talking about.

EARLY AND LONG EXPOSURE

As with animals, so with humans. If there is early exposure to disturbed behavior there is greater danger to the person. If it occurs later in life, there is little or less danger.

Let us start with the smallest unit of the family, a man and woman with no children. One couple may be giving, supporting, and affectionate with one another. They may tend to share their interests in a socially desirable manner. If so, they represent the ideal couple and their children are not likely candidates for mental disorder. There are no "sick" attitudes for them to catch.

But we may also see another kind of relationship between husband and wife, one in which the husband is cruel and domineering and persistently so. How does the wife respond to it? She may be submissive, compliant, even masochistic, and behave persistently in such a way.

In both couples we see a pattern of attitudes and actions which are consistent. In one we have a pattern of sharing, in the other, another type of complementary pattern. Such patterns go together, either for the healthy, well-adjusted couple or for the poorly adjusted couple. A complementary pattern may keep even a poorly adjusted couple together.

Now, you can carry over either type of relationship between husband and wife to the relationship between father and son, mother and daughter. If you wish, you can even carry this pattern outside the family confines. For instance, between employer and employee. You may have a domineering, rather sadistic type of boss, and a meek, compliant employee. The two may get along fine together! Why?

They are attuned to each other. They fit like hand and glove. They, too, have developed a complementary pattern. We have all seen this countless times. But, you may ask, why does an employee stay in an unhappy situation? We can certainly understand his remaining when it's a good situation, but why persist in the unhappy; why not change? His conduct is governed by the family pattern he experienced in childhood and which he carried over into adulthood.

Suppose we see an authoritarian, dominating, punitive father and mother. Naturally, there will be a tense, frustrating climate in the family. What sort of children would we expect from such a marriage?

The children may comply and submit. If so, you have a "contagious" pattern of compliance set against the established pattern of dominance and control. Or, they may rebel and you have another contagious pattern, one of rebellion against the parents. In either case, whether the children are overly submissive or overly rebellious, becoming defiant and destructive, we see a contagious situation.

Specifically, suppose we have two harsh parents who give no sympathy or understanding to their children. What may happen? If the rebellion gets out of hand, the situation can lead to delinquency in the world outside the family. Thus, in this case, delinquency would be considered an infectious pattern derived from rebellion against the domineering parents.

The Germany of the Second World War is a good example of mental contagion. There was a contagious pattern in which the Nazi attitude swept over a whole nation. It resulted from sheepish compliance with a pathologically authoritarian Fuehrer personality.

There are other examples of mass contagion in history such as the dancing epidemics of the Middle Ages, for example, where thousands of people marched through Europe dancing in a completely abandoned way. It was, if you like, mass hysteria. There, too, you had a pattern of the sharing of sick attitudes.

You can see contagion in girls schools when a group of girls develop an involuntary twitch as everyone suddenly has the same sort of tick. But this is a pathological example. Also, Rock and Roll is an example of contagion, although the teenager might not like this sort of statement.

As stated before, mental disorder is not catching in itself. But attitudes and behavior patterns which go on insidiously over years and years are handed from one generation to the other, slowly but surely helping to mold a compliant, or a

rebellious or a neurotic personality in one generation after
the other.

Is There a Way Out?

At this point, you may very well be asking, "Is there a way
out?" Yes, because fortunately things do not occur in such
rigid ways. Also, the fact is that people catch not only the
unhealthy attitudes but the healthy ones. Human nature is
such that we are also inclined to copy, catch and imitate
what is healthy and socially desirable.

The husband and wife who are affectionate, understanding and share positive ways of life with one another give
these same fixed attitudes and actions to their children. Here
is a pattern not contagious in the sense of sickness but of
health; laughter as well as sadness and sorrow may be
considered contagious.

Thus, the first thing that allows people to break the unhealthy patterns of living is the health potentiality in them.
Almost everyone has some measure of health potential.

Secondly — the fitting of hand and glove — a complementary pattern at work within the family and within society, allows the individual to get along to a certain degree with
certain people even when the going is bad — that is, when
they are pretty neurotic.

Previously, we mentioned a family where the husband is
very dominating and the wife submits. Perhaps it is the other
way around in another family, with a dominating wife and
a compliant husband. Yet, these marriages work. We all
know examples of this kind. Why do they work? Each mate
complements the other in what he needs and wants from the
other. They are happily matched in their mutual incompatibility, you might say.

There is another fact important to note once again. We
have found that it makes a great deal of difference at what
period of life a person is exposed to sick interpersonal attitudes. For the earlier the child is exposed, the greater his
risk of being infected. The later such sick (or well) attitudes
are brought to bear on the child, the lesser is the danger (or
the advantage).

This fact runs parallel with the basic psychoanalytic observation that it is the very early formative years of childhood

experience which determine a person's development. So, if a child is exposed very early to a very neurotic family, then the danger of "infection" is much greater.

Also, we have found that the longer the time of exposure to such influences, the greater the risk of infection. For instance, if a hostile, punitive stepmother comes into the lives of children who are 14 or 15, she cannot do much damage. But if the mother is, to begin with, a pretty neurotic woman and doesn't know how to handle her newborn baby because of her anxiety, her compulsiveness or her bossy ways, then the damage may be done in no time and we have a case of early contagion.

In effect, it is the time of onset and the duration of exposure that counts.

There is another way by which mental contagion is automatically reduced. There are those people so emotionally sick that they withdraw altogether from relationships with others. They are the lone wolves; they do not take social responsibilities. They do not marry, they do not have children. Some, who are extremely ill, become hermits.

No matter what the degree of illness, these people usually "quarantine" themselves (you might call it "psychological quarantine"); they retreat into their sheltered little neuroses or psychoses and stay there, and the sickness does not spread from them.

WHAT CAN YOU DO?

Let us say you recognize there are some patterns of behavior or attitudes in your life which you have "caught" and which are not good for you or for those around you. What can you do?

First of all, if you know the dangers of psychological contagion then you are, at least, no longer in the dark. You know the enemy, so to speak. You can take action. You have a margin of freedom in your behavior.

This means you have the capacity to change through small as well as large insights into your behavior. All psychotherapy is based upon this margin of freedom within a person.

However, those with more serious behavior problems may need help from outside. They may find it impossible to spotlight the exact problem or its causes. They may not be able to locate by themselves the focus of infection in their family. Nor may they be able to lift themselves by their own boot-straps.

In this case, they or the members of their family, will need to seek and find psychological assistance from someone with training and experience.

In summary, it is up to each one of us to make the best use of our own insights. All we can do is to make a little dent where we can — bringing our influence to bear upon as many people as possible. The psychologist, the psychoanalyst, the teacher, the social worker, the clergyman, each one can do his part. All of us have a chance to make a dent by conveying our insights to other people, provided our insights are valid and our attitudes socially desirable, not warped.

Above all, we must not forget that there is a margin of freedom in human behavior to which we may appeal, which we try to mobilize by good example, by persuasion and, if need be, by systematic psychotherapy. Psychoanalysis and psychotherapy presuppose the existence of this margin of freedom, this capacity to adjust to change through insight. It is this hope on which depend the insights that are the goods we analysts try to sell to the small consumer, trusting he will make good use of them.

23.

*"How important are the first feeding
experiences in the life of the child?"
we asked Dr. Lorand.*

XXXXXXXXXXXXXXXXXXX

RHODA L. LORAND, Ph.D.

Psychologist, specializing in the psychoanalytic
treatment of children and adolescents

In this interview Dr. Lorand also discusses:

"Can food represent love?"
  *"What happens to the baby without a mother to feed
  him?"*
    *"What happens to the baby with a tense, anxious
    mother?"*
"Do children outgrow their problems?"
  "Should babies be fed by the clock?"
    "At what age should a child give up thumbsucking?"
"Why is the first year of life so important?"
  "How are food and learning difficulties connected?"
    "Should children be forced to eat a balanced diet?"
"Why does a child demand excessive attention at mealtime?"
  "Does a child ever win a fight with his parents?"
    "Can aggression ever be healthy?"

RHODA L. LORAND, PH.D.

23.

This is what Dr. Lorand said when interviewed in her office:

The first activities the baby performs are sucking and swallowing. Intake of food is not only a fundamental physical activity — because obviously we must eat to survive — but it is also the function through which a loving bond is established between mother and child, starting at birth. Hence it becomes a fundamental emotional experience as well. The wisdom of nature has placed this, as well as other vital functions, within a tremendously satisfying setting.

Held against the mother's warm, soft body while being breastfed approximates for the child as closely as is possible the prenatal situation in which it actually was one with the mother and fed by her body. At the breast it is again being fed from her body, warm, safe, and completely dependent upon her.

These early beginnings are a crucial time in the child's life. During this time the foundation can be laid for a warm, secure, and happy relationship with the mother leading to trust in the world and to the development of attitudes of optimism.

As Anna Freud has pointed out, in the first weeks of the baby's existence food plays the most important part in his life, and at this time his mouth and everything connected with the mouth are the most important parts of his body to him. Sucking at the mother's breast produces delightful sensations in his mouth and leads the child to wish for a continuation of them, which he soon learns to obtain by sucking his own fingers.

Considerably before Freud's psychoanalytic explorations and discoveries led to this awareness of infantile eating pleasures, the great scientist Charles Darwin was making minute, careful and objective observations of his infant son at mother's breast. He published his observations in 1877 in an article entitled "Biographical Sketch of an Infant," in which he states, "It may be presumed that infants feel pleasure while sucking, and the expression of their swimming eyes seems to show that this is the case." Darwin further noted that ". . . a warm, soft hand applied to his face excited a wish to suck." Here he was referring to what was later termed the cheek reflex, which causes the baby to turn and take into its mouth whatever is put against its cheek. In this way the baby's face need only be held against the breast and the child will turn to suck. Darwin recognized the nature of this action in his remark, "This must be considered as a reflex or an instinctive action, for it is impossible to believe that experience and association with the touch of his mother's breast could so soon come into play." The illustrious father was surprised and puzzled to note that at the age of 32 days his son ". . . perceived his mother's bosom when three or four inches from it as was shown by the protrusion of his lips and his eyes becoming fixed. I much doubt whether this had any connection with vision. He certainly had not touched the bosom. Whether he was guided through smell or the sensation of warmth or through association with the position in which he was held, I do not at all know." But obviously the Darwin baby had learned to recognize that he was at the source of his most important gratification.

Anna Freud has called to our attention the fact that since the child would perish were his mother to withdraw her tender care of him during the first year of his life, it is not surprising that the maintenance of his maternal care begins to play a very important part in the baby's life. He needs his mother for the satisfaction of his hunger. Gradually the factor of needing the mother for sustenance broadens to a feeling of love for her. This is shown by the fact that the child wants his mother with him even when he has been fed. The child has begun to love her as a result of her ministering to his needs and making him feel safe and comfortable.

The younger the child is, the more surely it absorbs and reacts to the feelings and attitudes of the mother. Therefore it should not be surprising again that out of this early relationship can come some of the greatest difficulties in life if all does not go well. What happens when the mother is depressed or upset and handles the feeding situation with tension, indifference or anger? What happens when the child is allowed to suffer severe hunger pangs and become frantic with fear and rage?

In cases where the mother is withdrawn, anxious or hostile the child will feel it and become anxious. Babies thrive on the normal maternal feelings of loving warmth and affection which are communicated to them in the tone of voice, the manner of handling, and the general atmosphere of happiness generated by the mother who enjoys caring for her child. The sick or troubled mother who is in the grip of depression, overwhelmingly severe anxiety at the prospect of motherhood, or resentment at an unwanted child, will communicate these feelings to the baby who will then fail to develop trust in her or love for her in the same way as the well-cared-for baby. It will fail to develop the feeling of well-being which leads to the beginning of confidence and the ability to love other people. Its emotional and physical development will be retarded as compared with the happy baby.

Studies have shown that some babies refused food when fed by their own mothers who were anxious and in conflict, yet accepted the same food when it was fed to them by someone who was calm and relaxed. Experimental evidence thus proves that the child's ability to eat and his response to feeding are greatly influenced by the emotional tone of the person who is holding him and feeding him.

In those situations where matters have gone seriously wrong one can usually see much more clearly the factors which are involved. It is similar to studying some phenomenon under a magnifying glass — a slightly distorted glass since everything is not equally magnified. Through treatment and study of troubled children we know that a number of different kinds of neurotic problems can have their basis in the feeding situation during the first year of life. As a rule these problems continue and are reinforced and enlarged all through the various developmental levels of childhood and adolescence. (Contrary to popular belief, children do not outgrow problems. What leads people into this mistaken belief is the fact that the behavior which indicates the presence of a problem [in other words, the symptom of the problem] changes form. For instance, the child who would not eat as an infant, may demand to be spoon fed at the age of 4, and may at 6 insist upon being read to, or develop ever-changing food-fads.)

Today, fortunately, most babies are fed when they are hungry and are not left to scream in rage and panic for hours as were the "clock babies" of the 1920's and 30's. This practice created a never-ending struggle between many mothers and children, as was authoritatively demonstrated by the fact that in those years, high on the list of problems brought to pediatricians were feeding problems of all kinds. The fight that started during the first year of life in the mother's arms was carried on in the high-chair and over the dinner table for years. Now that most babies are fed on the self-demand schedule pediatricians are no longer beseiged with this type of complaint.

For the child, pleasure in eating is identical with pleasure in living and in loving. His life revolves around the loving provision of food. A punitive attitude on the part of the mother, distasteful foods, any unpleasantness connected with eating, make the child extremely unhappy and anxious and therefore impede his general developmental progress. Where the child should be motivated to come out more and more to the world, the anxiety and unhappiness foster a tendency to withdraw into himself and increasingly to seek comfort within himself. Too great frustration at this period can lead to distrust, anxiety, pessimism, selfishness and an insatiable craving for love while being unable to give love. Too great indulgence of oral pleasures, on the other hand, i.e., a nursing period extending beyond six months and bottle feeding until the child is three or four, can make the child too dependent upon infantile forms of gratification. The result will be too great a fixation on mouth pleasures, a reluctance to move on to more mature activities, and a tendency to be overly dependent upon others.

Parents should relax about thumbsucking. All babies and many young children need to suck. Drastic means to curb thumbsucking can destroy pleasure in eating and usually have far-reaching damaging consequences. The baby whose hands are tied or who has mittens covering his fingers becomes helpless with rage. For older children, it means subjecting them to searing humiliation. If by the age of five or six, a child is still sucking his thumb, the parent can very gently encourage the youngster to give it up as unworthy of his age. But if the environment is severely lacking in other gratifications which the child craves, he will be unable to deny himself this very great pleasure without a tremendous struggle. The six-year-old who still needs his thumb also needs a very strong incentive to give it up.

The importance of maternal love (or a substitute who will love and mother the child) in the feeding of the baby has been strikingly demonstrated by Dr. Réné Spitz's studies of infants in foundling homes, who had no mothering, but lay in cots all day looking at the ceiling, drank from bottles propped up on pillows, and were never spoken to, caressed or played with, although they were kept clean and given adequate amounts of food. These babies did not assimilate the food which they consumed. Many wasted away and died. The ones who survived appeared to be hopelessly retarded in every area of development. Obviously, food without love fails to nourish the baby.

A number of serious neurotic childhood, adolescent and adult problems have their roots in the first year of life, and center around the feeding situation. The most obvious are problems of obesity and the malnutrition caused by the child's refusal to eat. The least obvious is the problem presented by the learning block, or inability to learn in school. It must seem very strange indeed, to many people, to be told that the earliest oral intake is intimately connected with learning problems. To learn, the child must be able to attack the work, bite into it, chew it, assimilate it. He must be able to take in, eat with his eyes, and become the master of the work which confronts him.

Rage at the mother stemming from frustration in the early feeding relationship produces guilt feelings which can result in an inability to utilize oral aggression constructively. Unresolved difficulties in oral aggression can produce in the child guilt and fear of any kind of aggression. Strong conflicts about attacking and taking in or incorporating often lead to a tendency to avoid the "intellectual" foods. Children with learning problems, incidentally, are often obese. Instead of incorporating with their eyes, they can only incorporate on the most primitive level — with the mouth. Frequently, these children must have sweets in order to enable them even to approach the learning situation. They crave this infantile compensation for what is to them a highly threatening experience. (Most learning blocks are the result of a complex of factors, of which unsublimated oral aggression is but one component.)

It is important to remember that aggression means activity, not simply hostility. It means grasping and getting. When the child is nursing at the mother's breast, it is engaging in a healthily aggressive activity — it is actively sucking. Furthermore, when the child cuts his teeth he experiences a great deal of pleasure in using them and thereby acquires a feeling of strength and power. If the biting is angrily forbidden, the child may be severely frightened. If so, the upsurge of the need to bite will make him anxious. For all babies develop a need to bite when they cut their teeth, just as they develop a need to suck in early infancy — apart from feeding.

Newly teethed babies have the urge to bite everything and everybody. They bite when they want to kiss, show love, anger, playfulness, and for the pure pleasure of exercising the new equipment. From the manner in which people respond, the baby soon learns that his biting is regarded as a hostile act.

Babies are usually teething about the time they are being toilet trained, and if the mother is too strict in the process of training, the child may feel a great incentive to use his teeth as an aggressive weapon against her and everyone else.

If the child is being driven to use his mouth over-aggressively because of too much frustration, he will become guilty because his mother is bound to express her disapproval. Guilt feelings arising from over-aggression or too severely punished normal aggression in each phase of development, carry over to other, healthy aggressive activities, such as the learning of physical skills, i.e., skating, bicycling, climbing jungle gyms, baseball and later to intellectual learning. Thus when the child is faced with the need to be aggressive in these situations in order to master them, the old prohibitions

unconsciously descend upon him: "You're not allowed —
that's bad — you shouldn't do it. Your parents won't love
you." Faced with this threat the child is paralyzed in some
degree.

A Little Flag of Distress

When the mother nurses and feeds the baby, she is showing her love and care. Food is love and it never really loses
that meaning to us throughout life. That explains why eating problems and eating habits constitute a special language
of communication between mother and child. There are
many people who, when worried and anxious, eat continuously. Refugee children, for example, brought to the United
States between 1933 and 1939, gorged themselves until they
were shown affection and had acquired a sense of belonging
in their foster homes. In effect, they were giving themselves
the earliest form of love which they had once enjoyed. Feeling that they had no one to love them, they strove to give
love to themselves in this primitive form.

Sometimes children will eat voraciously to assuage a feeling of helplessness, weakness and smallness, or a feeling of
emptiness, all stemming from inadequacies in the relationship with their parents. One little boy who had many fears
about dying resulting from his guilt over hostility towards his
parents, found reassurance in continually stuffing himself
with food.

Some people find they are totally unable to eat when they
are deeply worried and upset. But whatever the reaction,
food is the vehicle of expression.

It should be apparent from the foregoing how mistaken
and cruel it is to deprive a child of a meal as a disciplinary
measure. To send a child to bed without his supper teaches
a child only that his parents do not understand his needs and
are capable of cruelty towards him. The counter-aggression
such behavior on the part of the parents arouses in the child
places him in an agonizing conflict of love and hate, and
gives rise to strong feelings of guilt, hampering the child's
normal development.

Before the baby can talk, it communicates with its body.
Therefore, feeding disturbances become a language of their
own. Later on, whenever the child has food fads, is finicky,

or is constantly dawdling and playing with its food, he is saying with his actions, "There is something the matter between me and my mother. Something is wrong, and this is how I'm saying it because, although I can speak I don't know how to explain it. I won't eat her food because I feel there is something the matter with the way she is giving me her love."

The fact that mother and child speak the same language is evidenced by the manner in which the mothers usually react to habitual rejection of the food they offer the child. It is clear from her upset, offended, angry manner that the mother understands the language of the unconscious, namely, that the food does in fact represent herself or her love, and that she is being rejected. Of course, in these situations mothers usually rationalize that their extreme reaction is caused entirely by concern for the child's health or character development, or the waste of food, etc. But the real reason is that they have rightly understood the child's message. Unfortunately, they seldom know how to reply constructively to the youngster because they themselves are helpless victims of their own early childhood experiences. Obviously, to find the villain in the piece we shall have to go back to Adam and Eve.

An understanding mother (which means one who is not full of conflicts about food) does not punish her child for not eating. She finds it possible to accommodate the child's preferences and even to make last-minute substitutions when requested. She doesn't feel compelled to make a battleground of the dining room and prove that she is the top-sergeant in charge of her platoon. (I know of one mother who forces her husband to eat everything on his plate and to refrain from expressing food preferences lest he set a bad example for the children who are subject to the same rules.)

Usually mothers who find it necessary to hedge mealtimes round with all kinds of rules and regulations have had a troubled relationship with their own mothers in the area of feeding and are themselves victims of an unconscious drive to even the score ("Now it's my turn to boss the children"), or prove something to their mothers or to themselves about their ability to be a better parent than the one they had. Convictions are strong, and feelings even stronger in such situations. Advice doesn't help alleviate the tension. Before they can change, these mothers need therapeutic help in order to understand what the feeding situation unconsciously represents to them as a result of their own childhood experiences.

Actually, there is no need for parents to worry about forcing their children to eat a balanced diet. Two experimental studies have shown conclusively that when given a free choice, even two-year-olds eventually select a balanced diet. Apparently there is an instinctive selection of food according to the body needs of the individual child. It was noted, for instance, that children with a calcium deficiency ate egg shell and plaster off the walls!

Sometimes, without any apparent provocation and no problem on the mother's part, a child will begin to be a difficult eater. In doing so, the child is waving a little distress signal. Some people say, "Ignore him, he's just trying to get attention." But if a child is trying to get attention, *there is a reason for it.* Something *is* the matter. The child feels deprived of the normal attention and love of the mother in some way.

If he is an only child, for example, doted on for four or five years, and then suddenly presented with a new baby, it can be very hard for him to bear. His experiences have accustomed him to the fact that the world centered around him, but when the baby brother or sister arrives, he is suddenly faced not only with sharing the mother but with taking a back seat while everyone makes a fuss over the (for him) unwanted baby. The child may never have been helped to endure the frustration of sharing his mother's attention and companionship with anyone else in the daytime hours. Under the new and painful circumstances he may begin to do all sorts of things in an attempt to gain the mother's attention. He is not a naughty child. He simply cannot cope with a painful reality for which he is unprepared. His attention-getting warrants serious investigation. The parent must ask, "What is wrong? What is he trying to tell me and how can I help him?"

Unresolved conflicts from one stage are carried over to the next phase of development and complicate the child's adjustment to it. Therefore, when a child has problems during the first year of life (which is known as the oral stage, since the mouth activities and sensations are of paramount importance during that year), they will color his reactions in the second phase, during which toilet training is usually accomplished. The child who enters this phase feeling hostile towards his mother will react to her attempts to train him with much more stubbornness and rebellion than a child whose desire to please his mother is unconflicted.

(The interview on "Sex and the Teenager" in this section contains a description of the effects upon later phases of development of a mishandled first year. If the stage has been set for difficulty at that time, it usually gathers momentum and complexity with the years, as I have tried to show in that interview.)

Youngsters entering adulthood with a complicated history of childhood disturbances are greatly handicapped in their sexual identity; and their choice of a mate (or inability to find one) is naturally going to be determined on the basis of the experiences and unresolved problems of childhood. When and if they become parents themselves, the whole cycle of difficulty will start all over again, because along with the conscious rejection of the parents as models, deep in the unconscious is the conviction that what their parents did was right and they will unconsciously be propelled in the direction of duplicating that despised behavior.

Mothers of children with severe eating disturbances often are heard to say that they had resolved never to do to their own children what their mothers had done to them. To their horror and despair, they find themselves doing the very same things. The patterns are repeated because where there are unresolved early childhood conflicts, the unconscious drives are the strongest determinants of behavior.

For those unacquainted with the studies in this field it must seem far-fetched indeed to attribute such great and enduring importance to events which have taken place in the first few years of life, especially the first. However, it has been established beyond question that the younger the child, the greater the impression made upon him by his experiences, even though they are lost to memory.

Development after birth follows in principle the physiological gradient of growth which governs the development of the fetus in the womb. The embryo does not develop in all of its parts at once, but follows a program of development which begins at the head, travels down to the feet, and from the center of the embryo outward. If at the time that the mouth is becoming differentiated, for instance, (which means that the tissue in the mouth area will be the most active part of the embryo for that period) something should temporarily go wrong, the result may well be a cleft palate. Although the fetal environment may right itself shortly thereafter, the mouth will never develop perfectly because the optimum time for it to develop is past — and irrevocably past.

The same principle applies to the very young baby. The younger the child is, the greater the damage when his needs are not met. This applies to both physical and emotional needs. A five-year-old can starve for a few days and be restored to perfect health within a very short time. A few-weeks-old baby may die as a result of such an experience. Similarly, a three-year-old may resent very much the absence of his mother for two or three weeks, but this confidence in her can be fairly soon restored after her return through proper handling. A sudden three-week absence of the mother from a six-months-old baby will create much greater anxiety and distrust and require much more time and effort to restore the baby's sense of security.

As Doctor Spitz's studies showed there is no healthy development without love, and food is one of the first concrete expressions of love for the child. It is a vehicle through which the mother gives her love. She is filling the child with love when she is filling it with food. Consequently, it is not too difficult to understand where certain childish fantasies come from.

Since children know that when they eat a lot, for example, they feel full in the stomach, and since they see that when mother is having a baby (or some other woman, for children are very observant), she becomes big in the stomach, the child easily comes to the conclusion that the woman got that way by eating something. Thus, food can become equated with the "something" which makes the baby.

Eating problems are sometimes caused by fantasies about pregnancy. The very thin and undernourished child may be making sure she (or he — for little boys often want to be able to have babies) is not having a baby because she wishes for one, yet fears that her wish may come true. The obese child may have the fantasy, "I'm having a baby. Mother isn't the only one who can have them!"

What determines emotional pathology is the degree of disturbance. Many people have idiosyncrasies related to food and feeding. It is the quantity, not the quality, which indicates whether help is needed. All children are somewhat dissatisfied with the amount of love they get from their mothers. There is no such thing as complete satisfaction, except during the first year of life. By the second year, the baby has made the highly disagreeable discovery that other people have a claim on *his* mother's time and love! Thus there is an amount of normal frustration every child has to learn to bear. And certain elements of the food problem may be present in every normal person.

WHEN THERE IS LOVE

All children start out in life with the ability to become hostile and angry. Frustration easily evokes normal aggression. As a matter of fact, the emotions of anger and hostility serve the instinct of self-preservation. If the baby did not scream with rage when it was hungry, for example, it could conceivably starve to death.

This rage is healthy aggression on the child's part. However, in order to become a civilized member of our society, the child must learn to sublimate his aggression and to direct it into constructive channels. He needs to learn to tolerate a certain amount of frustration without becoming unduly disturbed. This can be achieved only when the frustrations to which the child is exposed are appropriate to his level of maturity and are imposed by loving parents in whose good will the child has every reason to trust. For example, a five-year-old can wait for dinner a half hour if necessary but for a one-year-old, this is too difficult. The one-year-old will lose confidence in the mother because of the anguish one-half hour of hunger will cause him, whereas the five-year-old can tolerate hunger that long; he has a backlog of experience which enables him to understand the situation and cope with the frustration unharmed. His desire to please a beloved parent will provide the incentive to tolerate the discomfort of the delay without undue complaints and fussing.

But when aggression is so great that it cannot be sublimated, or the parents have not understood how to help the child sublimate his normally aggressive drives, frequently the child has difficulty in learning. All primitive forms of activity must eventually be curbed, and the energy and drive channeled into the learning of civilized forms of achievement and accomplishments. We all know how little children love to tear everything apart. But we teach the child to curb his raw, primitive hostility. He finds out that he cannot go on tearing things apart, but he can eventually learn to take apart and put together something which may be of scientific value and interest. Similarly he can't go around biting everyone, but he can learn symbolically to sink his teeth into things that will be of help to him in terms of learning and mastery. He can devour material with his eyes and mind and thereby acquire the internal and indestructible power that knowledge combined with self-control produces.

24.

"How does a boy become a man?"
we asked Dr. Schneer. "How does
a girl become a woman?"

XXXXXXXXXXXXXXXXXXXXX

HENRY I. SCHNEER, M.D.

Associate Professor of Psychiatry, Department of
Psychiatry, State of New York,
Downstate Medical Center

In this interview Dr. Schneer also discusses:

"Are females different from males in their sexual develop-
   ment?"
      "How do we master our sexual and aggressive urges?"
         "Can someone have both masculine and feminine
            feelings?"
"What are the biological urges of adolescence?"
   "Who are the natural love objects of childhood?"
      "What is a 'pseudo-hermaphrodite'?"
"When does the genital zone achieve primacy?"
   "Can passivity be hiddenly 'active'?"
      "What is the meaning of regression?"
"How significant to adolescents are the biological events of
   menstruation and seminal emission?"

24.

This is what Dr. Schneer said when interviewed in his office:

Recently, I asked an elementary school child how she thought a girl becomes a woman and a boy becomes a man. She answered somewhat embarrassedly, "It's what's up front. It's what's up front."

Of course, her answer is an obvious and simplified statement of what the difference is between male and female. In effect, the little girl said the difference is biological. But just as obviously, the difference between the sexes — and how they grow up — is much more complicated than an elementary school child's concepts. However, as this anecdote illustrates, a young child is more occupied with the physical, concrete, definite image of male and female than the later-developing adolescent who is attempting to get at the emerging image of being either man or woman.

The sexes are biologically definite at birth. There is no alteration of that fact, even by so-called change-of-sex operations which are occasionally publicized, because the entire endocrine physiology is rigidly fixed in the body from birth. In short, the individual is biologically male or biologically female for life.

But the mental aspect can be quite different. The attitude of an individual may contradict the biological, structural and inherited framework, even among what is known as "pseudo-hermaphrodites." That is, a person may have an outwardly confusing appearance of the genital organs ("What's in front," as the little girl would say). But such individuals seem to organize their minds and personalities in the direction of being more like the man if they have testes, or more like the female if they have ovaries, and this is true regardless of the external appearance of their genitals. Incidentally, the true hermaphrodite (one that could fertilize oneself) is a myth.

THE CRUCIAL TIME

The process of becoming a man or woman is an on-going one. It begins from the time the infant first smiles at either parent. The father has an image of himself as a man, the mother an image of herself as a woman, and both of these self-images are carried over to the child. Specifically, the father reflects and develops different attitudes toward his male child than to his female child. Thus, a male child, let's say, relates to the father in one way and to the mother in another way. A boy has his mother from the beginning, and in the entire epic of his life she is his natural choice of an object to love. Although he learns to feel as an opposite to her, in a sense, he seeks her out through his entire life. On the other hand, the father may be recognized by the boy child as someone who stands in the way of his being exclusively with mother.

The girl, however, does not immediately have her natural love object. She, the same as the boy, has her mother at first and she must make a transition from the mother to the father as the natural biological opposite in the love relationship.

During the ages of six to ten a kind of separation begins; girls stay more with girls and boys go more with boys. Group and gang formations often occur. This behavior seems to be some sort of preparation for developing a sense of individuality where maleness or femaleness is concerned. In effect, it is a period of consolidating and getting ready for being more the male or being more the female. But the preparation is going on in two worlds: the outer world, the world of everyday life, and the inner world of the child.

Broadly speaking, this inner world consists of drives and urges which create tensions which need to be satisfied. One of these urges is hunger; another, and a very prominent one, is the sexual urge. Since this is what we are talking about — sexuality — let us devote further thought to this sexual urge.

The stirrings preceding puberty, at the age of nine or ten, have to be kept under control, and this is another reason for the separating and grouping of boys unto themselves and girls unto themselves. But we want to focus our discussion on the time of puberty because it is the point of great change. Puberty is the crucial time for the boy evolving himself as a man and the girl evolving herself as a woman.

We know that at puberty the biological urges, which have been repressed since the ages of five or six, once again stir and become stronger. This increase of strength, in turn, causes a strain on the boy's or girl's controls of these inner drives as they are related to the demands and morals of the outer world. Furthermore, marked physical changes begin to take place. The individual's body assumes more the appearance of what is seen as male or female.

Along with the biological urges and physical changes there is also an organization of "the pleasure life." As stated by Sigmund Freud, this is the time in life when the genital zone achieves primacy. The genital area takes on a much more definite meaning. Bodily sensations are focused at this area of the body with profound psychological concurrences. Orgastic experience is possible.

Different things happen to the boy and to the girl. With the boy, this experience of orgasm is sharp and definitive and makes for a directness in attitude. According to the Kinsey Report, the average age for males to have first orgastic experience is slightly under fourteen. On the other hand, according to Kinsey, only forty percent of girls have first experienced orgasm by late adolescence. The point here is simply that there is more of a diffuseness for girls; bodily sensations are not as sharply differentiated. And while knowing what the boys want, they are more inclined to seek out a kind of self-value and an evidence of desirability, and to give expression to a desire to surrender to someone stronger. The girl does not view herself as just a companion for a little bit of fun, sexual or otherwise, because she is practicing for having a husband.

The girl has to establish her identity as a woman in receiving the "stronger" person. This is one aspect of femininity, passivity. But as Freud advised us, we should not identify activity with masculinity or passivity with femininity. Although femininity involves a preference for passive aims, it may also require a good deal of activity to achieve the passive ends. For example, adolescent girls may be very competitive with their girl friends in getting boy friends. The difficulty which can arise from such behavior, however, is that the competitiveness may become an end in itself, having nothing to do with the relationship to a man.

THE DAMAGING EXPERIENCES

There are all kinds of deviations and deviant possibilities in the emergence of manhood and womanhood. It has been found that an injurious experience at puberty, either physical or mental, can cause an individual to fall back upon and become fixed upon an early childhood form of the expression of maleness or femaleness.

For example, an aggressive and domineering mother may complain of her adolescent son that he will not wash himself for weeks on end. The not washing represents an earlier childhood form of attention-getting and an earlier form of relationship to the mother which is now persisting partially through the kind of experiences still encountered by this boy with his nagging mother. Some degree of untidiness may be a general characteristic of adolescents but it usually only indicates the in-between stage of growing from childhood to adulthood.

As an indication of her growing up, a fifteen-year-old girl said to me, "I am becoming more considerate to my mother. I don't leave my room such a mess." A woman, however, who had the unfortunate experience of viewing her parents in the act of sexual intercourse during her pubescence became fixed on an earlier childhood form of expressing bodily stirrings: she tended to become nauseous and vomit whenever in close proximity to a man.

With every adolescent, the development of the identity of being the man or the woman is crucial. Because of any number of damaging experiences, this identity formation may become interrupted. Instead of realizing oneself in relationship to the opposite sex, a tendency to keep with one's own sex may occur, as it does earlier in life.

In some cultures such an identity is recognized and has been described as the "berdache." For example, the American Plains Indians, as described by the psychoanalyst E. H. Erikson, allowed young men who could not become braves and warriors to do the things expected of the women of the tribe. They cooked, kept house, dressed like women, and had a "marriage" relationship with a man. In our society, the overt homosexual would be the berdache's counterpart, but the transvestite (the individual who dresses in the clothing of the opposite sex, and who may or may not be homosexual) is closer to the idea of the berdache. In our urban society such publicly acknowledged identity is not as easily found as in the Plains Indians, and consequently, in this sense of ostracism, a boy or girl has much more difficulty evolving as an adult.

The biological events of menstruation and seminal emission impose demands on the minds of a girl or boy to organize a pattern of reaction. The physical experience calls attention to the self as a sexual identity. How the experience is integrated in the recognition of oneself as a procreator, and counterpart to another of the opposite sex, is obviously vital in the process of becoming a woman or a man.

Does the boy acknowledge the genital part of his body, or dare he not know that the testes and penis are part of his body? Or a girl: Does she realize that she has a genital organ, or must she think there is nothing there?

Some girls, as taught by their mothers, look upon menstruation as a "curse," while others look upon it as the sign of their identity as a woman. A girl, for example, may stop menstruating for a period of time during her teens as a veiled protest against the emerging woman identity. Or, a girl may refuse to eat and become so thin that it appears she has the almost conscious aim of being neither a girl nor boy. The opposite may occur, also. The girl may become obese and, in doing so, perpetuate an infantile identity as well as making herself unattractive to men.

On the other hand, the boy's seminal emission may represent to him some failure in control of the body. According to the boy's development, it could be further misinterpreted as a weakening or losing of strength. This may happen especially where a guilt-ridden, punitive attitude is influencing the boy.

The task of becoming the man or the woman is to master the sexual and aggressive urges for the service of mature love, and to neutralize the surplus energies of sex and aggression for productive work. To be able to master these urges is to be able to control and direct them. The pubescent girl, for example, may see boys leaping over a high fence and she may wish to be able to do such things with her body. She may, however, be able to master and neutralize her urges in relationship to the boys by becoming, let's say, a ballet dancer.

The mastering of the urges, and the meeting of the expectations of the outside world may be costly in the sense of the anxiety and guilt generated in the process. To restrain their basic urges in adolescence and to meet the social demands around them, boys and girls require recognition by themselves — and by the older generation, also — of the conflict between their inner needs and the controls required of them. Such recognition will allow for the making of creative men and women rather than mere automatons or wild ones.

25.

"What forces mold the sex life of the teenager?" we asked Dr. Lorand.

XXXXXXXXXXXXXXXXXXXXX

RHODA L. LORAND, Ph.D.

Psychologist, specializing in the psychoanalytic treatment of children and adolescents

In this interview Dr. Lorand also discusses:

"Why are the teenage years of sex life crucial to the development of the adult?"

"Why does a teenager have to become emancipated from his family?"

"Why is too much gratification or too little equally unhealthy for a child?"

"Why do some adolescent boys feel hostile towards girls?"

"How is friction between teenagers and their parents related to the sexual development of the teenager?"

"What relationship does the early struggle over training in cleanliness have to a feeling of revulsion about sex in the teenage years?"

"Should parents take children into bed with them?"

"How is the sex life of the teenager related to his childhood?"

"What effect does the divorce of parents have on the sex life of the teenager?"

"Why is it dangerous to the development of a child when each parent tears the other down in front of the child?"

"What is promiscuity a sign of in the teenager?"

"Is masturbation during the teenage years normal and healthy?"

"Should a brother and sister ever share a bedroom?"

"What makes youngsters choose a partner who is unsuitable?"

"Should parents and children share off-color jokes?"

RHODA L. LORAND, PH.D.

25.

This is what Dr. Lorand said when interviewed in her office:

If teenagers sprang full-blown from their parents' foreheads one might begin with the teens in speaking of sex and the teenager. But every adolescent's sexual history starts in early infancy when the mother unknowingly prepares her baby for his adult sexual role by fondling, caressing and playing with him. The normal responses of the mother to her baby — the cuddling, holding it against her bosom, kissing, squeezing, tickling, rocking — all arouse delightful sensations in the child's body. Thus are awakened the first erotic sensations, which some day will be duplicated in adolescent and adult love-making. (One cannot help but be struck by the similarity of the mother's caressing of her baby and the amorous foreplay of adults.) The emotional tone and the manner in which the mother handles her baby from the earliest weeks of its life play an important part in determining the child's teenage and adult attitudes and responses to love.

Others in the child's environment, of course, also contribute to its education for love. Few adults can resist fondling babies and small children, usually speaking to them in endearing terms and in voices full of the affection and delight aroused in them by the child. And this is just what the baby needs in order to develop into a healthy young adult who can give and receive love in full measure.

The vitally important aspect of all the early childhood relationships with the parents is to be found in the psychoanalytic discovery that these become the pattern for all of the individual's later relationships. Freud's investigations of his patients' life histories enabled him to prove conclusively that there is in everyone a compulsion to repeat in later life the patterns of all the earliest reactions of love, hate, rebellion, submission, loyalty and disloyalty. Strange as it may seem to those who have never had the opportunity to observe this process, the child's later life is greatly influenced by an unconscious urge to choose his friends, his loves, and his life work so that he creates for himself almost a repetition of his forgotten childhood experiences. The emotional attitudes which arise in relation to his parents in childhood are later transferred to other persons.

Studies of children and adults who have been deprived, in varying degrees, of initial loving contacts with a parent figure — either through institutionalization of the child or mother, or severe emotional disturbance of the mother, such as deep depression — have yielded striking proof of the retarding effects of this deprivation upon every aspect of the child's development. Such deprivation makes the child turn back on to itself its newly burgeoning capacity to love, with a consequent overinterest and preoccupation with itself, its body and the products of its body.

Teenage is the time when youngsters begin to pour out to selected individuals outside their family the love they imbibed as babies and small children and which, up to adolescence, has been given to the parents (and in some measure to brothers and sisters). The child who has received love mainly from itself has correspondingly little to give and makes only shallow relationships. This has been shown conclusively by the work of John Bowlby, William Goldfarb and Réné Spitz, among others. The child who has been the recipient of love and devotion has a reservoir at his disposal. Before it is available to persons outside his family, however, he must first go through a process of breaking the childhood attachment to his family. This is often a very painful process for both the adolescent and the parent. In many cases it accounts for a large measure of the difficulties parents and teenagers have with each other.

Where the parent feels secure and understands that the youngster must give its most intense love to someone outside the family, it is very likely that the adolescent will achieve his emancipation with less upheaval than in families where the parents feel threatened by the loss of their child as he becomes a young adult. In the latter case the child may retain its childlike attachment to the parents and be unable to establish a mature love relationship with anyone; or, out of anxiety at parental restraint or anxiety at inner restraints stemming from over-attachment or conflicting attachment, the teenager may make a very sudden and ugly break with the parents. This is seen in those extreme situations where the adolescent becomes a churlish boarder in his own home, having no use for the landlady, the landlord and the other boarders, except to take money and borrow clothing from them.

A healthy teenage sex life, whether it be the sex life appropriate to a 13-year-old or that of the young adult of 18 or 19, is largely dependent upon experiences the individual has passed through at each important stage of his early development from birth to the age of six. Psychoanalysis has recognized three distinct stages of development in the young child, each determined by the primacy of a corresponding part of the child's body, which in turn has been determined by the physical development of the child.

In order for the child to achieve health in adolescence, the central goal of his parents and educators must be to steer a middle course in gratifying the drives which arise at each phase of development. Surprisingly, too little or too much gratification produce the identical result — fixation at a particular level, making progress to the next phase more difficult. Too little gratification causes the child to keep looking hungrily for more and he is thus emotionally not ready to move on to the next stage to keep pace with his maturing body. Too much gratification of instincts makes the child less willing to change the mode of gratification. He would like to keep things just as they are and his progress is impeded because he is encouraged to enjoy satisfactions which are no longer appropriate to his age.

It should be borne in mind that what follows is somewhat in the nature of a diagram. Human emotional development is a phenomenon of infinite complexity. Any one-to-one cause and effect explanation for a particular trait is bound to be, to some degree, an oversimplification. Qualities derived from one level usually undergo modifications at other levels of development, just as these primary qualities influence and color the characteristics which derive from later levels. A more comprehensive description would go far beyond the scope of this interview.

The interview on pages 230–242 contains a detailed explanation of the importance of the baby's experiences with the mother during the first developmental phase, known as the oral because the mouth and everything connected with it are of primary importance in the baby's life. Feeding, sucking and, later, biting pleasures are the center of the baby's interests and needs. Warm, affectionate and generous ministering to his needs, which involves a great deal of body contact with the mother, lay the foundation for the growth of a strong bond of love between the baby and his mother.

If all goes well during this period, the child will begin to feel trust. It can be dependent without fear; it begins to develop the rudiments of qualities of generosity and self-confidence and it will retain a normal enjoyment of mouth pleasures. As was indicated in that interview, too great frustration at this period can lead to distrust, anxiety, an insatiable craving for love while at the same time being unable to give love. It was also indicated that too great indulgence of oral pleasures, such as prolonged breast and bottle feeding can generate the trait of over-dependence on others and, further, fixate the child too strongly on mouth pleasures and other infantile modes of gratification.

It is not difficult to understand in what manner the qualities described above will color a teenager's relationships with the opposite sex.

The next level of development is called the anal phase because it begins with the physical maturation of the muscle of the anal sphincter. The child thus acquires the ability to control defecation. (Until about the end of the first year of life the anal sphincter has operated in reflex, responding automatically to pressure upon it of the fecal matter.) This newly acquired ability is immediately seized upon by most mothers to train the child to cleanliness. The child would, naturally, prefer to remain a little savage, depositing the products of his body wherever and whenever it pleases him. However, if the first year of his life has been a happy one, a very strong bond of love will have come into being. Out of love for his mother and the deeply treasured approval he wants from her, the child learns to deprive himself of his primitive pleasures of soiling and messing. Unromantic as this may seem, it marks his first renunciation for the sake of a beloved person. The child who in this way makes the vitally important first step of achieving control over his aggression through love, not coercion (although his mother's demands have aroused a certain amount of aggression since they run counter to his own desires) acquires the beginnings of independence and the feeling of strength which self-control gives, as well as freedom from the guilt and anxiety which plague the uncooperative or coerced child.

It is not difficult to imagine how different the situation is where the tie between mother and child is fraught with conflict, disappointment and distrust. In these cases the child does not have the incentive to exercise self-control. On the contrary, he derives a certain feeling of power and satisfaction from being able to thwart the wishes of the mother who has, during the first year of his life, thwarted him so often. If a fight was started in year one, it continues in year two, but in this round the baby has the upper hand, or so it may seem to the parent. Actually, the child is always the loser in a fight with the parents because when he does succeed in spiting them and apparently winning a battle, corrosive feelings of guilt and anxiety, which result from his aggression and parental disapproval, torment him and lower his self-esteem. He feels that he is a bad child and the feeling stays with him, exercising a continuing influence on his activities, behavior and personality.

Difficulties may of course arise for the first time during the second year of the baby's life. A mother who may have been relaxed and tender with a helpless infant, can suddenly become tense and demanding when active training is required. Special attitudes of her own towards cleanliness or towards the first signs of independence in her child can cause tension. The mother with unresolved problems of aggression towards her own parents may find herself severely handicapped in sensing just how much pressure she may bring to bear on her child without overwhelming him. But whether it is a continuation of an old struggle or begins with cleanliness training, discord between mother and child at this period leads to the development of such characteristics as spite, stubbornness, cruelty and disgust at sexual feelings and activities on the one hand, or at the other extreme, passivity.

In teenagers who have a history of conflict and struggle with the mother in regard to toilet training one finds these traits to a striking degree. Where the child has had the energy and the constitutional activity pattern enabling him to put up a big fight (Margaret Fries has shown that babies vary at birth as to whether they are very active, moderately so, or inclined to passivity) we find spite, stubbornness and cruelty. In the less active child, who has succumbed to overwhelmingly strong demands for conformity, we find passivity.

Adolescent boys of the active type exhibit very hostile attitudes towards girls, are incapable of tenderness and consideration for them, and hence are incapable of romantic ardor. These boys are baffled by their lack of success with girls despite conscious efforts to be agreeable. Girls usually sense the underlying hostility and lack of tenderness and feel repelled (except in cases where the girl's problem of masochism draws her to someone in whom she senses cruelty).

Boys of the inactive constitutional type who have become extremely passive as a result of feeling overwhelmed by their mothers' uncompromising demands for surrender, also find difficulty in relationships with girls. Unless they happen to be selected by aggressive girls who are not displeasing to them, these youngsters usually find themselves outside the stream of boy-girl social life of their peers. They also lack feelings of tenderness and devotion. (Both groups, active and inactive types, feel suspicion, hostility and distrust towards girls.) In extreme cases the passivity predisposes them to homosexual attachments to older men as well as to boys their own age.

How are teen-age girls affected by similar struggles with their mothers? The same personality characteristics of stubbornness and cruelty, or passive surrender are to be found, with the added complication of difficulties in acceptance of menstruation and a feminine role in life. They don't want to be like the mother towards whom they feel so much hostility. Girls with this type of history regard menstruation as disgusting. The menstrual flow is unconsciously regarded as excrement — they feel dirty for as long as their period lasts.

Also, since it is an ever-recurring reminder of the feminine role which they have automatically rejected along with the rejection of the mother as a model of the type of person they would like to be, it becomes a deeply resented function, the conflicts about it often being expressed in intense pain and discomfort. The problem is expressed by some girls in failure to establish a regular cycle, while in extreme cases menstruation is entirely suppressed.

One may well ask "What has this early struggle over cleanliness training to do with disgust about sex in the teens?" A great deal, although it is not the only developmental level from which feelings of disgust about the body and its functions can be carried over into adolescence. The child who refuses to cooperate with his mother and soils himself whenever and wherever he pleases usually provokes strong expressions of disgust and disapproval from her. He begins to think of himself as a bad child and his body then becomes bad and disgusting (especially the part which is causing so much trouble to his mother). Since voluptuous sensations are experienced in the anal region by the child during the process of evacuation, all voluptuous sensations eventually come under the cloud of disgust and disapproval, because a child takes over his mother's attitudes towards himself and his activities. Often these internalized attitudes which have been taken over from the mother, become even stronger than the mother's because they are reinforced by the child's guilt feelings caused by his anger and refusal to comply with her demands.

Another factor contributing to the feeling of shame and disgust about sexual matters is the reaction of the parents to the child's delight in, and curiosity about his body, and those of other family members. Starting at about one-and-a-half the child becomes actively interested in exploring his own body and finding out all about it. He also takes great pleasure in running about in the nude. If the parents are upset and disgusted at this curiosity and disapprove of his exhibiting himself, the child will surely begin to feel guilty and ashamed of his interest and will begin to feel that the hidden parts of the body are bad parts. These attitudes, like those previously acquired, carry over into adolescence, a time when every child is anxious and uncertain to a varying degree about the changes taking place in his rapidly developing body. Normal self-consciousness, which is usually outgrown and replaced by healthy pride in the possession of a young adult body, then becomes intense and painful, and greatly interferes with the teenager's feeling of confidence and attractiveness to the opposite sex.

Behind much of the agonizing over minor blemishes, hairdos, figure proportions, and height or lack of it, lies a deep fear that the maturing genitals are in some way defective and a conviction that they are disgusting. Such feelings stem also from the way in which early childhood masturbation was treated by the parents. In the third phase of development of the young child, which is referred to as the genital phase, since the child's interests, at around two-and-a-half or three, become centered on his genitals and in the sensations which can be derived from manipulating them, children also note with uneasiness the anatomical differences between the sexes. All children make up their own theories to explain puzzling phenomena. Apparently both boys and girls almost universally harbor the notion that they once all had the same apparatus as the boys, but that somehow the girls have lost theirs.

This belief creates special anxiety in little boys who begin then to wonder if the same fate will befall them. The anxiety will be greatly intensified if the parents threaten the child with punishment for handling his genitals. The amount of hostility and fear existing in the relationship to the parents up to this phase will also be a factor in determining the intensity of the fear of harm to the genitals. Particularly in this period of the child's life seeds of serious difficulties in adult sexual functioning can be sown. Fear that harm can come to his prized genital at the hands of a punitive mother or father can lead to varying degrees of impotence in adulthood.

Little girls who are convinced of having been deprived of a male genital by a punitive parent will also experience difficulties in achieving normal sexual responses. The mother of an anxious three-year-old girl reported that whenever the child watched her baby brother being diapered, she would clutch inside her panties and ask where her penis was, obviously unable to accept the explanation that only little boys have them.

The genital phase marks the beginning of an emotional relationship with the parents which Freud termed the Oedipal period because of the vividness of the child's attachment to the parent of the opposite sex, and the intense desires and fantasies of assuming the adult role. Anna Freud has drawn our attention to the great depth and intensity of this childish love and the agony of jealousy which the child may experience. It has by now become common knowledge that little boys want to marry their mothers, little girls their fathers and that during the period from about three to five or six, this struggle is in the foreground of their emotional life. Difficulties in the relationship with the parents prior to this period complicate the resolution of the Oedipal problems. Where the children have felt the parents to be hostile and frustrating, the normal type of solution cannot take place. In normal circumstances, after several years of playing house and pretending to be the wife, the little girl decides that she will become just like her mother and find a man for herself who will be just like Daddy. The little boy also resigns himself to the inevitable and strives to be a copy of his admired father with the hope of some day finding a girl as wonderful as Mother.

But in cases where mistaken parental handling has caused great hostility to exist side by side with love for the parent, the child cannot make the adjustment. In such cases, the little girl vows that she will be as different from her mother as day from night. She therefore continues to be her mother's rival for her father's affections and hence continues to be frustrated by her father's failure to give her the role she covets. She not only remains fixated in her little girl love for him, but at the same time develops hostile feelings towards him, which will color all of her future relationships with boys and men. Moreover, since she feels unable to identify herself with her mother, she will be ambivalent in her feelings about womanhood, motherhood and pregnancy. She will then unconsciously veer towards a masculine identification to some degree. In cases where the father is harsh to the little girl, she will carry over to teenage her fear and distrust of boys.

The boy in whom there is strong fear and anger towards the mother sometimes establishes a strong preference for the father, with unfortunate consequences to his adult sexual functioning. Where the father has been severe with the little boy, we find rejection of identification with the father's role and a consequent infantile clinging to his mother. The situation parallels in every detail that of the girl who remains fixated to her father through rejection of identification with her mother.

Sometimes difficulties in resolving the Oedipal problem result from over-stimulation or too great indulgence of the child's fantasy and desires. When parents appear nude before the child or take him into bed with them, this arouses confused and confusing longings in the child and increases the expectation of fulfillment of his fantasies, making it more difficult for him to relinquish the fantasies. When parents are seductive and derive too much pleasure from their children's Oedipal advances to them, the children become too much attached and find it difficult, in the teens, to break the attachment and give their love to someone outside the family. Parental seductiveness also increases the child's jealousy of the parent of the same sex, thus creating extra guilt and anxiety.

During the adolescent years there is a renewal, or second edition, of Oedipal strivings. A final resolution of them is most difficult to achieve in families where parents and teenagers engage in various kinds of mutual seduction, such as the exchange of off-color jokes, or a sharing of the teenager's love life through detailed reports of what has taken place on every date. These intimacies are of a sexual nature and are inappropriate to the parent-child relationship. They reinforce the sexual aspect of the childhood tie between parents and children at a time when the tie should be in the process of dissolution.

For similar reasons it is unhealthy for brother and sister to share a bedroom. The tendency to mutual seduction is strong. Frequent sex play gives rise to guilt feelings which later on hamper the teenager's relationships with members of the opposite sex, because they unconsciously represent for the teenager the first sex partner — who was forbidden. Therefore all sex partners become forbidden unless they are so far out of the teenager's social and religious circle as to enable him to reassure himself that the new love object is indeed not his sister (or his mother). Many of the strange and unsuitable choices adolescents make, to the bewilderment and despair of their parents, are determined by some type of early seduction in the home.

How the parents respond to the Oedipal strivings of the child determines to an important extent what kind of teenager will develop. If a father ridicules or becomes angry or overbearing with Johnny when he announces he is going to marry Mommy as soon as he grows up, the child will feel mortified, helpless and full of rage. If, on the other hand, the father respects his son's tender feelings for his mother, and explains that some day he will have a wife of his own just as lovely as Mommy, then the child can move on to the next step in the solution of the problem in deciding to bide his time and meanwhile be just like his Daddy. Both parents must let the child know they understand and appreciate his feelings. They should assure him that when he is grown up he is going to have just what he wants and in the meantime they'll both love him and take care of him.

Teenagers whose pre-Oedipal and Oedipal problems were sympathetically and sensibly handled are able to achieve a gradual acceptance of body changes without anxiety, and an acceptance of psychological changes as well. They stand at the threshold of adulthood with a minimum of anxiety about being lovable and finding someone to love. They happily accept their sex role, feel a sense of exhilaration in their growing independence of their parents, with whom they ultimately become good friends, and are capable of falling deeply and enduringly in love with a compatible person of the opposite sex (although they may have temporary homosexual crushes in the early teens). The teenager's attitude towards the boys and girls and the men and women he approaches will be colored by the attitudes his parents instilled in him in his early childhood, and also, of course, by the parents' attitudes towards each other, which he has been observing and absorbing from an early age.

Since all of these enormously important early experiences are lost to memory after the age of five or six, people who are not familiar with the voluminous evidence proving beyond doubt the connection between these experiences and the behavior of the adolescent and adult will find it extraordinarily difficult to accept. It is hard to believe that events which one cannot even recall can be influencing one's behavior vitally and consistently. But psychoanalysis has taught us that in adolescence all the forgotten relationships and emotions of the past are re-lived in a second edition. Therefore if we want to understand the sex life and behavior of the teenager we first must be acquainted with his early childhood sex life and love relationships.

An ever increasing class of teenagers who merit special consideration in a discussion of the love life of adolescents are those whose parents have divorced (either legally or emotionally) in the early years of the child's life.

We know that the ability to achieve a healthy love life requires the love of two parents who love both the child and each other. Part of the child's expectations and beliefs as to what a love relationship between a man and woman should be is learned from observing the parents' behavior to each other and sensing their true feelings towards each other. In the normal home, children are expected to emulate their parents and to identify themselves with them. Resemblances to the parents, both physical and behavioral are a source of pleasure and pride to the parents. And as has been explained, the resolution of the Oedipal problem depends upon the ability of the child to make a sound identification with the parent of the same sex. In doing so, he finds peace within himself and gains the additional reward of his parents' approval, which strengthens his motivation to continue along this constructive line. Every child needs to be able to take his parents as models in order to develop soundly and securely. In the process of identification certain qualities of the parents are taken over unconsciously and made a permanent part of the child's personality. The parents' estimates of each other form an important part of the child's estimates of them.

How very difficult it is to safeguard these processes under circumstances of divorce. Too little, if indeed anything, has been written to enlighten divorcing parents on the child's unconscious identification with a parent who is despised or hated by the spouse. To reach adolescence with self-confidence and the capacity to love deeply, the child must be allowed to love, respect and idealize both parents. Every parent, divorced or not, has the sacred obligation to allow and encourage these processes in the child. Healthy character formation depends upon it.

All too tragically often in divorce cases, the parents are so immersed in their own unhappiness and bitterness as to be unable to think about the effects on the children. The child who listens to vilification of one parent by the other is torn in his loyalties and confused in his evaluation of both parents — the vilifier and the vilified. Resemblances to one parent bring displeasure to the other and there can be no sharing of love (which is the most important item in the child's life) or admiration for both parents. The child does not know whom or what to admire and emulate. He loses confidence in his parents' love for him, and he therefore loses confidence in himself and in the world. In these situations he learns too early that love is not to be depended upon, and his capacity to love and trust is thereby greatly diminished.

Divorced or unhappily married couples need to be helped to understand that when one tears down the other, a part of the child's character and personality is torn down, too, because the process of identification goes on unconsciously; the child will identify with the degraded parental image just as surely as he will identify with an admired parent.

A 13-year-old girl who was told by her embittered mother that her father liked only tramps, began to exhibit sexually delinquent behavior in an unconscious attempt to win her father's exclusive love. It was as if she were saying, "If Daddy only loves tramps, then I will have to be one in order to be loved best by him." A teenage boy can be attracted to delinquent girls through identifying with a father who is thus described.

It is vitally important that the parent who leaves the home (usually the father) continues to see the children regularly and frequently. When the mother prevents it, or the father loses interest, the children cannot develop normally. They feel abandoned by the father, and hatred is slowly aroused towards him. They hold the mother responsible for his loss (even when she is innocent) and begin to distrust and have feelings of hatred towards her, too. Since they at the same time love and need both parents, these children begin to feel guilty, inferior, full of self-hatred and eventually become convinced that they are completely unlovable.

A teenage girl, whose parents had been divorced when she was five, found it impossible to believe that any boy could love or admire her, because of her father's neglect of her from the time of the divorce. She had been very close to him in the early years, and his sudden loss of interest in her so deeply hurt and wounded her self-esteem that she was unable to have any regard for a boy who showed interest in her. She always developed crushes on boys who were not attracted to her. It was as if she were saying, "The really wonderful men, like the Daddy I knew until I was five, wouldn't have any use for me. If a boy likes me it only proves that he is inferior and not worth having."

A young teenage boy, whose father showed little or no interest in seeing him after a divorce when the boy was 7, began to feel that men were bad and worthless. As a result of this conviction, strengthened by the mother's openly displayed anger and disapproval of the father's behavior, he slowly developed a strong feminine identification, to the great detriment of his normal sexual development and interests.

If parents were enlightened sufficiently on these vital points, the abuse to which children of divorce are subjected might be greatly decreased. Insight and understanding bring about modifications in parental behavior. Criticism and exhortation serve no useful purpose because feelings are too intense to be kept under control unless there is a powerful incentive for so doing. Knowledge and insight provide these incentives for any reasonably normal parent.

Much has been written on the dangers of over-attachment to the mother (who nearly always has custody of the children) in divorce, so it will not be discussed here, except to say that such over-attachment creates difficulties for the adolescent who must be able to detach himself before he can find someone else to love.

We have examined the crucial experiences of the child up to 5 or 6 in the light of their influence upon teenage. The years from 6 to 11 or 12 are relatively quiet. The past is forgotten (repressed into the unconscious) and the child's energies are directed to learning intellectual and physical skills. He still lives very much within the bosom of the family. He has become comparatively sedate and at peace, and it is possible to educate him.

The physiological and psychological changes which puberty brings, with its attendant strong upsurge in sexual feelings and the need to adjust to a changing body, shatter the peace. Enter the adolescent, carrying within him an indelible record of his past. Typical behavior of adolescents has been so often and so well described that it would be pointless to duplicate it here. Suffice it to say that since the function of the adolescent level of development is to prepare the youngster for adulthood, all of the behavior typical of the period is in some way related to that function.

It is probably fair to state that parents are troubled most about the question of morals and the degree to which their teenagers engage in sexual activities; and that what is of deepest concern to the teenager is the struggle over masturbation and anxiety about sexual activity with the opposite sex.

Lecturing about moral standards and ethics to adolescents will not reach them in the way parents hope. Teenagers have the standards of their home, by and large, molded to a varying degree by individual experiences as described in the first part of this chapter. Added to that are concepts taken over from peers. Where the child has observed love, tenderness, consideration and devotion between the parents, he will not need to be told that these are the qualities which give the deepest meaning and fulfillment to a sexual relationship. He will have sensed it for a very long time. Conversely, where infidelity, coldness, seething resentments, incompatability and lack of mutual respect have marred a marriage, the children of such a union have a very different view of the relationship between the sexes. These children cannot have the same expectations and attitudes and ideals as the children of a happy home. Often, in revolt against such a home a youngster will become overly idealistic and straightlaced or overly agreeable, but these will be largely surface attitudes. Identifications with the unfortunate characteristics of parents will be firmly anchored in the unconscious, forcing the youngster to fight a continuing battle with himself. This will deplete his supply of energy, energy which should be at his disposal for the mastery of normal developmental tasks, skills and intellectual learning, accomplishments which play a vital role during adolescence in building enduring self-confidence.

Parents with unresolved guilt feelings about pre-marital sexual behavior of their own often become arbitrary and strict with their teenagers in an unconscious attempt to expiate their own guilt. In such situations resentment and rebellion are provoked in the teenager, who intuitively senses the insincerity of his parents. These youngsters usually see their parents as mean and out to spoil their fun. As a result they often resort to lying, evasions and subterfuges of all sorts.

Promiscuity is always a sign of deep emotional disturbance. It is not caused, as some parents seem to feel, by trusting children too much or giving them too much freedom and information about sex. It is the result of a disturbed home, from which a teenager emerges feeling unloved and then desperately seeks expressions of affection. It can also serve to express rebellion against the parents. It is well known that promiscuous youngsters derive very little, if any, pleasure from sexual activities. They use them as substitutes for the longed-for expressions of parental love and acceptance. However, sometimes a teenager, in desperately trying to break an overly strong attachment to a parent who is finding it difficult to allow the child to become independent, feels impelled to seek exaggerated forms of attachment in the outside world in order to emancipate himself.

In some cases, of course, the adolescent fails entirely to break the childhood love ties to parents and is then unable to find anyone outside the home to love. Needless to say, this too is a sign of deep emotional disturbance.

The normal teenager's sex life consists not only of kissing and caressing, but also of a certain amount of masturbation. Teenagers must gradually be able to shed the guilt feelings which usually accompany these activities if they are to achieve normal functioning in adult love life. Through these experiences the adolescent learns to know more about the deep and wide range of emotion and feeling of which he is capable. He develops an important awareness of himself thereby, which enlarges his self-confidence and makes him more fully aware of others.

The combined qualities of awareness, confidence and ability to love enable the young adult to develop a sense of responsibility, which in turn provides him with the capacity to make moral decisions appropriate to his age.

26.

"What can the parent of a troubled child do for the child and for himself?"
we asked Mr. Lourie.

×××××××××××××××××××××××

NORMAN V. LOURIE

Deputy Secretary, Pennsylvania
Department of Public Welfare

In this interview Mr. Lourie also discusses:

"What causes a child to feel troubled?"
    "Why do children want to please parents?"
        "Why do we blame others for our mistakes?"
"How does a child learn from his parents?"
    "How can parents help a child to be himself?"
        "What is the meaning of 'juvenile delinquency'?"
"Why is it important for the parent to look closely at himself?"

26.

This is what Mr. Lourie said when interviewed:

One of the most important acts of love a parent can perform for a child is to look at him as a person, an individual in his own right: "Who is he?" not, "Look what he does!"

But this is difficult for many of us because it is hard to take a good look at ourselves. For, to be able to see someone else, you must first be able to see yourself. To know what values, attitudes and expectations your child has, you must know what your own values, attitudes and expectations are for yourself.

At one time or another we all daydream, and there are few parents who have not envisioned what their children should be. Some would like their son to be President of the United States, others a second Babe Ruth, and for the daughter, another Florence Nightingale, or Madame Curie. But this has nothing to do with the child as a person: it is the parent's daydream.

Recently, I talked with a professional man who had two sons in college. One had just quit in his freshman year. After the father had talked for a while about *what* the boy had done and *how he himself felt,* not about how the boy must have felt, I said, "Did it ever occur to you that maybe you have a boy to whom college is not a reality?"

"My other boy is doing fine," he answered.

"You know," I said, "This boy might turn out to be a good plumber and be very, very happy at it."

"It's a hard thing for me to accept that," was the answer.

Where was the man's son in all of this? Obviously, to his father he was non-existent as a person, just a blurred image of a shattered expectation which had been based on values and attitudes the father himself possessed.

This father reminded me of a story written by André Malraux, the French writer. In one of his books he describes a situation where, in a group of assassins, one of them is sent out to commit murder. This man performs the murder, and on his way back to the others he thinks that, although he has just murdered a man, he will be congratulated. He will be liked, he'll be clapped on the back.

"But that really isn't me," the assassin says to himself. "I want to be liked for what I am, not for what I do. For I myself don't like what I do."

The point is simply that there is no child who doesn't want to meet the expectations of his parents. Let's take a fairly common occurrence, a bad report card. The parents have expected "A's." The child comes home with "C's," "D's," and "F's."

"You flunked! Damn it, you flunked!" says the parent furiously. "You've got to do better!"

But let's turn it around. The father has a job where he is working for someone else. He thinks he is doing the best he knows how. But something goes wrong. The boss calls him in and says, "You're no good. You messed it up. Go out there and do it right!"

But, has anyone helped him to do a better job? Has anyone pointed out to him what he did wrong? Is anyone wondering why he may not have done his work correctly? Furthermore, the boss acts as if the father wants to do a bad job, doesn't want his employer's good will or a raise.

If the parent can turn the situation around, no matter what the trouble with his child, and realize that all children want to do the best they can, and that all children want to be loved by and to please their parents, then there is the start of understanding and help.

It's Easy to Blame

If parents are aware of and accept their own feelings, they can have some awareness of their child's feelings. Parents are no different than other people. Adult and child alike can be angry, can hate, can love, can be joyful, and can feel close or not close in relationships.

But it is often difficult to accept our own feelings. We don't like our thoughts and actions on occasion, and it is so easy to "blame" someone or something else. However, blame is wasted on many situations. It produces nothing useful. We are human beings, and if we are civilized, mature adults we should learn to control our actions and accept and use our feelings for constructive purposes. But this is not always easy to do.

Now, the child needs help. But the child cannot be helped by the parent if that same parent has not accepted or understood his own humanness. For if he hasn't done this, he cannot accept his child's humanness.

Parents can't help getting angry at children. But they can help with the anger by explaining it to the child if it is unreasonable. Parents are often ashamed of behavior with their child. It helps to tell this to the child.

Discipline is necessary for children sometimes. For a parent who loves his child there is no need to feel guilty. An old maxim is that the only one who has a right to punish a child is the one who loves him.

What do we mean by the word "trouble?"

When a child is in "trouble" of some kind it means that the child has gone against one or more standards of society.

In every society from the most primitive to the most civilized, the growing-up process from birth to maturity is essentially the same, and in every society there has been some form of delinquency. Every society has standards that can be violated.

The human animal is born into the world as a primitive thing. It has little control over its movements. It has little control over bodily functions; it has very little control over its anger, and it reacts sharply to physical comfort and to emotional tones through feeling.

The process of growing up in any society is the process of becoming civilized according to the values and norms of that particular society. The infant who is born into the savage tribe in a jungle and the infant who is born into the most civilized state, each go through a process of learning what is expected of him in that society.

The child learns primarily and most importantly from his parents. If you have parents who do not accept the standards of the society, you may very likely have children who do not accept them, either. If you have angry parents, you very likely will have children who are angry. If the parent hates, the child will learn this also. And if you have parents who love — and love themselves — you very likely will have children who love — and love themselves.

For to love yourself, to accept yourself as a human being, means to have a sense of worth about yourself. And a child "in trouble," whatever this "trouble" may be, is a child who is usually expressing, among other things, a feeling of self-worthlessness.

So many of us think that when we use the words "juvenile delinquent" we are describing a child. We are not.

A child is unhappy. He may withdraw from the world; he may become aggressive, "strange," or he may become what many call a "juvenile delinquent." But the acts of delinquency which he performs are merely symptoms of what is bothering a child.

The public holds attitudes about delinquency, and has visions about what a juvenile delinquent is, in terms of newspaper headlines. Actually, juvenile delinquency and the term "juvenile delinquent" are social and legal terms. When I think of children who commit delinquent acts, I think of the child and what has made him do what he has done.

I think we ought to get rid of these social and legal terms and start talking about the children and the love they need, rather than the acts which are merely symptoms of unhappiness.

In conclusion, a parent with a troubled child can do a number of things for that child, and for himself. First, the parent can take a good look at himself. What are his values, attitudes, and expectations for himself? Does he accept his own feelings as a human animal? Then, the parent can take a good look at the child, not only what he does but rather, "Who is this person, my child?" Possibly, the "trouble" might be with the parent's self-centered expectations rather than the child's behavior.

In other words, look at yourself for what you are, look at the child for what he or she is, and if you can understand and accept what the child is, then you can help him to help himself be himself.

27.

"What do a man's children need most from him?" we asked Dr. Scheidlinger.

NNNNNNNNNNNNNNNNNNNNN

SAUL SCHEIDLINGER, Ph.D.

Consultant In Group Therapy,
Community Service Society of New York City

In this interview, Dr. Scheidlinger also discusses:

"Can a father be a 'pal' to his children?"
  "Do fathers have to remain sexually 'good' to the child?"
    "What does authority mean to the child?"
"How many 'people' must a father be?"
  "Why must a child learn to control himself?"
      "How do children identify with the parent of the same sex?"
"Do children imitate the destructive as well as the constructive in their parents?"

SAUL SCHEIDLINGER, PH.D.

27.

This is what Dr. Scheidlinger said when interviewed in his office:

A little boy was trying to tell me about the first time he had seen his father drunk. He had been terribly frightened, but not because the father did anything "hurtful" to him. On the contrary, the father had laughed, giggled, talked baby-talk and danced around the room. The father evidently had been happy.

What had frightened the little boy? Simply, in the child's eyes, the father now also became a child. Here was a supremely important person on whom the little boy was supposed to depend as being strong and protecting, but who had lost self-control and was now like a child.

The need of young children and adolescents to have the adult remain the adult in all circumstances is of vital importance. In connection with this need of children there has recently been a tremendous emphasis on the importance of the mother, particularly in the early years. But what has been forgotten, I think, is the importance of the role of the father.

For most men, the amount of time spent in the home as a father is much less than the amount of time spent outside the home as the breadwinner. Thus, the idea has developed in many a home that the father might as well do only pleasant things with the children.

"Let mother be the one who takes care of them," he says, his wife agreeing. "Let her take the responsibility for discipline and guidance," they both may add, and what often happens is that father becomes chiefly a playmate.

THE FATHER'S MANY ROLES

We are all like actors upon a stage, in a sense. But the stage is life, and we are real. Each day, from the time we

274

wake until we sleep, we play many different roles in that particular theatre which is ours. Most of us role-play without conscious effort. We glide from being a lover, a companion and friend to our wife (and there you have at least three roles with one person) to our business and work scenes where we become a "different" person, and then to the poker and bridge table, or to the tennis court and baseball field.

In each case, our attitudes, feelings and actions are suited to the specific situation. The same is true of being a father. He must be "different" people to his children yet always be the "same" person.

The first role of the father in the family is the traditional one of being the economic support. Secondly, and just as traditionally, the father is the symbol of authority and protection. Thirdly, he is the source of male sexual identity for the boy, and male sexuality for the girl to learn to deal with as a female. And finally, along with the mother, he is the fountain from which moral and ethical concepts flow for the youngster.

It was not so long ago that most work occurred in and around the home. On the farms children were exposed to the day-by-day example of father's work and mother's work. The two were separate for the most part. To the child, daddy did certain things, mommy other things.

This has changed greatly in two ways. Women not only work and make money in many families, but the father's work is now invariably far away from home and a mystery to the child who does not see what his father does. Father comes home looking exactly the way he left in the morning, and the child's idea of the value of work as a contribution to one's self-fulfillment, as well as a contribution to the family and society, is lost.

The other role which was traditionally important but which is also changing, is that of the father as the symbol of authority and protection. By authority I do not mean the man with the big stick, the man who says children must be seen but not heard. For, what is the essential meaning of "authority" to a child?

Primarily, from the child's point of view he needs and wants to have authoritative protection against his own impulses. He needs to feel that if his own impulses get the better of him, the father and the mother will help him control himself.

Controls, protection, and authority are very much related. This is the way a child builds what has been called "controls from within." This is how he or she grows up, and it cannot be emphasized too much. It is vital to the basic mental health of the individual for both present and future.

With a young child you can see this process build up in a most dramatic and graphic way. At first, you can see the child say in effect, "I want to do this." (The "this" can be anything, and usually is.) What happens next?

When he attempts to do what he wants, if it is harmful to him, the mother and father tell him in various ways that he can't, he is not to do it. Thus, first he learns what he must not do when the mother and father are present.

But soon the child is saying to himself, whether or not the parents are present, "I want to do this but Mommy and Daddy say I can't." So, he doesn't, although he still wants to.

What eventually happens to all of us, if we are to get along in society and with ourselves, is that we no longer need to say anything to ourselves. The authority, the demands, the values, the expectations of mother and father have become what is called, in plain language, a conscience.

But throughout a young person's life, and even beyond adolescence, the external figure of the parent is still very much needed to reinforce the growing controls from within.

The third role of the father mentioned previously was male sexual identity and female learning. I once had a mother consult me about a six-year-old's temper tantrums. They were very severe, but otherwise the child appeared to be functioning well. It didn't take long to discover that the father had a tendency to vile temper also.

The child was doing what he was supposed to do, although self-destructively in this case. We imitate the good and the bad. This young boy was identifying with his father. It was his way of perceiving how to be a man, how to grow from a little boy into manhood. From his point of view, a man asserted himself by having temper tantrums.

In this case, I could do nothing about the father's temper. The only solution was for him to have his "tantrums" away from the child. He eventually managed to do this for the most part, and the temper outbursts in the child gradually stopped.

In the same way and by the same process of identification and imitation, the little boy gets from his father his sense of pride, of harmony and of being at peace with manhood. If you but listen, you can often hear your child using your phrases and gestures, and copying your acts. This occurs in little as well as big things as the child tries himself out. The little boy eventually picks up his father's razor and says, "Now I'm daddy." Or, he lifts the briefcase and says, "I'm going to work like daddy." Or, "Mommy, I'm going to marry you."

This identification with the parent of the same sex is a basic psychological process in growing up. But, just as important, the father has an equally vital role with his daughter. How does the little girl try for the first time to find out what it is like to relate to a being of the other sex? How does she for the first time experience a relationship with a male?

The father is the first male a girl encounters in her life, and it is through this contact that women experience the first emotions and feelings of the relationship between the sexes.

The last area in which the father plays an essential role is as the carrier of moral and ethical values. You might say he is God's and society's representative in the home. But in our world, our whole society is one of conflicting moral and ethical values. Our ideals, as we speak of them, are often quite different than our actual desires and actions. In a sense, this is the most complicated and difficult role the father must play.

For this conflict of values and standards is one of the dilemmas of our time, and there is no complete answer to it, at least from the individual's point of view. But the very young child needs a sense of consistency and needs to see harmony in the home. The same is true of the adolescent, although the adolescent has achieved a certain strength and can safely take a supervised look at the world, with its weaknesses and inequalities.

With this concept of the different roles the father plays

with his son or daughter — economic support and work; au
thority; protection and controls; sexual identity and learn
ing; morals and ethics — we can talk about the father who
wants to be the playmate, the pal. Why can't he be?

First of all, he can and should be a pal, if we mean hav
ing all types of fun together. But if this means the forgetting
of the adult roles of teacher and guardian while having
fun, then the so-called fun becomes destructive for the child
as well as for the father.

What we are talking about here does not relate to what
the father and son, or father and daughter, actually do.
They may be playing with toy railroads or kites, throwing a
baseball or engaging in any number of activities, some cooperative, where the father and child work together, others
competitive. It doesn't matter what they do. It is the parent's attitudes and feelings about the activity that are crucial.

Let us say that a father and his three-year-old son have
worked together for an hour on the beach building a sand
castle. The father turns his back for a moment, and the boy
smashes everything down. Now, the father can react in a way
which says, "*I've* put an hour's worth of work into this and
he destroys it."

Or, if the father understands that here is a three-year-old
who is asserting himself against something they both built,
the father will be pleased that his son wants to be an individual apart from him. Also he realizes the young boy is
learning to get rid of angry emotions in a way that does not
hurt anybody else, and in a way in which he, the father, is
not destroyed or criticized.

Think of the last time you saw fathers and sons playing
baseball, football or tennis with each other. For many it was
good fun, for those fathers who remembered their various
roles as fathers, but there were also some who argued angrily
about the play, who got excited beyond the value of the
game to them as adults, and in general behaved much like
the children.

A Number of Reasons

I have said it doesn't matter what fathers and sons do, but
that it is the father's attitude and feelings about the activity
which are crucial.

When the boy reaches adolescence, the father often wants to help him unravel the mysteries of sex. But if the father himself is insecure, guilty, or clumsy in regard to this part of life, he may take one of two similar roads, possibly both.

He may start to tell risqué and obscene jokes to his son, or he may even attempt to push him to find and act out his first initiation into a sexual relationship. The adolescent becomes very disturbed by either of these things because the still-young man needs to have his father and mother, and his teacher, remain ideally "good" persons with whom to identify. In other words, by such actions the father destroys himself as a father in his son's eyes.

Either one of these acts also may seriously disturb the adolescent's still-growing knowledge and acceptance of his father's and mother's sexual relationship.

When a father plays the mistaken role of the pal, forgetting the real roles of fatherhood, there may be a number of reasons. It may be that he is counteracting something that happened to him as a child. His parents might have been overly strict, and he has decided not to be so with his child.

Another motivation may be that to certain men it is much harder to play the adult role. If you just play with and kid around with your boy, you don't have to make decisions, and therefore you don't have to take responsibilities. "Let mother do it," these men say in effect. "Let her be the responsible one."

This is running away from the present, and wishing for the past when they themselves were children. This type of father will often get involved in little conspiracies with his children. "We'll do it," the father whispers. "But we won't tell Mommy."

Here, he is being one of the kids and the mother is the grownup. For the moment, the child will like the father. But when he becomes older and realizes that his father is nothing but a pal — another child — he will be afraid, unhappy, and not know where to turn for the strong teacher and leader he still needs.

In summary, it will be an impoverished father-son, father-daughter, relationship where the father does not fulfill his roles as an adult.

28.

"Should a parent appear nude before his children?" we asked Dr. Lorand.

SANDOR LORAND, M.D.

Honorary President of the
Psychoanalytic Association of New York

In this interview Dr. Lorand also discusses:

"Are children always curious about sex?"
  "What are some of the sexual desires and needs of the child?"
    "Is some frustration of sexual curiosity necessary to a child?"
"Why do some men exhibit themselves genitally?"
  "Why do some women think of themselves as 'injured' people?"
    "What do some men attempt to prove in looking at the naked female?"
"Can we defy conventions and not have guilt?"

SANDOR LORAND, M.D.

28.

This is what Dr. Lorand said when interviewed in his office:

Most believers in nudism think that when a child can "see" many naked men and women, or just the mother and father in the nude, he will be prevented from having many sexual difficulties in childhood and when an adult.

They think the child's natural curiosity with regard to the difference in sexes will be satisfied, and all his later problems regarding sexuality will be solved. But appearing naked in front of children, or allowing children to walk around naked, does not help the child to be free from neurosis and from a warped mental attitude regarding sexuality. Experiences — both of psychoanalysis and observations in general — show that even if a child learns, from early infancy on, the difference between the sexes, his curiosity in other problems of sexuality will not be eliminated, and later sexual disturbances may still develop.

The sexual reality of the adult is a world apart from the sexual aim of the child. No matter how free the atmosphere, the child's speculations and conflicts about sexual matters will develop regardless. Because the child cannot, and will not, escape attachment to his parents and the frustrations which must necessarily follow.

In other words, if the child "sees" the naked body, there will still be the mystery of "How does the baby get in? How does it grow in the woman? How does it come out?"

The child's curiosity in sexual matters will never cease nor will he be satisfied with merely seeing. It is advantageous to his development if this healthy and normal curiosity is maintained. The child's ever-curious and exploring tendencies will create many problems for him even though he already knows the differences between the sexes, and if he will be

permitted to see, he will want to see more. Then he will
want to handle and do things himself.

The child wants to discover, to touch, smell, feel and act.
Should the parent gratify the child's wish to see the naked
body and then, to explain more fully, have sexual intercourse before the child as a demonstration? And then what?
This line of reasoning may even lead to incest.

Actually, the parent who parades nude in front of the child
is unconsciously seducing the child. The manner in which
the nudist parent tries to solve the question of sex for the
child is dubious.

If the mysteries of sex are explained to the child, it is certain he will create other mysteries from which he himself
will want to lift the veil and thus find out in his own way
and manner of thinking and fantasying, what he wants to
know. This working of the child's mind is very important. It
is important for the child to be curious and to form his own
conclusions regarding the sexual mysteries, because it may
be the first attempt to develop the feeling of independence.

I recall a girl of sixteen and her brother of eleven whose
father was a doctor. At the request of the father, I saw the
girl, who had a slight tic and general "nervous habits," as
the father called them. The little boy, whom I also saw, was
moody, "shut-in," and neglected his school work. His problem was masturbation which he consciously and intelligently
tried to control but could not. His parents were aware of
this practice; his mother would discuss it with him and
frightened him by pointing out the possible evil consequences.

The girl was well developed for her age, both physically
and mentally. She indulged in friendly relationships with boys,
of which her parents were aware, and she even planned to
marry one young man she knew. What the parents did not
know, however, was that in their absence, she entertained
boys at home, one in particular, and had petting parties
which usually ended in both of them undressing completely,
going to bed and lying close to each other. There had never
been any intercourse. The boy, who was twenty, would
achieve sexual gratification. The girl was not at all interested in further contact. The primary reason for her actions,
according to her own statement, was that she knew the boys

enjoyed these intimacies. It was she who would start to undress.

During the time I saw her, she became engaged to a man who was many years her senior. She planned to postpone the marriage for a few years; it was important for her to be engaged in order to be admired and envied by her girl friends. She continued to indulge the practice of being together in the nude with her original boy friend without the knowledge of members of the family.

The attitude and behavior of the boy and the girl were easily traceable to the action situation which was then taking place and which had been going on in the family for a few years. One day the mother came to my office in a panicky state, accusing herself of the part she played in the boy's masturbatory activities. She was very much upset about it because she felt that she had done something wrong. She explained that, for a number of years, she and the children had been accustomed to spend time nude in their summer home. Her husband, who came out only on week-ends, did not participate in their nudist activities.

It was impossible to go into particulars with the girl about her feelings in the matter of nudism because she always avoided the subject by referring to her artistic interests (she was attending art school). The little boy, however, frankly admitted that his masturbatory fantasies always centered around his mother and sister whom he saw and visualized in the nude. The practice of walking around nude in the house had been in effect since the children were small.

In summary, in the child's world, there must always be frustration. In fact, there is not a world conceivable, whether in childhood or adulthood, where mystery and frustration can be eliminated.

THE CASTRATION COMPLEX

Love and resentment, fear, feelings of guilt, are all connected with the frustrations that must occur in everyone's life as he grows up and becomes educated to life. And these frustrations make for emotional tension which eventually results in "the castration complex."

How strong this complex is determines how much someone will want to exhibit his body or look at the nude bodies of others later in life. The reason for a man exhibiting himself in the nude is the constant need to deny his fear about castration. The male exhibitionist, and a nudist is an exhibitionist, is showing his possession of a penis to the whole world, emphasizing, in this way, the masculinity he is so very afraid of losing. In a deeper sense, by exhibiting himself, he encourages others to the same end, especially women, thus proving the difference between them sexually, and emphasizing his masculinity more than ever.

Also, the wish to have the woman exhibit herself contains the hidden desire to find the phallus which he desires to see on her in order to free himself of his own castration anxiety. (All children imagine both their parents, mother and father, have the coveted phallus.)

In woman, the aim of genital exhibitionism is quite rare. Instead, women exhibit various portions of the body, or the entire body, as an object of admiration. The genitals are covered, for women do not like to be reminded they do not have a phallus. Therefore they overemphasize the other parts of the body, or the body as a whole, to avoid being reminded of their "injury."

Sexual pleasure will be derived by the woman from the power which her body can exercise in attracting the male. In an indirect manner, while she may not actually enjoy sexual intercourse itself, she will enjoy the sexual relationship inasmuch as it means weakening the (male) partner, thus showing herself to be the stronger in sex.

In the male the sexual pleasure derived through exhibiting himself will center around the pride in possessing a phallus. He will emphasize this sign of masculinity to his partner. In the sexual relationship, he will derive pleasure by impressing his (female) partner with his masculinity, gratifying himself in seducing her.

Women are far less inclined than males to want to see the nude body (there are no women Peeping Toms, for instance). Wanting to "see" would mean the woman is reminded of the absence of a phallus in herself, which reminder she desires to avoid.

Wanting to look at the nude body is a natural childish wish, an expression of normal curiosity. But when an adult continues to have this wish so strongly that he receives sexual gratification from looking, rather than genital sex, it is easy to see he has held on to this childhood instinct and magnified it to a far greater degree than it deserves in adult life. This is what is called a "fixation" to an earlier stage of development.

To some extent the practice of nudism does have a beneficial effect on the minds and body of those who take part in it because their sexual tension achieves an outlet in the regressive manner which was the regular channel of gratification in childhood and which remains, to an extent, in the grownup. The sexual tension will be satisfied by seeing and being seen, and thus complete frustration will be prevented.

Psychoanalytic study and experience has shown that those persons who derive sexual gratification chiefly through exhibiting themselves or looking at others, are persons entirely dependent on the preliminaries of sex which, normally, serve merely to heighten the sexual tension. The component drives — seeing and being seen — become the main channel of their sexual gratification.

The nudist, however, will always feel guilty because his practice is not accepted by society and, therefore, he defies convention. Despite the partially beneficial effect in the release of sexual tension for the nudist, permanent and curative results, such as the cure of frigidity and impotence, will certainly not be achieved. The bathing suit, or its absence, cannot be considered crucial in the solution of neurosis or sexual problems.

It is the right of everyone to seek his salvation in the best suitable manner. However, at such times as this when sexual morality hardly permits exposure in private and tries to impose laws for one's sexual attitude and behavior, it is impossible to defy these social laws without adding to the complexity of the whole question.

There is no final evidence concerning the harm of nudism. But the basic structure of social life cannot be reformed by changing one phase of it. Too much indulgence of the instincts and too little repression may complicate the instinctual and emotional development of the child, just as too much repression may create morbid changes in the sensitive psyche.

29.

"Do parents have mixed feelings about children?" we asked Dr. Hulse. "If so, to what extent are these feelings sexual?"

XXXXXXXXXXXXXXXXXXXXXXX

WILFRED C. HULSE, M.D. (1901-1962)

Chief, Psychiatric Staff, Foster Care Division,
Bureau of Child Welfare, City of New York

In this interview, Dr. Hulse also discusses:

"Are mixed feelings about children natural?"
    "Do children ever seduce adults?"
        "What are some of the primitive feelings of children?"
"When an adult constantly teases a child what is he really doing?"
    "Why do children always want to touch others?"
        "Should a parent ever spank a child?"
"What is the meaning of 'pan-sexual'?"
    "Must we accept our savage feelings?"
        "Why are some parents undisciplined?"

WILFRED C. HULSE, M.D.

29.

This is what Dr. Hulse said when interviewed in his office:

All of us are composed of mixed feelings. So we cannot be very astonished if children arouse in us some of these mixed feelings. Having a child is a blessing, but it is never a complete blessing.

The child, especially the newborn child, is not really a good companion. It's no companion at all. It's a savage little thing that gives nothing and needs a lot for itself, with impulses and uncontrolled feelings that are selfish. It doesn't really care about anybody else.

All the concepts of how cute a little baby is are the parents' projection. They imagine, while the mother is pregnant, how the baby will later look and act and what he will say. But when the child is there, and even before, they also have feelings that are not so attractive.

But the attractive and unattractive feelings are very understandable psychological entanglements between the parent and the child. The experience of a patient of mine illustrates this point. He was a man who had had a very unhappy childhood. He had a mentally ill mother and his father, a man who struggled hard to support his family, although never making much money, died early and left this psychotic woman in the care of her sixteen-year-old son, an only child. For a few years they were absolutely destitute and he endured bitter poverty in his late twenties and thirties.

But he pulled himself out and now is a successful and a rather prominent man. He has a good income and a position of prestige in the community. He is married and has several children. His oldest son, who is very bright and well-adjusted, goes to a large college and wants to study medicine. He gets high marks in college and recently in his second year, on his summer vacation got himself a position as a hospital attendant, wanting to learn in advance about operating rooms and hospital life.

But his father has tremendous conflicts. He wants to be a good father but memory of his own childhood is strong and he feels that once again he is being exploited. First he was taken advantage of by his parents, who expected him to take care of everything, and left him destitute, and now he is exploited by his children, who want to use all his money for their education and leave him again destitute.

He is his late forties but he is thinking of his old age and wants to accumulate security, so great his fear of poverty. He worked hard to get through college and post-graduate school and his wife also struggled to put herself through college. Now the children expect him to send them to college and one son to medical school; he wants to send them, but he does not like their taking it for granted that he will. He feels no one is thinking of *his* needs and *his* pleasures, of his struggle to get ahead when he was young. His children have it far better than he ever had and take it for granted that certain opportunities are automatically open to them. You can understand his feelings of conflict.

Parents, even good parents, have both feelings towards children, the positive one, "I want to help, I love my child," and the negative one, "I hate him because he deprives me of certain pleasures," In the above case, the father also feels that in the end, he will depend financially on his son. As a doctor, his son will make more money than he ever dreamed of making, and he does not relish this feeling of dependence.

DISCIPLINE AND PUNISHMENT

Another psychological problem is the defiance of parental authority. There arises the question of what in our present language parents and teachers call "discipline," which, in my opinion, has nothing to do with discipline. I would call it punishment. For me, discipline is something different. It is an integrated concept of organized living. Discipline is something that the child learns from the parent because the parent is disciplined. Parents give discipline to their children not by being angry, but by living in an organized fashion. The child then learns to discipline himself, which means he realizes that his savage drives cannot be always gratified. Once in a while, yes, but not always.

In many cases, we are dealing with parents who are un-disciplined themselves but want to enforce on their children a discpline which they do not have themselves. This results in punishment. The parents themselves are antagonistic to the authorities that have parental status in our society — employers, government, church, whoever. These groups are actually defied by the parent, and then the parent wonders why the child defies him.

A certain amount of defiance is necessary to a growing child. I think a child who completely gives in to the parent on every issue without protest is not learning the struggle in life, a struggle in which all of us have to assert ourselves. Good parents want a strong child, a child who strives, one who heads toward definite goals and achievements.

But some parents block the child from certain goals, wanting him to give them up. They assume the child is always wrong and they are always right. Children, especially in adolescence where this problem of defiance is most prominent, have a need, in order to become well-adjusted, to defend certain of their strivings, even if the parental authority objects to them.

Conflict with parental authority in adolescence may be a good thing for the child, and the parent should not try to eradicate it completely. There should be an effort by the parents to compromise and not fall into such perennial attitudes as "youth is worthless" or "when we were young everything was fine and upright and good but today the young people are going to pieces."

I happened to read a quotation from a wall in an Egyptian temple, written 4,000 years ago, in which a priest wrote that the world was going to pieces because children don't obey their parents any more, use bad language and behave rudely. But the world is still with us.

Today the feelings parents have about children are very much the same as 4,000 years ago. All parents have to do is realize that while one should not deny these feelings, he should control them.

Let's put it another way. Let's assume a married man with children hires a secretary who attracts him very much. Or he has a feminine client, someone he sees frequently when he is alone, whom he starts to like very much. Is he going to dismiss his secretary, or refuse to see his client, just because she is an attractive person?

I think he has to face the fact that he will have such feelings when such a woman is near. Why shouldn't an attractive woman arouse him? He should realize he is tempted and that he will control his temptation. That is how we all have to live anyway. We don't steal, even though we would like to get certain things at times.

Many things tempt me but I don't do them because I have learned that between my feelings and desires and my social behavior, there has to be a difference. The difference has to be bridged by my adjustment and maturity, by my ability to control socially unpermissible drives.

I've had to keep myself from saying, as many parents do to their children, "I will kill you," or "You are killing me." Children do arouse violent feelings but there is no need to hurl that violence at them if one is mature.

This brings us to the topic of corporal punishment, in which we physically strike the child when we are aroused and angered. This very often has less relationship to what the child has really done than to how the adult feels. One does not feel like hitting a child when one is calm.

It is obvious that whoever is aroused and enraged cannot be very just. This is by definition not possible. In my opinion, corporal punishment is never justified because it is not necessary. It only serves the purpose of the parent, not of the child. If there is a good relationship between child and parent, things can be straightened out without corporal punishment. If the relationship is poor, beatings won't help anyway.

I never punished my daughter corporally and when she was in her teens, we once talked about punishment. I said to her, I never punished you by spanking. She said she had never thought about it, but now that she did, she realized I had never spanked her. It was interesting that she had not even been aware of it.

Children do not need corporal punishment. Since it is mainly an outlet for the parent's feelings, the latter should either control his anger or find some better outlet. It is never fair to the child because he is not physically able to defend himself. It would be much worse if he were, because then he would be tempted to retaliate and might physically defeat the parent. In our society this would be very dangerous, for it would mean a breakdown in the relationship between child and parent.

The child should also not be encouraged to use violence and should learn to control his feelings. We want the child to learn this control, yet how can he if his parents cannot control their own feelings? There is such obvious conflict in what we preach and what we do.

Parents are taking advantage of the child if they do not control their feelings toward the child and regulate them on a realistic level. For the child is in a position of depending on the reasonableness of parents. He is not equal to the father and mother. Parents should be aware of the responsibility that their parental status imposes on them, just as the teacher should be aware of the teacher status. If a child says to me, "Drop dead," and this has happened in psychiatric practice, I am not entitled to retaliate on the level of this childish undisciplined behavior. But many parents do just this.

Some actually believe that the child's voice may be heard by God or by whoever has authority over life and death in their opinion, and they will be killed just because the child wishes them dead. That's obvious nonsense. The child need not feel guilty, because his wish will not kill a parent.

Some parents may not go as far as saying, "Drop dead," to the child, but the child feels that his parent wishes him out of the way, á la Hansel and Gretel who were sent to the woods by parents who did not want them and consigned them to the witches and wild animals.

Parents say to children, "I will kill you if you do this again," and assume the child thinks this is a joke. But look at the face of the parent and you will see why the child does not think it such a joke.

REACTION AND SEXUALITY

When you touch a baby, he reacts, and then you react to him. We may be reluctant to admit that when we react, sexuality is involved in every one of our reactions. We like and dislike people, we are attracted and repulsed by people, and a feeling of sexuality lies at the bottom of both love and hate.

To parents who feel horrified by these sexual feelings aroused by a child, I would say: be aware of these feelings and do not be horrified by them. You can control them.

We have all been brought up to control ourselves; as we grow up, we become more and more controlled. One way we control our feelings with adults is to keep our distance. Most of our relationships are based on listening to each other and seeing each other, rather than being close to and touching each other. But with children this is not so. In our relationship to a baby or toddler, touching each other, smelling each other, feeling each other and mouthing each other are much more prominent than in adult life.

I base this comment on a recent study about blind children which I have just made. If there is no sight, the close-range relationship, or direct physical contact, becomes an important lead toward emotional contact.

Most adults put a distance between themselves and others, and this somehow relieves the sexuality which may be present. But as soon as we return to the primitive level in which animals relate to each other, mainly by physical contact, by smelling each other or by mouthing each other, we can see how much this contributes to erotization. Such erotization exists in the contact between mother and child, between everybody and the young child, because the young child is continually seeking physical contact.

Therefore, adults get aroused and are returned to the pan-sexual, undifferentiated feelings of their own childhood as soon as they have contact with the child. I will explain what I mean by "pan-sexual."

One of the great discoveries of psychoanalysis (I think the literary writers detected it first) is that a child is not without sexual feelings. And they are very strong feelings. But they are not what we call object-directed as in adults, for in the process of growing up, sexual feelings focus on one man or a number of men, or one woman or a number of women.

But for the child, as for the animal, everything is sexual if the mood is there. Animals, as you know, are in heat or not in heat. You know what a dog does with your leg if the dog is in heat. The dog doesn't really care for the object which he "loves"; any object that is mechanically usable will do.

So it is to a large extent with children. Masturbation in children is a common thing and why does it become so? Because no object is really necessary for a masturbatory act. If older children or adults masturbate, they usually have a fantasy object, someone whom they imagine they are loving. But younger children don't need that. Their sexuality is not object-directed. This is what I call pan-sexualism: everything can be sexualized.

For instance, a young baby gets an erection when he is handled and sometimes when he isn't handled. It might come from the diaper or something else. Now this might arouse the one who handles him, the nurse or the mother or father, if they are not prepared for such a feeling. It is amazing how little people are prepared to face a naked child and the unorganized feelings of the young child. They become shaken up by the experience.

Then they defend themselves, and what is the defense against? Very often they unconsciously accuse the child of being the seducer. Actually, you know, the child is a seducer. Every child is a seducer. It is the adult who has to protect himself and has to protect the child, also.

So if the parent gets angry because he is not controlling his own feelings when the child arouses him, then the parent is apt to develop a good deal of hostility. We have seen this in the parents of blind children who develop an enormous amount of negative feelings against blind children who are apt to act savagely and uncontrolled, who need, because they cannot see, their mouth, their hands, their whole body, for clinging, for continuous attachment. The parent is frightened, for as a child he was, against his own will, taught to give up this need. Now he sees his own child not wanting to give it up.

But this happened so many years ago that it has been "forgotten" by parents (or, as we say, "repressed"). When suddenly they are reminded of it, when their feelings come out of the unconscious, they become very, very ambivalent (caught in the grip of opposite feelings) and sometimes angry at the one who arouses these feelings.

ANGER, TEASING AND DISTANCE

One way they immediately put distance between themselves and the child is to become angry. I think that distance is the protective agent in our social structure, protecting us against anger aroused by too much uncontrolled closeness. This is especially so if the object is one which our society prohibits as the object of our sexual fantasies. I am quite sure that many people are gruff and hostile and haughty because they are attracted more than they can bear. Then they go the other extreme of rejection.

I think the woman we call a teaser (a man may be a teaser, also) is a person who is terribly attracted to others. The teasers want to arouse others, and themselves too, because this is pleasurable, but at the moment when it would turn into something serious, they get so frightened that they break it off. Then the "victim" feels betrayed.

Just in this way, adults tease children. Such interplay is frequently found between adults and children. The one who is teased is actually the object of hostility. For him, to be teased is a hostile act. It is as though he were offered candy and then not given the candy which was dangled before his eyes.

Take the mother or father who hugs, kisses and caresses the child excessively. When the child responds, which a child normally does, the parent then withdraws in anger. He is amazed because the child actually took the first part of the seductive play for the real thing. The grownup does not realize he has aroused the child's primitive feelings. This is what some do to a dog or other animal when they tickle him until he becomes very excited and then throw him out. What is the poor animal to do? He feels very angry.

There is a sexual core in all hugging and kissing of children. In parents it is well covered, well socialized, by what they have learned as they became mature. But the child is not mature. So, the mature person must take the responsibility of knowing how far he can go, and when to stop arousing primitive feelings in the immature person who has not yet been able to express his feelings acceptably.

The child is in the process of increasingly sublimating or channeling very primitive feelings into the socially acceptable feelings of adulthood. Instead of running wild with fury, the adult composes a very exciting piece of music or writes a poem in which the fury comes out. Then, he is again a social individual, and in the meantime may have produced a beautiful poem or piece of music.

But the child cannot produce beautiful music or poems. The child does not have at his disposal the organizing powers of the mature personality. The adult is a workman who has been trained to use many tools to create a better and better product. The child is clumsy with the same tools and may not even know some of the tools he possesses. It's a long process by which he becomes acquainted with them and learns to use them well.

THE FEELING AND THE ACT

Parents do not have to like everything they feel, only to control the expression of the feelings. Civilized, well-adjusted human beings cannot possibly like all their feelings. They should recognize that the savage animal, as it was represented by the baby, still remains in part within them. But if they are reasonable people, it is well under control.

Reason tells us that we have feelings in us which are not acceptable in terms of action but this does not mean that they cannot be acceptable in terms of feeling. In many respects, the morality of our present approach in child psychiatry is very much a return to certain Biblical concepts of conduct. But there's one very basic difference.

While the Commandments say that you should not *feel* this way, we say, we can't help but feel this way because that is how a human being is organized, but we cannot *act* this way. Our prohibition is that we act according to reason, although we realize that feelings may often not be reasonable. And we try to accept the fact that we are sometimes unreasonable in our feelings. We may not like it, but it is so. We accept the feelings — those that Freud called the "id," the savage core of our animal past — as being still with us and necessary to us, at the same time realizing we cannot always act on them.

We can wish we had no savage feelings, but in certain situations, such as the full enjoyment of sex, savage feelings are a necessary part. If we found ourselves without the savage and violent feelings in certain instances, our lives would be very poor and deprived.

For, without these feelings, how would we enjoy violent music, or painting, or acting? Or how could we laugh at the silliest slapstick comedy, in which actually a lot of violence appears? I do not restrain myself from laughing at such violence, but I wouldn't go around and slap people, even though I might occasionally feel like it.

In all creativity, in all physical processes, violent feelings are necessary. I think that all creativity deals with certain feelings of violence and develops from the conflict between, on the one hand, awareness of violence, and on the other hand, the organizing power which channelizes violence.

I think that in the next ten or fifteen years, we will see more research and some reliable findings about what happens in the creative process in all fields. I believe, that violence is part of all creativity and that we should not try to eradicate it in children, but help the child to compromise, to control it. If we make the child repress his violence completely and push it down too far, we will not have a creative adult in the years to come.

30.

"Do accidents just happen to children?"
we asked Dr. Spotnitz.

xxxxxxxxxxxxxxxxxxxxx

HYMAN SPOTNITZ, M.D.

Fellow, American Psychiatric Association

In this interview, Dr. Spotnitz also discusses:

"Why is love so important in marriage?"
   "Do love and hate always go together?"
      "Is it possible to love everybody?"
"Do families have definite patterns of behavior?"
   "Are aggression and accidents related?"
      "What are the disadvantages of corporal punishment?"
"Must frustration and gratification be balanced?"
   "Is the over-protected child healthier than the neglected child?"
      "May colds and cancer be caused by anger and hate?"

30.

This is what Dr. Spotnitz said when interviewed in his office:

When I was an intern at a large metropolitan hospital many years ago, I recorded the following family history related by a mother who wanted us to admit her twenty-eight-year-old daughter as a patient.

The daughter was the third of her three children. The mother had married a man whom she had quickly come to hate, but for a number of reasons she had found it impossible to leave him.

The first child she had with this man was only a few months old when it developed pneumonia and died. A few years later, the second child was sleeping in bed with the mother when she accidentally turned over and suffocated the child to death. The third child, this particular patient, was being admitted in a psychotic condition following an attempt to abort herself with drugs.

The mother told me that she had devoted her "whole life" to the raising of her only surviving offspring. But everything she had tried to do for the girl had turned out "the opposite."

"I gave her the best of everything," said the mother. "But she turned out bad!"

The series of unfortunate and apparently unrelated events in the history of these three children ended a year later, when the patient died of an inoperable brain tumor.

Today, when I think of how intense hatred within a marriage contaminates a parent's reactions to children and can leave them a legacy of illness, accidents and death, I recall this unhappy family. For accidents may be more than just accidents. Often some aggressive motive appears to be related to them. The history just told suggests that children conceived in a hateful marriage may come to an untimely end because of their mother's inability to neutralize the effects of her own poisonous feelings in the course of raising them.

But it is true that, although the emotional relationship between the mother and the father is of prime importance to the child, accidents do occur which appear to have nothing to do with this relationship. A sudden and unexpected explosion, or an airplane crash, or a flood or hurricane are examples of accidents of nature or man which you would not ordinarily expect anyone to prevent. Nevertheless, many men, women and children seem to possess the ability to avoid such catastrophes or emerge from them relatively unscathed, whereas other individuals seem to have an affinity for danger and death. Last year, for example, in the great hurricane and consequent flood which swept the Gulf States, some people insisted on ignoring the advice of local authorities and, in one well-publicized case, almost an entire family was drowned because the father refused to leave his home at the proper time. Although we can only guess at the many motives for his refusal, we can reasonably surmise that part of his unconscious motivation was a need to defy the authorities.

In addition, there are people who have a sort of "sixth sense" whereby they seem to anticipate an accident. Some persons, for example, at the last minute before departure, decide not to board a train or plane that is about to meet with disaster; or a child will suddenly — and for no reason of which he himself is aware — change his mind and not venture out on thin ice with his playmates. But the nature of this special sense is not entirely known, and at the present time study and research continue to try to determine why and how it operates.

My own impression is that it has something to do with the love factor in the marriage. A very strong love component in the paternal relationship seems to inculcate in children an intense interest in survival and to heighten their awareness of themselves and the world around them. On the other hand, many youngsters learn to protect themselves against the destructive effects of a hateful marriage by going contrary to parental advice. Often, these are the so-called disobedient children. But these impressions must be studied a great deal more carefully before any definite conclusions can be drawn.

A Magnifying Mirror

We all know that some children have the ability to avoid accidents while there are other children who actually seem to court accidents or, at least, experience them repeatedly. But what many of us don't realize is that one of the factors involved in the behavior of the accident-prone child is corporal punishment. For when the mother and father physically punish the child for misbehavior, he takes on this attitude and incorporates it as his own.

The child has a very strong tendency to identify with the significant adults around him. He tends to imitate his parents. Consequently, if he is away from them and does something of which he knows they would not approve, he will tend to punish himself physically as though they were present and knew he had committed the particular act. But the real trouble comes when he tends to exaggerate or distort the parental attitude. Whereas the mother may punish the child by giving him just a light spanking, the child, away from her, may very well break his arm or leg when he finds himself behaving in some way of which she would not approve. For the child is a sort of magnifying mirror. What gets implanted in his mind by his parents is not necessarily what they meant to deposit there, but what the child imagines they did.

This fact is one of the many reasons psychiatrists do not recommend corporal punishment for children. It may tend to produce a tragic situation when an individual takes over the punishment for himself. Of course, it must be understood that the child does not "think" these thoughts of self-punishment. This is an entirely unconscious process on the child's part. It is completely "unknown" to him in a conscious sense. One should also understand that this self-punishment does not necessarily take place immediately. It may very well be a cumulative thing, one forbidden action following another (or a series of "crimes" that the child imagines he has committed) until, in a moment of fatigue or inattention, he acts on a hostile impulse directed toward himself. In this way the self-aggression may eventually break through the barriers of survival.

But the chance of an accident taking place may be increased by all sorts of circumstances. Lack of sleep, hunger, poor ventilation, anger and rage, or extreme concentration on some activity are some of the factors which help to release the potential for an accident. All too often we read in the newspapers about a child who, while deeply absorbed in a game with a playmate, runs out into the street in front of a car, temporarily "forgetting" that Mommie has said hundreds of times, "You must never run across the street."

In addition to the fact that children tend to identify with and imitate their parents in an exaggerated manner, families themselves tend to set up and follow certain patterns of behavior. For example, when a child has an accident and suffers a cut finger, let us say, his mother may give him a beating or she may make the accident an occasion for a dramatic display of affection and excitement. The tension and excitement, whether associated with a beating or with hugs, kisses and caresses, may be very rewarding to the child. In that case he may demonstrate a strong tendency to initiate the predictable pattern of action and reaction.

I knew a little boy whose mother worked herself into a frenzy whenever he played with matches instead of simply taking the matches away from him and telling him not to take them again. So whenever this boy wanted excitement and attention, he managed to get hold of a match and light it. Through the histrionic display he could very well anticipate, he always got the desired excitement and attention. On the other hand, some children have a great craving for punishment. If they know that it will be forthcoming for a particular act, such as walking with muddy boots on the carpet, they will tend to repeat that "bad" act in order to get the wanted punishment.

Accidents are usually both self-punishing and attention-getting. I once had in treatment a little boy whose parents physically punished him whenever he was naughty; and he had a great craving for attention. One day, during the course of a birthday party for another child, this boy found an old uncovered well and decided to walk precariously around the edge. Naturally, he fell in and managed almost to drown before he was eventually pulled out, a great deal of fuss and excitement accompanying the rescue. By accomplishing the comparatively simple act of falling into the well, this little boy captured the major share of attention at somebody else's birthday party and, at the same time, acted out his self-punishing tendencies.

However, what is most difficult for mothers and fathers to understand and accept is the simple truth that we all have a reservoir of love and a reservoir of hate for the people around us. We just don't "love" people one hundred percent of the time, nor do we "hate" one hundred percent of the time. Every husband has some negative feelings for his wife and children, however strong his positive feelings for them. Ordinarily, when he is not tired, disturbed or depressed, his love is powerful enough to hold any destructive act in check. But let me cite an example of what may happen when other factors combine with the aggressive tendencies which normally lie within all of us.

The father of a two-year-old boy was painting his living room in the early evening after a day at the office. He was using turpentine to thin the paint, leaving the pure turpentine on the floor in an open coffee-can. The little boy, toddling about, was told a number of times not to touch the can. The man had, in fact, pointed out the danger to his wife, who was busy doing things around the house. However, when the father became thirsty, he momentarily "forgot" the danger and went into the kitchen to open a can of beer. In those few seconds, the child drank a quantity of turpentine and had to be rushed to the hospital.

A number of factors contributed to this accident, the crucial one being that the somewhat tired and harassed father became thirsty. In addition, the aggressive component of his personality could have operated to help him "forget" that the child might injure himself. In the moment of "forgetfulness," the aggressive act of neglecting the child took place.

But at the time of the accident, this father was not aware of any negative feelings for his child or for his wife. For there are many individuals who are not aware of their hatred, and probably just as many who are not aware of their love. Frequently, for example, they are so oblivious to the impact on them of someone they know that the great sense of loss and sorrow they experience when he dies is very shocking to them.

It seems, too, that the more intensely a person loves or

hates, the greater the likelihood that he will be totally unaware of his reservoir of opposite emotions. The most dangerous situations are apt to develop if the intensity of his
love stifles any recognition of his anger or hatred. The
newspapers occasionally report such situations. A typical
story concerns the man who never quarrels with his wife,
who is always kind and loving to his children, and who has
earned high respect for his many contributions to his community. No scandal has ever been linked with his name. He
is successful in business, also active in the P.T.A., the Boy
Scouts and the local churches. Then one day he comes home
from the office early and, without the slightest warning or
any evident provocation, he kills everybody in the house and
finally commits suicide. In effect, here is a man who was
totally unaware of harboring any hostility toward his wife
and children, and himself. He had suppressed his anger
so completely that, when it finally erupted, it led to the
most extreme behavior.

A mother consulted me recently about one of her two teenage daughters, a girl who was very emotional and flew into
a temper tantrum whenever she was seriously frustrated.
This behavior worried the mother. On the other hand, she
approved of the behavior of her other daughter, who was
described as a "nice and quiet" girl who never indulged in
any emotional explosions. Naturally, this teenager was not
a source of worry to her mother. However, in the course of
the interview, it became apparent that the girl who charac-
teristically displayed her emotions so openly actually was not
difficult to get along with, whereas her "nice and quiet"
sister, whenever she talked, seemed to have a "bad taste in
her mouth," as if constantly exuding a little poison or hatred.
She turned out to be the more emotionally disturbed of the
two girls. Her behavior, as the mother eventually recognized,
was what was really making her parents uneasy because it
was vague and hard to pin down, whereas the emotional
explosions of the other daughter were manageable and, in
a sense, "quite normal."

The point is that we all have a little aggression within us,
and if we know about it and discharge it in socially approved
ways, we can function more healthfully. But if we are not
aware of our hostilities and tell ourselves that we love every-

body, we are in a much more dangerous situation. Love is comparable to the milk and food provided by the good mother, and you might say that the aggressive component of the personality is analogous to the stool in the body and similarly "bad and evil" if we retain it within us. But just as human beings must have, and accept the need for periodic bowel movements, they must learn how to release their aggressions regularly in ways that will not cause harm to themselves or others.

HATE, ILLNESS AND CANCER

What we have been saying about physical accidents may be applied in a broad sense to physical illnesses as well. Allow me to cite an example of how aggression, anger and hate may be related to the common cold. In this family, the mother and father were frequently embroiled in violent quarrels. Concurrently, their two children had many colds; being run-down appeared to be their chronic state. It was not one, but a number of factors, which led to the children's sicknesses.

There was a negligence factor. When the mother was absorbed in an argument with the father, she was not aware that the children were playing in a drafty room or were not dressed warmly enough when they played outside. Moreover, the excitement between the mother and father stimulated excitement in the children so that, when they went outside to play, they could quickly get overheated and take off some of their clothing. And what was possibly the most significant factor, the quarreling and screaming which went on so often inside the house was tormenting to these children. They would feel very unhappy, wanting to cry frequently.

Many of us carry cold viruses around with us at times, and emotional stress appears to be an important determinant of when we become ill. From what we know today, it seems that a situation which tends to create great unhappiness and misery also tends to deprive us of our natural immunity to viruses. As a matter of fact, a subject of current research is the extent to which cancer may be a product of loss of immunity to the cancer-producing viruses. Evidence appears to be accumulating that children and adults — all of us —

have different degrees of immunity to cancer, and there is reason to believe that emotional factors can increase or decrease our resistance to the development of cancerous conditions.

Many years ago, I encountered the most unusual situation of a boy who had never been sick until he came down with his first cold at the age of eight. His mother, whom I interviewed, loved him very much and had always taken the greatest care of him. He had never been permitted to get dirty; she had kept his food sterile, and had seen to it that he bathed every day and always put on clothes fresh from the laundry. Until this infection, he had been the picture of health and had, in fact, won a national health contest. However, when he was eight he came down with a simple cold which quickly spread through his entire respiratory system, and in a matter of hours he was dead. Apparently, he was a victim of a total lack of immunity.

It is well known that the child who is overprotected from dirt and illness may not develop the immunities he needs to maintain good health. When he later encounters a situation of stress, he tends to have little defense against it. Too much protection and care lavished on a child can in this respect be even more disastrous than too little, and it is a mistake to equate them with the love and understanding care which is his birthright. Often, the so-called deprived or neglected child brought up in a poor environment develops a high degree of emotional and physical fortitude, and this must be attributed in part to the fact that he was exposed to illness and infection early in life. Children need to experience various diseases common to childhood and to have some acquaintances with dirt in order to build up immunities and other defenses against the various stresses of life.

It is a tough job to be a good parent. You have to use good judgment, intuition, and do the best you are capable of doing. Maximum care and maximum protection are not the answer. The child needs parents whose attitudes are moderate, who give him a moderate degree of care, and who know when not to "protect" him.

31.

"Must a handicap be a disability to a child?"
we asked Dr. Blank.

§§§§§§§§§§§§§§§§§§§§§

H. ROBERT BLANK, M.D.

Contributing Editor, The Psychoanalytic Quarterly

In this interview, Dr. Blank also discusses:

"Are most people afraid to face life?"
  "Can a gifted child be turned into a handicapped child?"
    "Why are parents unprepared for a handicapped child?"
"What is the difference between a handicap and a disability?"
  What is the meaning of 'abnormal' and 'normal'?"
    "Should the handicapped be segregated?"
"How does our society tend to handicap the gifted?"
  "What may be the psychological meaning of the birth of a handicapped child to the mother?"
    "Should the mentally defective child always be institutionalized?"
"Why do some of us reject the handicapped child?"
  "What are the 'global feelings' of children and adults?"
    "Why are parental attitudes important to the handicapped child?"

31.

This is what Dr. Blank said when interviewed in his office:

An immediate and clear distinction must be made between the words "handicap" and "disability." These two words are confused even by doctors, and it is not just a confusion of words. The distinction has to do with ideas and attitudes toward handicaps of a physical and mental nature which either favor rehabilitation of the person with the handicap, or contribute to regression and a worsening of the disability.

A handicap is something fixed. It is a physical state such as blindness, an amputated leg, a state of paralysis or of mental deficiency, which has remained constant following the best of medical treatment. In short, a handicap is a fixed condition.

It is a principle of rehabilitation that a fixed handicap does not itself produce a fixed degree of disability. Therefore, we should never speak about a handicap in the same terms that we talk about disability. Allow me to give you a real and immediate example of what this means. Within the past two years, two men of the same age, with relatively similar social backgrounds and intelligence, were suddenly handicapped by total blindness. In both cases there was no injury or disease of the brain or vascular system.

One of these men, two years after the accident, is now a complete failure in the rehabilitation center in spite of all of the efforts of the competent professional staff. He doesn't learn Braille; he remains fearfully attached to his teacher who is attempting to train him to get around by himself with a cane, and everyone in his family takes it for granted that his blindness is adequate reason for his total disability and dependence two years after the blinding accident. This misconception is similar to that held by many people about a man who, losing all of his money, jumps from the Empire State Building. "Sure, he lost all his money, and that's why he jumped," they explain. However, during the depression of the 1930's there were thousands of men who lost all their money, and only a very few killed themselves. In the same sense, the handicap of a total blindness is not the cause of this man's almost total disability.

The second man reacted quite differently to his total handicap. Although the blindness was a deep shock and was followed by severe depression, two months after the accident he could walk alone fairly well with a cane, and also had a beginning grasp of Braille. He didn't keep to himself; he didn't sit there and wring his hands and say, "Why did God do this to me?" At the end of eight months, this man was again working at his old business, as a salesman. The only help that he now needs is a chauffeur because he must travel by automobile. In addition, he objected strenuously to having conditions changed in his work by his employer so he could sit at a desk. At present, one year after becoming blind, he goes alone into New York City from the suburb in which he lives with just a cane, and he can use the subway system almost as well as anyone.

These two contrasting men make the point of not confusing handicap with disability. Let us go into an orthopedic ward of any large hospital where we may see an old man with multiple fractures. He has just barely survived an automobile accident, let us say, and he is lying there in traction, one hand and one leg up in the air. But he is having a fine time of it. He is entertaining other patients with fantastic stories, he listens to the radio, and he reads a good deal. Twenty beds down the ward there is another man with a simple fracture of the femur where no big nerve is pinched, but he is, naturally, howling for attention from all the nurses.

Why "naturally?" Why are there these differences between people?

Today we know there are profound and complex psychological factors which account for one person overreacting to a simple fracture of the femur, let us say, as compared to another who does not permit a serious injury to be a complete disability. Furthermore, what we have said about the differences between adults applies even more strongly to children. A child with a handicap is in that physical and mental state when his personality is not fully developed.

Thus the parental and school attitudes toward the handicap are the fundamental determinants as to whether the child will remain disabled to any real degree, or whether he will become a productive human being in spite of his handicap.

GLOBAL FEELINGS

The infant and the young child are dependent upon the parents for physical and psychological survival. Newborn infants who are well fed but who do not get body handling and stimulations, and psychological affection and love from a parent or from a parental substitute, will waste away and will die. This has actually happened to countless foundlings in hospitals.

In the process of development, the child is dependent upon parental attitudes toward him for the attitudes he develops towards himself. In infancy the child absorbs feelings about his body first, and then about his total self (feelings which may be called "global" feelings of good and bad, of worthy and unworthy) that are largely based on parental approval and support on one hand, and/or parental disapproval and dissatisfaction on the other hand. Parental attitudes are unconscious as well as conscious, and there is a transmission of both to the child.

We can see this most clearly in extreme cases. One child is valued by his parents and develops nicely, with self-acceptance, self-confidence and poise. Another child may come from a home where there is callous neglect, no standards and little love; under these circumstances it is not too difficult to understand that a child will acquire few constructive attitudes towards himself or society. Most of the problem children come from homes where the adverse influences are not quite so apparent, for most children are not totally rejected. Their parents, consciously and unconsciously, react to them with mixed and inconsistent feelings and attitudes.

Every infant and child has conflicts. There is, for example, the normal and inevitable power struggle with the parents, especially with the parent of the same sex. The most balanced and healthy child will carry certain residues of these childhood conflicts into adulthood. In some children and adults the conflicts and residues are relatively minor, remaining unconscious for the most part. But in other individuals they are so major that they result in what is called a "neurosis" or some other more severe personality disorder.

The point here is simply that all of us, no matter who we are, are initially unprepared when we are subjected to some very severe stress or blow such as loss of control of a body part or the loss of the body part itself. We have unconsciously developed a whole set of attitudes toward ourselves. We have expectations of a life in the future, which depend upon our intactness and the way we have been in the past. All this is included in the term identity. Thus, when there is an accident to ourselves, what we regarded and accepted as our body and bodily function is suddenly no longer our body nor our function.

Everyone who suffers a severe physical handicap, especially if it is a sudden accident, goes through a shock reaction, a sense of loss, disorientation and, to some degree, disintegration of certain psychologic functions. But gradually, as the person recovers from the shock and disruption of psychic functioning, what becomes apparent in the way the individual handles his handicap is what was apparent in the way he handled his major problems before the handicap.

I believe that it would be fair to say that to some degree all of us tend to moralize about a handicap. This moralization goes back to ancient conceptions of illness where sickness and injury were regarded as punishment for sins. Regardless of our modern education and objectivity, there is still a hidden tendency to think along these lines. The reason for this is partly that children are brought up on a very simple moral code which is actually divorced from reality. We tend to say to children, "If you are good and you behave in the right way, you will get pie in the sky." In other words, the child gets certain rewards for being good; if he has good manners, eats his supper, helps old ladies across the street and goes to church, then — and only then — will he be rewarded.

But the reality of the world does not always support this childish concept: good and nice children do get sick; they do die; they do lose an arm or a leg, or are blind from birth. You frequently hear an individual who has suffered a sudden handicap (or the birth of a handicapped child) say, "What did I do to deserve this? Why, God, did you do this to ne? Me!" In short, the handicap is seen as a punishment for a sin. The child, or the man or woman, was picked out by God or by Fate — the powerful father — and he cries, "I didn't deserve this!"

The individual's psychological make-up will govern to what extent he views a handicap, or the birth of a handicapped child, as a punishment. If he has been suffering from guilt feelings which are due to his own unconscious conflicts, or which are due to actions for which he has not adequately atoned according to his own moral codes, the punishment reaction to the handicap will naturally be much more severe and intense than in the case of the individual who is relatively free of irrational and essentially childish guilt.

These are the reasons why it is extremely important to get at the roots of the guilt which existed before the illness or injury. Unless these are uncovered and dealt with in psychological treatment, the guilt-ridden reactions and attitudes will persist and preclude healthy change. This is particularly true in the case of parents, especially the mother, of a child who is born with a physical handicap.

Every girl grows up with a conscious and unconscious backlog of experience about motherhood. These experiences prepare her, for better or for worse, for pregnancy and giving birth to a baby. The young girl sees women with normal babies; she handles, feeds, and kisses them, and they are just wonderful. Consequently, when she herself gives birth to a handicapped child her conscious and unconscious training and experience leave her completely unprepared. How can the average girl know, for example, that a blind child, or a deaf child, or a child born with some other congenital abnoramlity, is not totally defective? How does she know that the child is capable of growing up with her help to be a desirable, productive person? This is obviously very difficult in itself.

But if you add to this lack of knowledge the unconscious conflicts which predispose her to inordinate guilt, and which go back to her own childhood, there is often created the classical situation where the mother holds herself responsible for the congenital defect. Such mothers often say, "If I hadn't run around with men I wouldn't have had such a child." Or, "If I hadn't tried to have an abortion two years ago, the baby wouldn't be defective now."

However, in the vast majority, the real sources of guilt and self-recrimination are completely irrational. They are based on unconscious conflicts which the mother does not recognize as existing. The newborn baby is an extension of the mother — an extension of the self — and the mother of the handicapped child is sure that she is somehow responsible. "After all," she unconsciously says, in effect, "if I were good, I would be rewarded the way all other mothers are rewarded, with nice healthy babies."

This unconscious feeling is particularly strong with women who have been subjected to an over-moralistic training in their childhood. As married women, they may tend to still believe that sex is dirty, even that sexual thoughts are dirty. Such a woman is very predisposed to have inordinate guilt reactions and hold herself responsible for any defect in the child.

I have heard it mistakenly said that congenitally handicapped children are "emotional abortions," that is, unwanted children. I don't think there is a shred of truth in the generalization, not a shred. However, I do think that it is true that no one wants a handicapped child. The initial emergency reaction of "I wish I didn't have this child," is a universal one. It is quite normal, but the average parent can be helped to overcome this reaction, especially when he learns it is supremely rewarding to love, teach and play with his child.

Mothers who are, by all standards, very well-balanced and stable also have an initially helpless and depressive reaction. The reasons for this are two-fold. First, all mothers are completely unprepared for the handicap and they cannot but feel saddled with a permanent disability, for there is a great sense of loss right from the very start. Secondly, the best balanced parent, to some extent, has an unconscious tendency to expect the child to be a reward or punishment. Unconsciously, a nice healthy baby is a reward for goodness and a defective baby is a punishment for sin, somewhere and somehow. It is not too difficult for anyone, no matter who he may be, to pull out of the past evidence of his being a "sinner."

Because of this fact, and because of the initially helpless and depressive reactions, every mother in this situation requires and should have a good deal of professional help so that her child's fixed handicap does not become a fixed disability. With professional help, the unconscious and unreal reactions can be undercut and not be allowed to become chronic. Thus, it will then be entirely possible to get the maximum development out of the positive resources that the handicapped child does possess.

If guilt and rejection are not dealt with constructively, the mother may then approach the child in one, or a combination of destructive ways. There may be abhorrence, a total rejection of the child; this is often irresponsibly catered to by people who advise institutionalization for children with serious congenital abnormalities regardless of the actual need for institutionalization. Or, what more frequently happens because of the guilt reactions, is that the mother is overprotective of the child, tending to keep the child to herself and withdrawn from participation in normal social activities. In effect, the child is treated as some terrible family secret. There is an excessive fear about the child hurting himself, and consequently, constant limitations are set up that block the child's normal spontaneity, growth and development. On the other hand, the handicapped child who is not limited by such parental attitudes, often develops with very little retardation beyond the nonhandicapped children. Often, by high school age there is no retardation whatsoever.

NORMAL AND ABNORMAL

It is characteristic of psychoanalysts, psychiatrists and psychologists to speak more definitively about what is "abnormal" and "desirable." We mean by "pathological," a disease state which may be objectively observed. For example, in the psychiatric sphere a hallucination is a symptom of a disease state. When a person walks around talking to someone who is not there, we can say this behavior is pathological. It is a symptom and a sign of abnormality upon which the overwhelming majority of experts and laymen alike agree, although there might be disagreement as to cause.

Circumstances and the necessities of reality and standards do change from time to time, and we are even looked upon differently by different people at the same time. But there seems to be an unconscious vote taken by the majority of us to agree on certain realities. In many abnormal conditions, however, there are certain criteria which transcend social and cultural considerations. For example, I believe that neurosis (an impairment in the total functioning of the personality resources of the individual) is pathological in the widest sense of the word. I believe that most people in our society today suffer from serious and unresolved neurotic conflicts which do not necessarily show themselves in the ways we usually associate with pathological behavior. On the contrary, neurosis can most usually be observed in the limited degree of development of the individual's interests, intellect, and creativeness.

But the fact that ninety-nine percent of us suffer from neurosis does not make it "normal." However, I want to differentiate here between the two meanings of the word "abnormal." Strictly speaking, when the scientist uses the word "abnormal" he is referring to a statistic. For example, the average height of an American male today is five feet, nine and one-half inches. This is called the normal, and consequently, a man who is five feet tall is abnormal because he deviates significantly from the average. In the same way, a man who is six feet, four inches is also abnormal in the statistical sense. But neither man is abnormal in the pathological (undesirable) sense of the word.

When the average layman uses the word "abnormal," he means "undesirable." He makes no distinction between what is different from the average and what is pathological (undesirable). The reason for the confusing of abnormal in the statistical sense and abnormal in the sense of undesirable is that none of us are free from one terrible compulsion which runs through almost everything we do and think.

We have to have people look alike, act alike and talk alike. Anything different than the so-called "normal" is something we tend to look upon as queer or ugly and strange. A typical example of this is the beautiful woman who has feelings of inferiority because she is six feet tall. Although she may be the envy of other women, she was always taller than every girl in school, and therefore, felt abnormal. Yes, she is abnormal to the extent that she belongs to the one percent of females who are six feet tall. However, there is quite obviously nothing pathological about a beautiful girl, no matter what her height, except that unconsciously determined thinking makes it so.

At this point I should like to pause a moment and speak of the gifted child. For, as with the beautiful woman, a gift can be turned into a handicap. Furthermore, the family of a gifted child often reacts to his special talent or high intellectual capacity as though it were a handicap. Although the gift that a child has in the way of talent, creative ability and high intellectual capacity, does not in itself constitute a handicap, the net result can be partial or serious impairment of function.

The gifted child tends to be superior physically as well as intellectually. For example, a child who is artistic in painting, generally tends to be artistic musically, and to have superior neuromuscular coordination. However, many people falsely believe the creative person, or the genius, is somehow queer and defective. At the very least, they often believe he is unstable. These beliefs are myths and many people persist in believing in them because it gives them comfort, not being creative or endowed with genius themselves.

It does happen frequently that the parents of a gifted child make a handicap out of the gift because they are overwhelmed by it and, in their lack of objectivity, seek to exploit the child. We all know the stereotype of the mother who is constantly hammering away at the child to play the piano. But in the process, she often effectively ruins his interest in the piano and in music in general.

Conformity is another factor which may turn a gift into a handicap. Because the gifted child is outstanding, often following his own inclinations, the mother and father are deeply concerned because he is not becoming the "All-American Boy." They are fearful lest he stand out as an exception.

There is absolutely nothing pathological or abnormal about the gifted child following his particular bent and not being interested, at any given time, in what the other children are doing. Characteristic of the gifted child is his ability to motivate himself, to plan out his own day, and not be dependent upon his fellow playmates or his parents. The healthy gifted child is never bored; you never hear that complaint from him. If encouraged to follow his own gifts, he is self-motivated, self-stimulated, and creative.

I believe there are many more talented and gifted children than we ever hear about. These "mute and inglorious" Miltons and Shakespeares are crippled by those forces in the typical family and in the culture at large, which go against individuality and exceptional functioning.

Look closely at any high school or college situation. Look closely into adolescent groups and you will see tremendously destructive pressures against individuality and creative expression. You will see the pressures to conform to the model of the Little League, the high school football player, cheerleader, or social butterfly. These pressures limiting creative expression begin in the family. The destructive pressures emanating from outside the home operate on parent and child, and on the child through the parent. While the task is difficult, it is the parent's responsibility to define his own values and goals, and live with a minority viewpoint if necessary. This will provide the parent with real satisfactions, provide his children with a worthwhile model, and enable the parent to see more clearly the needs of his individual children.

But there are many factors beyond the control of the parent and the child, e.g., unconscious conflicts and special problems in the school and the community. The fact is that we are frequently confronted with a highly talented, intelligent child who is emotionally disturbed and performing far below his capacity. As in the case of the handicapped child, what is indicated here is the most thorough diagnostic study of the child — medical, psychiatric, and psychological. The family, school, and community have to be evaluated. Psychoanalysis, or psychotherapy based on psychoanalysis is often indicated in disturbed gifted children but this cannot be prescribed without thorough diagnosis. Similarly, the child might require an educational milieu radically different from his current school.

I repeat, all of us tend to look upon anything which is significantly different from the average as queer, or ugly and strange, and this is especially true when we look upon the handicapped adult or child. When we meet someone — anyone — we are usually unaware of the fact that identification takes place. If the person is familiar, or his type is familiar, the identification is acceptable to us and we don't take notice of outstanding and special things about him.

But when we meet someone for whom we are completely unprepared — a man without a nose, a child without arms — there may be a strong revulsion because we identify with that person and are unconsciously and momentarily losing our own nose or arms. This losing of a part of ourselves is completely unacceptable to us. We project this rejection back to the handicapped person in the form of a revulsion. In other words, if not for this process of over-identification there would be absolutely no basis for the revulsion. We would be able to see that this handicapped person is just a *different* person, and we would deal objectively with the difference.

Allow me to make this clearer. I am sure that most of us know men and women who can't stand to read about someone being operated on for cancer. Or who cannot visit someone who lies dying in the hospital. This type of person attributes his behavior to "being over-sensitive." But that is the sheerest nonsense. These people are not sensitive enough, in a sense, because they are over-identifying and not psychologically separating themselves from the other person, and seeing that person as a different person.

Thus, it is not the friend or relative who is dying of cancer — "I am dying," says the unconscious.

On the other hand, it is quite normal to feel with a suffering person. We mean by "identifying" having sympathy and feelings for the person. But when there are gross bodily handicaps with which we are not familiar, there often occurs this instant revulsion and rejection because of the highly irrational over-identification. In short, these people cannot see other individuals as individuals. They can only see deformed images of themselves.

Medical students, for example, may vomit and have panic reactions when they first see gross bodily pathology. But most of them get over it; they have to in order to function as physicians. The classical form of unconscious identification is exemplified in the little boy who, for the first time, sees a nude little girl and instantly grabs his own genitals — "I don't want to lose mine," he says in effect. At the age of two, my own little girl first saw a nude little boy. She grabbed herself in front and in back and said, "I no got it," that is, "I lost it, or it was taken away."

The Bearer of Ill Tidings

Generalizations cannot be made about the handicapped child, nor can broad statements be made about specific handicaps, except in the small group of mentally defective children who are uneducable. The handicapped child and his family must have the best available diagnostic services. Regardless of their own irrational guilts and other reactions, parents need to be told just what is wrong, and then, with further aid, they can be helped to accept the objective facts.

By the time a child is three years old it is possible today (in most instances) to determine objectively whether he is mentally defective and uneducable. It is not too strong a statement to say that it can prevent the ruination of a family for parents to know this fact authoritatively and unquestionably, and to be helped professionally to cope with the problem. An uneducable mentally defective child should be institutionalized early in life. It is better for the child, for the parents, and for the brothers and sisters.

The parents of a seriously mentally defective child are doing something very constructive by placing him in the proper institution. If kept at home, the child will not get the best care to which he is entitled, and eventually, the parents will be confronted with institutionalizing the child at the onset of, or during adolescence when his or her behavior will become intolerable to the community at large, let alone to the family. It is a great tragedy when a family keeps an uneducable defective child at home and by doing so, cripples the entire family.

No one wishes to be the bearer of ill tidings. Consequently and regrettably, there are some physicians, and others, who are fearful of interpreting the known facts to parents. As a result there are families who say of a child, "He will grow out of it." They believe this because they want to believe it and their doctor has told it to them. The child may or may not be standing up, although he is a year and a half old; he grunts and doesn't have anything resembling speech; his coordination is impaired; he is flabby. These are just a few of the symptoms which warrant a very thorough psychological and neurological examination. It is completely nonsensical to say that a child of this type will "outgrow it" without the most thorough diagnostic study.

There are specific criteria that can be presented. There are objective tests and observations which can determine whether a child is uneducable. Approximately 95 percent of children who are mentally abnormal are educable to some degree, and consequently, should be educated within the public school system, some in special schools in the community, not segregated in some distant institution. Unfortunately, too many handicapped children are institutionalized because of the paucity of adequate multi-disciplinary diagnostic treatment, educational resources and foster homes.

I wish to stress that diagnosis and treatment of the handicapped requires a multi-disciplinary diagnostic and treatment team. At the very least, the team should consist of a pediatrician, psychiatrist, neurologist, psychologist, and social worker. Under these circumstances, after the child and the family have been very carefully studied, much may be said about the child as far as educability is concerned, and sensible recommendations made for treatment and further study.

Reliance on institutional placement is also due to a cultural lag in our society. Following the European tradition, we tended until recent years to institutionalize our deaf, our blind, and our mentally retarded children. Here in the United States, however, we have now demonstrated conclusively that this is destructive and wasteful of human and economic resources. The majority of blind children, for example, can do beautifully in regular public schools when there is an itinerant teacher program in which the regular teachers are helped by specialists in the utilization of materials and techniques for the blind. A notable accomplishment is that of the Industrial Home for the Blind of Brooklyn, which supervises the education of several hundred blind children in the public schools of four counties. This shows just what can be done if we will only put our collective minds to work to really help the handicapped. Sustained high-level prog-

ress depends on the public and our elected officials realizing that so-called expensive rehabilitation programs for
handicapped children and adults are far cheaper than cus-
todial care for chronically disabled.

There is no reason on earth, or in heaven, why a blind or
deaf child, or a child born with stunted feet, cannot be educated and become productive, earn a living, and turn into
a responsible member of the community. I do not say they
can be "happy," because that word is often used in the sense
of "slap-happy." I prefer the word "productive," because
you are truly happy when you are fully utilizing your capacities for work, love, and play. Also, many people think that
happiness means the absence of anxiety. That is ridiculous.
We all have anxiety-producing problems in life.

Also, I am opposed to the use of the word "exceptional"
child to describe a handicapped child. Many people use
"exceptional" because they don't want to face the facts of
life. They are afraid to use the term "mental retardation,"
for example. But I believe in using descriptive and diagnostic terms that are very clear, so that the parents and the
child himself become accustomed to the words and the
ideas. If a child is blind, refer to his blindness. If a child is
paralyzed, refer to his paralysis, crutches and braces. Get
him used to the words early in life so that he will accept
the realities of life. All of us have to deal with what is true
about ourselves. If we do not, we pay the penalty of living
with terrible shame and fears which are needless.

It frequently happens that the parents of a blind or a
deaf child will automatically assume that the child is also
going to be mentally defective. This is where a large problem arises. Parents of children who have a single handicap
need strong reassurances that just because there is blindness,
let us say, there is not necessarily mental deficiency. There
are some children who do have multiple handicaps. But let
me repeat — just because there is one handicap it does not
necessarily follow that there will be other handicaps, and
only through thorough multi-disciplinary study can the true
facts be diagnosed.

For handicapped and gifted children there can be only
one slogan: the needs of the individual child have to be
evaluated and met.

5. WORK

Introduction

Man must work to eat. If he is unable to work, there is something emotionally wrong with him. He needs work not only to earn his daily bread but also to fulfill a part of himself that gets prestige and satisfaction out of using his mind and body at something productive. Work offers many rewards.

"What is the meaning of work to man?" we asked Theodor Reik, Ph.D. "Why, at times, does it seem a curse rather than a blessing?"

For, there are many people who consider their work a chore, achieving very little satisfaction out of it. They go to their job each day with a heavy heart, expecting little from it. Year in, year out, they work, but with resignation, wasting what amounts to, in actual hours, one-third of their lives.

"Why do so few people find their work satisfying?" we asked Harold Greenwald, Ph.D. "Does work have to be meaningless except for the pay check?"

One great change in our society today is the number of women who work. Of these, fifty-five percent are married. Many of them must work to help support families if their husband is unable to do so. But a large number work because they want to.

"What does modern woman get out of her work?" we asked Geraldine Pederson-Krag, M.D. We also wanted to know, "Does the highly educated or skilled woman have special problems?"

Often man (and woman) finds he has not given his full potential to his work. He operates, in a sense, at only thirty or forty percent of his capacity, although he would like to be far more efficient and productive. Something holds him back, something he cannot fight because he does not know what it is.

"Can the unconscious overhead be the biggest expense of all?" we asked Leo L. Orenstein, M.D.

One of the most important things in our lives, not only our work lives, but our lives as a whole, is money. It represents many things to us, both consciously and unconsciously. From the time the child understands anything, he learns the value of money, and as he grows up, he tends to place even more value on it.

"What does money mean to us?" we asked Phillip Polatin, M.D.

A large fortune — approximately one billion dollars — is stolen from American business every year, but there is seldom a prosecution or conviction for the crime. Sociologists have called this phenomenon, "white-collar criminality." From all available evidence, it appears that millions of Americans are involved to some extent.

At one extreme stands the sales clerk who, over a period of years, steals thousands of dollars from the cash registers, and the "blue-collar" worker who systematically takes thousands of dollars worth of tools home from the factory in which he works. At the other extreme, there is the secretary or office worker who goes home with an occasional box of pencils and ream of bond paper.

Stealing occurs not only in terms of money but in the form of "featherbedding" on the job, spending too much time at the water cooler, or going out for coffee or resting or talking in the lounge.

For the most part, none of these people consider themselves criminals, certainly not in the same sense as the pickpocket or bank robber. "White-collar criminality" seems to be part of the culture. "Everyone does it," we tend to say. We have many popular jokes, for example, about padding expense accounts. In short, we are talking about "something for nothing."

We asked Ludwig Eidelberg, M.D. to discuss, "Why do people want something for nothing, to get something without working for it — which is for nothing?"

We in America are living longer and are more healthy in our older years than ever before, and the future holds an even greater promise. But, as with automation in industry and business where the future may promise a twenty-hour work week or less, so with longevity. Some have said it may prove to be as much of a curse as a blessing.

"What makes for a successful retirement?" we asked Alvin I. Goldfarb, M.D. "What are some of the facts, and some of the fictions, related to the problems of the elderly?"

If we learn to handle our feelings about work and money, we can work more effectively and put to far greater use the money we earn and save. Then, as the experts above tell us, we will be neither hoarders nor profligate spenders but will use money and time to enrich our lives.

32.

"What is the meaning of work to man?"
we ask Dr. Reik.

XXXXXXXXXXXXXXXXXX

THEODOR REIK, Ph.D.

Founder and Honorary President,
National Psychological Association for Psychoanalysis

In this interview, Dr. Reik also discusses:

"How do we value ourselves through work?"
    "Do men and women look at work differently?"
        "Is man's image of himself related to his work?"
"Why do some lose themselves in work?"
        "What is the 'work' of the child?"
"Should man's work be separate from other parts of himself?"
    "How do actors and actresses use their unconscious?"

32.

This is what Dr. Reik said when interviewed in his office:

The self is larger than we know. It is, so to speak, deeper and wider than we think, and it reaches further than we would perhaps like to think. When we look inward toward the self we see only some small part of it. In addition, if you are honest with yourself, you must agree with the German philosopher Schopenhauer, who made a distinction between the character people pretend to be, the character they think they are, and the character they are in reality.

I have recently read some correspondence between Freud and the French actress and diseuse, Yvette Guilbert. Guilbert and Freud were friends for many years, and at one time, when she wanted to write her life story, she asked Freud for his advice on the following matter. She had a theory, she said, that when an actress plays a street Arab, or a prostitute, or an old lady, the actress obliterates her own personality and puts in its place another personality which is entirely alien to herself.

Freud answered that, although he did not know much about acting or actors, he did not think she was correct. Rather than obliterating her own personality, Freud said, the actress is presenting emotional or intellectual potentialities which are in the self but which are unconscious or disavowed. Thus, the impressions and experiences which are unconscious are made realities for a moment, as in a dream.

Freud used Charlie Chaplin as an example of the use of unconscious or disavowed experiences. Chaplin always acted the same part. He was the unhappy, the handicapped and the underprivileged man. Freud pointed out that in this comic-tragic part, Chaplin was bringing to life, or re-living, experiences which were not necessarily always conscious but which were experienced by him as a little boy in the Jewish quarter of London.

So, this is, in part, why I say we are several people at once and the real self is much larger than we know. Both of these truths are intimately related to work.

We must speak differently, in a certain sense, of men and women. For, as a French writer once remarked, "One of the minor tragedies of life is that women love men but men love work."

The self-image of women, in general, is not as intimately connected with everyday work as that of men. A woman is much more identified with her children, with the happiness she gives to her husband and others. Although she may be a secretary during the day, this work usually plays a much smaller role than her "work" as a mother and her physical attractiveness as a giving and feminine woman.

USEFULNESS AND BLISS

Work is only meaningful if it is useful. The Nazis had a group of prisoners knock down a brick wall, carry the bricks a few hundred yards away, and then, when finished, carry the bricks back again and build the same wall. That was, of course, adding insult to injury, because it showed the prisoners their work was useless.

I would say it is necessary for our self-esteem that our work be understood and recognized as useful, if not by the external world then, at the very least, by ourselves. I would even go beyond that. I would say that the self-image of man changed when he was compelled to work. Adam had a different self-image before he was driven out of Paradise, before he was cursed to work by the sweat of his brow, than afterwards. As a matter of fact, some commentators think that what was conceived of in the Old Testament as a curse — mankind having to work his fields of grain — was in reality a blessing.

In childhood, play is work. For play is the "work" of the child. When a little boy pretends that he is a fireman driving a huge red engine, he forgets himself, and for the time being he is the fireman. It seems that one of the elements of happiness is to forget oneself, and as adults we do forget ourselves in some states — for example, when we are in love. At that time, the self is not very important any more. All interest is centered in the love object. We also forget ourselves when we are enthusiastic either for a "cause" or for our "work." In these states, the self becomes unimportant and the person concentrates on a high state of interest.

Gustave Flaubert, the French writer, once wrote to his friend, George Sand: "The man is nothing, the work is everything." Flaubert himself is a good example of a man who found a blessing in his work, for he was a fanatical worker and when he wrote he forgot everything else. This shift from oneself to one's work is favorable for creativity whether it be for the writer, the scientist, the carpenter or the office worker.

Henrik Ibsen, the Norwegian playwright, spoke about the blissfulness of creation and saw a job well done as a creative job. It is apparent that most everyone has a feeling which at least borders on happiness when a job is well done. The French writer, Emil Zola, commented: "Une phrase bien faite est une bonne action." ("A well-made sentence is a good deed.")

Freud once said: "Thought is action in small quantity." Freud also made a distinction between the man and the work. He said, for instance, that the discovery of America by Columbus was a great deed, while Columbus himself was nothing extraordinary. In the same sense, he considered psychoanalysis as great scientific progress, and although he didn't know what eventually would become of it, he was sure it would live on in future generations. Yet, he said of himself, that he was an average man. In my opinion he was far from an "average man." He said of great men, such as Beethoven and Moses, that their work was only a part of their lives. But the great go beyond their work; no distinction is possible between themselves and their accomplishment, I believe.

I would like to continue in this direction by saying that there is a discernible change in self-evaluation from childhood to old age. It is necessary, said Freud, to listen to the voices of self-criticism very acutely, while one should listen to the critical voices of others with "some" attention. But the child is inclined to over-appreciate himself and what he does. This loving of himself and his product is based upon the way he sees himself — all powerful, all knowing and godlike.

This omnipotence he gives himself is finally hesitantly restricted and when the child is to grow into a mature adult,

THEODOR REIK, PH.D.

329

is given up altogether. The older you get, the more you realize the narrow limitations everyone has with regard to achieving something. Even Albert Einstein spoke of himself in his advanced age as a "has-been." Freud once remarked that every scientific advance at the end appears only half as important as it seemed at the beginning.

An Apparent Contradiction

Arthur Schnitzler wrote, "Posterity exists also only for the living." This is an epigram full of *esprit*. But it seems that great geniuses like Beethoven or Freud can, at least, in imagination, conceive a continuation of their work and its value into the future. This is not given to the rest of us, because, in our society, most of us are compelled to divide our activities between what has to be done for financial reasons and that which we like to do and in which we are interested.

Yet, if we conceive of our work as useful, even if only in a restricted sense to ourselves, we have gratification beyond the self. In childhood one wants to be acknowledged and admired by his parents. "I am," the child says. "Therefore, I am lovable and to be admired." Later on, the circle of people by whom the child wants to be approved and admired is enlarged to include his teachers and friends. When he becomes a man he wants to have the approval of a still wider circle which may, eventually in some men, include a nation or the world at large.

But the approval does not come because one says, "I am, therefore I'm lovable." It comes, rather, through work and accomplishment, and although self-love is certainly present, it is not so much narcissistic reflection that gives us pleasure as the process of actually working and the end result of that process. In effect, although the process of work and the end product are separate from the self, they make the self meaningful if we conceive of the work as useful.

As I have said, we are not only several people at one and the same time, but the real self is much larger than we think. Although it seems to be a contradiction, the blissfulness of work, the meaningfulness of useful work, and the end result of the work, all conspire to take us away from the realm of interest in ourselves. By doing this, they give meaning to the real self at the same time by fullfilling its potentialities.

33.

*"Why do so few people find their work
satisfying?"* we asked Dr. Greenwald.

XXXXXXXXXXXXXXXXXXXXX

HAROLD GREENWALD, Ph.D.

Faculty member, Training Institute,
National Psychological Association for Psychoanalysis

In this interview, Dr. Greenwald also discusses:

"Why is much of modern work meaningless?"
> *"Are work problems connected with other problems in
> life?"*
>> *"Who are the poorest adjusted members of the labor
>> force?"*
"Is work part of the essential nature of man?"
> *"Why are some unable to accept success?"*
>> *"Why do so many people just drift into jobs?"*
*"How important is money in the satisfactions offered by
work?"*
> *"What is the importance to the employee of feeling val-
> uable to the employer?"*
>> *"How are aggression and guilt related to work?"*
"Does the unconscious affect our work?"
> *"What are the immediate gratifications in work?"*
>> *"Does psychological treatment destroy the artistic
>> drive?"*

HAROLD GREENWALD, PH.D.

33.

This is what Dr. Greenwald said when interviewed in his office:

Work is one of the major problems that many people are faced with in life. Yet, while Freud said that the healthy person was the one who had the ability to love and the ability to work, most psychoanalysts, psychiatrists and psychologists have spent a great deal of time on problems of love, but have devoted comparatively little time to problems of work.

There have been studies on talented, artistic individuals, but the work problem of the woman at the typewriter, or the man wielding the monkey wrench, or the office worker or teacher has been treated very sketchily by those in our field.

This fact is difficult to understand. Work, and the problems of work, take up a major portion of the time of most individuals. Many serious, emotional problems are centered around the problems of earning a living and around the problems of doing work that is satisfactory.

One of the major tragedies of our time is the fact that so few people find their work satisfying, rewarding in any way. For example, in working with some "Bohemian" patients, it has become very clear to me that one of the things against which they are in rebellion (self-destructive rebellion, perhaps) is the meaninglessness of so much of modern work.

But the problems of work are not new problems. Perhaps they are exaggerated by our present way of life where so much work has been sub-divided that no one sees the results of his labor in a productive, fruitful manner. However, work has always been a problem for man. Even in the Bible, the Lord punishes Adam by saying, "Hereafter thou shalt earn thy bread by the sweat of thy brow."

Yet we know work can often be a blessing rather than a

curse. Many retired men and women feel they have been robbed of the opportunity to work, and look upon their leisure as a curse. Man is essentially a social animal. This is one of the features that distinguish him from all other animals. In order to realize his true humanity, he has to participate with others in purposeful activity which is meaningful to him and which contributes something to the social good.

OTHER FACTORS INVOLVED

At a General Electric plant, the management became interested in discovering the effect of improved lighting on the productivity of workers. It was found that as they improved the lighting conditions and checked with the workers in this particular assembly operation, productivity increased and so did workers' happiness with the job.

Then, someone suggested, "Let's see what happens if we decrease the lighting." To everyone's amazement, productivity still improved! Further research indicated that improvement was due to the interest shown in the employees, rather than better lighting conditions.

As a result of this experiment and other research, knowledgable management today attempts to make the worker feel that he is of value as an individual and is participating in something of value.

The reality may very well be that the worker is of little value as an individual in relation to the product, and the product may have no real value. In this case, there may be serious work problems for both management and the individual worker.

In addition to the meaninglessness of many jobs, people have the problem of dealing with aggression. Work involves the shaping and manipulating of the environment to the advantage of those in it. It involves struggle against the environment.

Now, if for one reason or another we have been made to feel very guilty about aggressive attitudes, we may tend to be very cautious about expressing aggression in terms of work. In relation to this, there is also the problem of being successful.

Many of us learned in childhood that to be successful would cost us love. If we did better in school than our brother or sister, or if we did better than they in completing the chores around the house, we may have found that, instead of earning appreciation and love, we received anger and hate.

Very often this denial of success arises out of the relationship of the child to the father and mother. For example, the sons of unsuccessful men sometimes find it difficult to be successful themselves because they are fearful of succeeding where father failed. And to succeed where father failed might arouse his anger, thereby losing the opportunity of getting the acceptance and love which most of us still desire from him even far into our own adulthood, and even if he is dead.

Therefore, work and success may become equated not with joy and fulfillment but with sorrow and fear and hostility. In apparent contradiction to this, but actually closely related, is the entire problem of rebellion. For the individual who has never solved his rebelliousness against the dictates of the family finds it very difficult, indeed, to take orders from his foreman, or his office manager, or his editor, because he is still engaged in a senseless and often meaningless rebellion against his father or mother.

Along with the meaninglessness of much work, the problem of handling aggression, the fear of success, and rebellion against authority, there is also the problem of immediate gratification.

Work requires a postponement of pleasure. There are many of us who feel put upon when we have to get up in the morning. But we have to get up, we have to get dressed, and we have to go to work.

Not too surprisingly, this is one of the most difficult decisions many of us have to make. Why do we call it "Blue Monday?" It is the day after two glorious days of leisure in which you could do whatever you pleased. If you wanted to make love, or listen to music, or eat at odd hours, or whatever, you could do it. But on "Blue Monday" none of these things is possible, and the infantile individual finds it difficult to postpone immediate gratification and difficult, therefore, to go to work.

In addition, there is the unconscious wish of so many people to return to that wonderful state of infancy where all of our desires were anticipated and taken care of by the everloving hands and breast of mother. To many of us, to be required to give up this happy state for one of work seems intolerable.

Why should we have to do anything? Why should we have to give up that period in our lives when all our needs were satisfied and expend the extra energy of disciplined effort to get something we once received without any effort at all?

This infantile attitude is reflected in our advertising. It is played upon by the advertiser, who is often well aware of man's childishness. We can now turn our television sets on and off without stirring from our bed or easy chair. There is one cereal that advertises itself as "easier to eat." We have frozen foods, instant mixes, and countless other items which all tend to make eating and living effortless.

WHAT CAN BE DONE

At this point, we can say that a work problem — like any other problem — is a product of the sum total of the individual's experiences. However, there are a whole variety of things that a person can do to help solve a vocational problem.

One of the most serious problems we face is that many of us often drift into jobs. We don't make an effort to pick the job that is right for us. In this respect, the vocational advisory services, many of which are connected with our major universities, can be extremely helpful in showing a person where his abilities and talents lie.

Unfortunately, some of the vocational advisory services do not pay attention to finding out whether a man or woman is emotionally suited for a job. For example, someone might discover at the vocational advisory service that he has excellent finger dexterity and is advised to become a watchmaker. Yet, his emotional make-up might be such that it would be very difficult for him to tolerate the intricacies and details of watchmaking.

Thus, in checking to see whether we are suited for an occupation, it is a good thing to check both our emotional suitability and our talent suitability.

Interestingly enough, it is those who have an ability to do all kinds of work who are sometimes among the worst-adjusted members of the work force. These are people of considerable intelligence who are capable of doing almost any kind of job but who often speak of not "having found" themselves in their work.

They are really saying they have not found themselves as persons, as individuals.

Here is one area in which psychotherapy is extremely important. My experience has been that people of this type who come for therapy because of work problems find therapy one of the most financially rewarding activities they could undertake. They discover that rather than therapy becoming an added expense, they are better off financially after therapy because they can earn more.

But I would not like to leave it at just that. There are situations in which a person may be emotionally happier at a job which earns him less than at one which would pay more. Money itself is not enough of a reason to spend one third of our lives in an unhappy situation.

I have heard it said many times that psychotherapy will "destroy the artistic drive." Now, I do think that there have been a number of one-book writers and one-painting painters who were not able to create after therapy. But this is no indication they would have continued creating without therapy.

I can think of a man who for twenty years was a waiter and hated every minute of his job. As a result of several years of therapy, he was able to write two successful novels. I can think of a woman who was interested in the dance but never able to get beyond working in the chorus of a Broadway show. After therapy, she was able to choreograph and direct. I can think of a musician who played in large orchestras. After therapy he was able to conduct and compose.

My experience has been that for most people, therapy frees the creative ability rather than destroys it.

In general, however, there are certain realities that all of us must face. There is no occupation or job where the work is completely pleasant at all times. We have to accept this and be content that in doing our work we reach certain other goals.

It is true that a lot of work is meaningless. But this can be overcome in a number of ways. Our relationships with others at work and outside of work can be rewarding. The man who has a good family life, who has a wife and children that he loves will, for example, be willing to make sacrifices by standing at the assembly line for, what is to him, the greater good.

However, if a man or woman finds his work completely impossible, there are still a variety of new occupations which he can take up. Or he can expend the effort and energy to learn other interests in life which can be just as creative as work.

34.

"What does modern woman get out of work?"
we asked Dr. Pederson-Krag.

XXXXXXXXXXXXXXXXXXX

GERALDINE PEDERSON-KRAG, M.D.

Medical Director,
Huntington Township Mental Health Clinic

In this interview, Dr. Pederson-Krag also discusses:

"What is a victim of 'Westchesteritis'?"
    "What is a woman's first job?"
        "What feelings do some women express in work that do not belong there?"
"Does the highly educated or skilled woman have special problems?"
    "What is the 'preconscious'?"
        "Why are some frightened of success?"
"Why do some women feel they must work although they do not need to for financial reasons?"
    "Does the private secretary usually look at her boss realistically?"
        "What does it mean when a woman uses a masculine nickname?"

34.

This is what Dr. Pederson-Krag said when interviewed in her office:

Usually one thinks of a woman who has to work as unfortunate. But today it is often more of a benefit than a disadvantage, as shown by the fact that over half of the married women in this country contribute to family earnings and most unmarried girls do something useful, whether paid or not. The era when people had nothing to do but amuse themselves is over.

Why do women work? First of all, most women, whether married or single, have skills. They possess the drive, just as men do, to express themselves in work. I believe it is an axiom that we all can express in work many of our aggressive impulses and other drives, such as the need to show off, to create and, as we say in analysis, to "sublimate" feelings we could not otherwise express.

Also, many women have a desire to become people in their own right, just as men do. They find they get status and satisfaction from working. Even society women take jobs, espouse charities and join women's auxiliaries. So you cannot say it is altogether for economic reasons that women work.

This is particularly true, I think, for educated women. Women who go to college spend their late adolescence and young adult lives in getting training comparable to a man's and are trained to use their minds, frequently creatively, or to attain a skill. For them it is irksome to give up all this achievement.

The young college woman who gets married, either right out of college or after one or two years of working as a secretary or at some other job, suffers frequently if she does not work, especially if she marries a well-to-do man who can give her household appliances that cut down housework to a great extent. Her husband wants her only to take care of the children, and to be a companion, an ornament, but she has no occupation for her mind, and often not very much for her body. She feels depressed, useless and guilty because she is not using her talents. If she can find part-time activity, she usually feels better. This is particularly true when the children become old enough so that she is no longer needed as a taxi-chauffeur or dressmaker or telephone-answering service.

If a woman's drive to work, however, is too urgent, too compulsive, we may find that in work there is for her a repetition of bygone emotional situations. She is repeating childhood patterns, including a drive to be masculine in a man's world. Very often a girl who believes her brother was the preferred one, or more important, who felt inadequate when growing up, imagines that if she only were a man, she would attain the sense of dignity and self-sufficiency that she fancies a man possesses. This is particularly true if a woman has received an education which allows her to do work comparable to a man's, say as an engineer or doctor or lawyer; in some factory jobs women can run the automatic machines as well as men.

These are often the women who adopt certain male characteristics. They love wearing slacks. They call themselves rather masculine nicknames, such as "Billie" instead of Bella, or "Hank" instead of Harriet. These women find an outlet in work which they would never find by staying at home.

"I Remember Mama" — Too Clearly

All our adult lives we try to repeat experiences we had when younger even though we have consciously forgotten them. Or we may tend to regard our experiences as though they were repetitions of something that happened earlier, even though they are not. When we consider employment, we find that we tend to regard the company for whom we work as if it were another home.

The company itself plays a sort of maternal role with our immediate boss playing the paternal role. Just as, when we were children, Mother was responsible for the set-up of the home, for the rules, and for three meals a day, so is the organization for which we work. The boss, or Father, whom the children saw only at night and in the morning, is the stern authority, the one who makes plans and is powerful (at least in the stereotype of the household, although very often Mother is actually the boss). The point is that when people work in industry, they tend to regard the set-up the way they did the home when they were children.

This takes place not in a conscious sense, not even in an unconscious sense, but rather largely in a preconscious sense. The unconscious, to my mind, refers to basic infantile drives which are largely physiological and so alien to our adult self that we hardly ever recognize them. Preconscious feelings are those which, you might say, sort of flit through our minds but which we push out of awareness because they are distasteful.

Unconscious drives are more on the level of desire — for food, for equality between the sexes, to see certain people killed whom otherwise we love — the jungle kind of impulses. Preconscious drives are the ones which might have come into our minds but which we just don't wish to see. Similarly, when you meet somebody, perhaps you have several feelings. One is, "I'm glad to see you," but another is, "My goodness, what a dreadful dress you're wearing. Why do you have to come out in an outfit like that?" You quickly brush the latter thoughts aside because you like the person, but the feelings still exist in the back of your mind.

In discussing the ways in which people in industry tend to regard both the company and their boss as they once did their parents, for instance, many have a kind of loyalty to the company which they do not have to the superior. They dislike the boss as overbearing and stupid, but they like working for the particular firm and look forward to the firm's caring for them with pensions for the rest of their lives when they retire.

This is particularly important; I think, for the woman, because all women have strong attachments to their fathers. The woman in industry tends to have a stronger attachment to her boss than the man, I believe. The outstanding example is that of the many women who work as secretaries, devoting themselves to their bosses. The bosses' lives become their lives as they immerse themselves in the office situation. It isn't just that they are conscientious and enjoy their work.

They place an emotional investment in their work far beyond what they are paid.

Take the secretary of one prominent man. She enjoys the same prestige and satisfaction in working for him as does his wife in her position. This, of course, is different from the middle-aged, rather drab woman who works in a factory, although she often has a kind of semi-flirtatious, semi-insulting relationship with the foreman, that is to say, her boss. He kids her along, and she kids him. She feels she is enjoying a sort of prolonged flirtation with him on a somewhat sadistic level which she would not be able to achieve in an ordinary social relationship because conventions are against it. Here is a kind of intimacy and ambivalent working relationship which she finds very satisfactory. In a sense, it is a repetition of earlier experiences with her father.

Why is there a need to repeat the earlier experiences? I don't know that I would exactly call it a need. Rather, it is something inherent in the human psyche, which is somewhat like a piece of raw rubber — you can press it, you can mold it, but it always springs back to its original shape.

To go into what we call a need for the "repetition compulsion" would really require a dissertation on psychodynamics such as described in Freud's "Beyond the Pleasure Principle." You can see an example in those who suffer from the effects of the war, soldiers who have endured a horrendous experience, perhaps having been shot down or under bombardment for a long time. You would think they would like to forget the experience. But instead, they dream about the horror almost every night as they tend to repeat something which would be best out of their mind. It is, in a sense, an attempt to master the dangerous experience.

We also, in daily life, tend to make our adult situations repetitions of our earlier situations, if they were harrowing. I knew a young man, the only child of doting parents who were never so pleased as when he could bring home a good mark from school. That was the big day. He later went into industry and became the junior partner to a rather insecure older man. He had a lot of good ideas and kept running with them to his boss because, in his repetition compulsion, he said to himself, "Father was always pleased when I got a good mark. Therefore, my boss will be pleased when I come up with a bright idea."

But this was not true, because the boss was not only his father, he was his competitor. To a certain extent he was a father; to a certain extent he was a competitor who felt less secure when the younger man came up with bright ideas. Friction developed between them, although both were doing their best to get along.

The place where we find feelings most marked is in our relations with our parents. We have a certain amount of rivalry with parents, as well as a certain amount of erotic stimulation from them and desire for them. We work this out in one way or another, according to our culture. Different cultures are based on different ways of working out the Oedipal situation. We tend to use the same mechanism in later life.

I had a patient once, an only child, who always dreamed of three people engaging in some criminal activity. This was how he thought of his relationship to his parents. He thought his mother and father were up to something devious. This carried over into his work life. He was always at loggerheads with his boss. He felt his boss was inherently wrong although he couldn't find any basis for disagreement. When he attacked a project, he felt guilty, as though the project represented an attack on his mother.

This was a man who, although fairly well gifted, for he always had high qualifications and could land a good job, could never remain in it more than a few years. The emotional tension which arose between him and his employers was such that he would rather go somewhere else and lose his seniority. He had several different skills, so he could move from one company to another. Unconsciously, he looked upon each job as if the work was really an incestuous attack on his mother, spiting and competing with his father. Therefore, when he approached success in any job, he felt guilty and extremely anxious (for the son cannot defeat his father sexually) and moved on to something else.

This seems illogical, yet many things we think and feel seem illogical and we banish them from our conscious thinking because we do not want to face that part of ourselves. It is as though you suddenly found yourself picking somebody's pocket or doing something rather unspeakable, and you say, "No, this can't be me. I hate to think of myself as doing this." So you say, "I never did such a thing. I wasn't there. It isn't me." And thus, the feelings become preconscious. But they are still operative, even in the chrome and glass walls of industry where all is terribly logical and modern and very respectable.

SLAVE TO TWO MASTERS

The working woman expresses her preconscious drives in an acceptably social way that she could not otherwise do. Whereas to the man, his work is an affirmation of manhood and a symbol of his place in society and acquisition of status, to a woman it is the second job she has to do, and she often has to do both at the same time.

A woman's first job is to be feminine, especially a married woman. This entails making herself as charming as possible and her home as livable as possible. She has to do this in competition with the demands of her job if she works, and perhaps a certain sacrifice of excellence follows both in work and in her home. A woman can be extremely well groomed and well dressed and a good hostess, if all she has to do is to be feminine. But if she also has to compete with men at work, she's not going to be as effective either in the home or on the job. It is more complicated to be a woman than it is to be a man in industry. We all have only a certain amount of energy at our disposal, and the married woman who works is trying to do two jobs at once.

Her job, though, can help make her feminine in this respect. If she is married, her husband's income usually goes to pay for the necessities of life, whereas her salary goes for luxuries, for the things about the home that give her status and comfort.

There is an old saying. "You cannot live by bread alone." You can have a roof over your head and food on the table, but if you lack a carpet under your feet and other luxuries, it is the woman's income which will provide it, in many instances. It also provides the college education for the son and pretty dresses for the teenage daughter. Sometimes these things are also very important for the woman's self-respect. They afford her a feeling of stature. A woman who is perhaps adept at keeping a room clean does not feel the satisfaction she would if she were a good secretary. Why that should be I don't know. But it seems to be that way.

Many women are victims of what I call "Westchesteritis," of technological unemployment. They have been good secretaries. Perhaps good stock-broker clerks. But now there is no need for them to work. Their husbands earn enough money. So they are faced with twenty-four hours a day changing diapers, sweeping floors, dusting, shopping. They're not as competent at dusting as the average cleaning woman, and they feel humiliated. In addition, they don't like the work, because it is harder than what they have been trained to do. They can play a good game of tennis, but that's not comparable to scrubbing a floor.

The result is they feel very disappointed in married life, which was their goal, when they find it does not produce the satisfactions for which they hoped. This is one of the dilemmas of women today. They feel they should get the education their brothers and cousins have, but when they get it, what do they do with it?

Another thing, if they don't go to college and don't get married, they are on the unskilled, not the skilled labor market. That is, they don't get either academic training or preparation for highly skilled work, and they are not married either. It is quite a problem for them. There are no easy answers.

Another problem is that of the girl who works for some outstanding industrialist as a secretary, who gets in the habit of regarding him as a kind of model and develops an admiration for him. She compares his image unfairly with that of the young man she married, who is in a much lower income bracket and has far fewer responsibilities. She thinks, "Mr. Smith, who is the Vice President in charge of Whatsis for the Whosis Corporation, is a much more godlike figure than Bill Jones whom I married and who is just a shipping clerk or the second assistant to the second assistant Somebody Else."

Such a woman usually does not have any choice, though, because the Vice President has usually married someone else years ago. Yet, in her mind he remains the hero, the father figure. He never becomes a real person. She transfers to him all the feelings she had as a child for her father. If she is not aware of this, she is likely to be unhappy in her marriage. She is still Cinderella, waiting for Prince Charming.

To sum up, women in industry face the same difficulties and the same psychological problems as men, only more so. Perhaps the demands on a woman are not quite so rigid, as a rule, as on men. Theoretically, the woman can choose more freely what she wants to do.

Industry offers women a sort of social background they would not otherwise have. For instance, the rather timid woman who shrinks from playing either a male or female role, often finds a niche in industry, earning her living and gaining status and respect in a neuter role, the typical worker-bee.

Then there is the type of woman who feels intensely feminine in an organization where there are many men. There she faces less competition than if she worked in a factory or a store where there are many other women.

So it adds up to this: In industry, a woman does not only earn the necessities of life. Her wages are often the means of acquiring luxuries, her occupation a means of social contacts and of making a place for herself in society. More than this, a job gives her scope to use talents that have little place in domestic life, and express drives which otherwise would have to be suppressed and wasted. But most important, perhaps, through her relations with her fellow workers and superiors, she can relive those forgotten and unknown memories that are always striving to reappear.

35.

"Can the unconscious overhead be the biggest expense of all?"
we asked Dr. Orenstein.

LEO L. ORENSTEIN, M.D.

Associate Clinical Professor, Department
of Psychiatry and Neurology,
New York University School of Medicine

In this interview, Dr. Orenstein also discusses:

"What is our 'unconscious'?"
   "Is the unconscious rigid and fixed?"
      "Why do some men fail in their work?"
"What causes people to be indecisive?"
      "Is unhappiness often caused by the unconscious?"
         "What is the meaning of conflict?"
"What is a compulsion?"
      "What determines our choice of work?"
         "Why is adolescence such a stormy time of life?"
"Is our psychic energy limited?"
      "Does the unconscious control our motivations?"

LEO L. ORENSTINE, M.D.

35.

This is what Dr. Orenstein said when interviewed in his office:

In a broad sense, the unconscious is the sum total of the mental and emotional experiences of a human being. It can be compared to a collective storehouse. At the present state of our knowledge, I cannot say this storehouse is anatomically located in the brain, although it may very well be, because the brain is a very important storage space for impressions, attitudes and experiences which occur over the years. Actually, "the unconscious" is a concept of a part of the mental functioning of a human being.

This idea of the unconscious might be easier to understand if I discussed for a moment the conscious part of our mental life. All of us hear, see and do things which, in turn, give us impressions, feelings, attitudes and ideas. These are part of our conscious awareness, and although consciousness is a very important part of our experience, it is only a small part of the total mental apparatus.

There may be feelings, for example, which arise from a physical experience at the little finger, or in the viscera. Outer parts of our body and internal organs and systems also have their impact on the mental functionings of the moment. The breathing of the lungs, the beating of the heart, the process of digestion and our entire metabolism are only a few of the bodily functions about which we have very little conscious awareness. To be sure, when we are hungry, for example, we have a conscious awareness of this fact, and when we are terribly hungry we may even experience certain painful sensations.

But although conscious thought and impression may appear to contain a great deal of awareness, psychoanalysts know that the greatest quantity of total mental functioning is not available to the conscious state at any given moment because of the many physiological and psychological limitations within the human being.

In summary, the unconscious is a store of energy which determines much behavior. If there is a lot of unconscious conflict, this may become a liability to an individual. The word "conflict" means the same thing in psychoanalysis as in the English language in general — a struggle between opposing forces. We know that there are many struggles on in — and rooted in — the unconscious part of the mental life of the individual. There are wishes of a kind, and fears of the wishes, and the result is conflict, sometimes an impasse kind of conflict where nothing constructive can result.

At the conscious level an individual may be aware of a conflict. Allow me to use as an example of unconscious conflict the rather well-known "hand washing" compulsion. There are some people who have a need to wash their hands all the time. In itself, the actual washing and scrubbing may prove a serious liability because it can very likely lead to abrasions and infections of the hands. But in addition, it wastes a lot of energy and takes up a great deal of time. In short, the symptom of hand washing is an attempt to solve a problem uneconomically.

Furthermore, such a compulsion means that although the victim of the symptom is consciously aware that something is wrong, that something is going on which he doesn't want to go on, nevertheless he cannot help doing it. What determines his compulsive behavior is a complex and complicated arrangement of forces about which he is not at all aware. These require fairly extensive and detailed psychiatric and psychoanalytic investigation to bring them into conscious recognition and understanding so that the patient may understand and control them wisely.

WASTE IN TIME, ENERGY AND HAPPINESS

With this brief background on conscious and unconscious conflicts, I will now attempt to show how the unconscious can interfere in basic life adjustments, including work and business, and how it may at times become the biggest overhead of all.

In the first place, the motivations which drive us to choose and perform in all areas of life, including love, work and business, are the secrets of the unconscious. The great majority of us do not know why we do what we do in the ways we do it. I might even add that the motivations behind choice and performance are rigidly controlled by the unconscious. Every sensible person, for example, has given up making New Year's resolutions. This type of resolution is a universal joke, for unless the resolution just happens to coincide happily with our basic motivation, it is quite useless to make it.

Let us suppose we ask a man to tell us why he is a salesman. "I haven't the slightest idea," he might answer quite honestly. "It somehow just happened." In thinking about the question, however, he might add, "Well, my father was a salesman — and a darn good one." Part of the answer to why he was motivated to become a salesman might be as simple as that. In effect, there was a conscious effort to be like the father because the father was successful.

Behind this motivation to imitate the father, however, there is quite likely to be found the fact that the father was successful in his relationship with the son. Consequently, what the father was doing became a very pleasurable and wonderful thing for the son not only to watch, but also to experience and share with his father, even though he may in no way have helped the father sell anything.

The opposite may also be true. The son of a successful salesman may not want to be one and thus does not become one. Here also the motivations stem from what has been formulated and solidified at a very early age in the father-son relationship. To the son, for example, to be a successful salesman may mean being away from home a great deal, having little time to share family experiences. While such a family may enjoy tremendous success in the sense of a nice home, respect in the community, and the like, very little time may have been available for the ordinary and rather simple commonplace exchanges that are very necessary for every child to experience.

A youngster is not necessarily proud of his father because the father is the world's most successful businessman, or professional. He is often much prouder of his father because he could take time out from his business and check on how things are going at school, or watch him play ball, or play ball with him.

In other words, a positive identification with the father, or a complete disappointment in the father, may determine the choice of a vocation. Simultaneously, it can lead to other steps of development and to the ultimate capacity for functioning in adult life. We all know that parents, knowingly and unknowingly, exert important influences on the choices their children make. Whether these influences are constructive or destructive, is a matter of how the influences are exerted and experienced. Parents as well as children have conscious attitudes which are colored by their unconscious conflicts, so that what parents do with their children is very much determined not only by their daily awareness but also by the hidden sources of the unconscious.

A young man recently told me about his difficult relationship with his parents. On one hand, they constantly complain about his very apparent lack of independence, and it is true that at times he is so completely dependent that he is afraid to say yes or no even though the answer is obvious to all, including himself. But to give an answer would mean to take a position and he is too frightened to do that.

As he was discussing this unfortunate situation, he recalled that when he was a youngster, he and his mother and father visited a place where his parents were very much interested in taking photographs. He himself had never used a camera before, he was seven years old at the time, and he remembered that when his parents attempted to teach him how to take a picture they could not stop yelling at him about all the mistakes he was making. As he recalled this incident it was easy to see that what he was really saying was, "If they wanted me to learn how to take pictures, why didn't they give me a chance to experiment a little and find out?"

Assuming, however, that a youngster has a fairly good experience in the course of growing up, he is then prone to have relatively few conflicts and can use his energies for productive work. It has been demonstrated time and again that the more inner conflicts there are, the more energy will be used in the struggle with them. Since every person has only a certain quantity of energy available to him, the less he wastes, the more he can use wisely. The corollary is also true: The more he must waste, the less he can use productively.

For example, many a driver at some time or other has become lost while traveling, spending more energy and time in ultimately arriving at the destination than necessary. The result is that there is less energy and time (they are interrelated) to be used at the destination. In the same sense, a boy may start out in school with the ambition to be like his father, a successful lawyer, let us say. But at around the age of fifteen, a typical age for the turbulence of adolescence, he discovers he cannot concentrate on academic work and possibly becomes greatly interested in sports.

When the father is called to school, the teacher tells him, "We know Johnny is very smart, but he is not working up to par and we are quite disappointed and displeased with him." The father becomes displeased also. Everyone treats Johnny as if he were deliberately not studying, as if he were a bad little boy. What is ignored time and time again, is that something is happening to Johnny at the age of fifteen which the boy also dislikes.

In a sense, what ultimately will prove to be the adult personality of an individual is being established during puberty. At the same time, this is a period of great difficulty because, in part, this is unfortunately the time when a person has his first real clash with reality. Johnny may have done very well in the first few years of high school, then began to slump because what happened prior to this period has already established certain conflicts in the struggle which now overwhelms him. His apparent loss of interest in academic work and turning to sports may be his way of holding on and staying above water, so to speak.

For the majority, however, these years are a stormy period which they weather and emerge stronger and with a more solidified personality. But the point is that emotional turbulences occur at this time because of what is going on in the unconscious, and if the conflicts are severe enough and last long enough, there will most certainly be failure and waste, possibly throughout life.

Most of us have come across the person who is puzzling in the sense that although he is very clever, he seems to be a constant failure on the job. For example, a man may choose to study medicine and do very well until such time as he goes into private practice. Then, one disappointment follows another, and he, as well as everybody about him, is completely mystified.

One medical doctor who came to me for psychoanalytic help had actually graduated from medical school at the top of his class, was highly successful as an intern and resident physician at a large hospital, but, thereafter, had been an almost constant failure. In this case, psychoanalytic investigation showed that, up to the time he entered private practice, he had existed in a basically dependent state of living. Somebody was taking care of him in the area of money and in the area of work, where he was constantly supervised. When he went into private practice, however, he was on his own completely. That was when he began to run into difficulty.

Many bright young talented lawyers, dentists, artists, writers and actors and actresses have started out with tremendous success, only to end in failure. I think we have to place the responsibility for this huge waste on the unconscious. Whatever conflicts were operating before reality began to demand more mature behavior and accomplished performance from the individual, may have become more crippling afterwards. The conflicts may become overwhelming. Then the total personality of the person slumps and he cannot keep up with the frustrations with which reality is always confronting us in our daily lives.

From early childhood, frustration is part of daily civilized living. It is inevitable and unavoidable. Frustration means some form of interference with expression of an instinctual drive. We cannot live in a very complex society while at the same time giving constant expression to every impulse that arises. It is obvious that any interference with an impulse requires some frustration of the impulse.

It is my opinion that were it theoretically possible to lead a totally frustration-free life, an individual would be extremely unhappy in terms of our cultural patterns and ways of life. There probably is a very short period of life without much frustration and without very much awareness, the first few months of life where parents take care of most of the needs of the child. In these early months, conflicts are almost nonexistent, the unconscious is undeveloped, and therefore, there is little, if any, unconscious loss and waste.

I point this out because, if we compare the first few months of life to adult life, it is possible to see why it becomes very difficult for some people to move into adulthood with reasonable certainty and why they cling stubbornly to some of the patterns of earlier life. It is, unfortunately, true that some people grow physiologically but are stunted in their emotional and psychological growth. I do not mean to imply that an individual really stops growing and remains like a six-month-old infant. I simply mean that because of what happens early in life, because of the conflicts which develop, and because of the way the individual attempts to deal with these conflicts, certain rigid patterns are formulated which carry over into the adult personality.

The word "infantile" is used quite frequently in an attempt to describe what I mean, but it does not tell the whole story. An adult individual may be afraid to make a decision, for example, not because he never in his life knew how to make a decision, but perhaps because he grew up in a home where the parents maintained the attitude: "Children should be seen and not heard." While such parents might make many demands on a child, at the same time these demands might be frequently contradictory and not allow the child to experiment, to risk making a few mistakes.

We know, for example, that if a child just learning to walk falls but gets up and starts walking again, pretty soon he falls less and less. Should a child have a very anxious mother, however, one who cannot tolerate seeing him fall and creates a terrific scene the first time he does fall, the child will very soon sense his mother's anxiety and stop walking. This is an attempt on the part of the child to please the mother, but at the child's own great expense.

If we now translate this rather dramatic example into less dramatic form, we can see how indecisiveness can develop in response to parental demands. A conflict does not occur because of one event happening at one moment. It is, rather, a cumulative thing. The indecisive man is not that way because he was not allowed to learn how to walk by making mistakes, nor because his history may show that he had a very strong, demanding and moralistic father. We have to know more about what kind of relationship existed between father and son.

To give another example. If every time a boy wanted to do something and sensed that the father was displeased, he might have little by little begun to withdraw from his relationship with his father. This withdrawal goes on over many years as the unconscious stores more and more reactions to this type of father. By young adulthood, the individual may unconsciously be reacting to all men irrationally and basically in a childlike manner. I hardly need add how wasteful and expensive this type of reaction may ultimately prove to be.

Another good example of how very costly an unconscious conflict can be is illustrated in the following case. I once knew a very bright and capable middle-aged woman who was most successful in her career. She had a younger brother who was ineffectual and having a difficult time in making financial ends meet. Although she had many alternatives available to her to be helpful to him — and it is understandable that a person would be eager to help a close relative — she allowed her unconscious to exploit the realities. Instead of helping him get a job, she chose instead to pass secretly on to him her employer's merchandise, which he then sold illegally.

Most of us would call this stealing, which it was, and she was eventually charged with a crime and prosecuted. But at the time, she herself did not consider it stealing. She had somehow consciously rationalized her behavior which came essentially from unconscious conflict. Because of these unconscious conflicts she had destroyed her own professional position, which had taken many years to achieve, and she had also failed to help her brother. By her own acts she destroyed herself and him.

While this woman did not undergo psychoanalytic treatment, it is nonetheless my opinion that analysis would have disclosed intense ambivalent feelings towards her brother which compelled her to behave in a most irrational manner, the unconscious once again proving to be extremely costly.

THE FEAR OF SUCCESS

Unconscious waste and expense can be thought of not only in terms of lost time and money, but also in loss of happiness. The incidence of divorce, for example, has enormously increased in America, and divorce is most certainly both an economic and emotional waste and expense. I do not mean to imply that a particular divorce necessarily spells out something bad and shouldn't take place under certain circumstances in which the mental health of the two parties, or of their children is seriously threatened. I am not here to moralize but rather to look at issues — I trust, objectively.

Divorce is the result of incompatibilities which may have even been apparent during courtship but which were "deliberately" either ignored or not recognized. People can frequently go on doing the very things they know are not best for them. Neurotic reasons always have their roots in the unconscious.

It often happens that the very thing which will make life quite incompatible a few years hence is what attracts one young person to another. It is often very disturbing for a person to discover that negative attitudes begin to appear either right after marriage or sometimes just after the decision to get married. But it usually takes a few years for those unwanted feelings to become so pronounced as to make divorce inevitable.

There are times, however, when two people could live very happily together if they were willing to do a less costly thing than divorce — seek psychological treatment. It is interesting to note that not infrequently when the husband or wife decides on treatment because of incompatibility in marriage, and stays in it long enough to show improvement, that is the very time the other partner begins to object to the treatment. This sometimes vehement objection, which may become outright interference, is not difficult to understand if we know that the root of the trouble lies within the unconscious where possible marital success may loom as much too frightening.

We all know people who are actually so frightened of being successful in all areas of life that they constantly do everything within their conscious power to hurt themselves and avoid success. In addition, we may have seen individuals who, having reached success, have dramatically and rapidly fallen into depression or other types of illness almost as if they had deliberately arranged their lives to hurt themselves. I have seen this happen to both professional and laboring people. I know of a man who waited for twenty years to become a foreman and within a few months after he became one, fell acutely ill. The illness does not have to be psychiatric, because many physical illnesses such as blood pressure, heart disease and ulcers of the stomach have many of their determinants in the psychic organization of a human being. I have also seen instances in marriage where, as long as the husband is not very successful and is struggling hard, the partners get along reasonably well. But as soon as the man is promoted to vice president, let us say, he may become depressed, or the wife may develop a severe anxiety state and the marriage quickly falls to pieces.

There is no area of life where I could not document how frightening it is for some people to allow themselves success, and how "preferable" failure may unconsciously be. Millions of people struggle all the time, waste energy and avoid any semblance of happiness. It is as if they had only one goal in life, to prove to themselves that they could never be happy. Although no one can be perpetually happy, I do believe that every human being is entitled to some happiness.

In summary, I wish to point out that although the unconscious is rigid and fixed because of life experiences and conflicts which take place over a long period of time, it is, nevertheless, an essentially elastic institution with many reversibles. If this were not true, psychoanalysis as a form of treatment would not have become a possibility. Employers, among others are more and more realizing that psychological treatment can be a good investment for their employees. In short, both in terms of happiness, and of dollars and cents, psychological treatment, if needed, pays off to the individual, to the employer and to society.

36.

"What does money mean to people?"
we asked Dr. Polatin.

XXXXXXXXXXXXXXXXXXX

PHILLIP POLATIN, M.D.

Professor of Clinical Psychiatry, College of
Physicians and Surgeons, Columbia University

In this interview, Dr. Polatin also discusses:

"Why do we like to shop at the supermarket?"
"Are we all emotionally deprived in childhood?"
"Why do some people think of money as 'dirty'?"
"Can hate and rage be related to money?"
"When is money an end in itself?"
"Why do some boondoggle on the job?"
"Do some men control their wives through money?"
*"Why does a 'good-time Charley' always want to pay the
bill?"*
"Why can't some men ask for a raise?"
"Can money be a magic weapon?"
"Why are maids often mistreated?"
"Why do some people want to get rich quickly?"
"What kind of person is the irresponsible credit buyer?"

PHILLIP POLATIN, M.D.

36.

This is what Dr. Polatin said when interviewed in his office:

Most of us at one time or another have shopped at a supermarket. And most of us have often come away from the store with more foodstuffs and household supplies than we originally intended to buy or actually needed.

This overbuying is what the owners of the market were shrewdly banking upon, and it is one of the chief reasons for the tremendous success of the large chain stores. For the supermarket operator knows, either consciously or by intuition, three important characteristics which all of us possess to some degree.

Some of us are wasteful, some of us are hoarders, and most of us are impulsive in our buying. However, in most of us these characteristics are well diluted and quite mild, and present no problems either financially or emotionally. Before we talk about the psychological meaning of our impulsiveness, our wastefulness and our miserly hoarding tendencies, let me tell you about a man who recently came to consult me.

"One year ago I saw an $85.00 suit for sale," he said. "But I bought a $45.00 one instead. You know, I could have afforded the $85.00 one, which I liked very much. And I've just bought *another* cheap suit after a year of regret over buying the first one!"

This may sound unimportant and seem trivial on the surface. But this man's entire life was wrapped up in his conflicts about spending hard-earned money which he had increased through wise investments. He was like a squirrel hoarding for the hard winter ahead. However, in this case it was as if the squirrel had been transplanted to Florida but still persisted in preparing for a Maine winter.

Love, Security, Money

All of us, to a greater or lesser degree, have been deprived in childhood. Most obviously, there are some who did not have adequate food, shelter, or clothing. The man mentioned above had lived through a very difficult childhood financially, and he illustrates the fact that early conditioning by deprivation can establish patterns of behavior which persist even when our living conditions have changed and we no longer need to struggle for physical survival.

But not so obvious as this is the fact that all of us, no matter what our experience, have been deprived to some degree of the total love and security which children crave.

That is, no matter how loving and tender a mother may be, part of growing up is to experience the frustration of many of our wishes, of what we want at the moment. The new-born infant, for example, may have a nurse dancing attendance twenty-four hours a day but that infant must, by necessity, experience hunger, if only for a few seconds, before the bottle or breast is thrust into his mouth.

However, most of us, in the process of maturing into healthy adults, learn to postpone immediate gratification. We learn that being "frustrated" is not necessarily a deprivation of love and security. Yet, with some individuals who have not neutralized either the physical or emotional deprivations inherent in growing up, there may be all sorts of difficulties and symptoms. These may be expressed directly in terms of anxiety or depression, or indirectly in terms of attitudes and feelings about money or people, or they may be incorporated into the character structure of the individual.

The adolescent is a good example of confusion in regard to money, as well as other things. Often a boy or a girl is given an allowance which is adequate and which is spent or saved wisely for the most part. Let us say that the money is given once a week by the parent, but every month or so and for no apparent good reason, at least as far as the mother and father can discern, the young boy or girl "needs" extra cash.

The child will have some story as to "why" he "needs" the money "right now," and he will also have a ready explanation of "why" he hasn't saved ahead or planned in some way for this "extra" expenditure.

At this point the parent is very likely to attempt to explain patiently, or not so patiently, that part of the purpose of an allowance is to teach the wise handling of money. Yet, the intelligent teenager will not understand. He cannot comprehend.

"I need!" he says.

The parent should not be surprised at this evident dullness on the part of his child, for quite simply, *the direct giving* of money represents an expression of love and affection, and by giving the parent gives security.

We can also say that to adults, as well as to children, money can mean physical or emotional security. When you buy too much food in the supermarket, or when you don't spend enough, or when you ask people to give you money, you may be unconsciously acting out, in a very mild degree, unresolved childhood conflicts about love and security.

"Valuable" Possessions

The man who couldn't bring himself to spend $85.00 on a suit which he could well afford but bought instead a $45.00 one which he did not like, could not in any way be called a miser. After all, he did spend the $45.00. What we mean by "miser" is a person who places such value on money that possessing it alone is pleasure. It is an end in itself.

The miser may live in filth or squalor, or he may be a beggar who has money in the bank. Most of us are familiar with such sickness through sensational newspaper stories, the Collier brothers in New York being perhaps the most publicized in recent years.

If you remember, when the police finally broke into the brothers' two-story house, they found not only a considerable amount of hoarded money but hundreds of burned-out light bulbs, yards of tiny pieces of string, mounds of old newspapers and magazines going back 50 years, rotted food; and among other things, and most significantly, the police found that the brothers had not used the working toilet facilities.

Very frequently in the process of early bowel training, a mother will be intimidating, prohibiting and punishing. If she is very punitive during toilet training, it may arouse considerable anxiety in the child and it may give him the idea that his feces are extraordinarily valuable.

Now, in circumstances of this type the child often develops constipation — he holds back this very valuable possession. This attitude may be carried over in the unconscious into adulthood, where feces may then be equated with money, or with absolutely everything with which the person comes into contact, as happened with the Collier brothers.

Most languages have the expression "dirty money." The same connotation is expressed by the phrase "filthy lucre." In effect, money may mean the "filthy valuables" which a person may want to hang onto at all cost, or else throw away with hate and rage.

Some time ago I was treating a young man who had considerable unconscious hate and rage towards his parents, especially his mother. He had little contact with her after his father died but upon her death he discovered she had left him a legacy of about ten thousand dollars.

This young man had no other money and poor job prospects, but in one week he had spent or given away the entire ten thousand. He bought clothing, then burned holes in it with cigarettes — not "deliberately," of course — and in general "threw it away."

Here, his mother's money represented to him a weapon of aggression and a means to express hate and rage. He flouted his mother, annihilated her, and showed that he valued her no more than he did the money.

In relation to money as a symbol of aggression, there is the employer who is paying a salary and who has the feeling that he is giving up something very precious. He wants excessive value for his expenditure and he often becomes what is called "a slave driver," a Simon Legree.

This aggression is very common in women who employ domestic help, whether by the day or week, and possibly most severe where the domestic help "sleeps in." There is often the attitude on the woman's part that she is spending a sum of money and she must get "full" service, which actually means exploitation. The worker is now her slave because she is spending money on her.

In the case of the employer in business who uses money to take advantage of his employees, or to intimidate or coerce them, the money again represents the hate and rage which the employer experienced in childhood. For the woman who uses money as a weapon of aggression against domestic help, there is often a direct getting-even process in relation to her own mother.

The woman has now reversed roles, she playing the part of the mother, the domestic the part of the child, and she constantly whips the domestic just as the mother whipped her, hated her and exploited her psychologically. In this sense money is power, but in its deepest sense, it is a weapon of aggression.

On the other hand, and very similar to the young man who "threw away" his mother's legacy, there is the employee who has extreme hate for his immediate boss, or for the person or company which employs him. Again, this is childish defiance and rebellion expressed in boondoggling, prolonged coffeebreaks, going to the bathroom, hanging around the watercooler, or other time-wasting devices. The employee "gives" as little of his services as possible, regardless of what he is being paid, because this childish defiance and rebellion causes him to keep back what is "precious."

In direct relation to the above there are the men who control their wives through money. They dole out sums to them, they put them on allowance instead of entering into some sort of partnership where the money will be shared.

I've repeatedly had wives come to me and say, "I can't stand my husband's attitude toward me. I can't tolerate the way he manages me. Everything is doled out as if I were his belonging, as if I were his mistress. He's paying me. I can't stand it!"

Interestingly enough, there is usually no quarrel with the amount of money doled out. The man may be very generous, but nevertheless he is using money as an instrument of power, aggression and masculine superiority.

And often men who use money as power, as in this way, are the very ones who are basically most insecure about their aggressiveness and masculinity.

Self-Value

In apparent contrast to the man who doles money out, yet closely related in actuality, is the one considered "the great sport." He buys treats for everybody, he picks up the bill on every occasion, he's always giving gifts and presents, and often expensive ones.

He's "the good time Charley" whom everybody loves, whom everybody compliments, and whom everybody takes advantage of, but he doesn't care; he loves them regardless.

In this case, money is used, not as with the adolescent who wants the "gift" of security and love, but as a payment, to buy affection. This type of person can't tolerate the possibility of people rejecting him, not loving him, even if they are mere leeches, and so he calls attention to himself in an exhibitionistic way. "Look at me!" says he. "I'm here, so love me because I'm great, wonderful" — and so forth.

But from the point of view of the unconscious, this represents an insecure individual who feels inadequate and inferior. In order to make up for the insecurity which he feels so strongly, and which derives from the unconscious feeling that he never had enough love and affection in childhood, he now attempts to obtain what is forever lost by "buying" false good will.

His actions make him happy and gratified, temporarily. His gratification can only be temporary, however, because he must repeat the process over and over in order to keep making sure of something of which he can never really be sure.

Using money to express insecurity or devaluation of self are those who take underpaid jobs or never ask for a raise, and professional people who don't charge enough for their services.

Not asking for enough money, even when lacking enough of it to live on, is an expression of low self-esteem conveyed in terms of money. In effect, such people are saying, "I'm not worth much." They manage to explain their misfortune to themselves by thinking that others are more capable or more deserving, or by rationalizing that they might lose their jobs if they asked for a raise.

But the fact is, they cannot set a value on their financial services because they cannot set a value upon themselves as worthwhile human beings. This type of man or woman is expressing unconscious feelings of unworthiness usually related to some lack of love in his relationship with his parents.

If there has been emotional deprivation, the child may develop a fantasy that the parents do not love him *because he is not worthy of love.* He is not lovable, he feels, and this is carried over into a conscious expression in relation to money.

"I don't deserve a good salary."

"I don't deserve a big fee."

"I'm not much good."

This is thought regardless of the person's mechanical, professional or intellectual abilities and qualities.

Let me give you a brief case history. One man, who is very successful in business, some years ago worked very hard, very long hours, and was seldom home with his wife and children. He had signed a business contract which gave him such a small profit that he lost money on his services, which were worth a great deal more.

He couldn't understand this apparently foolish act of his, but in the course of treatment the following became clear to him and to me. Part of the reason he worked such long hours was unconsciously to avoid contact with his wife and children with whom he was uncomfortable as a husband and father. The responsibilities of marriage and parenthood disturbed him.

Furthermore, an older woman was the head of the other company. In his fantasy, the contract and the money did not matter at all. To him, this woman would always take care of him, provide for him for ever and ever; money was of no consequence, the contract insignificant.

Thus, he had signed anything that she and her attorneys had specified because she was "protecting" him. Of course, this was his fantasy, the fantasy of the powerful, all-receptive, encompassing, lovingly protective mother.

It was a fantasy of a mother he never had.

When this became clear to him and the contract expired, he demanded and received a new contract which was worth three times his former one and which realistically represented his rendered services.

Here was a man who had previously lost a great deal of money by an unwise contract which had been imposed upon him *and which he had accepted* because of his immature and unrealistic attitudes.

MAGICAL DOLLARS

While speaking of fantasy we must talk of those people who *WANT TO GET RICH QUICK.* I know a man who represents this type very well. Ten years ago he started to invest in penny stocks. If the stocks went up, he worried lest they go down. If they went down, he would be beside himself with anxiety as to whether they would go up.

He was always buying and selling, always worrying, and always working. But by the end of ten years, when most people had increased their holdings substantially by wise investment for long-term gains, he hadn't earned or lost a penny and was right back where he had started.

We all know people of this type. The setting in which they invest their money and time and effort may not be the stock market — it may be in fly-by-night businesses or inventions — but no matter what the setting, the money and energy are invested in such a way that the investors are always worried and anxious.

All children have the fantasy that whatever they wish for will be accomplished, will actually take place. Such a magical formula may run from pulling a string and thinking that now the cloud won't cover the sun to construing the momentary wish of death to the parent as a real threat to the parent's life. Of course, we all must learn that we are not the center of the universe, nor is anyone a Divine Being.

But the get-rich-quick individual has not gotten beyond the childish fantasy of magical thinking, of rubbing his Aladdin's lamp in the belief that merely thinking a wish will have it instantly gratified. However, this person is so insecure in his infantile magic that he is constantly anxious and never satisfied.

He goes in a circle, time and time again, and although there are rare exceptions where the get-rich-quick really does get rich quick, this type of individual can never win psychologically, for his basic insecurity and infantilism have not been touched or resolved.

But the fantasy of money as a magic weapon is not by all means restricted to this type of person. Far more common is the irresponsible credit buyer, and as a matter of fact, also the so-called "responsible" one.

Hundreds of millions of dollars a year are borrowed by families and individuals who, in effect, want what they want when they want it, not a moment later. Of course, in our contemporary inflationary approach to living this is socially acceptable behavior. "Everyone does it," goes the reasoning, "why not me?"

Actually, for the most part, credit buying is subject to some controls. Yet there are many individuals who have no controls of their own, and they often allow themselves to be exploited.

"I must have it now," these people say. "I want because I want."

Again, here is the use of money as magic — the infantile need to acquire, to own, regardless of any external circumstances; it is the childish inability to postpone immediate pleasure.

In conclusion, we may now say that all of these phenomena can be demonstrated to exist in all of us. But in most of us these qualities are so diluted that they cause no anxiety or difficulty within us or in our relations with others.

Most of us are fairly normal in our attitudes and feelings about money. After all, we tend to save for a rainy day, or we invest in life insurance, or we provide for our children's education. All of this can be said to be within the framework of attitudes towards money which, with a little exaggeration and distortion, can lead to miserliness and hoarding. Primarily, it is motivation which determines whether we are behaving in a healthy or sick way about money.

If an individual's basic attitudes and feelings and actions about money cause no conflict, no anxiety, depression or other unhealthy reactions, and if these same attitudes, feelings and actions afford satisfactions so that the person is relaxed and tranquil about the whole monetary transaction, then it can be said that the individual is behaving in a perfectly normal way. Unhappiness, tension, frustration, lack of satisfaction, mean there is a problem.

37.

"Why do some people want something for nothing?" we asked Dr. Eidelberg.

XXXXXXXXXXXXXXXXX

LUDWIG EIDELBERG, M.D.

Clinical Professor of Psychiatry, Department
of Psychiatry, State University of New York,
Downstate Medical Center

In this interview, Dr. Eidelberg also discusses:

"Is there a hidden pleasure in stealing?"
　　*"Do most people who steal, swindle and rob do so because
　　　　they need what they take?"*
　　　　"How does the conscience of man function?"
"Why won't many of us take something for nothing?"
　　*"What does it mean if a man always allows others to pay
　　　his bill?"*
　　　　"Is the taking of one pencil an act of stealing?"
"Is the Mann Act realistic?"
　　"Why are some only too willing to be 'suckers'?"
　　　　"What is an unconscious masochist?"
"What is the difference between guilt and remorse?"
　　"What function do our jails serve?"
　　　　*"Why do many of us not separate aggressive from
　　　　sexual pleasures?"*

LUDWIG EIDELBERG, M.D.

37.

This is what Dr. Eidelberg said when interviewed in his office:

It is true that many of us have a conscious or unconscious desire to get something for nothing. But it is also true that the large majority of us desire to get something for something. In other words, most of us are perfectly willing to pay in one form or another for what we receive. Also, a number of things in life are freely given to us, and there is nothing wrong in our accepting them.

The problem arises, however, when a person tries to obtain something which is not given to him, but which he attempts to get by some form of subterfuge. A descriptive explanation of such a person is: "His morality is not very strong. He does not have enough inhibition." Also, this type of person uses various excuses for himself, and society does the same for him. "Everybody does it," people say, and that is supposed to be the explanation of his behavior. Or, another excuse: "He is a poor man. He didn't have any money or skills, and there was no other way for him to get money except by stealing, robbing and swindling."

Many years ago, kleptomania was singled out as an example to demonstrate conclusively that purely rational causes cannot be considered responsible for that form of stealing in which there is a compulsion on the part of the person who, able to pay, steals an object where the risk taken is far out of proportion to the value of the object. Yet at the same time, we had a great deal of trouble in using a similar approach when the person was poor and the stolen object highly important.

But today we know that in every crime, large or small, some kind of unconscious motive is responsible. There is no doubt in my mind that the simple need for an object will only rarely produce stealing, swindling and robbery. In addition, it will only rarely produce dishonest behavior which may or may not be considered legally as theft.

The Unconscious Factors

The first unconscious motive which we may mention in relation to stealing is the individual's insistence on having an aggressive pleasure, only obtainable if he does something forbidden. All of us possess such tendencies, all of us are able to experience pleasure from the forbidden. (Ludwig Eidelberg, "Studies in Psychoanalysis," International Universities Press, 1952.) But those of us who are ideally normal are able to sublimate this wish. Instead of stealing, we are able to achieve things by legitimate methods. For example, a scientist is able to experience aggressive pleasure by discovering a secret of nature, an engineer, by building a tunnel or a bridge.

There are various forms of pleasure. One person enjoys smoking a cigarette, another reads a book, and still another drinks whiskey and soda. But psychoanalytic theory divides all pleasure into two groups. First, there are those pleasures in which the person is interested in sharing his enjoyment. These are the so-called "positive" pleasures. (They may be called "sexual" only if it is clearly understood that "sexual" does not mean genital sex exclusively, but rather anything and everything connected with the positive life forces within us all.)

The second group of pleasures are the aggressive ones experienced by the victor who defeated the victim. For example, when you play chess with a friend, you are interested in winning the game, and you obtain your aggressive pleasure only if you do win. It is impossible for both players to enjoy the aggressive pleasure at the same time in the same game. On the other hand, when a man makes love to a woman — if he is normal — he is interested in making love in such a manner that it pleases both.

Most neurotics, however, for reasons connected with infantile wishes, are interested in having aggressive and sexual pleasure at the same time with the same object. Consequently, a man will be attracted to a woman who is the wife of his best "friend" because in making love to her he is not only partly enjoying sexual pleasure but also aggressive pleasure because he is cheating his friend. We very often find in an-

alysis that should this woman, for example, divorce her husband and marry the friend, the ex-lover-now-husband suddenly finds that her caresses lose their "aggressive" glamour.

It should be made clear in connection with the study of
love and aggression that the original gratifications of the so-
called infantile sexual wishes are first encouraged by our
parents in childhood training. However, after a certain time,
an act which has been considered to be something good becomes something disgusting or forbidden — sitting on the
pottie, for example. Thus, to the child, the same act can
serve not only a sexual but also an aggressive pleasure.

Under normal conditions, most of us discover in growing
up that it is wise in our actions to separate the pursuit of
aggressive from that of sexual pleasure. If a man, for example,
is interested in necking with a girl, it is wiser on his part if
he refrains from playing tennis with her at the same time.
Tennis would interfere with his necking and vice versa.

Mixing aggressive and sexual desires causes a decrease in
the intensity of both. There are many people who are afraid
of being overwhelmed by very intense sexual or aggressive
desire. They try to avoid this danger by uniting the two, thus
diluting both.

Some people who are interested in obtaining sexual pleasure
mixed with aggressive pleasure are interested in obtaining
sexual pleasure mixed with some kind of punishment. A
girl should know, for example, that if she allows herself to be
picked up on the street by a man, he will be more interested in
a proposition than a proposal. If she allows herself to be picked
up, she is in a sense inviting and seducing the man to bedding
instead of wedding.

We all know about the overt masochists who themselves
are aware that they can only experience a genital discharge
while being humiliated by the sexual object. But there are
many unconscious masochists unaware that they desire non-
genital pleasure connected with humiliation. This may apply
to the owner of a store, for example, who unconsciously sets
up a situation (or allows one to exist) in which his employees
can easily steal from him.

All of these people are acting out an unconscious desire to
humiliate other people, humiliate themselves, or both. There
was a patient in analysis, for example, who gratified his un-

conscious prostitution fantasy by never paying a bill in a restaurant when he was with others. In other words, there are people who can be seduced into abusing others, and also, people who will always find those whom they can seduce into mistreating them. Franz Werfel wrote a book called "Not the Murderer But the One Who Was Murdered Is Guilty" in which the point is clearly illustrated.

The second unconscious factor related to getting something for nothing stems from childhood. When we are infants we receive all kinds of things "free of charge." While I do not wish to deny that a mother who feeds her child may be considered to be "paid" by the smile of the child, it is obvious that, on a conscious level, this form of paying is not considered legal tender for an adult.

All of us are born immature and dependent upon the care of grownups, but during the period of growing up we slowly have to learn to give and to reciprocate when we receive. But adult individuals who have repressed the infantile wishes keep on behaving as if they really were children and entitled to be fed and taken care of without contributing anything in return. A simple example is the number of people who when they lunch with another person, will continuously "allow" the other person to pay the bill. If these people are analyzed, it is very often found that they have an idea their company is "so marvelous" that the other should be pleased to pay for it. In summary, they behave like children who rightfully assume that by being nice, polite and loving to their parents, they are thereby entitled to the parents taking complete care of them.

A third factor in getting something for nothing is the idea of the "sucker." The United States Government, for example, expects that a great number of citizens will cheat on their income tax each year. It is estimated that if everyone paid his proper tax, income taxes in general could be decreased by at least twenty-five percent. This means that when I, as an individual, pay my proper tax according to the present inflated rates, I am really being discriminated against and in this sense, I could, if I choose, look upon myself as a "sucker." It cannot be denied that it is very difficult to have a completely different standard of morality than everyone else in the society.

It is an unpleasant feeling to think of oneself as a sucker. Consequently, we tend to eliminate this feeling by doing something which proves that, in fact, we are not suckers. But somebody has to start, and so you say, "I will begin being honest and the others may follow. But even if they don't follow me, I will do what I consider to be proper."

On the other hand, some people are only too willing to be "suckers." It is perhaps well known that in Europe and America there was a time when any sale in any shop which sold merchandise was preceded by twenty minutes of bargaining because the shop keepers always put an inflated asking price upon the items, and everyone knew it and acted accordingly. No one thought this practice could be eliminated. But the Quakers, because of their high ethical-religious beliefs, were made so uncomfortable by the fact that some people paid the asking price, not the selling price, that they fixed one price which would be final for everybody, no bargaining acceptable. Although only a few other merchants thought that this fixed price policy would work, it turned out that it was simpler for all concerned and soon most other shops had no choice but to imitate the Quakers.

A fourth factor is that every neurotic act has a moral innuendo. A patient of mine some years ago "suffered" from overeating. The analysis disclosed that one reason for this overeating was the moral wish not to be slim and attractive. To this woman, to be slim and attractive meant to be able to seduce all men and to produce envy in all women because of her "beauty." Therefore, it was moral to overeat. What happened when she began to control overeating? She had to take the bitter disappointment that, although slim and attractive, she did not mobilize the love of all men and the envy of all women.

In many criminal acts, or minor transgressions, the moral innuendo plays a great role. A man may do something — anything — to another man and unconsciously believe it is moral because "he is a son-of-a-bitch and abuses his employees." Or, a grocer may send bills thirty percent higher than the merchandise delivered. He will admit, "Yes, I do it. But look at all of my customers who don't pay their bills!" He cannot see that the two things do not logically make sense, because the higher bills go to customers who always pay their bills.

I would say there is no crime without a moral innuendo, and always the decisive factor is unconscious. There was a patient in analysis, for example, who specialized in holding up brothels, his reason being that brothels were immoral places anyway. While pointing the pistol at the other man, he was unconsciously saying, "It is not true that I am a homosexual interested in playing with the penises of other men. The truth is that I am, on the contrary, depriving them of their money."

This man partly cured himself when one day he discovered the entire loot in a particular brothel to be four dollars. He said to himself consciously, "Am I really this kind of an idiot who, for four dollars, takes the risk of going to jail?" Thus, he started to realize his actions logically did not make sense.

People will very often steal from the rich, or from big companies, or from the state, and their conscious excuse is, "It doesn't matter anyway, for they are rich." But the conscious excuses would not be sufficient if it were not for the unconscious innuendo that this rich person, firm, or state, represents the parents. For, a child is entitled to take from the "rich" parents. Here again we see the repressed infantile wish carried over into adulthood.

Another essential factor related to getting something for nothing is that of guilt and punishment. All individuals have an organ which we psychoanalysts call "superego." The superego is approximately what is referred to in everyday language as the conscience. This organ, as yet, has not been anatomically located but its function can well be described.

Under normal conditions, whenever I have a wish I consider immoral, my superego sends me a signal called a feeling of guilt. With the help of this feeling I am able to reject or modify the immoral wish. However, if I go ahead and gratify this wish I have still another signal called remorse. As a result of the feeling of remorse, I have the need to undo what I have done.

As a matter of fact, it is interesting that in most (if not all) good dictionaries, the difference between the feeling of guilt and the feeling of remorse is not adequately explained. Yet, many of us would agree that we have a different emo-

tional signal when we want to do something than when w
have actually done it.

However, in psychoanalysis, we have found that our pa
tients react to the wishes not with the feelings of guilt bu
with the feelings of remorse, and this necessarily leads to co
fusion. This reaction is explained by the fact that the infantil
wish does not differentiate between the wish and the actio
In other words, when an infant and a neurotic (who is un
consciously an infant) wish someone dead, they behave as i
they had actually killed that someone. And if, by bad luck
the neurotic reads in the newspaper that this somebod
died, he has a feeling of remorse. But what he should feel i
a feeling of guilt that he had such a wish, rather than "boast
he was able to kill the poor fellow. In short, the neurotic -
as the child — is essentially narcissistic and omnipotent.

In many criminal cases, or in minor transgressions, it i
easily provable that the crime was discovered because th
guilty person behaved in such a way as to disclose the crim
and provoke the punishment. This apparently illogical be
havior on the part of the criminal is not illogical, for there i
a "need to confess."

The child learns that his fear of punishment, which goe:
along with his disobedience to the rules of parents, disappear
when he accepts the punishment. Furthermore, the punish
ment is preferable to the fear of punishment because every
thing is "wiped clean" afterwards, all just as it was before th
act of disobedience.

Because they want to stick to unconscious aggressive wishes
and avoid feelings of guilt, many neurotics will instead accep
various kinds of self-provoked punishment, and will consequently feel at ease after being punished. This is similar to the
criminal who, having spent his "time" in jail, feels he did
what society demanded as punishment and now can go out
and once again commit crimes against society.

SIGNIFICATION OF ANALYTICAL INTERPRETATION

Many people have the idea that psychoanalysts have
analytic interpretations for everything. For example, they
claim that the analyst says that whenever you love somebody
it is actually a defense of a wish to hate that person. This is
not true. No analyst, properly trained, will say that whatever

someone experiences actually represents the opposite of what he feels. Every analyst has been trained to refrain from offering an analytic interpretation unless something occurs which does not make sense. There is no reason for analytic interpretation as long as something does make sense, and no analytic interpretation should be attempted in that case.

Why a man will select a particular object to steal can only be ascertained by a detailed and careful analysis of what the object represents to him. It would be superficial to jump to the conclusion that the stealing of a hammer from a factory, for example, represents to the worker the penis of his father or the nipple of his mother.

We have first to prove that the act of taking the hammer did not make sense. We would have to get the worker's co-operation to recognize that what he did was irrational and then, with the help of his associations, we would be able to see why he selected a hammer and not something else. There are specific psychological reasons why a person will select one object and not another, and there are just as specific reasons for the conditions under which he will act. Some people will only steal, for example, under the condition that what they steal is not used by themselves or by their immediate family, but rather by strangers. In that manner they are able to eliminate part of their feeling of guilt.

Psychoanalysts have proven that in certain cases the object the criminal stole was actually a defense against stealing something far more dangerous. Consequently, the actual stolen object represents a relatively harmless compromise. It is much better for example, for a vice-president to embezzle bank funds than to castrate the president of the bank. But you cannot say that gross embezzlement, or the stealing of one pencil from the boss, represents the penis. It may, or may not.

That witty French author, Jean Anouilh, said that if one man dies nobody cares, if ten men die we are surprised, but if one hundred thousand die, we are really shocked. The point here is that there is a difference between the secretary who "steals" one pencil from the boss, or even an entire box of twelve, and the secretary who makes an arrangement with a shipping clerk to steal ten cartons of pencils.

The quantitative approach is legitimate. If a man who has a compulsion to knock once on the door when he leaves his apartment would come to me for advice — and he had no other problems — I would say, "Leave it alone." However, if he has to knock on his door one hundred times and then still has some doubt whether it really was a hundred times, and thus knocks ten times more to make sure, then I would advise him to see a psychoanalyst.

In the same sense, if a man transgresses the law by taking away a pencil from the office every day, and if he has no other problems, there is no reason for society to regard him as a potential sinner because he may gratify his infantile wishes by this relatively harmless act. If this same man is analyzed for some reason, however, then this act of having to take the pencil will be treated as something important. In this case, I would ask the patient to try and not take the pencil today, and then we could see what kind of emotional trouble he will face tomorrow.

From the society's point of view, it is not necessary to assume that everybody who transgresses the rules is a potential or actual criminal. The man who kisses the new bride a bit too passionately is not necessarily going to rape her an hour later. In the same sense, the man who steals pencils and paper from the office is not necessarily going to take company funds nor act in other immoral ways. Even the police are aware of this. In other words, the burglar has his line of work, the pickpocket his line, and very rarely will either of these two commit an armed robbery (let us hope).

The man who compulsively knocks on his door one hundred and ten times is not necessarily (in fact, very rarely) a pervert exhibitionist, and the chances that either he or the pervert will ever commit rape is quite remote. Each has a different "line." For the exhibitionist, many specific factors make him defy the law in exhibiting his genitals. Exhibiting is his line, and he will stick to it through thick and thin.

When people exaggerate everything, then all becomes nonsensical. It is the nihilistic approach to life which tries to eliminate any kind of knowledge. But if we are to make any sense we must use our common sense. It is obvious that a man who arrives in the office two seconds after 9:00 A.M. is not the same as the man who arrives forty minutes late. It cannot be argued that "if he is willing to be two seconds late he will also be an hour late."

I repeat, before we attempt to analyze and look for unconscious factors, we must decide on a conscious level whether an act does or does not make sense.

WHO DRAWS SEXY PICTURES?

I would say that the majority of people do not want to become involved in getting something for nothing. A few years ago a movie company tried to publicize a motion picture about counterfeiters by having men give away genuine one dollar bills. Not so strangely, they found that only a small number of people were willing to take the money.

The normal man does not want to get something for nothing. Although I am not absolutely sure that the act of giving is better than receiving, I would say that both are equally good. Furthermore, if I value myself then I certainly don't want something for nothing. I want to give because I am able to work and produce. I don't have to be kept.

Many people don't realize there is really no such thing as getting something for nothing. In one way or another, they pay. I don't know whether human beings do or don't go to hell when they die, although I think it is a mistake to try to keep people moral by threatening them with a future hell.

I think you can keep people moral by opening their eyes to the fact that the moment they behave in an immoral manner, hell is here in this world in the form of unconscious guilt and punishment which may appear in a variety of ways that spell out unhappiness, misery and self-defeat. Although this idea is difficult to explain to a neurotic, or to a criminal, I do believe it can be sold.

Psychologically speaking, it would be a great advantage if the standards of morality were more generally observed. In order to achieve this goal, we should only insist on that morality which makes sense. For example, our society says that adult men and women who are not married should never have sexual intercourse. That idea does not make sense to me. Or, society says that it is a greater crime for a man to take a girl under eighteen across a state line in order to make love to her than it is to take the same girl some place within the same state for the same purpose. Why should the fact of going across a state line make the act any the worse?

In addition, I should like to add it would be of great advantage to society — and to the individual — if in the handling of criminals, society did not deprive the criminal of his feelings of guilt by punishing him. In psychoanalysis, where the conditions are obviously completely different than in jail, because the neurotic patient is interested in cooperating, we are able to achieve a final aim in which the neurotic is no longer interested in obtaining punishment so he may be relieved of the feelings of guilt. The patient in psychoanalysis is eventually able to eliminate the desires responsible for the feeling of guilt. Therefore, ideally, when a man kills another man, the killer should be treated in such a manner as to free him from the desire to kill. No punishment would then be necessary: actually this would be the worst punishment.

Jesus Christ said to forgive our enemies and turn the other cheek. When we in fact do that, we try to embarrass the person committing the crime. We make him feel guilty, and consequently, we take away his desire to continue committing the crime. In old China, for example, if you were rich and didn't take care of your poor relatives, they would come and commit suicide on your doorstep. This act was an appeal to the superego, nothing else. We have the expression, "To shame him into it." What does it mean but that you are able to mobilize his feelings so that part of himself says to another part of himself, "You son-of-a-bitch, look how you are acting!"

If this would also work with the criminal and the murderer, society would not need external forces such as police. At the same time, I do not wish to imply here that in present-day society, criminals are actually not criminals. They most certainly are criminals, and although they are sick people who should be treated, we must keep on jailing them until such time as most society is willing to grow up, face the facts of life and understand and accept that man is not entirely a rational creature without an unconscious.

Gertrude Stein said, "A rose is a rose is a rose." But in neurosis the trouble is that the rose may not be a rose entirely. It may be something else, too, and therefore, it may mobilize feelings different from feelings which a rose mobilizes. There are great numbers of people who do not want to understand this idea. These people either say that the unconscious is "a lot of nonsense and psychoanalysts are all crazy," or they claim that psychoanalysts think "everything is a penis."

It is such people themselves, however, who are over-sexed. There is a story which illustrates the point. A man came to a doctor because he was having trouble, and the doctor made one dot on a piece of paper. "What is that?" asked the doctor. "Well," answered the patient, "that is a penis." The doctor then made another dot next to the first one, and the patient said, "Those are the tips of the breasts." The doctor then made a third dot. "That's easy," said the patient. "It is the eternal triangle — husband, wife and lover."

The doctor said, "It seems to me that you are over-sexed."

"It is not my fault," said the patient, "that you draw sexy pictures."

38.

"What makes for successful retirement?"
we asked Dr. Goldfarb.

ᗡᗡᗡᗡᗡᗡᗡᗡᗡᗡᗡᗡᗡ

ALVIN I. GOLDFARB, M.D.

Chief, Department of Psychiatry and Neurology,
The Hospital and Home for Aged and Infirm Hebrews

In this interview, Dr. Goldfarb also discusses:

"Why are many afraid of retirement?"
    "What is a 'Sunday neurosis'?"
        "What are some of the real reasons for retirement?"
"Can you 'retire' into something?"
    "Why do some elderly people complain a great deal?"
        "Should the elderly try to act 'young'?"
"Can a man really prepare for retirement?"
    "Do some people give retirement a bad name?"
        *"Is there a difference between the problems of men
        and women when they retire?"*
"Why do the young tend to criticize the old?"
    *"What are the dangers of retirement to Florida or Cal-
    ifornia?"*
        *"What is the difference between the laborer and the
        professional man when they retire?"*
*"How is childhood experience related to adjustment in old
age?"*

ALVIN I. GOLDFARB, M.D.

38.

This is what Dr. Goldfarb said when interviewed in his office:

For many men and women in our society the idea of retirement from work is synonymous with retirement from life. But this does not have to be so, for retirement is often an opportunity to retire into another way of life and, in many of its aspects, a more fulfilling way of life. Nevertheless, there are too many who look forward to "retirement" as if it were a killer, not a time of possible pleasure and fulfillment.

There are a number of reasons for this negative and frightened attitude. One is related to the fact that for many men retirement is often an abrupt and marked change from being a wage earner to becoming a completely "leisure-ridden" person. I say leisure-ridden because in our society we have a high regard for work and for performance; we are measured, and tend to measure ourselves, by what we do, how much we earn, and by how well we do our work or impress others. We believe just as strongly in work and performance as we believe in monogamy, being good mothers and fathers, taking good care of infants and children, early toilet training, and the importance of success and of cleanliness.

This high regard for work and the tendency to measure oneself by performance can be so marked in some individuals that when they retire they develop symptoms similar to the "Sunday neurosis." I'm sure far too many of us are familiar with the man who, after working very hard for five or six days a week, on Saturday and Sunday when he could relax and enjoy himself, promptly gets a headache, or feels completely worn out, and at the same time is tense and anxious. Psychologically, this type of man has a sense of worth and self-respect only when he is performing, doing something. On Saturday and Sunday he is just "Daddy." Possibly his wife orders him to get out of bed early so she doesn't have to make three breakfasts, perhaps he has to do chores around the house, rake the lawn, or take the kids some place, duties he regards as non-productive and degrading. He may, of course, get some pleasure out of compulsive golfing, gardening, repairing, or "do it yourself" activities or even from excessively enthusiastic "fathering" attentions to his children. It is usually characteristic of these substitutes for work that they are not "bad," they are sensible and gratifying, but they are overenthusiastically entered into and pursued — it is "too much of a good thing." However, in general such a person feels downgraded and doesn't feel "good" when away from the job which identifies him as a wage-earner, a doer, and a succeeder even though he may feel physically well.

Thus, for many who retire, the "Sunday neurosis" becomes a constant state which they suffer for their remaining years. They fret, complain, fruitlessly hunt for gratifying pursuits, insist they would feel better if they were given work which, unfortunately, they may no longer actually be capable of, and they drive themselves too hard in seemingly purposeful but actually purposeless activities.

But "retirement" is a big word. It covers a great many changes that occur toward the end of life. Let us first talk about how and why people retire.

In this country men tend to retire at 65 and women are entitled to their old age and Social Security benefits at 62. These are arbitrarily chosen ages, supposedly representing the point at which, for men, fifty percent of the population has died and fifty percent still have some years to go on living. Looking at it another way, the early sixties is the time of life when everyone begins to show signs of aging. It is also the time of life when many people begin to feel their years, develop the attitude that they are living on borrowed time, and want to reap the harvest of their years of work and effort.

There are three large categories of those who retire. One large group, about one-third of the men and women who retire, do so because they are forced to stop work by employers, private businesses or government agencies that have an arbitrarily chosen retirement age. When the person reaches that age he is automatically released without regard to whether he be in poor or good health or whether he has a continuing value to the enterprise.

In the second category are those who retire because their health is so poor that they are delighted when the earliest age arrives at which they can retire on pension or Social Security. They are sick but not so sick that they had to stop work before the retirement age determined by regulation. In this second group are persons who have suffered less-than-severe illness which has left residual impairment — "heart attacks," "strokes," and many other disorders which would have permitted continued work but offered a convenient opportunity to retire.

Third is the group of individuals who give retirement its bad name. These are the men and women who retire because they are very ill, or are quite sick by the time they reach retirement age. Many of them die soon after retirement. They would have died in any case, and retirement had nothing whatsoever to do with their ill-health or their subsequent death. As a matter of fact, in these cases, as in many of those in the second category who are not quite as sick, retirement actually prolongs life because there is less strain on the organism. Unfortunately, illness which precedes retirement has often impoverished the retiring person and his family so that the later years are a time of deprivation and brooding discontent.

There are also psychological, social and economic differences which greatly influence the effect of retirement upon the person. Let us contrast the college professor and the laboring man, both of whom are retired.

From the psychological point of view the uneducated, or relatively poorly educated, man's work is his chief means of gaining and holding family and community status. His main role in life is that of provider. You ask him what he is and he answers, "I am a working man." Often, if not usually, this man has little ability to divert himself and to keep himself pleasurably occupied. Most, if not all, of his entertainment comes from outside himself, by way of television, movies and watching sports. Even in all of these his choice is circumscribed because of his limited capacity to appreciate and enjoy things that are relatively complex. He is prone to boredom and lassitude and may be over-addicted to food, gossip and alcohol. By and large he had gained his chief pleasure from his contacts with his fellow workers, from prideful adherence to a routine, and in varying degrees, from the work itself. Of course, he may say that he "hated" his work, but it was, nevertheless, important and satisfying to him and he may have measured himself in terms of the wages he earned.

What is this kind of man to do when he stops working? Unfortunately, he has little or no capacity to find things to do himself, and he has great difficulty remaining active and interested in people and things. Because of the fact that his income has usually been sharply reduced, he has difficulty in maintaining his status in terms of his financial contribution to the family. Often, as a matter of fact, he is forced to fall back on his sons and daughters for partial or full support. It is his further "class" misfortune that usually his children married young, stopped their formal education early, and are themselves in need of all the money they earn. At best, there will be some internal family discomfort, sacrifice and conflict, and all too often there arises disappointment, open hostility and guilt.

Contrast this far too frequent situation with that of the college professor, or other professional such as the doctor, lawyer, and teacher. Very often retirement for them means retiring *into* something. For them education makes for a better old age. There are many things they can become interested in — writing, research, or public service, for example. Usually, this kind of man has an active and alert mind because he has been trained in, and has maintained, alertness and mental activity. He can find things for himself to do, gaining a great deal of continuing pleasure out of life. Then his children tend also to be better educated and to be of "higher" occupational status. They are more likely, therefore, to have the time, energy and money to be of help to a father or mother without undue strain.

In addition to the differences within the retirement population which have been mentioned there are differences between the sexes. For the most part, women in our society, contrary to popular belief, whether they are married or single, work because of economic necessity. But when the housewife or unmarried woman retires she often has something more than the man. She either has a home of her own or family relationships which she has tended to maintain and cultivate, and within this setting of friends, or family, she can often be of very good use. She is usually a good baby sitter, and most important, a welcome one. She can cook, bake, sew, clean house, or just listen to other people talk. On the other hand, the man at home — in anyone's home — is more likely to be and to feel he is a burden and an annoyance. He has little or no domestic utility and he is, in effect, a displaced person who lost his status when he lost his role as wage earner, father or husband.

A Sense of Purpose

No matter who or what you are, the important factor in sustaining morale is a sense of purpose. A person who has an interest in and a desire to live, demonstrates this by way of activity and assertiveness. But the attitudes which are formed as one grows up are important determinants of adjustment in old age. For example, individuals who, correctly or not, think of old age as a time of decline, as a period of life with a decreased capacity to withstand stress both physically and emotionally, do not do as well as those who believe that in old age you can be youthful, active, and useful, no matter what may be physically wrong with you. My co-workers, among them Muriel Oberleder, Helen Turner, and Max Pollack, have studied attitudes of the old and have helped demonstrate that people who espouse youthful views tend to make a better adjustment than people who are convinced that age is synonymous with deterioration. People who have been cynical, pessimistic, and worried about what would happen to them when they were young, do much worse toward the end of life than those who have been optimistic, active and serene. If you are neurotic when you are young, it will work very much to your disservice when you are old.

Dr. Robert L. Kahn, another colleague, conducted a study of older people's ability to recognize or identify a figure in a diagram with an unclear, ambiguous background. He compared the ability, or inability, with the older person's tendency to complain, and both of these with the person's actual state of health. The study strongly suggests that individuals who are assertive and able to get at the task and pick the vague figure out of the unclear background quickly are those persons who tend to complain less than those who are unable to do this simple task well. Furthermore, this is true irrespective of the actual state of health.

The importance of this is that the individual who is assertive and problem-solving tends to be, and to become, less of a complainer than a passive, wishful-thinker type, despite misfortune such as illness. I am inclined to regard a minimum of complaints as one important sign of good mental health.

The ability to be assertive and problem-solving is something which can be developed at any time of life. One usually finds, however, that the general tendency to be self-assertive rather than passive is an early development. The capacity to use one's resources effectively is very much affected by an individual's relationship with his mother, father, and other persons who cared for him in childhood. Healthy self-assertion is either encouraged or impaired within the context of the parent-child relationship. The child wants to grow up in his own way. He wants to eat when he's hungry and what he likes, to develop control over his bladder and bowels in his own way, and he wants to do almost everything when he wants to do it and not at some other time. However, for his protection and comfort, and to help him learn the things which will make him a tolerable member of society, the mother or parent-person who cares for him attempts to get the child to do things in another way — "her way," as the child sees it. Right there you have the setup for a fight.

In this parent-child situation a child may develop fears and angers, or he may develop stubborn and obstinate characteristics which tend to persist throughout life. Unfortunately, in our society a surprisingly large number of people tend to keep on setting up relationships with other people in the pattern of their early relationships with their parents. With wives, husbands, brothers and sisters, and with their own children, many individuals behave as though they were still in the fight with their mother. They fight to be permitted to do things in their own way, but at the same time they want to retain the mother's protection and assistance, even as a child wants to stay within the mother's good graces so he can command her powers and manipulate them for his own use, that is, transfer them to himself.

If this simultaneous fight to be free and fight to be close

persists throughout life, as I have suggested, we would expect to see it in old age. We most certainly do see it as an
important behavior pattern in some of the elderly persons
who have actually begun to need physical and emotional help
and support. When these people begin to feel helpless and
in need of protection their behavior will tend to be polarized
around that core of emotional organization which was laid
down early in life which can be described as a child-parent
struggle. Dr. Sandor Rado, a distinguished psychiatrist, has
described these child-parent struggles as "the battle of the
pot," because it is so frequently and clearly seen in relation
to bowel training.

In later life, when one loses the work which has sustained
one's sense of worth and contributed to one's self-confidence,
and which moreover has given one a sense of purpose and
identity, one may feel weak, helpless and frightened. In a
search for help experienced as "loneliness," behavior may
have as its central point the tendency to get into struggles
with others who are regarded as potentially helpful. This
may lead to such behavior as anger, complaining, sullenness,
helplessness and feelings of pain and disability which impair
the ability to get along with others easily and to receive and
give affection easily. It is a paradox that those who are frightened and want help, because they try so hard to show their
need for help, may behave in inefficient and maladjusted ways
which tend to deprive them further of what they desire.
Conversely, even in old age, people who retain a sense of
worth and confidence in their own ability to deal with problems and to solve them, who receive pleasure from the process of activity as well as the result of the activity, tend to at-
tract the support and assistance of others.

CRITICISM FROM THE YOUNG

The young often criticise the elderly for what they regard
and may call "acting foolishly." They may say to the elderly, in effect, "Why don't you act your age?" There are many
people who feel that in our society it is common for the elderly to deny their years in dress, action and thought. I don't
like this tendency to regard retirement of the aged as proper,
to encourage "conservatism" of dress and action and withdrawal from life. It is true that at times some aged people

may act as though they hope that, magically, by acting young they will recapture youth. But it is more usual that persons take too much to heart their chronological age and, by acting old, prematurely encourage old age. The individual who espouses youthful views, who is hopeful and confident, makes a better adjustment and lives longer than the so-called "realist."

I recall that when I was fifteen years old my father came home one day with a very light gray herringbone suit. He put it on and asked me what I thought of it — he meant the fit. Being young and critical, I said I thought he was rather old to "wear that kind of thing." My father was a very tactful man, and didn't say anything to me about my tactlessness. He just kept right on wearing that suit and similar ones. Of course, I was upset. I thought he should wear dark blue suits, or black ones, but he himself didn't feel particularly old. He maintained youthful views and youthful vigor until the end of his life in his seventies. Today I am older than he was when he modeled the light gray suit and, I am happy to report, I find that "youthful" clothes seem to suit me admirably.

Although some elderly people do attempt to recapture youth as though by magic through clothes, games, parties, or cosmetic illusions, many wear bright shirts and slacks because, although old, they really feel young. Many are doing what they enjoy and what is natural to them when — as in Florida colonies or even in old age homes — they play shuffleboard, dance, and are youthfully companionable. In doing so, they are, in all likelihood, prolonging their lives by way of exercise, and because pleasure has salutary effects upon both body and mind.

Retirement to a distant place with a "better climate" is not always good. A certain religious group in India believes that when a man and wife have married off their children they have accomplished their major life task and should retire. This happens when they are about fifty-five years old. According to these views, retirement almost literally consists in getting a cabin in the woods, turning over most of the wealth to the younger generation, and from then leading a simple life.

In a sense, this is equivalent to the bungalow in Miami

Beach for many Americans. Many who emigrate from their old homes in later life are not remaining a part of life, but are rather retiring from life. This may even be planned for, looked forward to, longed for, because we in America have an idea similar to that of the East Indians, that the old have to give way to the young. There is no basis for objecting when the old act young unless we wish to "throw them out of life." Objections may, of course, be motivated by economics or ambition, for we tend to encourage old people to get out when times are economically bad and they compete for scarce jobs, but to keep them around and at work when times are good and we need them to fill the many jobs open in an expanding economy. In effect, our retirement ideas are not rigid, they tend to change when it "pays" to change them. Our views of the old and their view of themselves may fluctuate with the times and with conditions.

I do believe that many people who move into the so-called retirement communities in Florida or California should behave differently, but not by acting in a manner befitting old age. I would rather have them stay at home and behave in a youthful fashion there, actively remaining a part of the community in a vigorous and effective manner. I have seen many men and women who have come back home from the retirement havens greatly disappointed and disillusioned. Men especially hate to leave their homes. Ordinarily, a woman can tolerate a change of house better than a man. She appears to be a more social sort of individual, whereas a man feels torn away from his roots after thirty or forty years of living in a house and building it into a home. In this connection, I should add that it is a poor idea to move a widower until you are very sure he has adjusted to being left by himself. In contrast, a widow also may not do well if you move her too soon after the death of her husband, but she does adjust better when moved from the actual apartment or house than does a man who has lost his wife.

I think we should here touch on the question of institutions, nursing and old age homes. I do not encourage homes for the aged as a place for healthy old persons. In fact, neither do they. In our society, entering a home is felt as a great affront to an individual's dignity. Usually, people don't go to them to retire, but only when they are in need. Need

for money, food and lodging, and, most important, for medical attention and health care which they or the family cannot provide, are the chief if not the only reasons for apply-
ing to old age homes. One type of need for medically directed institutional care is the development of severe memory loss and emotional disturbance. At times the old person
is frightened and wants to be in a secure situation.

Whatever the reason, the elderly who enter old age homes
most often do so with great bitterness, anger and resentment;
these feelings "can eat them up alive" unless they find an
understanding staff within a home which reminds them of
their own homes because of its program, its residents and its
furnishings and even its architecture. Consequently, despite
this negative attitude, those who need a home can often find
a very pleasant way of life within a modern, well-staffed
home for the aged.

PREPARATION FOR RETIREMENT

There is no simple answer to the question, "Can one prepare for retirement?" for it is both "Yes" and "No." Early
opportunities in life to become self-reliant and assertive, and
good early opportunities which have provided good education, are very important. These two factors are the best preparation for a good old age. We see that people who have
"naturally" tended to develop hobbies and interests in the
middle years are better off in their old age than those who
have not done so. However, it may do little or no good to
attempt to force people "to take outside interests" in their
middle years. By then, if they don't have the resources to find
satisfaction and reasons for living, then it is often too late.
Techniques which "motivate" them, to use the now popular
term, may subtly encourage them to develop new interests
and a new sense of purpose. Exhortation, inspirational techniques and threats, however soundly and medically based,
are usually ineffective. Such motivation toward expanded interests, and purposeful feelings, is occasionally achieved with
psychiatric help.

But on the other hand, there really is such a thing as preparation for retirement. Many people retire without knowing
how, without having learned basic facts. Simply and briefly,
they may not know their pension rights, or about the Social

Security laws and benefits due them. Also, many people who retire have an adequate income but they don't know how to spend it; they can benefit from counsel. These people need to be re-educated or to educate themselves so they can get the most out of every dollar in a time when inflation tends to overtake increases in pensions and Social Security and defeats thrift and frugality.

In addition, many aged people worry continuously and needlessly about non-existent physical illnesses, yet tend to ignore significant symptoms. They have to be reassured by their family doctor that, although there is nothing which can be done about much of the fatigue which occurs with aging except to gain more rest, nevertheless all physical symptoms and aches and pains should not be glibly dismissed as due to old age. An old person who does not feel well should check with his doctor. It is not true that illnesses in old age are hopeless and incurable. Although it is true that, as Dr. Frederic D. Zeman has aptly put it, "Diseases in old age are characterized by chronicity, multiplicity and duplicity," an old person may very well have an illness which can be cured. Pneumonia in old age may have few symptoms but be readily curable. It is good to know that as one ages, certain diseases are less threatening rather than more so. Many cancers, for example, are so slow growing in the aged that they are much less harmful and more easily treated than in the young.

Some old people complain bitterly all the time, yet do not complain correctly. They are not well but they don't take their specific complaints to their doctor and, consequently, needlessly and foolishly worry when action and self-assertion would ease their fear and dismiss their discomfort.

In summary, retirement can kill you if you allow it to kill you. Only the individual himself can make of retirement a time of worth and health, and a time of deep personal wealth.

6. TREATMENT

Introduction

We hear much about mental health these days, in newspapers and books, on television and even in the movies. What *is* mental health? It has been defined in many ways, probably as many as there are people who have been asked for a definition.

We asked several authorities for a definition of mental health, to start off a section that describes the various kinds of psychological help that are available.

There seems to be great confusion in the public mind as to the different types of therapy and what each attempts to achieve. In the following pages, there is discussion of the most important kinds of help.

Otto E. Sperling, M.D., and Henriette Klein, M.D., discuss Freudian psychoanalysis. Phillip Polatin, M.D., describes psychiatry's approach to mental health. Theodor Reik, Ph.D., tells us about lay analysis, which is analysis conducted by someone who does not have a medical degree. The late Wilfred C. Hulse, M.D., and Bernard F. Reiss, Ph.D., describe psychotherapy and supportive therapy. S. R. Slavson gives us a picture of group therapy.

We hope these interviews clear up a number of questions that may be puzzling people as to the different kinds of help available.

HOW CAN YOU FIND HELP IN YOUR AREA?

By writing to:
1. National Association for Mental Health, 10 Columbus Circle, New York.
2. American Psychiatric Association, 1700 18th St., N. W., Washington 9, D. C.
3. American Psychoanalytic Association, 1 East 57th St., New York.
4. American Psychological Association, 3536 Appleton St., N. W., Washington, D. C.

39.

"What is mental health?"
we asked.

A SYMPOSIUM

XXXXXXXXXXXXXXXXXXXXXX

WILFRED HULSE, M.D.
HENRIETTE KLEIN, M.D.
PHILLIP POLATIN, M.D.
THEODOR REIK, Ph.D.
BERNARD F. RIESS, Ph.D.
S. R. SLAVSON
OTTO SPERLING, M.D.

39.

This is what Dr. Hulse said when interviewed in his office:

I think everybody who has tried to define mental health has failed. The reasons they fail are: First, there is never an ideal state of emotional affairs in man, or anywhere else in nature; second, all conceptions of mental health are very subjective, based mainly on what one person would like to see in others.

When we ourselves feel best we should not automatically decide that others will feel best if they are in the same situation we are in. On the contrary, I believe that mental health is often best achieved in highly individualized emotional situations which the person keeps as a secret — even to himself. If you take one hundred people, they will all feel differently when they are in the "best mental health." Also, some people may not like it when others are in their best mental health. A child feeling his best mental health, for example, may run around a lot and sing at the top of his voice or dance and blow a whistle but the child's mother may not be happy about his behavior.

Mental health has usually been defined in the negative — not being ill. In other words, what is it *not* to have emotional illness? Primarily, it means to possess an adequate balance of comfort, contentment, "happiness" and an optimistic outlook for the future, at the same time not disturbing others too much by what one is doing or not doing. After all, if a child or adult has his best feeling of mental health only if he can play seven drums from morning to midnight, the other people in the house and the neighbors, might not consider this promoting the best state of communal mental health.

When we psychologically treat adults who are not in good

mental health, our yardstick is completely individualized. A man comes to me and says, "I can't take it any more." Although I may think that he can take it very well indeed, he obviously feels he needs help, and this is, in itself, one indication for me that I ought to try to help him. The difficulty with treating children is that they are always brought to us by their parents or sent by schools. The children themselves are at first rarely self-motivated in seeking help; they are brought not because they themselves are unhappy, but because others are.

Only in New York will it occasionally happen that the child says, "Mommy, take me to a psychiatrist. I feel so unhappy." But even in New York this is extremely rare. Children are usually brought in by their parents, or sent by school, or courts, because somebody has complained about their behavior, rarely because of their own feelings. However, it is up to us to show them, in the very first contact, that we are able to give them the help they need.

Essentially I think a definition of mental health is impractical and meaningless. One could, of course, elaborate a very theoretical, high-sounding philosophical concept, but it would have little practical application. Although there is a good amount of literature which tries to define mental health, I think most of it is merely a shuffling around of words and philosophical concept.

This is what Dr. Klein said when interviewed in her office.

The mentally healthy individual might be described as one whose motivation and behavior are geared to serve his best interests, who is able to withstand stress and strain, who operates effectively as a member of the community, and finally, who derives his maximum satisfaction from the use of his own resources.

Definite standards beyond those related to capacity to withstand stress cannot be arbitrarily stated for all because of the many factors involved. For example, generosity would ordinarily be considered a sign of mental health. When generosity is carried to extremes, however, it can operate against the individual's own welfare and could then be considered psychologically unhealthy. On the other hand, extreme withdrawal is generally considered an index of severe disfunction in most people. But it might be generally accepted as the prerogative of the truly creative artist.

In a concept of mental health there must be room for individualism — the unique characteristics of each individual, the circumstances of his life, his need for self-realization and pride.

This is what Dr. Polatin said when interviewed in his office:

Mental health is a state of well-being in which the individual has a satisfactory capacity for work, for relations with others, is able to love someone other than himself, is free of disabling symptoms such as severe tension, anxiety, depression and phobia, and is unhampered by serious mental conflicts.

Mental health is achieved when an individual learns to have a balanced flexibility in his adjustments to all spheres of living. This flexibility is based on an understanding of his own capacities and limitations so that he can attain the maximum of what he is able to achieve. At the same time he avoids straining beyond his capacities.

Mental health is variable. It does not have to conform to a set pattern. For example, a man who never gets married but who is happy, relaxed and well-integrated, is in good mental health. Everybody does not have to get married and have children.

As a matter of fact, I know of a man who maintained his mental health in the single state until his middle fifties. Until then, he had lived with and supported his widowed mother; he had a good job, had gone out with women, had many friends, and had lived happily and comfortably with no serious conflicts. But then his family, who had been after him for years to get married, put a great deal of pressure on him and, against his better judgment, he married a woman whom he had known for some time. In a few months, however, he found himself in a profound depression. He couldn't work or sleep, and didn't know what was wrong. He had, in fact, strained himself beyond his emotional capacity, gone beyond his own particular normalcy.

The variability of normalcy is the point to understand

here, for all of us tend to be pushed into a pattern of conformity by the forces of public opinion and social values. Our society says, among other things, that we all must get married, all must have children, go to college, be financial successes, and the like. But not every individual can conform emotionally to this pattern, and if he strains to do so, he may very well go beyond his inner strength and then develop symptoms of mental illness.

This is what Dr. Reik said when interviewed in his office:

I would say that mental health is evidenced by behavior which is appropriate to the necessities of reality. However, what is considered "real" may change from one century to another, even from one decade to another, and the necessities of reality may be viewed differently by different people at the same time.

In the 10th Century A.D., a man would have been considered insane if he had denied that the Devil existed and if he had insisted that there was no possibility of meeting him in the village square. But today, if you said you met the Devil at 42nd Street and Broadway, and if you believed that you did in fact meet him, you would also be considered insane.

In our own time, however, Lord Bertrand Russell recently went to jail because he thinks that nuclear weapons should be abolished. In other words, he sees the necessities of reality in a different way than many other people who may very well think Russell insane. But as a matter of fact, he may be considered a genius by these same people ten years from now.

This is what Dr. Riess said when interviewed in his office:

The question, "What is mental health?" has bothered innumerable psychoanalysts, psychiatrists, psychologists and social scientists. I will try to give some dimensions of what mental health means to me. First of all I would say that it involves a series of attitudes toward other people and toward oneself. It is basically a combination of how one sees oneself as an individual, and how one sees one's own relationships to other individuals.

A mentally healthy person is an individual whose pictur of himself is consistent with the picture others who know him well have of him. His attitudes toward other people to be healthy, must involve a respect for others and a firm disinclination to abuse them.

Although the things I have just said are gross generalizations, they do constitute in some small way what I think of as positive mental health. Another way of expressing it, however, is to say that mental health is the absence of unhealthy symptoms. I think this is what most therapy aims at. This is actually a medical-health concept. We, as well as the general practitioner, try to get rid of the patient's disturbing symptoms. This is one of the limitations of psychotherapy today; mental health concepts should also include how to help patients toward positive mental health.

This is what Mr. Slavson said when interviewed in his office:

Mental health is a state of being in which a person's responses are appropriate to the situation. The healthy person deals with a situation in a way advantageous to himself and to others, thereby avoiding difficulties. An unhealthy person, however, either over-reacts or withdraws. That is, one may tend to become over-emotional and over-involved; instead of resolving problems he intensifies them. Another withdraws, fleeing either pychologically or physically, sometimes both.

In other words, the unhealthy person resorts either to fight or flight. He does not deal with problems realistically. On the other hand, the healthy person recognizes the facts with which he is confronted, views them objectively, evaluates them, and deals with whatever realities are involved in such a way that no further problems are created.

There are two facets to mental health. There is the area of function in the outer world, and the area of inner being. But function is a reflection of the self and if the person is inwardly balanced and integrated, his function will then be healthy. The person who is imbalanced (not "unbalanced") in any way will show it in his behavior, and the stresses of life will tend to become more difficult for him.

This is what Dr. Sperling said when interviewed in his office:

Once during the winter, when I looked through one of those seed catalogues, I was attracted by the picture of a certain strain of petunia; the flowers were very large, approximately three inches, the petals were beautifully frilled and the plant seemed all covered with blooms. When I grew these petunias myself, they looked measly. The flowers were hardly more than one and a half inches wide and not nearly as profuse as the catalogue had promised.

When I discussed this with an experienced gardener, he showed me what I had done wrong. I hadn't put the seeds in the proper soil. I hadn't added enough fertilizer. The flowers didn't get enough sun. When I placed these same petunias in the right place with the right soil, with enough water and enough fertilizer, they flourished and looked like the pictures in the seed catalog.

Now, to return to the question of mental health, I would say that the goal of all psychotherapy, including psychoanalysis, is to help human beings look like the pictures in the seed catalog. This means to make it possible for them to reach the optimum of development in terms of their endowment and the civilization in which they live.

One cannot, of course, get a rose out of a petunia. If you plant petunia seeds, the best you can do is to grow a petunia. Thus, we cannot expect to make a man a genius if he doesn't have the endowment for it. But if he has the endowment, yet because of inhibitions and repressions cannot develop in the right way, it should be possible to help him to become that which he was truly destined to be.

Some articles on mental health say it is the job of the psychiatrist to enable people to adapt themselves to their environment or to develop the right adaptations. Freud did not agree with this, nor do I. I would say that mental health is not only the ability to adapt yourself but also to influence others to adapt themselves to you. That means to induce them to make those adaptations desirable from your point of view.

The popular view of the mental health goal of adaptation means that people suppress their originality or ability as leaders. In my opinion, it is part of mental health for those who possess the ability to be original or to become leaders to be free to do so. Those who have the ability to influence others should develop the courage and strength to influence others. It is not always desirable that the individual adapt himself to the society. Otherwise, you would never change the society. There have to be individuals who influence society to change.

40.

"What is Freudian psychoanalysis?"
we asked Dr. Sperling.

OTTO E. SPERLING, M.D.

Associate Clinical Professor of Psychiatry,
Department of Psychiatry,
State University of New York,
Downstate Medical Center

In this interview, Dr. Sperling also discusses:

"What is a Freudian psychoanalyst?"
    "What is the meaning of psychoanalysis?"
        "What is the drive, or instinct theory?"
"What is the meaning of sexuality?"
    "Does aggression stem from frustrated love?"
        "What is transference?"
"Why does a patient have to lie down to be psychoanalyzed?"
    "Does the psychoanalyst 'influence' the patient?"
        "How much does an average psychoanalysis cost?"
"Who is most suitable for psychoanalysis?"
    "Can the average person benefit from psychoanalysis?"
        "Where is the unconscious located?"

40.

This is what Dr. Sperling said when interviewed in his office:

Q. What is a Freudian psychoanalyst?

A. A Freudian psychoanalyst is a psychiatrist who has had at least two years of psychiatric training and then undergone additional training in a psychoanalytic institute or school supervised in this country by the American Psychoanalytic Association, or in other countries by the International Psychoanalytic Association.

There are a number of men and women who are graduates of institutes and schools not supervised by the American Psychoanalytic Association. Those of us who were graduated from accredited institutes do not consider them Freudian psychoanalysts. The training at an institute takes some four to six years of post-graduate work and includes a personal analysis of the student, theoretical courses and supervised work with patients.

It is unfair if anybody who is not a Freudian calls himself a psychoanalyst. The law protects the consumer from being fooled with inferior merchandise by punishing anyone who would usurp a brand name unlawfully. The public deserves also to be protected from being fooled by those who call themselves "psychoanalysts" and cash in on the renown that psychoanalysis has acquired in the course of its existence, without having the proper training and without basing their activities on the scientific principles which Freud has established.

Q. Could you describe the meaning of the word "psychoanalysis?"

A. The term "psychoanalysis" covers several meanings. Psychoanalysis is a technique of therapy. It is a technique of research. It is a body of knowledge encompassing all the things psychoanalysts have observed and discovered. And it is a theory.

Let us start with the last point — psychoanalytic theory. Freudian psychoanalytic theory is all-inclusive, taking in not only the phenomena observed in the normal person but also the psychological phenomena observed in those suffering from all kinds of mental ills and physical diseases with accompanying psychic changes.

Psychoanalytic theory covers the psychology of development from the infant through childhood, adolescence, maturity and old age. It covers the psychology not only of our civilization but all kinds of different civilizations, including today's primitive societies and societies of past centuries.

It covers also the psychology of the criminal and of the deviate personality. It helps us in the understanding of group behavior, history and sociology. The psychoanalytic theory also provides a bridge from mental function to biology, and to physiology. This seems especially important because, as scientists, psychoanalysts are of the opinion that body and mind cannot be separated. Both the study of physiology and psychology consider man as a whole, although the approach is different.

Psychoanalytic theory was slowly developed by Freud. In the beginning he was only trying to explain what he observed in cases of hysteria. But soon he recognized that the same phenomena could be observed in normal people, that there was really not a deep cleft between normalcy and pathology.

With this observation came a different attitude toward the patient. In the 19th century it was easy to see from the writings of the physicians that they looked down on mental patients, regarded them in one way or another as degenerates. Freud analyzed himself and recognized that the patient is not so different from the psychoanalyst, that it is advisable to believe what the patient says and not gloss over it highhandedly.

The discovery of the unconscious had been prevented for centuries because observers did not believe what the patient said. They did not believe the patient did not know what was really going on inside himself. The new respect for the patient made it possible for them to realize that he actually did not know what went on within himself.

The psychoanalytic theory of "drives" made it possible to explain changes which occur in character, not only as it develops from early childhood on, but also the changes which we can observe in adults. According to the earlier psychology, a miser was a miser. But people observed that a miser could suddenly change and make a very generous gift. The psychoanalytic theory explains this change. It can be understood when we realize that our drives undergo vicissitudes, that the same energy which in one case has been directed in a sadistic direction, for instance, can at a moment's notice be changed to a masochistic direction, which, to the observer, seems to be a complete change of character.

Psychoanalysis is a dynamic theory of human personality. It assumes that there are conflicts going on between one drive and another — for instance, between an aggressive drive and a sexual drive. Psychoanalysis is concerned with the defense an individual has established to prevent himself from being overwhelmed by his drives.

It is not necessary to separate psychoanalysis as a research tool from psychoanalysis as a therapeutic technique because the two go hand in hand. Psychoanalytic treatment in every case is research, without prejudice, to find out the truth. We discover in people a number of similarities, but it also has to be emphasized that no two individuals are ever identical.

Even in identical twins, when we have reason to assume that everything which is inherited is identical, we find two different individuals. For example, usually one twin is the stronger, taking on the dominant role in the twinship. This, in itself, has a very important influence on the development of character. Also, it is impossible that parents always behave exactly the same way, even with twins. The fact that people are so diverse makes it necessary to treat them individually. In psychoanalysis one analyst treats one patient at a time.

Q. Could you explain what a "drive" is?

A. The "drive" or instinct theory, has caused quite a bit of controversy. When I was a student, I attended lectures in psychology where the professor would recognize only needs, never anything behind these needs, because he was so afraid of psychology ending up in philosophy. This fear of abstraction made the academic psychology of the 19th century completely useless in explaining pathology or the motivation of people. It also kept it from being of any help in the understanding of history or sociology. Such psychologists were afraid to make use of their ability to think.

It is only a step from the observation of a feeling of hunger at a particular moment to the abstract thought of a need for nourishment. This need for nourishment whenever the concentration of glucose in the blood went under a certain level would be the constant driving force causing a real sensation of hunger.

It is not enough to acknowledge only the immediately observable sensation of hunger. We have a right to come to the conclusion that if such a sensation occurs regularly, under specific circumstances, there is a driving force, namely, a drive for nourishment behind it, even if we do not always feel it and cannot always observe it.

In a similar way, it is possible to observe in human beings such manifestations as love for one's own body, or love for a part of one's body. Or love for another person, or for a part of another. Or sexual pleasure in the narrow sense of the word. Or pursuit of certain individuals for the purpose of sexual pleasure. Or a great number of different perversions, or a number of so-called bad habits in children which are precursors of later sexual activities. All these phenomena can be grouped together under the name of "sexuality." Sexuality, in this sense, is an abstraction, the driving force which can show itself in many different ways from childhood on in the emotion called love, as well as affection, and as sexuality in the narrower sense.

Similarly, it is possible to observe hatred, destructiveness, prejudice, dislike, sarcasm in a child or grownup, and to group all these emotions under the heading of aggression. Then, there are also phenomena where there is a high degree of mixture of aggressive energy and sexual energy, as in the will for power or need for glory, or sadism and masochism.

Q. Are aggression and love a dual instinctual drive? Or is your implication that aggression comes out of frustrated love?

A. Freud originally thought aggression to be of a reactive nature. But later on he convinced himself that human beings are not angels. It is not the "bad" society that causes "good" human beings to become criminals or prostitutes. If, even under favorable social circumstances, undesirable developments take place, then the aggressive drive is the force which makes people react to any kind of pain or frustration with hostility.

Aggression can express itself in all kinds of hostility or destructiveness, or anger or rage, or murderous impulses. There is an admixture of aggressive energy in all kinds of activities. Even if a young man is in love with a girl and extremely unselfish, if there were no aggressive energy in his courtship, he wouldn't get anywhere with her. Similarly, a man and a woman could not have sexual intercourse if they did not have aggressive energy, because an admixture of aggressive energy is necessary to love.

Q. What does "transference" mean, a word about which we hear so much?

A. If a boy is told that his mother loves him but she nevertheless places him in an orphanage, it might well prejudice him to expect later in life that the same thing would happen again: if a woman says she loves him, she intends to abandon him. He would also expect this to occur in all kinds of situations, even in his psychoanalysis. He would believe that although the analyst pretends to be interested in him, one day he, too, will throw him out of the office.

"Transference" is the repetition of an emotional sequence, or sequence of emotions and expectations, usually beginning in childhood and projected into new situations. If the new situation is like a blank screen — as for instance, it is in psychoanalysis, where the patient doesn't know much about the psychoanalyst or what he is thinking — then it is very tempting for the patient to project onto this empty screen a sequence of emotions that are a repetition of experiences in childhood. It could be first love, then hatred. Or it could be first hatred, then love. Or a sequence of trust then disappointment and disillusionment. All kinds of emotions are repeated.

Q. Why does a patient have to lie down to be psychoanalyzed?

A. Psychoanalytic treatment is usually performed on the

couch in order to permit the patient to develop his own ideas, uninfluenced by the expression on the face of the psychoanalyst. Anybody who has taken part in an oral examination knows it is possible to see on the face of the examiner whether he likes something or dislikes it, whether he is interested or not. The psychoanalytic technique is based on free association, which means it is necessary for the patient to say everything that comes to his mind, whether it seems right or wrong, sensible or nonsensical, fitting or ordinary, strange, tactful or tactless. Only in this way is it possible to bring out the full truth. Facing the analyst would tend to block the patient's associations.

It works both ways. There is as little point in the physician lying to a patient as in the patient lying to the physician if he hopes to get something out of his treatment. Psychoanalysis is an education in the direction of truth.

The psychoanalyst is not free of values. He upholds the value of truth, without which treatment cannot be effective. He further emphasizes that health is important and worthwhile. But otherwise, he is careful not to interfere with the values or religion or political opinions of his patient. In this way he is no different from the physician in general, whose Hippocratic oath demands that he give equal treatment to the good and the bad.

Psychoanalytic treatment is usually arranged for four or five times a week. It is necessary to cover such a large amount of material that treatment only once or twice a week would take so much time that it would be impractical. Furthermore, it is desirable to make psychoanalytic treatment an intensive experience, an important experience. If the patient does not go wholeheartedly into it, it will take him much longer than if he is enthusiastically involved.

The goal of psychoanalysis is a high one. If one really wants to achieve mental health, it is necessary to do a good job, and this takes time. How long cannot be predicted. In general, the probability is that somebody who is very sick, suffering very deeply, will finish earlier. It is believed he will put more energy into the treatment because he suffers so much from his disease.

Those who are normal or almost normal and undergo psychoanalytic treatment face more difficulties and a longer time

of treatment. That is one of the reasons why the treatment
of psychiatrists who want to become psychoanalysts usually
takes a long time. It is one of the principles of psychoanalysis
that nobody has a right to undertake the treatment of others
who has not undergone a psychoanalysis himself. First, this
is the best way to learn the method, to experience it first
hand. Furthermore, it is necessary to overcome the many prejudices and predilections or idiosyncrasies, a part of human
nature, which the prospective analyst may have.

Psychoanalysis usually takes two years or three, perhaps
more. This does not mean a shorter period of treatment
could not be very helpful and free a patient from the symptoms which torture him most. But if a change in the personality is to be expected, then it is desirable to have more
time available.

For the treatment of children, adolescents and psychotics,
certain modifications of the Freudian technique of psychoanalysis have been invented. But the more modifications of
this classical technique are used, the more the treatment becomes, instead of a psychoanalysis, a psychoanalytically oriented psychotherapy.

Q. How much does psychoanalysis cost?

A. Fees are arrived at according to the income of the patient.
Psychoanalysis should entail sacrifice of some sort to be effective. In a clinic where people get treatment without having
to pay a fee, it is assumed that traveling to the clinic and
having to be there at specific times is enough of a sacrifice.
Even so, in most clinics, the patient is expected to pay a
small fee if he can possibly afford it. In private practice, the
average fee is usually $25 a session. It is possible to get psy-
choanalysis for $15 or $20. There are a number of psychoanalysts who ask a higher fee.

Q. Do symptoms ever return?

A. If symptoms return, this indicates that the psychoanalysis
had not been completed. It is then advisable to return to the
analytic couch for a limited time to supplement an analysis
of the problems which manifested themselves in the relapse.
On the other hand, there are many people who, even after a
short treatment, do not have a return of the symptoms. With
some personalities, as one specific problem gets solved, the

neurosis falls to pieces and the person can develop normally from then on.

Q. Who is most suitable for psychoanalysis? The "seriously ill," the "neurotic" or "almost normal?"

A. Psychoanalysis was invented for the treatment of neurosis. This includes people who suffer either from an apparent physical illness, such as writer's cramp or headaches, or those inhibited by painful ideas or nonsensical habits which force them to waste time and often cause anxiety. In addition, there are a number of psychosomatic diseases, like ulcers, nervous asthma, ulcerative colitis and skin disorders, which nowadays can best be treated by psychoanalysis.

Psychological treatment of schizophrenia has also become possible through psychoanalysis. But the technique has to undergo certain modifications to reach the mind of the person suffering from this disease. The treatment of the criminal has been attempted, in some cases successfully, but the probability of success is not as high as in neurosis.

Psychoanalysis also had to undergo certain modifications to be used in the treatment of children. Child analysis employs play instead of free association, but there also the child learns to understand himself better and in this way is enabled to overcome his suffering.

Q. Can the "normal" person benefit from psychoanalysis?

A. Psychoanalysis has made it possible to overcome those inhibitions which reduce the usefulness and efficiency of the normal person. Especially in writers and artists, it has been a frequent experience that talents inhibited by repression are set free so they can be richly developed and a work of art created.

It has been suggested that people playing an important role in public life should undergo psychoanalysis. During the Civil War in Spain, for instance, it was observed that the neuroses of the generals on the Loyalist side contributed to the defeat of the Loyalists. The same is true in many other situations, probably. It is to be expected that, if energy has to be used for the purpose of keeping certain knowledge repressed, the person then does not have as much energy available as after analysis when these repressions are relieved.

Q. Can only the "strong" be analyzed? Is undergoing psychoanalysis an act of strength?

A. No. Psychoanalysis is not a treatment for the strong one only. Because psychoanalysis aims at giving strength to the personality, we naturally expect a person to be stronger after treatment. But there are all kinds of personalities. A division into weak and strong personalities is not really a scientific division. A general, for instance, can be a strong personality before his soldiers and fellow officers, who fear and respect him, yet the little Mrs. can regard him as a very weak character.

Q. How does "suppression" differ from "repression?"

A. We all face temptations and are subject to passionate emotions which we have to learn to control. The control is a conscious act, something we do deliberately and with full awareness of our motives and purposes. For example, a man may be tempted to look at television while at the same time he has to write a report or an important letter. He might deliberate for a moment, then decide that he has to fulfill his obligation. He *suppresses* the temptation to watch television. This is conscious; it is on the surface, and quite clear.

Repression, however, is the process by which some temptation or knowledge is not only prevented from being put into action but also is eliminated from consciousness. Let us say a husband has good reason to be angry at his wife. In his unconscious mind, the temptation to kill her might be very much alive but his conscience would prevent him from doing it. The fact that he loves his wife makes it intolerable even to acknowledge the temptation to murder her.

In this case, not only would he not murder his wife, but he would not be aware that any of these murderous impulses existed in him at any time. This conflict may take a lot of his energy so that he would have less available for his business. He might overcompensate in some way. He might become very dependent on his wife and unable to defend himself against her. Or he might develop an unjustified hatred for his mother-in-law, unconsciously displacing his hatred from his wife to her. Then, whatever he doesn't like in his wife would be his mother-in-law's fault, however perfect the behavior of the mother-in-law might be.

Q. We know the unconscious can't be anatomically located with a scalpel. Where is it and what is it?

A. Since all conscious psychological phenomena go on in the brain, we have reason to assume that the unconscious phenomena also take place there.

Before the advent of psychoanalysis, people were aware that a number of things went on in the mind of which they were not always conscious. If we play the piano, for instance, we do not deliberate every moment which finger to use to play a certain note. Our action is automatic. This is not the unconscious. When we speak, in psychoanalysis, of the unconscious, we mean truly psychological phenomena, not things that are of reflex nature or of an indifferent nature. We mean a phenomenon, such as a murderous impulse, which has a specific psychological nature. It has motivation. It has a certain intensity and can undergo displacement or substitution.

One quality can be very clearly observed, that is, whether someone is conscious of an impulse or not. Every individual knows very well whether something is conscious. But the man who had the impulse to murder his wife, if asked whether he had such an impulse, would have denied it. He would have been honest in saying "No!" Some, who do not understand the unconscious in themselves, might claim he was aware of the impulse and just didn't want to admit it.

But one who undergoes psychoanalysis successfully, convinces himself that an unconscious really exists, that the man in our example was not lying when he said he didn't know about his murderous impulse toward his wife. For it is in psychoanalysis that we become acquainted with our own unconscious and realize the power it can exert over daily living As we make conscious the unconscious impulses, we are then able to deal with them better and live happier lives.

Thank you, Dr. Sperling.

41.

*"What are the differences between
Freudian psychoanalytic treatment and
other forms of psychological treatment?"
we asked Dr. Klein.*

xxxxxxxxxxxxxxxxxxxx

HENRIETTE R. KLEIN, M.D.

Clinical Professor of Psychiatry,
College of Physicians and Surgeons,
Columbia University

In this interview, Dr. Klein also discusses:
"Can everyone be helped by psychological treatment?"
"What is the theory of psychodynamics?"
"How is a method of treatment selected?"
*"How can an individual get the type of help best suited to
his needs?"*
"Who is most eligible for psychoanalytic treatment?"
*'Why does the analyst assume a variety of roles for
the patient?"*
"Who is the 'typical' person who seeks treatment?"
"Can 'problems' be eliminated and 'symptoms' cured?"
"What are the goals of psychoanalysis?"
*"Does the analyst impose his own values and standards on
the patient?"*
"What qualities make an effective analyst?"

41.

*his is what Dr. Klein said when interviewed in her *ffice:*

). Can everyone be helped by psychological treatment?

A. I think we can assume that a decision to seek psychologi-
*al help implies in itself that the individual is to some degree
*aware of certain difficulties which may stem from faulty atti-
udes toward himself. Others may have arisen from unresolved
*emotional problems which have long been present. Conse-
*quently, once the decision to seek help has been made, the
*prospective patient has taken the first step toward change and
*growth. Of course, the actual benefits he is likely to derive
*from therapy will depend on many crucial factors, especially
*the nature of his problem. These factors determine, in part,
*the goal of therapy in each specific case.

To illustrate, medical treatment for a badly cut finger would
be limited to repair of the damaged finger, while treatment of
a chronic heart condition might have a broader goal. Here
the physician might attempt to reconstruct the functioning of
the patient's entire body, in order to make it possible for him
to live a longer and more comfortable life within the bounds
of his illness. Similarly, the diagnosis or apparent nature of
the patient's underlying emotional illness will determine the
most suitable type of psychological treatment to be recom-
mended.

Furthermore, the goal of treatment may be limited by certain realistic factors. Theoretically, an older person, who may
have longstanding symptoms or is "set in his ways," is less
likely to be able to alter substantially some personal attitudes
held from early childhood than is a more plastic younger person. Not all emotional dysfunction is reversible. In fact, certain irreversible life circumstances, such as previous faulty
commitments or crippling family responsibilities, may inhibit
the fulfillment of personal therapeutic goals.

Finally, the success of treatment will largely depend on the strength of the patient's desire to "get better" and to grow. Ultimately, the credit for the success of treatment belongs to the patient himself. Therefore, it is widely believed that wherever feasible, the patient himself should be willing to seek psychological help of his own volition rather than as a result of external pressures.

In general the success of treatment will depend on the degree of understanding and guidance supplied by the therapist.

Q. *Do the various types of psychological help which are currently available differ essentially in terms of basic underlying theory?*

A. Therapeutic approaches tend to differ widely. It is fair to say, however, that all current types of psychotherapy are bases on the theory of psychodynamics, that is, the body of theory and knowledge which attempts to describe and explain why people feel and behave the way they do. Psychodynamics is derived from Freudian psychoanalytic theory. Over the years, Freud's basic work has been expanded and modified by subsequent workers. These modifications include contributions from sciences which are not directly concerned with human behavior, e. g., physiological work on anger, experimental work on dreams, biological work on instinctive behavior, cultural studies, etc.

Q. *Why does individual's behavior differ from another's?*

A. In general, the adult's behavior and attitudes are based on motives and needs, many of which he is not conscious. In turn, these drives can be understood in the light of his developmental history and the nature of the specific experiences to which he was exposed, particularly in his earlier life. Once the effect of these early experiences are emotionally re-experienced, understood and discussed, they need no longer govern his behavior in adulthood inappropriately.

For example, a loving and tender relationship with the mother or a mother substitute is all-important to the helpless infant. If at some stage in his early development, the mother was forced to withdraw her protection, thus depriving the infant, he may suffer from the effects of these unsatisfied dependency needs well into later life. His attitudes toward, and perception of, other people in his environment may be colored by his fear of repeated desertion and rejection, although this fearful expectation may be without any realistic basis. Even his marital choice may be predicated on a woman's "motherly" qualities, on her willingness to take care of him. Although some of these marriages may prove successful, they are based on decisions which were predetermined by unfulfilled infantile desires, rather than adult needs. Hence, such a marriage may not fulfill all of his healthy adult needs.

Q. In what way do methods of psychological help differ?

A. For the most part, a so-called classical or standard form of psychoanalysis will be conducted in accordance with Freud's original theories. This means that analytic sessions are scheduled four or five times a week for a period of 3 to 5 years. The patient is encouraged to express whatever thoughts and feelings may come into his mind. One uncensored thought will lead to another, ultimately providing the clues to the true nature of his feelings. This chain of "thinking out loud" may also be stimulated by the patient's account of dreams.

Throughout treatment, the psychoanalyst interprets the patient's introspective feelings and thoughts whenever appropriate. As a result, they may lose their abstract quality and emerge as a more clearly defined set of feelings, enabling the patient to re-experience these feelings more intensively. Usually, the psychoanalyst will not make direct suggestions regarding the patient's tactics in handling individuals in his environment or with regard to other specific life situations. However, he will constantly try to help the patient to clarify the issues involved. Moreover, the analyst may have to intervene in order to prevent the patient from following a course of behavior which would be particularly detrimental.

Other methods of psychotherapy call for less frequent sessions and the therapist's more active participation in the patient's treatment and current life experiences. This participation will usually be limited to a certain readiness to interpret the patient's assertions in the light of his immediate life situation. Some forms of psychotherapy are thus more "directive" than the non-interventionist policy of the psychoanalyst, although the degree of this participation may vary considerably. For example, in "supportive" therapy, the patient may obtain substantial relief merely by virtue of being able to tell his troubles to a sympathetic person. Wherever appropriate, the therapist may actively support the patient's efforts toward a particular goal.

At the other extreme, the therapist may actually intervene in almost every phase of the patient's life. For example, he may provide detailed instructions as to how other people in the environment might be handled effectively. Although he will not force the patient to make a specific decision, he may lead him to that decision by emphasizing its advantages. He may even offer suggestions as to how the patient might effectively manage certain activities, for example, his leisure-time activities or the management of finances.

Other approaches may fall somewhere between these two extremes. As a rule, a directive therapist will not restrict his activities to just one of these methods. Instead, the approach will vary according to the overall needs of the patient at a particular stage in treatment.

Q. *Is it essential that an emotionally troubled individual obtain psychoanalytic treatment?*

A. There are many persons who have been helped, and helped permanently, with other forms of therapy including drugs. Also, a treatment method should be selected on the basis of each patient's capacities and limitations. By the same token, a method which is selected to fill the needs of an individual with similar potentialities should not be considered less effective than a method such as analysis, which is able to bring about dramatic changes in a patient's personality or life situation. The effectiveness of a treatment method can be judged only on the basis of whether it has fulfilled the goals of therapy. These goals are determined by many factors, including what the patient is like and what the nature of his dysfunction or problem is.

Q. *How can a prospective patient be sure that he will get the type of psychological help best suited to his particular needs?*

A. If he consults someone with regular training in psychiatric disorders and the theory of psychodynamics, he can expect to have prescribed for him the kind of psychotherapeutic

elp needed for his particular problem. He should request to
pe referred to someone with a particular kind of professional
xperience and skill.

). *What specific factors will determine a therapist's choice of
ne treatment method?*

A. Some of the factors involved have been mentioned previously, such as the characteristics of the illness — type,
everity, duration — or the age and intelligence of the patient.
Let us assume that a middle-aged woman who has always
unctioned fairly well, has decided to seek psychological help.
She has a mild depression which she attributes to her current
nability to get along well with her employer, and wants help
vith this phase of her life.

However, before making a valid decision as to the most
effective treatment method for this limited problem, the
therapist would have to evaluate her emotional make-up, her
previous level of functioning in life, and other factors, This
patient does not want to be analyzed; she feels she "could
not afford to spend years being analyzed." In addition, the
therapist doubts that the patient would profit sufficiently from
intensive long-term analytic therapy. The goals of therapy,
therefore, are limited in this case. The patient's symptoms
will have to be alleviated by helping her to understand the
factors which precipitated her recent difficulty with her employer. Also, the therapist will try to reactivate the strength
which had enabled her to cope with previous life problems.
However, even by treatment with limited goals, the patient
will gain some awareness of her motives and needs. In the
very process of working out her mild depression and the poor
relationship with her employer, she may expect that her
functioning in other areas will to some degree improve as
well.

For example, the reasons for the patient's overreaction
to her employer will be partly explored in treatment. This
reaction may have been motivated by conscious or unconscious feelings of envy, or it may have been precipitated by her
own wish (and fear) to assert herself and resign. As a result of
treatment, the patient may gain the courage to look for a new
job, or may decide to make the best of her present situation.

Whatever her decision, she may hope to be no longer sus
ceptible to symptoms which seem to "come out of the blue
Also, treatment will probably entail some exploration of th
patient's relation to others, and the insights gained in th
process may prove equally profitable.

*Q. Is it necessary that a person possess specific qualities i
order to be suitable for psychoanalytic treatment?*

A. No one could say with certainty what makes someon
"right" for analytic treatment. We are better at knowing wh
would not be. However, one could take a general shot a
what makes a person eligible. First, it may be said that h
would need to be capable of a high degree of cooperation. Fo
example, he should be willing to forego other activities in th
interests of treatment.

He is expected to have some degree of self-reliance and
should possess the capacity for functioning effectively in a
least some of the major areas of behavior such as work o
marriage. He should somehow demonstrate the inner capacity
for deriving pleasure from these activities, although he may
not be fulfilling his true potential in *any* of these areas at tha
time.

The life situation of the patient eligible for psychoanalysis should be relatively fluid, e. g., without chronic physica
illness. The eligible patient must also have some awareness o
his problems and conflicts, and he should realize that they are
interfering with his functioning. Of course, he cannot be expected at the onset of treatment to have deep insight into the
actual nature of his problems, but he should have the intelligence and aptitude to think in terms of his emotions and behavior. Only if he has enough desire to change will he be
willing to involve himself in a lengthy, sacrificing, and at times
uncomfortable treatment procedure.

The patient should be capable of tolerating some degree
of frustration in order to profit from psychoanalysis. For example, he may realize how important his father's love was for
him as a child, re-experiencing this longing for paternal affection and support on a conscious level. However intense, this
desire is no longer appropriate. In fact, it is undesirable —
even impossible — for an adult to create this longed-for situation, which properly belongs to childhood. Thus, the patient

should be prepared to renounce this wish. Instead, he will have
to devote his efforts to developing his capacity for emotional
fulfillment on an adult level.

Finally, the eligible patient is expected to have the ability
to form an emotional attachment to another individual (including the therapist). Success or failure of treatment will
ultimately depend on this capacity.

*Q. Earlier, you portrayed the psychoanalyst as needing to re-
main "aloof." Wouldn't this "aloofness" inhibit an emotional
response on the part of the patient?*

A. Perhaps I haven't sufficiently clarified the meaning of
"emotional involvement" in this context.

In the course of treatment, the analyst will assume a variety of roles for the patient. For example, at one point, the
patient may "make him into" a loved and loving mother or
father; at another, a hated sibling, and so forth. The patient
will behave toward the analyst just as he behaved, or would
have liked to behave, toward this loved parent or hated sibling
in the past. The patient will eventually gain some insight into
the sources and meanings of this behavior. He will become
cognizant of his tendency to behave similarly toward other
people who, for a variety of reasons, represent those persons
in his present environment who played crucial roles in his
early development. It is through "aloofness" that the patient
is enabled to attribute this wide variety of roles and qualities
to the analyst. If, instead, the analyst were to assume the role
of a supportive parent throughout treatment, it would be
difficult for the patient to react toward him as a censoring,
inhibiting father. The patient's ability to re-experience the
feelings elicited by these original parental attitudes — and his
reactions at the time — would be limited to an intellectual
awareness, which could not have deep or long-lasting benefits.

Only when such insights are experienced on an emotional
level, may they have a true impact on the patient. For one, he
is able to vent pent-up hostility onto the analyst, without fear
of retribution. Secondly, once he understands and feels the
true nature of his family relationships, he will refrain from re-
enacting blindly these relationships with others in the outside
world.

Q. Could you describe the "typical" person who seeks psycho-analytic treatment and what symptoms he is likely to present?

A. It is hard to think of a "typical" patient. The majority of patients who come for analysis have no organized symptoms. There are changing patterns in all fields of medicine. For instance, pediatricians report a marked decrease in feeding problems as compared to those in the 1930's. Also, many of the pediatric clinical pictures have changed over the years, if not the underlying process.

Patients who come to analysis today are likely to complain of being discontented. They are dissatisfied with their lives; they complain of uneasiness and tension, vague fears and worries; they derive very little pleasure from life; they live with a great deal of rage; they feel they have not fulfilled themselves in work or love. But, while it may be particularly his marital or job problems that are stressed by the patient, none of them will prove to be isolated from all others.

Q. What are the chances that the patient's problems will disappear as a result of treatment?

A. There is a very good chance that the patient, through this emotional experience, will be helped to help himself; that is, to use his own resources to solve his conflicts. As a result, he will get more pleasure out of life and operate with more social usefulness. Or he may have to learn to live with what is "not reversible" within himself.

Q. Where the symptom is more specific, can the patient expect analysis to "cure" his symptoms?

A. The psychoanalyst's interest is not restricted to the symptoms which merely represent dysfunction, though it is to be hoped that the patient will indeed become free of them. The more common "symptoms" presented by patients on admission to psychoanalytic treatment, such as anxiety and headaches, usually disappear.

However, when symptoms are excessively severe, or of long standing, the ultimate prognosis as to their complete disappearance should be guarded. Through treatment, however, the general level of the patient's adaptation may be raised. We assume that treatment will be more effective if it is aimed at the variety of causes giving rise to a particular symptom.

Q. How would you define the goals of psychoanalysis?

A. The psychoanalyst's goal is to help the patient reconstruct his life and to raise his self-esteem. In order to derive pleasure and gratification from work, in marriage, in sexual adjustment, in social relations in the family and community — above all, to build up his self-esteem — the patient's excessive guilt must be relieved.

Q. Isn't it possible that the analyst will impose his own values and standards on the patient?

A. Inevitably, since the analyst does have personal values and moral standards, the patient will become cognizant of them. But the analyst does not aim at imposing them on his patient. He does not assume the role of a moral god who judges, punishes, or approves.

Rather, he attempts to help the patient fulfill his own particular potentialities through understanding. Individual differences must be understood and accepted. For example, some people derive maximum pleasure from living essentially in the present, without worrying about the future. Others are oriented toward saving and planning ahead.

Q. In the interest of the patient, however, shouldn't the analyst discourage such a trend in the ones who want to live only in the present?

A. Except for the fact that the analyst will always see his objective in preventing the patient from inflicting damage on himself, his efforts along such lines will be based on the assumption that gratification and satisfaction depend upon an absence of fear, conflict, guilt, and so forth. The analyst's function is to help the patient to identify and resolve his fears. Then, the patient will become free to make his choice, which may go in any number of directions.

The differences in maternal attitudes would be another example of the patient's "personal choice." We can start with the biological fact that some women are fundamentally more maternal than others. This is a fact, but fear and guilt, for example, might interfere with a woman's motherliness. It is not the analyst's goal in such a situation to persuade the patient to become more maternal. Instead, he will help her resolve th fears which may affect her maternal attitudes.

Q. One popular conception is that people, after analysis, ar too free of duty and responsibility.

A. I consider this a misconception. Hopefully, after th treatment is terminated, the individual's behavior will b based on free choice. But this will be predicated on disciplin and conscience. Freedom from pathological guilt does no mean absence of personal conscience or social conscience. Fo example, behavior based on free choice may result in eve greater pleasure in fulfilling responsibilities.

The term "pleasure" does not mean the gratification o every whim. It refers to satisfaction gained from the use o inner resources, from pride in achievement, and self-realiza tion.

Q. Since your professional work has included a particular in terest in the selection and teaching of applicants for psycho analytic training, would you be good enough to define those qualities which you regard as essential for the analyst-to-be?

A. In spite of the public's hope that the analyst be perfect, he cannot be, nor does he need to be, even if he may be expected in some ways to provide a "model." He will have to possess a thorough knowledge of the nature of mental illness and should be well grounded in psychodynamics. In order to work with patients effectively, the analyst in particular must have a knowledge and insight into the motivations which govern his own behavior. For clinical competence in psychoanalytic technique, he needs certain basic emotional qualities, above all the quality of empathy which is the capacity to recognize and understand the feelings of the patient. Needless to say, he must possess a high degree of integrity, since he deals with problems of a highly personal nature in a relationship of close dependency.

Finally, because analysis is a highly personal and some what solitary process, the analyst must have the personal security to evaluate the effectiveness of the analytic treat ment with each patient all the time. In this process, he will assess his own competence to implement the goals of psychoanalytic treatment.

Thank you, Dr. Klein.

42.

"What is psychiatry?"
we asked Dr. Polatin.

XXXXXXXXXXXXXXXXXX

PHILLIP POLATIN, M.D.

Professor of Clinical Psychiatry, College of
Physicians and Surgeons, Columbia University

In this interview, Dr. Polatin also discusses:

"What is a psychoneurotic?"
   *"What forms of psychiatric help are available to the
      public?"*
      *"What can an individual reasonably expect from
         treatment?"*
"Is there an average length of time in treatment?"
   "What is the average cost of treatment?"
      *"How can an individual find and choose a psy-
         chiatrist?"*
*"Is there a difference between the private and public mental
   hospital?"*

42.

This is what Dr. Polatin said when interviewed in his office:

Q. *What is meant by the word "psychiatry?"*

A. Psychiatry is a branch of medicine in which the doctor specializes in mental and emotional diseases. It differs from "neurology" in that neurology is a specialized branch of medicine which deals with diseases of the brain and spinal cord, namely with the central nervous system. Psychiatry differs from "psychology" in that psychology is not a branch of medicine, since it does not deal with disease processes but merely with the study of the normally functioning mind. To be a psychiatrist one has to study medicine and, after obtaining a medical degree, then go on for several more years in the specialized study of mental diseases.

Q. *What is the meaning of the word "psychoses?"*

A. Psychoses are severe mental diseases which were previously called "insanities." In the psychoses there are disturbances of thinking, feeling and behavior. A psychosis is a serious maladaptation of the individual to his surroundings.

Q. *What is the meaning of the word "psychoneuroses?"*

A. These are emotional disturbances in which anxiety occurs as a result of unconscious conflicts, and which lead to uncomfortable symptoms such as morbid fears (phobias, obsessions, compulsions, severe tensions, depressions, and even physical symptoms which have no organic causes. The psychoneuroses never involve the total personality, as most always occurs in the psychoses, nor is there the marked involvement of thinking, feeling and behavior almost always seen in the psychoses.

Q. *What are the various forms of psychiatric help? Who is most suitable for each type?*

A. The main form of psychiatric help is psychotherapy. Psy-

otherapy is to the psychiatrist what the scalpel is to the
urgeon. It is a relationship based upon verbal contact beween the patient and a psychiatrist which results, in due
me, in alterations in the symptoms, personality and adjust-
ent levels of the patient. There are many forms of psy-
hotherapy, only one of which is psychoanalysis. But unfor-
nately, the public has gained the impression that psycho-
nalysis is the only form of treatment in psychiatry. This is
bsolutely false. Psychoanalysis is a very small part of the
otal scheme of psychiatric treatment; furthermore, there
re relatively few people who are suitable for the classical
orm of psychoanalysis. The mild psychoneurotic is amen-
ble to psychoanalysis, but the severe psychoneurotic and the
sychotic individual are helped more by a modification of
sychoanalysis which is called "analytic psychotherapy."
This is not classical psychoanalysis in which the patient must
e seen at least three or more times a week and must lie on
he couch with the psychoanalyst seated behind and out of
iew. Rather, analytic psychotherapy involves a one-to-one
elationship in which the patient faces the therapist and
reely discusses his feelings, thoughts, wishes and desires,
nd the therapist uses his psychoanalytic knowledge to un-
lerstand what the patient is trying to convey about his unconscious (dynamic) conflicts. Then, when it is indicated as
ecessary and appropriate, the therapist interprets the
lynamics for the patient. In other words, this is an active
orm of treatment in which the therapist whole-heartedly
enters into the situation. Psychotherapy can be utilized in
any emotional problem, such as marital difficulties, work
difficulties, social inhibitions, parent-child problems, adolescent problems, or in any instance where a person is
chronically unhappy, maladjusted and constantly tense and
anxious. I should mention in connection with this another
form of psychotherapy, namely group therapy. Since the last
war, group therapy has found a great popular appeal, and
deservedly so, because many more patients can be treated
effectively as a minimal financial cost. In addition, it has
in several instances a more specific value than individual
treatment, particularly in cases showing social and work inhibitions.

Q. What are the other forms of psychiatric help? When ar
they best used?

A. There is *insulin shock* and *electroshock.* The former *
used in the schizophrenic diseases, whereas *electroshoc*
treatments are used in severe depressions, retarded states, an
extremely overactive and excited states. There is a *continuou*
sleep therapy used mainly with schizophrenic patients, whicl
is applied very little in the United States although exten
sively in Europe. *Narcotherapy* is used with patients who hav
difficulty in verbalizing, or who have reached a stalemate i
therapy and can't go on. But this also is used rarely i
America. In addition, there is *chemotherapy* (use of drugs
which is utilized in psychotic conditions, particularly
schizophrenia in any form, and in the depressions of any
type. *Chemotherapy* is also used in any neurotic condition
with a large anxiety component, but it is always combined
with psychotherapy. *Chemotherapy* utilizes the new tran
quilizing and anti-depressant drugs quite successfully. *Hypno*
therapy (hypnosis) is essentially valuable in states of dissocia
tion such as amnesia, multiple personality, somnambulism, and
other similarly unusual conditions. For the most part, when
mechanical or drug treatments are given to the patient they
are combined with psychotherapy.

Q. What can individuals and the public at large reasonably
expect from any of these forms of treatment?

A. Good results can be expected if a skilled psychiatrist makes
a correct diagnosis and fits the proper treatment to the particular condition. In other words, in psychiatry there is as
much training and skill utilized as there is in general medicine
or in surgery. If a surgeon misdiagnoses an appendicitis and
takes out a gallbladder you will have a poor result for the
patient. In the same sense, if a psychiatrist misdiagnoses a
psychotic for a neurotic and consequently uses classical psychoanalysis, there will also be a poor result for the patient.
Successful treatment depends upon accurate diagnosis.

Q. Is there an "average" length of time of treatment?

A. Not really. Treatment may only take a few weeks if it
is a question of merely eliminating certain symptoms by means
of brief psychotherapy or chemotherapy. On the other hand,

may last five years if it is a question of reconstructing the ersonality by means of psychoanalysis.

. Is there an "average" cost of treatment?

. The average cost in a psychiatric clinic attached to a priate or general hospital is very moderate, often as little as one or two dollars a session. In a semi-private clinic, however, the ost varies from five to ten dollars a session, while with a rivate psychiatrist the cost may vary from fifteen to fifty ollars a session, depending primarily upon the experience, ge and training of the therapist, as well as geographical cation.

. How can an individual best find and choose a psychiatrist?

. The first recommendation would be to consult with the amily doctor who is well qualified to recommend a specialst in any specialized branch of medicine. If there is no amily doctor, however, the individual can call his local County Medical Society, and they will give him the names of hree psychiatrists from which he himself can choose one. Or, person can contact The American Psychiatric Association at 270 Ave. of Americas, New York City, and obtain from it he names of three psychiatrists in his community. If the ndividual wants a psychoanalyst, he can contact the American 'sychoanalytic Association at 1 East 57th Street, New York City. Or, if he lives in a large city, he can call his local ospital and obtain the names of the psychiatrists on its staff.

. Today, what are the significant differences, if any, beween public and private mental hospitals?

A. Briefly, with the use of new tranquilizing drugs and with he advent of the era of chemotherapy, the previous wide gap etween the private and the public mental hospital has narrowed markedly. The number of patients leaving the public hospitals as a result of excellent treatment with drugs is now very high. Financially, of course, there is still a very wide gap, because the public hospital is supported by local, state and Federal funds and charges relatively small fees based upon the ability to pay. The private mental hospital and the psychiatric pavilions of general hospitals charge about two hundred dollars per week, this figure varying from as low as one hundred and fifty to as high as four hundred and fifty per

week. Nevertheless, both the public and private mental hosp
tals are today places where individuals may go with a stron
hope of getting well.

Thank you, Dr. Polatin.

43.

"What is lay analysis?"
we asked Dr. Reik.

XXXXXXXXXXXXXXXXXXXX

THEODOR REIK, Ph.D.

Founder and Honorary President, The National
Psychological Association for Psychoanalysis

In this interview, Dr. Reik also discusses:

"What type of person is most suitable for analysis?"
   "Who are the people who consider themselves different
      from others?"
      "Are there limitations to treatment?"
"What is the importance of money in treatment?"
   "Are analysts too concerned with sex?"
      "Does the analyst mold the patient in his own image?"
"Why is the analyst a symbolic person to the patient?"
   "What are compulsive thoughts and actions?"

43.

This is what Dr. Reik said when interviewed in his office:

Q. *What is meant by "Lay Analysis?"*

A. To me, it means analysis made by men and women who have not thoroughly learned the theory and methods on analysis, who have not had adequate supervisory training, and who have not been thoroughly analyzed themselves by an experienced and perceptive psychoanalyst.

Q. *What is "analysis?"*

A. That is too broad a question to answer here. But put briefly, analysis is a therapeutic method of treatment of neuroses, character deformities and borderline cases. It is a method used by the analyst to find unconscious forces in connection with conscious feelings, attitudes, thoughts and actions. And last, but certainly not least, it is a body of knowledge which has accumulated through five decades and which is still increasing.

Q. *What type of person is most suitable for analysis?*

A. To begin with, I would rather say who is least suitable. First of all, there is the "psychotic" person. The man, for example, who comes and tells you that he has just met the Devil outside your door; upon questioning, it develops that he does indeed believe that he has met the Devil. He saw him with his own eyes, he says. Secondly, there is the "psychopathic" personality. A psychopath is a person whose disturbances are of such a kind that they can be called moral insanity. It very often approaches the character of the criminal. Another type of person who is not suitable for analysis is the one with serious physical as well as emotional illness or defect. If a man has lost both of his legs in an accident, let us say, no amount of analysis will change that fact. And ast, there is a group of people who are very difficult to treat ut not necessarily impossible. These are men and women who consider themselves "exceptions." They feel that they need not accept the general regulations and necessities of ife. They behave as if they had a special claim on life, and hey feel that life must make amends for congenital injuries n early childhood for which they are not responsible. In alking of this type of person, Freud gave as an example Shakespeare's interpretation of the Duke of Gloucester, later Richard The Third. In Shakespeare's play, Richard has a great monologue in which he explains that he can do "whatever" he likes because of his hunchback, for which, of course, ie is not responsible. Richard says that he is beyond the law, beyond morality; he is an outsider and an "exception," all because of his hunchback.

Q. What can a man or woman reasonably expect from analysis?

A. An individual can expect that the disturbances, emotional and mental, will be slowly improved and finally removed. I mean by this that there will be a kind of cure, with formations of scars, and I mean also that certain symptoms of the previous neurosis will remain. For example, I treated a woman who was obese as a result of overeating. The overeating was a substitute for a lack of sexual satisfaction in her life, and this in turn could be traced back to a traumatic experience she suffered in early childhood when an old male relative seduced her into performing fellatio. Although I managed to reduce the obesity and to ameliorate her defeatist emotional outlook on life, I did not entirely succeed in stopping her overeating. It was a left-over symptom which would remain.

But each case is different. You can't make generalizations too easily, for in certain cases we do enough when we improve the patient's mental health, and in other cases it is enough to keep him where he was with the help of analytical methods.

Psychoanalytic therapy has, of course, certain limitations, for instance constitutional factors. It is often possible only to improve an emotional disturbance without removing it; you can play only with the cards that were dealt to you. Let me give you one other example. One of my cases was a frigid woman who, like the woman I just mentioned, had been sexually mis-used as a little girl. The patient remembered that when she was a little girl she had the very strong wish that her father would die. You see, when her father was absent from the house this male friend of his would come and "play" with her, and the most terrifying thought to this little girl was that her father would find out about her shame. So, as a matter of protection, she wished him dead. As in the other case, I did not entirely succeed in removing certain neurotic symptoms which were expressed in her sexual life.

Q. *What is the average length of time of treatment?*

A. Often this is the first question a patient will ask the analyst. "How long will all of this take?" they want to know. However, the length of time will depend upon a number of factors, and to a great extent upon the moral courage which the patient possesses. It depends upon how soon and how ready he is to talk about himself and others with fullest sincerity, and whether he is ready to face the unpleasant realities of his life. In order to evaluate the patient's moral courage, Freud suggested that there should be a trial time of five or six weeks, in which it can be ascertained how much, or how little, can be done and how long it will take. Freud used an Aesop fable to illustrate the meaning of this. An Athenian walks towards Sparta, and when he first catches sight of the city in the distance he stops and asks a peasant how far it is to the center of town. "Walk," is the paradoxical answer the Spartan peasant gives him. The meaning is, of course: "Walk. And when I see how fast you go I can tell you how far Sparta is from here for you."

Q. *What is the average cost of treatment?*

A. It depends on the age and experience of the analyst. An elderly and experienced analyst, because of age or illness, is often restricted in the number of hours he may work. But at the same time, he must make a living from those hours, and therefore he will charge more than the beginner. You know, the famous painter Whistler once finished a commissioned portrait of a gentleman in three or four hours. The "customer" was unhappy about the price Whistler charged, complaining to him that he only "worked" a few hours. Whistler answered by saying that indeed the time was short but for him to learn his art had taken many years at great expense.

Q. *What is the importance of money in treatment?*

A. First of all, money gives a certain sound motive to the patient to move his analytic progress forward. I would say, furthermore, that those people with the best chance for success in treatment are those who pay from their own means and who have to sacrifice a certain amount of pleasure to do so. Those individuals who are dependent upon others to pay for their treatment, or those who are unwilling to pay, have poorer chances of success. Also, people who generally prolong payment, or who are unwilling to pay, have an unconscious guilt feeling toward the analyst and they behave accordingly. This means that the guilt will come out in self-destructive behavior in life, or in the process of analysis. That guilt feeling toward the analyst is, of course, based on their debt. The German word "schuld" has the double meaning of debt and guilt.

Q. *Many people claim that analysts are much too concerned with "sex." Would you give an answer to that?*

A. It seems that our society is hypocritical, especially in certain areas of life. We have hypocrisy in man's sexual life, man's economic life, and in the area of aggression. In the ordinary education of children in our culture the child is taught to be "good and nice" in all of these three areas. Thus, when he is aggressive, jealous, mean and sexual (all of which are quite natural for him to be) he considers himself an outcast and an especially "bad boy." This leads to early guilt feelings, and consequently we are hypocritical in that we keep on denying our guilt in sexuality, with money, and in the handling of our aggression. We see this hypocrisy at work not only within individuals and families; entire nations behave in the very same way, assuring everyone that they are peace-loving while they are, in fact, full of aggressive drives.

Q. *Do you believe that anti-Semitic feelings and attitudes play a part in many people's negative opinions of Freud's life work, and in general in their attitudes towards psychology?*

A. Yes, I would say, to a great extent. But this is a generally defensive attitude. I remember a Christian American who went to Europe for consultations with Freud. Freud referred him to me, and at our first meeting the patient complained that analysts were too "inquisitive." The answer to that is that a physician cannot make an operation without cutting; or, one could say that you cannot make an omelet without breaking eggs. But Freud himself attributed to his Jewishness two advantages. First, that he had the courage to remain in the minority against a compact majority; that is, when he first presented his ideas to the world, the overwhelming majority of medical doctors, and others, laughed at him and were violently opposed. Secondly, he attributed to his Jewishness the fact that he was free from superstitions in which others were still involved — for example, a belief in the hereafter, or similar ideas.

Q. *Is has often been charged that an analyst cannot help but mold the patient into his own image. For example, could you have treated in 1939, a Nazi Storm Trooper?*

A. No, I couldn't have treated him. In the 1930's in Vienna, for instance, there were great political storms between the radicals (the communists and the socialists at the extreme left) and the reactionaries. The favorite color of the radicals was red, the conservatives' color was black, and Freud said to his students, that we should avoid taking into treatment people who belonged to either of those extreme camps. He said. "Man should not be black or red, he should be flesh-colored."

Freud also said that you have to make a distinction between psychoanalysis as a method of therapy and psychoanalysis as a body of scientific insights. But if you consider only therapy, not the science, then certainly you have to have values at the onset. The physician who does not have value for life will not pay enough attention to the possibilities of healing the sick. While science does not acknowledge moral values except truth, practical life cannot be led without values. A surgeon who is convinced that life is not worth while, will not consider that an operation will be life-saving. Also, it nakes a difference whether you educate someone in the Soviet Union or in Western Democracy. "Education" means educating someone for something, whether Fascism or Democracy. If the aim is different, the education must be different.

Now, if an analyst would say that mental health, or a certain emotional balance, is not important, then he would forego all effort in this direction and he would not care how the patient lived. I would say that whenever you do anything in therapy you have to choose certain values, although they do not have to be the same values as those of conventional society. I can, for instance, treat a playwright who puts into his plays moral values which are different from our conventional ideas, or possibly different from my own.

Q. Nevertheless, many people believe that the analyst does "mold" the patient.

A. But that is not correct. The analyst is not God who created man in His image. The analyst's proper task is to remove inner disturbances so that the patient can work and live according to his own best potentialities. The analyst does not try to be a pattern, or mold, for the patient to follow or fall into. As a matter of fact, it is often the case that the patient does not have a clear picture of what the analyst even looks like, let alone a clear picture of his personality. This is because the analyst is to the patient a figure whose features move between those of a real person and a symbolic person. A good example of the use of the symbolic person — and the confusion between the real and the symbolic — is illustrated in a patient of mine who accidentally found out that my daughter was twenty-three years old and a student of mathematics. Without any other information whatsoever, and without my once mentioning her to him, the patient decided that I had hatched a plot for him to marry her. After a few months of brooding he finally accused me of this plot; however, although I may be many things to many men, I am not, and never was a marriage broker.

Q. You have lived your own life with certain moral values and concepts. How can you help but impose these upon your patients?

A. There is a certain justification to this question. I would say that the process of analysis is not only a method of treatment but also of re-education. Freud called it a kind of "post-education," and in this sense analysis is not different from other methods of education. Parents at first educate the child to give up things out of love for the parent. In the same sense, the transferred love of the patient for the analyst works in a certain direction, especially in that the analyst endeavors to prevent the patient from doing things which would harm himself.

For example, I once treated a very religious young man who suffered under obsessive blasphemous thoughts. He would see, for instance, a picture of Christ at The Last Supper and he had to think "Drunkard!" He would see a figure of the Holy Virgin and he had to think "Dirty Jewess! You spread your legs to allow Joseph to have sexual intercourse." When he thought such blasphemies he would pound himself on the forehead until he was bloody. In this extreme case I forbade that self-punishment. If you call this "interference with the patient's behavior," then I agree. The main thing is to prevent the patient's self-destructive behavior.

But consider the case of a woman in Western culture, let us say, who is promiscuous. This kind of woman has a low opinion of herself as a woman, because a woman expects to be treated not only as a sexual object to satisfy the sexual appetite of the man, but as a human being. But if a woman is promiscuous she shows that she values herself very little as a feminine human being. And I would therefore say that if I had such a patient I would try to the best of my knowledge and conscience to educate her this way: I would want her to react in a sexually responsive way only if the man respects her and does not consider her merely as a sexual object. This would have, I might add, nothing to do with her being married or single, nor would I consider "adultery" sinful in the Christian sense.

Thank you, Dr. Reik.

44.

"What is psychotherapy?"
we asked Dr. Hulse.

XXXXXXXXXXXXXXXXXXXXX

WILFRED HULSE, M.D. (1901-1962)

Chief, Psychiatric Staff, Foster Care Division,
Bureau of Child Welfare, City of New York

In this interview, Dr. Hulse also discusses:

"Are there basic differences in treatment methods?"
"Is psychotherapy a science?"
"What is 'noodle soup' psychotherapy?"
"Is supportive therapy the same as psychotherapy?"
"Do patients fall in love with the doctor?"
"Are sexuality and genital action the same?"
"Do patients have magical expectations in psychotherapy?"
"What are the average costs of treatment?"
*"What is the best way for a person to find and
choose a psychotherapist?"*

44.

This is what Dr. Hulse said when interviewed in his office:

Q. What is psychotherapy?

A. Psychotherapy is a scientific method used to alleviate emotional stress and mental disbalance. Ideally it cures people of psychopathological ailments. It is geared toward a process of rearranging, by psychological means, the feeling and thinking processes of the one who seeks help. It has as its goal for the patient the more satisfactory use of his feeling and thinking processes in relation to himself and his environment.

Within this wide frame of reference it is possible to use a number of various methods. However, during the past sixty years, as psychotherapy has developed into a scientific instrument, all the workable methods have become pretty well based on a few basic concepts (with the exception of the purely non-scientific magic procedures).

In other words, there are not as many differences in approach as many of those who invent and introduce new methods of psychotherapy would like to pretend. Practically all methods can be reduced to a very few basic factors which make for psychotherapeutic effect. The relationship between the patient and the therapist, I think, is one basic factor. What always develops is that the patient sees the therapist in terms of his own thinking and feelings, which originate in his childhood. This phenomenon is called "transference," and the therapist uses this ubiquitous phenomenon to help the patient understand his own unconscious. Our chief aim is to make the unconscious conscious. We want to substitute reality for magical thinking.

Transference is the basic factor in all psychotherapeutic approaches, whether this is recognized by the therapist or not. It is much better, of course, if the therapist does recognize the phenomenon of transference.

There is one important difference between a scientific procedure where the therapist understands what he is doing and why the patient does or does not respond and a purely emotional, unscientific process. It's like the difference between chemistry and alchemy.

In chemistry, the man knows what he is doing, in alchemy he does not. The difference between recognizing what one is doing and not recognizing what one does is a development of science. Alchemy was not scientific, although occasionally the alchemists had some surprisingly successful results through sheer good luck or coincidence. One could say with truth that chemistry was not, at first, any more successful than alchemy. Yet, chemistry had hypotheses and was not based on magic.

All scientific work must start with hypotheses. You have to set a goal, and then do some theoretical thinking about how you can reach that goal. It does not matter that the hypothesis is not correct. As a matter of fact, within the last one hundred years in all scientific fields in the natural sciences, most hypotheses have been found to be incorrect. It is only in the humanities that thinkers like Aristotle and Plato are still alive. No natural scientists have had anything except historical development to teach after a hundred years or so. This will probably also be true of psychotherapy. We know that our hypotheses today will be greatly modified and proven untenable, for the most part, within one hundred years. This is progress.

In short, our psychotherapeutic methods today are not the last word. As far as they go, I think they are doing a very useful job for those who can use them rationally. But the therapist as well as the patient must be able to use them rationally. Regrettably, there are some practitioners who claim they don't need any relationship to science. They believe that measurements are not necessary, that one can just go out and do good. But that takes the method out of scientific procedure, and consequently, out of psychotherapy.

All theological procedures, all procedures which base themselves on non-scientific methods and, therefore, are not open to scientific investigation, belong to another field — the field of magical procedure. This is certainly widespread, and not without success in many areas of human distress. But it has nothing to do with psychotherapy as a scientific method which is part of the practice of medicine.

I would like to mention here what Dr. Leo Kanner has called "noodle soup psychotherapy." A mother who gives her child good hot noodle soup because the child is cold and wet and miserable is not giving him psychotherapy, just good hot noodle soup. In the same sense, the doctor is not practicing psychotherapy when he comes into your bedroom when you are laid up with the grippe, pats you on the back and says, "You're not so badly off!"

In my opinion, the doctor is doing what ministers do in similar situations. They hold people's hands. But that is not psychotherapy, either. Although it is a very nice and kind gesture, it is not a scientific application of the concepts of the functioning of the human mind to an emotionally ill person.

There are some men, for example, who think that when they make love to a girl they are also doing psychotherapy. Although it may make the girl feel better, it is not at all the same thing. When I talk of psychotherapy, I mean a scientific method that has a plan and is aimed at the rehabilitation of the emotional disturbances of the patient. This is certainly not accomplished either by the doctor who pats his patients on the back, nor by the man who necks with his girl. Nor is it achieved by the mother who gives good hot noodle soup to the cold, wet and miserable child.

Q. Does what you have been saying also apply to supportive therapy?

A. Yes, it does. Because to a certain extent all psychotherapy is supportive. If it were not supportive, the patient would possibly break off therapy and not return to the office after a very few sessions. Consequently, as we help and often manipulate the patient, we also have to support him.

I do not think that any method geared toward support alone actually is exclusively supportive. When we talk about supportive therapy it simply means that we reduce the other aspects of the psychotherapeutic method to a minimum. But at the same time, certain aspects cannot be completely left out because of the hidden and unconscious phenomenon called transference.

Support encourages the patient, to a certain extent, to take the attitude of a child who is looking for support — and primarily for support. Thus, a patient who is only supported is in danger of regressing to a lower more childlike state of function. Consequently, some other elements of psychotherapy are always mixed in with support.

On the other hand, classical psychoanalytic procedure, which is often considered the least supportive of all, is supportive by the very fact that the patient is seen four or five times a week. That is enormous support for the patient because he knows that the process is a continuous one. But a patient who is in so-called "supportive therapy" and is only seen once every two weeks is actually not supported much.

The differences between "supportive" or "non-supportive" psychotherapy are more or less technical, introduced in order to have certain effects upon the patient. We do not say, "I support you," but in good psychotherapy we act in such a manner that the patient feels he is not alone.

Q. Many people think that the word "transference" means "falling in love with the doctor." What does it actually mean?

A. When two people have any kind of relationship, each views it in his own unconscious in terms of his own significant childhood experiences. For example, no one deals with the grocery clerk merely as a grocery clerk. There is always some other feeling. Possibly, he may remind you of someone whom you liked or didn't like when you were a child. This reminder may be entirely unconscious and we tend to push such unconscious feelings away from conscious awareness. All of us act in a kind of pseudo-reality. We tend to deny that adult life has anything to do with our childhood and operate as if life were truly realistic. If we are not too disorganized, this pseudo-reality works moderately well.

In the therapeutic process, however, the unconscious is recognized and used, because the therapist cannot do good psychotherapy without understanding how his patient operates in relation to other people and in relation to himself. The therapist must understand why his patient acts in certain ways and how his patient, unaware of his unconscious projection of infantile feelings onto other people, does harm to his emotional state and to his daily living by acting in such unrealistic ways. The psychotherapist needs to understand this projection of infantile feelings. After he has started to understand, he can treat the patient in various ways — supportive, psychoanalytic, existential, or whatever it is called. In short, the understanding of the patient's mode of operation is the basis for all psychotherapeutic procedures.

Q. Then transference is not "falling in love with the doctor?"

A. No, not necessarily. The misunderstanding of the concept of transference, I think, comes from the idea that love and sexuality mean genital action, and genital action means sexuality and love.

Freud never thought that sexuality and genital action were the same, nor do we think so today. As a matter of fact, Freud developed the theory that sexuality has many other infantile manifestations before it becomes genital. But this idea is difficult to understand and it is usually misunderstood. People tend to equate genital action with love, and then they equate transference with both genital action and love. But genitality is not identical with love, although there may be a good deal of love accompanying it. Nor is transference identical with genitality, although there may be a good deal of genitality accompanying it, also.

Eros, often called the God of Love, is the little fellow with the darts. However Freud's use of the word "love" held the meaning of life force. The life force is the positive force, the drive for living, which is within us all. It is contrary to the death force, Thanatos, which is also within us all. One can say that the total life and death forces are unconsciously projected upon the therapist by the patient. This may or may not include desire for genital action which in common language is confused with love.

Q. What can a patient reasonably expect from psychotherapy?

A. It all depends upon how eager the patient is to change. It also depends upon how many other motives a patient may have which bring him to treatment.

Many adults come and say, "I am here because my wife says if I continue to do what I am doing, she is going to leave me. I need her, so I better go into treatment." If I say to such a man, "Well, what do you expect from treatment?" he would probably answer, "You have to change me, somehow, so that my wife will not leave me."

Although this might possibly be accomplished, at the moment the man is expressing openly ulterior motives which cannot fit in with his own needs — because I cannot provide him with a steady wife. I can only help him achieve the emotional ability to have a steady wife.

Such a man is skipping around in his own thinking. He would like some manipulation so that his wife stays with him, but the chances are that he feels that his own behavior is quite satisfactory to him. He thinks, "Why should she not do for me, or tolerate in me, what she doesn't want to do, or tolerate, but what I want to have done for me?"

Most people who come into the psychotherapeutic process for the first time have some magical expectations, not quite understanding the process. They come often, because they are at the end of their rope. They really do not know what to do next. Nor do they know how to get out of the many conflicts and enormous life or inner difficulties in which they find themselves.

When you throw a rope to a drowning man he will not examine the material for good workmanship before he grabs it. Many people start psychotherapy with the idea that it is the last piece of rope that will be thrown to them. It is up to the therapist to reverse this negative motivation into positive motivation. The first step may be taken as the man comes after a visit and says, "I felt better during the last hour with you than I felt before." You have to make him feel better until he realizes that psychotherapy's purpose is not to make him feel better during the session but to make him better fit for life.

Q. *Are you saying there is no general answer to the question, "What can a patient reasonably expect from psychotherapy?"*

A. If you went to a construction firm and told them your house needed many repairs, and then asked how long the repairs would take and how much they would cost, the chances are that a good construction firm would say to you,

"We will have to see your house. Give us time to look it over, and then we will make an estimate of what we can and can't do, of how long it will take, and of how much it will cost."

It is the same thing in the reconstruction of a personality. I might say to a patient in the first session, "I don't know much about you. Let me find out more and in about a month or so I will tell you what I think we can do. But I can't tell you more at this time."

A peculiar thing may happen after that month is over. The patient will not ask what he can get from psychotherapy, nor will he ask how long it will take. After a number of sessions, he may very well say, "You know, I am afraid my house is in much worse shape than I thought when I first came to you. I now see many holes in the walls which I actually didn't see before." Furthermore, after a month or so the patient will very often tell the therapist it will take much longer than he, the therapist, thinks.

What has happened is the process in which the eyes of the patient are opened a little bit and he becomes more aware of himself and his problems. Thinking that they support the patient, some therapists will tell him they will repair everything in a very short period of time. But this superficial reassurance, this so-called support, actually may frighten the patient because, if the patient is not psychotic, he will soon become aware of his large amount of emotional disability, and think, "This construction man does not even know how badly my house is damaged. If he thinks he can repair it in such a short period of time, I better go to someone else because I don't think it possible."

A lifetime maladjustment cannot be turned into a paradisic state of happiness in a short length of time. After a few sessions a patient will want to have someone conscientiously repair him rather than to undergo a slap-dash job.

Most people who come for therapeutic treatment know that a good deal is wrong. Patients very often say, "I have actually been this disturbed ever since I can remember. How long will it take to change?" The answer depends to a large extent on the forces to change that we can mobilize in the person. This has to be carefully understood and investigated. It is not so much what the therapist can do in psychotherapy but what can be done by the patient himself. Of course, there are people who only need a little advice and then they can get out their do-it-yourself kit and repair their own house. But this type of patient is the minority.

Q. *Is it possible for you to give an estimate of average costs?*
A. There is no average cost because the range is so very wide. In New York City, for example, a person today can find a large amount of free treatment. I mean by "free" that he pays a clinic a fee of fifty cents or a dollar, and gets good treatment once a week. On the other hand, a person may go to a privately practicing psychotherapist or psychoanalyst who charges a very large fee for his hour of treatment. Usually, I might add, this type of practitioner devotes a considerable amount of time to community and hospital services and public research projects for which he receives no fee. Therefore, the high hourly fee represents only a small part of his total professional activities.

Insurance companies are becoming increasingly more interested in covering psychotherapeutic treatment. There is a research project underway at present which is assessing the costs of psychotherapy and they are found to be much lower than the public and the insurance companies previously had assumed. I think the greatest financial burden is placed on the middle-income class. The high- and low-income groups are much better served than the middle brackets who, if they go to a so-called low cost clinic will be charged about ten or twelve dollars a session, and will be charged approximately the same, or a little more from young private practitioners.

Generally speaking, I would say that the high cost of psychotherapeutic treatment has been grossly exaggerated. The same is true of the so-called unobtainability of treatment. I personally have never failed to place a patient in treatment, either privately or in a clinic, within a three month period if the patient was willing to contribute a certain amount of his income which would ordinarily go into other not absolutely necessary items of living.

Q. *Beyond the obvious fact that the doctor has his own economic needs, what is the significance of money in treatment?*
A. The number of missed appointments in free clinics is

much higher than the number of missed appointments in any other setting in which the patient has to make a financial contribution. In our culture, rightly or wrongly, many hold the concept that whatever is given free cannot be worth much. Many people are firmly convinced of this idea and so they derogate all service given free.

Professional people who work in clinics today are very often paid adequate yearly salaries. They don't do clinic work because they can't make a living in private practice. They do it because they like that kind of work, and consequently, their motivation to treat is not diminished by the fact that the patient does not pay for treatment. But from the patient's point of view, he often thinks that if it does not cost much it cannot be worth much and this is a real handicap in treatment of this type.

Q. What is the best way for a person to find and choose a good psychotherapist?
A. The patient who has little or no money must go to a clinic where his own choice of a psychotherapist is limited because clinics cannot allow the patient to choose freely. However, most clinics transfer a patient from one therapist to another if conditions are such that a transferral would be in the best interests of the patient.

When an individual can afford a moderate fee, he should not choose his own psychotherapist by shopping around from one to the other. Preferably, a person should rely on a referral by someone in whom he has confidence. The family physician could be such a person, but unfortunately, some general practitioners turn down such requests because they are ignorant of or against psychotherapy. The reason they are against it is simply that they do not understand it.

Most medical societies have referral services and will give the names of qualified therapists. Many of the analytic psychotherapeutic institutions and organizations also have such services. If an individual will call or write to them, they will give him the names of three qualified people in his geographical area.

Thank you, Dr. Hulse.

45.

*"What is the basic difference between
psychotherapy and supportive therapy?"
we asked Dr. Riess.*

BERNARD R. RIESS, Ph.D.

Chairman, Research Department
Postgraduate Center for Psychotherapy

In this interview, Dr. Riess also discusses:

"Who is most suitable for supportive therapy?"
  "Who can best benefit from psychotherapy?"
    "What kind of therapist is best for an individual?"
"What do patients want from psychotherapy?"
  "How long does treatment take?"
    "Can symptoms be removed?"
"Are 'normal' people similar to 'sick' people?"
  *"Must there be conflict between the patient and the
  therapist?"*
    *"Must there be conflict between psychotherapy and
    religion?"*
"What is the meaning of the sexual drive?"

BERNARD R. RIESS, PH.D.

45.

This is what Dr. Riess said when interviewed in his office:

Q. *What is psychotherapy? What is supportive therapy?*

A. I believe there is no such thing as non-analytic therapy. The basic problem in all patients is that they do not know why they are doing what they are doing. The first function of the therapist is to make them aware of the motivations behind their symptoms which are unhealthy, self-painful and destructive.

To me, these are the basic roots of therapy: first, making the patient aware of the meaning of his symptoms; second, making the patient aware of alternatives to the symptoms; third, helping the patient to elect alternatives which lead to better adjustments.

Within the broad area of therapy there are different types of approaches. The basic difference between supportive therapy and reconstructive therapy (psychotherapy) is that the therapist's function in supportive therapy is that of a continuing prop for the patient who keeps on feeling well as long as he has the therapist. While in reconstructive therapy the aim is to enable the patient to achieve a strength he will continue to possess after he no longer sees the therapist.

Supportive therapy is comparable to certain situations in physical medicine. There are people, for example, with anemia who must continually take drugs in order to keep the anemia at a given level. In this case, obviously, the drugs are supportive and not curative.

The problem with supportive therapy, however, is that the patient frequently does not move beyond the point where he feels comfortable with the therapist. When the prop is taken away the symptoms recur. There are some therapists who believe that the function of supportive therapy is to offer the patient a prop until the patient's instinctive potential for healthy development takes over. These therapists say that the purpose of the supportive treatment is to keep the patient in a state of relaxation while his natural desire to get better helps to overcome his difficulties. In short, there is a school of psychotherapy which believes that if the healthy growth potential of every patient is simply allowed to come into operation, the patient begins to become better. The evidence cited for this belief is seen in people who are on waiting lists at clinics and for whom nothing is done. Merely the fact that somebody has extended this small amount of assistance to them helps them lose their symptoms.

I do not think, however, that this is real therapy. It does not seek the cause of the difficulty, nor does it select a method of changing it and getting the patient better.

Q. Who is most suitable for supportive therapy?
A. Chronic schizophrenics are the first group that comes to mind. These are people who have been extremely isolated from the world of personal relationships. But even though they may never feel any relationship with their co-workers, friends and immediate family, they nevertheless have the feeling of some contact with the therapist — a person who does understand them. In these cases, supportive therapy has been found to be of importance, and it is not uncommon for a patient of this sort to remain in treatment for ten to fifteen years. Fifteen years of treatment is not a criticism of supportive therapy. For without support the patient would very often end up in a state institution, a hospital or jail.

The second group for whom I think supportive therapy has been found to be effective are the terribly anxiety-ridden patients. Support suppresses the anxiety for the time being. The ultimate goal is to move into analytic therapy. With the chronic schizophrenic, however, the situation is different. I am not sure how effective analytic therapy can be with a long-established chronic schizophrenic.

But I am sure that there is one group of patients for whom supportive therapy is not very good. That is the passive-dependent patient whose goal in life is to find somebody to lean upon, and who, if gratified in that goal, will never change.

Q. Who is most suitable for psychotherapy?

A. I cannot think of any individual who would not benefit from psychotherapy. I think it is one of our classic myths in psychology that psychotherapy is a potentially harmful instrument. It is no more harmful than any other procedure when it is skillfully used and when its specific application to a specific patient is kept in mind. No therapist ever uses the same technique or the same approaches to every patient, and the more skillful practitioner recognizes what type of treatment is effective for what type of patient.

The basic question, in my opinion, is not who is most suitable for psychotherapy. The question is, rather, what kind of therapist is good for what kind of patient? All of our experimental studies have shown that it is probably the personality of the therapist more than any other factor that determines his success or lack of success in the treatment of patients. In addition, a second factor of importance in evaluating the success of a therapist is his amount of experience. There have been any number of experimental studies which indicate that the so-called orientation, or school of therapy to which the therapist belongs, does not seem to have any relationship to what happens to his patients. There is a significant difference, however, between an inexperienced therapist and an experienced one in relation to the success of treatment.

Q. What can a patient reasonably expect from psychotherapy?

A. People do not come and say, "I want to be made over again." They come to a therapist because they have headaches, or because they cannot get along with their superiors and have lost a series of jobs, or because they have sexual or marital difficulties. We regard these in a broad sense as being symptoms, and certainly a patient should expect that at the end of a reasonable period of time the symptoms will be removed. That is the goal of the initial stage of therapy.

At the point where the symptoms have been clarified or removed, there is an option open to the patient. He must decide whether or not he wants to pay for the more elaborate and time-consuming process of finding out why the symptoms existed, and he must decide whether he wants to get involved in a joint enterprise with the therapist to change his personality.

His initial expectation, however, should be: "I want to feel better. I don't want to have these difficulties which bother me." I do not wish to imply here that this is necessarily the easiest phase of psychotherapy. The removal of symptoms is often impossible without helping the patient to reconstruct himself. On the other hand, it sometimes happens that the symptoms can be removed very simply. In either case, however, at the time when the symptoms have been removed the patient has the right to say, "This is satisfactory to me."

It should be pointed out that if there has been no real reconstruction — and if there is no continuing supportive therapy — there can be no guarantee that the symptoms will not reappear, or new symptoms develop. As a matter of fact, this has been one of the problems with chemotherapy and shock therapy. There have been no sound studies to show that mechanical therapies of any type — including the newest drug therapies — induce lasting change in patients. On the contrary, even the most recent studies indicate that the new drugs simply make the patients more amenable to psychotherapy, but do not effect a cure of themselves.

A doctor can tell a patient to take two aspirins every time he has a headache. But even though the aspirin may temporarily cure the headache, a symptom of this sort may very well be indicative of a focal source of difficulty. First of all, the source may be physiological, such as brain tumor. But a man can also have headaches because he has to live with his mother-in-law, and by simply changing the environment the therapist may allay the symptoms. At the same time, however, the research-minded therapist would want to know why the mother-in-law produced a headache — rather than a stomach ulcer, let us say. For there is significance in the location and choice of symptoms which may reflect upon the strength or weakness in the patient's personality.

Furthermore, if the patient's life experiences tell him and the therapist that he gets headaches whenever he is in contact with a woman, or whenever he is in a situation where he has to prove himself, then this suggests that there are character and personality problems involved in the symptom. Consequently, the therapist goes on almost automatically into reconstructive therapy.

Cost may be a factor in whether the patient should go on for reconstructive therapy or be satisfied with the alleviation of symptoms. If the patient has to reduce his area of life functioning because he has to pay for his therapy, it may backfire and the symptoms become worse. The reality of the patient must always be taken into account in deciding how far to go and at what cost.

Q. What would you answer if a patient with chronic headaches, let us say, asked you how long it was going to take to relieve his symptoms and make him better?

A. I do not believe that we should ever duck a patient's questions. To say, "I don't know," is only part of the answer. I put it this way to my patients: "I don't know how long it will take us to get you better, and I will not know until I know much more about you and know what we mean by 'better.' On the other hand, if you don't feel any relief from your symptoms after a certain amount of time — and this is related to how many visits per week you can afford — then I will think there is something wrong with our relationship, or I will think that I'm not the therapist who can best help you with your problem. But there is a period of adjustment to each other within which we ought to be able to find out whether the two of us can help you feel better."

Q. In other words, there is no average length-of-time of treatment?

A. I could make some generalizations if the question were put in the following manner: What is my prediction as to the time it will take if a patient's symptoms are due to relationships with other people, and if we do not have to go back into the patient's childhood and go over all of his past in order to find out about the symptoms?

I am connected with a clinic where we see substantial changes in patients after one and a half to two years of treatment, when the patient is seen twice a week. I have to answer this way because some therapists see patients five times a week and others see them once a week. But unfortunately,

he frequency of treatment is partly determined by the eco-
omic circumstances of the therapist and the patient.

Q. *Can you make any generalizations as to the average cost
of treatment?*

A. In private practice in New York City, the average cost per
session is around fifteen dollars, and the average number of
sessions per week is two or three. In taking a very broad
average, therefore, with a privately practicing psychologist a
patient with the ordinary type of presenting complaint may
expect to spend between thirty and forty-five dollars per
week for a minimum of a year and a half.

Q. *What is the significance of money in treatment?*

A. The most orthodox practitioners believe that therapy is a
kind of contract entered into by the therapist and the patient. The validity of a contract in a free enterprise economy
is determined by the amount of money paid, and it is therefore important, in these practitioners' opinion, to have the
patient recognize the building force of the contract because
he must pay for it.

On the other hand, I am sure the vast majority of therapists have some patients who either do not pay the standard
fee, or do not pay it regularly. I think, however, the question should be, "Should a patient be forced to pay anything,
even if it's only a token payment of, let's say, fifty cents a
session?"

This is difficult to answer because we have little evidence
one way or the other as to what happens with patients who
do not pay as compared to patients who pay. The Veterans
Administration, for example, has achieved results by treating
patients within a framework of government subsidy in
which the patient does not pay directly. One could say, consequently, that unless we are willing to discount the millions
of people who have been treated and helped by the Veterans Administration, the amount of actual transfer of money
from the patient to the therapist does not appear to be an
important item.

The attitude toward money is like an attitude toward anything else. If I have a wealthy patient who admits he is
wealthy and then quibbles about a fee, I would expect to
have to deal with a problem about an attitude toward man-

kind which expresses itself in money. Money becomes impor
tant when we find a personality which has been popularl
characterized as either miserly or spendthrift, or when ther
are fetishes attached to money. The symbolic significance o
money to some people, for example, is that it is dirty anc
unclean. I have had as much trouble with people who thin
money is something undignified to talk about, as I have hac
with people who want to question whether they get thei
money's worth from treatment.

Here again, the personality of the therapist is important
A rigid therapist will have a rigid system of fees. A flexible
personality in the therapist implies a more flexible attitude
toward fees. We all have an annual income toward which
we aim, and we feel we deserve to earn that amount of money when we do the work. It certainly has to be made clear
to the patient that the therapist has his needs, both in terms
of money and in terms of time available.

Q. *What is the best way of finding and choosing a therapist?*
A. This question can be answered in several ways. As a rule,
patients find therapists through the recommendation of the
family physician, or the recommendation of friends who
have been patients of the therapist. Referrals come basically
from these two sources.

The real question is: "How does the patient evaluate the
competence of the person he has selected?" To that question
we have no valid answer at the present time. A patient can
and should check on the training and experience of the therapist through his membership in professional organizations.
But the matter of the selection of the right, competent therapist for a particular patient is a real problem. Granting that
the therapist has the paper qualifications, has been out of
school for a considerable number of years, has had an analytical training beyond that of the Ph.D., or M.D., and has an
affiliation with a professional association which evaluates the
minimum qualifications of practitioners, how does the patient know that the therapist he sees for the first time is going to be the right person for him?

It is the duty of the therapist and the patient to consider
whether they can operate together. A thoroughly experienced
therapist knows his own biases and limitations, and he will

not take a patient with whom he feels he cannot work. In that case, he will simply say to the patient — without any discredit whatsoever to the patient — that he himself is subject to considerable internal pressures and it would be best if the patient went elsewhere for help.

When a therapist deals with a patient who comes from a very religious orthodox Protestant, Jewish or Catholic background, for example, the values of the therapist are bound to come out in what is said in the therapeutic sessions. If these values are going to be offensive to the values of the patient, there is a question as to whether this is the most effective patient-therapist combination the patient can find. I do not mean that every orthodox Catholic or Jewish patient, let us say, must be treated only by orthodox Jewish or Catholic practitioners. I simply mean that the two people, in their initial contacts, will have to explore the areas in which they may come into contact, and if the areas of conflict are relevant to the treatment indicated, the patient ought to seek someone else.

I think it would be very difficult, for example, for a Southern white psychotherapist to deal with a Northern Negro patient unless the therapist himself had examined and sifted his biases and attitudes. As a matter of fact, in New York City the training centers for psychotherapists are beginning to realize that it is important to give trainees cultural and anthropological training as well as training in psychodynamics. When the therapist deals with foreign cultures it becomes necessary to have some feeling for what goes on in the actual life situations of people. We are not all the same. We are a pluralistic society. We must recognize and appreciate the differences in people; they are what make life so exciting.

If we rule out racial, religious, cultural and economic differences, then the question of whether the therapist is the right person for the patient depends upon the needs of the patient. These may include a need for an authoritative therapist instead of a permissive one, or for a male therapist and not a female one, or for a therapist with status instead of a beginner. All of these considerations, and others, are part of the problems the patient brings to treatment, and either they can be worked out with the therapist, or the patient can decide to go to a therapist where any, or all of these will not become a problem. Many patients, for example, say, "I can't discuss my problems with a woman." This is part of the patient's over-all problem, and whether he discusses things with a woman or a man, they will have to come out anyway.

Q. In your opinion, is there a serious conflict between psychotherapy and religion?

A. I think there is an irreconcilable and basic conflict between psychotherapy as a science of personality and organized religion. In therapeutic practice, however, this conflict rarely becomes an issue because the therapist tends to avoid an open discussion of value-conflict areas when they are not related to the symptoms of the patient. As a matter of fact, most of the time these conflict areas do not come up.

Nevertheless, one of the essential elements in human behavior is a need to believe in something, and both psychology and religion believe in belief. The conflict between the two is what each believes in, the kind of belief we have. To me, a belief in the supernatural and the transcendental is inconsistent with the scientific world in which we live. The beliefs that the scientist possesses are in the value of inquiry, in the possibility that one can get facts which are subject to observational agreement, and finally, that the ultimate explanation of phenomena must be material. Thus, when we have these kinds of beliefs as opposed to the religious beliefs, there is an irreconcilable conflict, and of course, I believe that my point of view is right.

Q. Yet, many critics of psychoanalytic theory maintain that psychotherapy is not a science because the basic beliefs and assumptions are not scientifically provable.

A. I disagree with that criticism. I think that what the critics have said about psychoanalysis and psychotherapy is that it has not yet stated its assumptions in such a fashion that they can be scientifically tested. Few critics have said the assumptions themselves are not scientific.

In other words, we have not been able as yet to state our assumptions in such a way that they can be put to a rigid scientific test. But the assumptions we do make do not violate any scientific concepts. One of the areas about which we have had conflict, for example, is Freud's insistence on an instinctual basis for human behavior. The question is: how can we test this belief? How can we test, for example the existence of a concept such as the Oedipal relationship?

Although we do not have a clear answer to this problem at the present time, we are beginning to see from the studies of the animal behaviorists that it is possible to study instinctive behavior from an objectively experimental point of view. It is now a problem to state the Oedipal situation, let us say, in a manner that would allow us to test it. But there is nothing in the Oedipal concept which is non-material. We simply have to find a way of getting therapists to look at their data and to agree upon ways of presenting it so that other scientists can test what therapists have to say.

In short, no one has said that psychoanalytic concepts are untestable. On the other hand, the practitioners of religion say that religious concepts are untestable and have to be accepted in terms of revelation and belief.

Q. *One often hears the comment that psychoanalysts, psychiatrists and psychologists are much too interested in sex. In fact, many laymen seem to believe that "Freud explained everything by sex."*

A. To answer the question about the place of sex in psychoanalytic therapy I must talk about the many varied ways in which Freud used the words "sexual drive." Sexual drive is an English translation of a German word which carries with it many more meanings than our English word "sex."

Freud never talked about the sex drive. He talked about a sexual instinct and then endowed it with an element inseparable from it which he called the "libido." The libido he then defined in terms of almost anything that was constructive, and although genital sexuality (sexual intercourse) is included within the total constructive life force, it is nevertheless only a part of the libido.

Certainly the therapist is concerned with sex because in the relationship between a man and a woman the totality of feelings are expressed. On the other hand, to say that a therapist uses sexual relationships as the sole test of healthy adjustment is not true. Or, to say we believe that biological sex is the cause of all human adjustments and maladjustments is not true either.

The misunderstandings that people have arise in large part because the English word "sex" does not describe what we are talking about. Few people allow themselves to use the word "copulation" freely. But if they did, they could then better understand the total concept of "sex" which includes copulation.

This difficulty of words and language is an over-all problem in the field of psychology. On the one hand, for example, we are accused of using jargon which no one can understand. On the other hand, we are also accused of confusing people because we use popular words in technical senses. I am quite sure that if we could speak in the language of the physicists, where a "half-life," for example, is an incomprehensible concept to anybody on the street and has meaning only to the atomic physicists, we would be far better off in psychology. But unfortunately, we do not have this special language, and consequently, many popular misconceptions have developed.

In addition, I think that one of our difficulties in psychotherapy has been that the dramatists and playwrights, as well as newspaper and magazine writers, have taken hold of psychoanalytic insights and have used and abused them in public presentation. Many of our current writers evidently think that by presenting a case history they automatically present drama, also. In the first place, this is not true artistically. Secondly, the case histories which are presented are so extreme and distorted that it is then assumed that therapists look at human beings in the same extreme and distorted manner.

Q. *Some friendly critics of psychoanalytic theory maintain that what can be said about neurotics and psychotics should not be said about the general population. In other words, everything that the therapist believes is based upon clinical work with mentally ill and disturbed people, but the non-sick population might be quite different.*

A. Each year the Federal Government spends forty-three dollars per case on basic research on cancer. Only thirteen cents is spent by the government on schizophrenia. In view of this fact, the reason for the criticism that we talk about a sick population and not necessarily also about the so-called well population, is apparent. In order for us to investigate the non-patient we need a great deal of money and time. What therapist, for example, can give up half of his practice and spend that time with people who are not sick? The people who are not sick, obviously, are not going to pay to be investigated.

All psychoanalysts, psychiatrists and psychologists would be delighted to be able to answer this criticism and the questions which arise from it. In some senses, we have already found some of the answers. In the matter of dreams, for example, it is often said that patients who come to therapists dream what the therapists want them to dream. But a study was made in which thousands of dreams of college students were recorded, and many of the symbolic things which occurred in the dream lives of patients in treatment were found to be duplicated in the lives of these non-patients. The researcher was a university man who could afford to take the time out to do the necessary work.

The truth is, however, that we do not have at the present time the facts one way or another on most of the important issues that arise in psychotherapy because we do not have the facts on the large group of people we do not and cannot see.

In other words, I am answering this criticism with a plea for more money to be spent on basic research in psychology because this is where we need it the most. I also think that we need another type of research where therapists of different persuasions check their conclusions against each other, because nothing produces boredom as easily as devotion to a theory.

Thank you, Dr. Riess.

46.

"What is group therapy?"
we asked Mr. Slavson.

XXXXXXXXXXXXXXXXXXX

S. R. SLAVSON
Consultant In Group Therapy

In this interview, Mr. Slavson also discusses:

"Does group therapy reach as deeply into the unconscious as individual treatment?"

"Are there different kinds of group therapy?"

"Are children more easily helped in group therapy than adults?"

"Can most of us look at our real feelings without help?"

"What is the essential difference between group therapy and all other types of therapy?"

"How do patients act and react to each other in groups?"

"Are patients reasonable people?"

"What is the 'ego'?"

"Do most men and women really want to change?"

"Can a person know the type of psychotherapy most suitable for himself?"

"What are the costs of group therapy?"

46.

This is what Mr. Slavson said when interviewed in his office:

Q. What is group therapy?

A. Group therapy is a psychotherapeutic process for establishing inner equilibrium in a person. Its special characteristic is that more than two patients are being treated simultaneously, the minimum being three patients who interact with one another. What is more important, they stimulate one another to reveal inadequately repressed memories from the unconscious which generate tensions and create inner turmoil, feelings of guilt and resultant anxieties and hostilities. We call this "interpersonal stimulation," "vicarious catharsis," and "spectator therapy." These processes occur in a group but not in individual treatment. In individual treatment the person has to recall memories out of his own unconscious through his own "free associations." In group psychotherapy a patient can use the free associations of another by identifying with him and by empathy. Such "emotional resonance" aids each individual in reaching his unconscious with much less effort and pain and in a shorter time than he might require in individual treatment.

On the other hand, and because of these processes, patients in group psychotherapy cannot reach quite the same depths of the suppressed layers in the unconscious to examine themselves and work through many of the traumatic experiences and suppressed memories and feelings. The reason for this is twofold: there is the inevitable interference from other patients who cut into the "free association" of one, as their own memories and feelings are activated. Secondly, there are many areas of his life which an individual may find extremely difficult or impossible to expose in the presence of others. Consequently, there are a great number of adult men and women requiring psychotherapy who cannot benefit appreciably from group therapy alone. Some may require exclusive individual therapy while others could gain most from a combination of the two, or "parallel treatment."

Q. *What role does the therapist play in group therapy.*
A. The therapist is the center of the process here as in all other types of therapy. He is the recipient of all of the feeling and fantasies toward parents, both negative and positive. These feelings are usually distorted and exaggerated; they are all projected onto the therapist, a phenomenon that is known in psychoanalysis as "transference."

The value of transference in psychotherapy lies in the fact that the therapist, being a trained person and one who understands what goes on in the mental life of the patient and the hidden significance of what he says (latent meaning), deals with his attitudes and statements in a way that helps the patient clear up confusions and exaggerations and eliminate distortions of reality. The most serious problems with which we are all destined to live stem from distortion of reality, exaggerations in relations and feelings, projections onto others through which we seem to allay our guilts and diminish our anxieties. In patients these are greatly magnified.

In group psychotherapy, the therapist does not play as important a role in aiding the therapeutic process as in individual treatment. The transference is *diluted* because it is divided among the other people in the group. The other patients are also used as targets of hostility and projection rather than only the therapist. Thus, a patient can project his hostile and destructive feelings towards another patient as a substitute for his mother, father, or for his brothers or sisters.

This diluted transference is very helpful for certain patients because their quantum of fear of, and guilt about, their intense hostile feelings toward their parents creates so much anxiety that they cannot bring themselves to direct their hostility toward the therapist, who represents in their unconscious their original parents.

Q. *Are there different kinds of group psychotherapy?*
A. Group psychotherapy with children, for example, is in every regard different from that done with adults. Similarly,

on-psychotic adult patients are treated differently than the psychotic, though there are some common elements in the therapy of psychotic adults and non-psychotic children.

We have developed four types of psychotherapy groups for children: activity, play, activity-interview and transitional groups. Each of these has special techniques and special procedures, and requires specific training on the part of the therapist. The one common element, however, is that in all of them reliance is placed either solely or partially upon the *activity* of the child, rather than on verbal production only. Depending upon the type of problem and age, the sessions are designed to provide children with play or work activities of various kinds. In some there are discussions, too; in others, activity only. In a similar sense, adult groups also function on different levels. Physical activity, however, although not completely eliminated is discouraged and frequently prohibited for adult patients.

There are also four types of adult group therapy: group counseling, group guidance, group psycho-nursing and group psychotherapy.

In group counseling we attempt to help the group members to work through specific problems in their immediate lives, rather than internal conflicts. For example, groups can be employed in vocational counseling, premarital and marital counseling, and parent-child relations. In these groups practical situations are discussed by the group under the guidance of a trained leader who supplies specific advice and information from time to time as it becomes pertinent and necessary to clarify a point that would lead to a better understanding of a situation and how to deal with it.

It is, nevertheless, important that this work be done by psychologically knowledgeable people, because during these discussions some emotionally charged elements are brought out, and to avoid entering into them requires great skill. As a matter of fact, tactful avoidance of arousing strong feelings sometimes requires greater skill than discussing them. In short, in group counseling the person is not deeply involved, for the group members speak only of external situations and how to deal with them.

In group guidance, however, feelings and attitudes are explored. But we do not enter into the background of these in

terms of early childhood experiences and relationships. If a
individual is in constant conflict with his boss, let us say, w
would explore how he *perceives* the boss. Does he see him a
an enemy or a friend? What does his boss stand for in hi
own feelings? Is he a strict father figure, an exploiter, a perso
who takes advantage of his employees?

We would consider all these feelings and attitudes, thereb
helping the individual think them through, separating the rea
from the unreal on a rational, objective basis. However, many
people cannot be objective where authority figures are in
volved. They are too emotional and too set in their feelings
Their conflicts arise from deep-rooted unconscious neuroti
feelings, as a result of which they exaggerate, distort and
project much that is really not there because of their intensity, hostilities and defenses. Some of these people require
individual psychotherapy, while others can be treated in
groups.

In group psychotherapy we help patients to recall childhood
experiences and trace the origins of their intense feelings and
recognize how they relate these to their current life situations.
Although we do not do this as profoundly as in psychoanalysis,
we do retrace the individual's childhood and bring to consciousness what is in the unconscious and the early reactions
which have become ingrained in his psyche and nervous
system. We say that we "work them through"; that is, through
catharsis and communication, thorough interpretation and
conceptualization, the patient begins to understand what he
is doing in the light of what he has done, his new insights and
emotional freedom.

As the name implies, in psycho-nursing, we nurse those
patients along whom we know we cannot help toward permanent change. This process is similar to medical nursing. We
reduce the psychic burdens which are unavoidable and irreversible that a patient carries as a part of life and from which
he cannot escape. His psychologic organization or state of
health does not permit of a permanent or lasting change.
Through psycho-nursing we help him carry the load, and we
supply opportunities for release of feelings of sadness and
tragedy by unburdening himself and being supported by an
understanding, sympathetic person, the therapist. This can be
done more effectively in a group where the members can

hare their troubles and find support in one another. An an-
ient Hebrew adage says, "The anguish of the many is half
ur consolation." I have suggested the term "universalization"
or this experience, for relief comes to an individual when
here is sharing and revelation in a group.

The senile are an example of persons who need psycho-
ursing rather than psychotherapy. As a matter of fact, clubs
nd centers for the old are actually intended for it, although
hey usually do not define their work in such terms. Patients
f all ages with physical or psychological handicaps, the men-
ally deficient, the seriously ill or dying patients who may need
sychological attention are candidates for psycho-nursing.

Psychotherapy is the only process of those outlined which
ims at basically changing *the inner being* of persons so that
hey can get hold of their lives and live in accordance with
eality. In counseling, guidance and psycho-nursing, such basic
hanges cannot be achieved. Persons undergoing these experi-
nces leave them the same as they came, though they are
etter able to deal with specific problems or situations. Should
hey meet up later with difficulties either of a similar or dif-
erent nature, they will once again require help. But in psycho-
herapy, our aim is to make the patient strong enough and
elf-reliant enough to satisfactorily deal with any stressful sit-
ation which may arise in the future. As to the extent to
vhich we succeed in doing it, of course, that is another matter.

Q. *In the context of your previous answer, is it possible for
you to say what type of person is most suitable for group
psychotherapy?*

A. Group psychotherapy addresses itself predominantly to the
ego rather than to the libido. As a matter of fact, this is the
pivotal difference between psychoanalysis and group psychotherapy.

The group provides to patients an arena for action as much
as an arena of introspection. In classical psychoanalysis, for
example, only introspection is employed. The field of action
is outside of the therapeutic situation. The patient brings for
analysis his feelings, actions and reactions as he experiences
them in his daily life. In the group, the patient cannot only
talk about these, but he also can act them out. He need not
just talk about hostilities; he can also attack fellow patients

and the therapist. These actions then become the subjects fc examination by the other members of the group, and if nece sary, by the therapist.

.Also, in the group patients react directly to each other behavior and pronouncements, thereby creating an action - interaction process. Here, there is not only examination c feelings and behavior, but also a revelation of the person i action. Thus, his character, or what we term, his ego functior ing, is laid bare to the group and to himself through th reactions to him by the others. We call this "mirror reaction.

We place in groups patients who are socially maladjustec because of character disorders, that is, where the ego functior ing is unsuitable to the life situations with which the individua is faced. Patients with mild neurotic states are suitable fo group psychotherapy, but not true or massive psychoneurotic whose problems stem from sexual disturbances or who suffe: from massive trauma of a deep or profound nature. These re quire individual psychoanalysis or psychoanalytically orientec individual psychotherapy.

There are adults and adolescents who need a preliminary group therapy experience before individual treatment can be effective, because this preliminary group experience "loosens up" their rigid defenses and allows them to express hostile and murderous feelings without guilt or fear. Without such a preliminary group experience, they would be inaccessible to individual treatment. On the other hand, there are patients who cannot face a group because of the great discomfort and uncontrollable hostilities they feel toward groups (as family substitutes) and their fear of revealing themselves to others. The anxieties which early family relations have created in many individuals who seek out psychotherapy are so intense as to make participation in groups quite impossible for them. They often have developed specific fears of multiple relations and, although they can sustain individual relations, they be- come very disturbed in groups. Such patients require varying periods of individual therapy to work through their fears. They then should be placed in groups, preferably with the same therapist, to work through their social-phobic states.

Q. *What is specifically meant by the term "ego?"*

A. The ego is the understanding, selective, integrative, planning, administrative and executive function of the psyche. It operates toward the outside world and within the personality of the individual. It regulates feelings, deals with frustrations, controls tempers. The ego also mobilizes the individual's powers for action, directs them toward a chosen goal and selects suitable means for achieving the goal. The intellect is an instrument of the ego. In group psychotherapy the ego is more involved than in individual treatment and for patients with psychogenic ego deficiencies, group treatment is the treatment of choice.

The ego is derived basically from the bio-chemical processes of the body, or soma, but its pattern, strength and functioning are determined by imitation, identification and internalization of the parents' attitudes and behavior. Later, cultural values and practices and national patterns of conduct and responses are added to these early impressions. If, for example, a child is constantly exposed to a parent's loss of temper, or his or her becoming easily upset and panicky in a difficulty, the child's ego will be shaped by these. He will model himself after the parent and grow up to be irascible and intolerant, fearful or aggressive. That is, his ego controls and judgments will be weak.

Group psychotherapy, in a sense, acts as a substitute family. It accepts and mirrors the patient's behavior. The therapist demonstrates by his impassive, calm and controlled conduct how one should behave in a difficulty. The patient accepts the corrections and the code of the group because he is convinced that they are trying to help him rather than being critical and punitive. As he understands this and controls his feelings and behavior, his ego is modified and strengthened.

Q. *What can a patient reasonably expect from group psychotherapy?*

A. Every patient who seeks help expects to rid himself of his troubles and suffering. At the same time, he violently struggles against changing his personality. All psychotherapy is faced with this problem, and the therapist must skillfully break through the patient's resistance to change. Unconsciously, everyone wants to remain as he is. This is a reasonable wish because the individual does not know what he will become when and if he changes. This tenacious holding on to his neurosis or special character is partly a result of his need for security. The only security the patient has in the giving up of some of his characteristics, neurotic though they may be, lies in the interest which the therapist has in the patient and of which he must be sure. This attitude is what is called "positive transference."

But patients are not reasonable. If they were, they wouldn't be patients. Consequently, although all of them wish and expect to feel and to be better, there are nevertheless limits to the goals we can realistically set for any given patient. In this connection, a note of warning has to be sounded. There is a comparatively small percentage of adult patients who can be "cured" or fundamentally helped by group psychotherapy. My estimate is about twenty percent of the adult patients can benefit from it, which is nevertheless a very large number of people. The suitability of children and adolescents is perhaps four times that percentage, because of the malleable nature of the child and his capacity for personality modification.

Nonetheless, there seems to be a tendency at the present time for many prospective patients to seek group psychotherapy quite on their own. People constantly inquire about this type of treatment. But from what we have already said it should be obvious that the choice of suitable treatment for any given patient can be made only on a diagnostic basis, requiring an investigation by a qualified psychotherapist before a choice of treatment can be determined. An individual cannot refer himself to groups. The inquiries are usually somewhat like, "I would like to have group psychotherapy. To whom shall I go?" Our answer usually is, "Did you ever prescribe medicine for yourself?" We might also add that not infrequently some persons who seek treatment by a group are unconsciously attempting to evade the rigors of psychotherapy by escaping them through a group.

Q. *Why is group psychotherapy so much more applicable to children than to adults?*

A. When you work with clay and the clay is still soft and moist, you can easily mold it and shape it; once the clay hardens, you have to use a chisel and then rough edges remain. The adult personality is similar to the hardened clay. It is rigid. It has established psychological and neurological networks of engrams or configurations and conditionings and habits of behavior and responses that give each his specific defenses, his preferences and prejudices which have become organized and structured into an integral part of himself. A chief characteristic of neuroses is their persistence and autonomy and their extreme resistance to change. Patients, therefore, resist change even more rigidly than does the average person. Children, on the other hand, make experience a part of themselves. They are in a constant flux of change and gain immeasurably more from properly applied group psychotherapy than adults ever can. And change in children is basic and fundamental.

Psychotherapy is very effective with children, and with adults only when they become children in the process of therapy. In other words, adults must regress. They have to become children, and the therapist their parent. As long as they hold on to their rigidities (resistance), they are inaccessible to treatment. The couch universally employed in real psychoanalysis serves the purpose of regression. While originally introduced by Freud as a means of avoiding facing patients for ten hours a day, it was discovered that the prone position caused regression in patients, that is, they more easily returned to a state akin to childhood. This immeasurably aided in the process of therapy. Regression is the rule also in other therapies, but it occurs differently and on lesser levels.

Children are naturally susceptible to change. They are malleable and take on whatever the environment around them favors. In addition, to be in groups is part of the self-preservative instinct in all of us, but in children this instinct operates much more strongly than in adults. In effect, groups are the most natural therapeutic instrument for most child-patients.

Q. *What are the advantages of group psychotherapy for the general population?*

A. As I have already implied, a great number of people, though not requiring profound psychoanalytic treatment in which the unconscious is probed, overreact to life situations and create difficulties and tragedy for others. By becoming aware of their behavior and their effect on others, they can recondition themselves. This, of course, can be achieved by persons with sufficient ego strengths, and when such persons alter their conduct and gain insight into their customary behavior, their personalities improve and they are easier on their families, colleagues and neighbors. By helping people to affect such changes, group psychotherapy can be of great service to the community. As to society as a whole — the application of group therapy principles to dealing with personnel in industry, in education, in government, in recreation, and in family and marital guidance has proved of great benefit. Group therapy has been used with varying degrees of success in the treatment of alcoholics, drug addicts, criminals and delinquents as well.

Q. *What are the costs of group therapy?*

A. In community clinics fees are set according to income of the patients. It is available free or for as little as fifty cents a session. Some psychotherapists charge fifteen dollars per session. I would say, however, that the average fee in private practice is from five to seven and a half dollars per session.

Thank you, Mr. Slavson.

7. ABOUT THE CONTRIBUTORS

EDMUND BERGLER, M.D. — (1900–1962)

A psychoanalyst in private practice, Dr. Bergler was a graduate of the Medical School of the University of Vienna. He was on the staff of the Psychoanalytic Freud-Clinic in Vienna from 1927 to 1937, serving as assistant director the last four years.

He was lecturer at the Psychoanalytic Institute in New York from 1942 to 1945. He held membership in various psychoanalytic and psychiatric societies and published many books and studies on the theory and therapy of neurosis.

Among Dr. Bergler's books are: "The Basic Neurosis", "Principles of Self-Damage", "One Thousand Homosexuals", "Homosexuality: Disease or Way of Life?", "Counterfeit-Sex", "The Revolt of the Middle Aged Man", "The Writer and Psychoanalysis", and "Divorce Won't Help". His most recent book was "Curable and Incurable Neurotics".

H. ROBERT BLANK, M.D.

Contributing editor of The Psychoanalytic Quarterly, Dr. Blank has had as his chief research interest the psychological problems of the physically handicapped child and adult, particularly the blind. He is in private practice.

He conducted a series of lecture seminars in Israel in 1960 on "Psychological Problems of the Physically Handicapped" and "The Multidisciplinary Treatment Team in Rehabilitation".

He is attending psychiatrist at Grasslands Hospital, Valhalla, New York. He has contributed to many professional journals and books, and his professional memberships include: consultant to the Family Service of Westchester and the American Israeli Lighthouse; fellow, American Psychiatric Association; fellow, American Orthopsychiatric Association; fellow, Academy of Child Psychiatry, and member, American Psychoanalytic Association.

SMILEY BLANTON, M.D.

Associate founder and director of the American Foundation of Religion and Psychiatry, Dr. Blanton worked with Sigmund Freud in Vienna and London during the 1930's. He is in private practice.

Dr. Blanton is a diplomate of the American Board of Psychiatry and Neurology, and associate professor (Emeritus) of clinical psychiatry at Vanderbilt University College of Medicine, Nashville, Tenn. He has contributed many articles to professional and popular magazines, and his published books include: "Love Or Perish", "Now Or Never — The Promise of the Middle Years", "The Healing Power of Poetry", and, with his wife, Margaret Gray Blanton, "Speech Training For Children", "Child Guidance", and, "For Stutterers". In addition, he has written with Norman Vincent Peale, "Faith Is The Answer", and "The Art Of Real Happiness".

RALPH MANNING CROWLEY, M.D.

Fellow and supervising and training psychoanalyst of the William Alanson White Institute of Psychiatry, Psychoanalysis and Psychology, Dr. Crowley's professional memberships include: charter fellow, Academy of Psychoanalysis; fellow, American Psychiatric Association; member, American Psychoanalytic Association; member, William Alanson White Psychoanalytic Society; member, The Association for Psychoanalytic Medicine, and, member, The International Psychoanalytic Association. He is in private practice.

Including among Dr. Crowley's many published journal articles are "Psychoses with Myxedem", "A Low Cost Psychoanalytic Service: First Year", "Human Reactions of Analysts to Patients", "Clinical Research in Psychoanalytic Treatment — Some Experiences and Points of View", and, "The Role of a Psychoanalyst in a Psychoanalysis".

GEORGE DEVEREUX, PH.D.

Professor of research in Ethnopsychiatry at Temple University School of Medicine, Dr. Devereux is also lecturer in Anthropology at Columbia University. He is in private practice.

His professional memberships include: The American Anthropological Association, the American Ethnological Society, the American Psychological Association, the New York State Psychological Association, the New York Society of Clinical Psychologists and the Philadelphia Association for Psychoanalysis.

Dr. Devereux has carried out field work among American Indians, Melanesians, pygmies in Papua, New Guinea, and the Moi of Indochina. He has held fellowships, scholarships and research grants from the Rockefeller Foundation, Harvard University, the National Institute of Mental Health and other organizations.

In addition to two hundred papers in professional journals, Dr. Devereux is the author of "Reality and Dreams: The Psychotherapy of a Plains Indian", "A Study of Abortion In Primitive Societies", and "Therapeutic Education".

LUDWIG EIDELBERG, M.D.

Clinical professor of psychiatry, Department of Psychiatry, State University of New York, Downstate Medical Center, Dr. Eidelberg is the author of "The Dark Urge" and "Take Off Your Mask", both of which have been translated into foreign editions. He has also written many articles and books for both general and professional audiences. He is in private practice.

Dr. Eidelberg's works in progress include the book, "How Not To Treat Neurotics", and he is editor-in-chief of the forthcoming "Psychoanalytic Dictionary". He has been chief of the Psychiatric Clinic of Mount Sinai Hospital, New York, and president of the Psychoanalytic Association of New York.

JAN EHRENWALD, M.D.

Attending psychiatrist, chief, Adult Psychiatric Outpatient Department, The Roosevelt Hospital, New York, Dr. Ehrenwald is the author of "From Medicine Man To Freud", "New Dimensions of Deep Analysis" and "Telepathy and Medical Psychology". He is in private practice.

MORTON M. GOLDEN, M.D.

A psychoanalyst and president-elect of the Brooklyn Psychiatric Society, Dr. Golden is the training program director,

Psychiatric Education of Physicians, Kings County Medical Society. He is in private practice.

Member of the American Psychoanalytic Association, Dr. Golden is also a diplomate, American Board of Psychiatry, the editor of "Suggestions For the Management of Emotional Problems Encountered In Private Practice", and psychiatric consultant to the New York City Board of Education and the Brooklyn Psychiatric Centers.

ALVIN I. GOLDFARB, M.D.

Chief, Department of Psychiatry and Neurology, The Hospital and Home for Aged and Infirm Hebrews, New York, Dr. Goldfarb is consultant on Special Services for the Aged, Department of Mental Hygiene, State of New York. He is in private practice.

He is associate professor, New York School of Psychiatry, associate professor and associate attending psychiatrist, New York Medical College, assistant attending psychiatrist, Mount Sinai Hospital, New York, and chairman of the Committee on Aging, Group for the Advancement of Psychiatry.

Dr. Goldfarb's professional memberships include: member, American Psychiatric Association; member, American Medical Association and fellow, American Acedemy of Neurology.

HAROLD GREENWALD, PH.D.

Faculty member, Training Institute, National Psychological Association For Psychoanalysis, Dr. Greenwald is the author of "The Call Girl, A Social and Psychological Study", and, with Lucy Freeman, "Emotional Maturity In Love And Marriage", and editor of "Great Cases In Psychoanalysis". He is in private practice.

His professional memberships include: past president, Association For Applied Psychoanalysis; member, American Group Therapy Association; member, American Psychological Association, and, member, Association for Clinical Experimental Hypnosis. He has also been director, Group Therapy, Stuyvesant Polyclinic Hospital, New York.

MARTIN GROTJAHN, M.D.

Training analyst, Institute for Psychoanalytic Medicine of Southern California, and clinical professor of psychiatry at the University of Southern California, Dr. Grotjahn is the author of "Beyond Laughter" and "Psychoanalysis and Family Neurosis".

He has also written numerous scientific papers on psychoanalysis, therapy, psychoses, the family, and humor. He is in private practice.

MELVIN HERMAN

Executive Secretary of the National Association of Private Psychiatric Hospitals, Mr. Herman serves as editorial consultant and writer for hospital and medical journals. His interest in this field developed during the Second World War when he was assigned for a year to write a weekly radio show at Welch Convalescent Hospital, an Army hospital at Daytona Beach, Florida.

Educated at Columbia University and New York University, he has worked on the editorial staff of several magazines, on the Brooklyn Daily Eagle, at the J. Walter Thompson Advertising Agency and as a public relations counsellor.

WILFRED C. HULSE, M.D. — (1901–1962)

Chief of the psychiatric staff, Foster Care Division, Bureau of Child Welfare, City of New York, Dr. Hulse was associate attending psychiatrist at Mount Sinai Hospital, New York, and psychiatrist for the Jewish Guild For The Blind and Sheltering Arms Children's Service. He was in private practice.

Dr. Hulse was also associate clinical professor of psychiatry at Albert Einstein College of Medicine and co-author with Lucy Freeman of "Children Who Kill". His professional interests and specialties included child psychiatry, psychoanalytic psychotherapy and group psychotherapy.

PAUL KAY, M.D.

Assistant clinical professor, Department of Psychiatry, State University of New York, Downstate Medical Center, Dr. Kay is adjunct attending psychiatrist at Hillside Hospital, Queens, New York, and co-author of "Suicidal Behavior in Adolescents". He is in private practice.

Dr. Kay's specialty is child psychiatry. His professional work includes the training of residents in child and adult psychiatry. He is a member of the Psychoanalytic Association of New York and assistant attending psychiatrist, Pediatric Psychiatry, North Shore Hospital, Manhasset, New York.

HENRIETTE KLEIN, M.D.

Clinical professor of psychiatry, College of Physicians and Surgeons, Columbia University, Dr. Klein is a member of numerous professional organizations, including the American Psychoanalytic Association and the American Psychiatric Association. Currently she is president of the New York Society for Clinical Psychiatry (New York County District Branch, American Psychiatric Association), the first time in its forty-one year history that the Society has elected a woman to this office. Dr. Klein is in private practice.

She has written numerous articles and been co-author of others, covering a range of interests including "Nursing Behavior" and "Psychosexual Factors in the Paranoid Phenomena." Her interest in teaching and training is reflected in "A Development in Psychoanalytic Training," Chapter I of the book, "Changing Concepts of Psychoanalytic Medicine."

PETER LADERMAN, M.D.

Member of the Association for Psychoanalytic Medicine, Dr. Laderman is a psychoanalyst in private practice. He is consultant psychiatrist, Board of Cooperative Educational Services, District number 2, Westchester County, New York.

Dr. Laderman is also a member, Westchester Psychoanalytic Society; member, Association for Psychoanalytic Medicine and fellow, American Psychiatric Association.

RHODA L. LORAND, PH.D.

Psychologist, specializing in the psychoanalytic treatment of children and adolescents, Dr. Lorand was formerly clinical psychologist and child psychotherapist, Department of Psychiatry, Vanderbilt Clinic, Presbyterian Hospital, New York.

She is author of "Therapy of Learning Problems," a chapter in "Adolescents: Psychoanalytic Approach to Problems and Therapy," and is currently writing a book on learning problems. She is in private practice.

Dr. Lorand is a member of the American Psychological

Association, the New York State Psychological Association
and the International Council of Psychologists.

SANDOR LORAND, M.D.

Honorary president of the Psychoanalytic Association of
New York, Dr. Lorand is past president of the New York
Psychoanalytic Society and Institute. He is in private prac-
tice.

He founded and organized in 1948 the Division of Psychoanalytic Education, State University of the New York College of Medicine, for teaching psychoanalysis and training
psychiatrists in psychoanalysis. He was the director of this
division and, up to 1960, professor of Clinical Psychiatry at
the University.

Among his books are, "Technique of Psychoanalytic Therapy", "Perversions, Psychodynamics and Therapy," which he
edited with Michael Balint, and "Adolescents: Psychoanalytic
Approach to Problems and Therapy," which he edited with
Dr. Henry Schneer. His scientific contributions and books
have been translated into many foreign languages.

NORMAN LOURIE

Deputy secretary, Pennsylvania Department of Public Welfare, Mr. Lourie is president of the National Association of
Social Workers.

He has contributed to many professional journals, books
and conferences. His most recent publication on children in
trouble appeared in "Values and Ideals of American Youth".
His professional memberships include: fellow, American Orthopsychiatric Association and board member, Child Welfare
League of America.

SOLOMON MACHOVER, PH.D.

Chief psychologist, Kings County Hospital, Brooklyn, New
York, Dr. Machover is also professor, Department of Psy-
chiatry, State University of New York, Downstate Medical
Center. He is in private practice.

His professional memberships include: diplomate, American Board of Examiners in Professional Psychology; fellow,
American Psychological Association; past president, Brooklyn

Psychological Association and member, American Academy of Psychotherapists.

Formerly professor, Division of Graduate Studies, Brooklyn College, Dr. Machover is co-director, Mental Health Education Project, Research Foundation, State University of New York, and research consultant, State University Alcohol Clinic, Downstate Medical Center.

Preston G. McLean, M.D.

A teacher at the American Foundation of Religion and Psychiatry, Dr. McLean is also a training and supervising analyst for the National Psychological Association for Psychoanalysis.

Among his published work is "Psychiatry and Philosophy" in "The American Handbook of Psychiatry". His teaching courses include seminars in "Masochism", "Character and Affect", and "Theory of Organism". He is in private practice.

Leo L. Orenstein, M.D.

Associate clinical professor, Department of Psychiatry and Neurology, New York University School of Medicine, Dr. Orenstein is the author of numerous publications in the fields of psychiatry and criminology. He was formerly psychiatrist-in-charge, Psychiatric Clinic, Court of General Sessions, New York City.

His professional memberships include: member, International Psychoanalytic Association; member, American Psychoanalytic Association, and fellow, American Psychiatric Association. He is in private practice.

Geraldine Pederson-Krag, M.D.

Medical director, Huntington Township Mental Health Clinic, Dr. Pederson-Krag is the author of "Personality Factors in Work and Employment" and numerous articles in the "Psychoanalytic Quarterly" and other scientific publications.

Her professional memberships include membership in the American Psychoanalytic Association. She is interested in the application of psychoanalysis to modern living and to literature. She is in private practice.

Phillip Polatin, M.D.

Professor of clinical psychiatry, College of Physicians and Surgeons, Columbia University, Dr. Polatin is also the clinical director, New York Psychiatric Institute, and attending psychiatrist, Presbyterian Hospital, Columbia-Presbyterian Medical Center.

Co-author with his wife, Ellen C. Philtine, he has written "How Psychiatry Helps", "The Well Adjusted Personality" and "Marriage In The Modern World".

Dr. Polatin is a psychoanalyst, a psychiatrist, a teacher, a research worker, a hospital administrator, a consultant and a therapist. His private practice is limited to consultations.

THEODOR REIK, PH.D.

Founder and honorary president of the National Psychological Association for Psychoanalysis, Dr. Reik was a student of Freud. He is a diplomate of the American Psychological Association.

In recent years, he has been particularly interested in archaeological psychoanalysis, especially research in early Semitic civilizations. At present his professional practice includes private consultations and the training of psychoanalysts.

Dr. Reik has contributed to many professional publications. Among his books are "Listening With The Third Ear", "From Thirty Years With Freud", "The Secret Self", "The Haunting Melody", "The Search Within", "The Psychology of Sex Relations", "Surprise and the Psychoanalyst", "Masochism In Modern Man", "Of Love and Lust", "Sex In Man and Woman: Its Emotional Variations" and "The Ritual", with a preface by Freud.

BERNARD F. RIESS, PH.D.

Chairman of the Research Department, Postgraduate Center for Psychotherapy, New York, Dr. Riess is president-elect of the New York State Psychological Association, and editor of the "International Newsletter In Mental Health Research."

His professional memberships include: diplomate in clinical psychology, American Board of Examiners in Professional Psychology; member, American Psychological Association; member, American Academy of Psychotherapy; member, American Orthopsychiatric Association; member, International Council of Psychotherapists and member, American Association for the Advancement of Science, New York Academy of Medicine.

Former associate professor of psychology, Hunter College, Dr. Riess is co-editor of the biennial series "Progress in Clinical Psychology". Including in his research work is the personality analysis of psychotherapists in training. He is in private practice.

LEWIS L. ROBBINS, M.D.

Medical Director, Hillside Hospital, Queens, New York, Dr. Robbins' professional memberships include: member, American Psychiatric Association; member, American Psychoanalytic Association and member, American College of Physicians.

SAUL SCHEIDLINGER, PH.D.

Group therapy consultant, Community Service Society, New York, Dr. Scheidlinger is the author of "Psychoanalysis and Group Behavior" and has written numerous articles for professional publications dealing with child psychology and group psychotherapy.

His professional memberships include: fellow, American Psychological Association; fellow, American Orthopsychiatric Association; fellow, American Group Psychotherapy Association and member, National Association of Social Workers. Child psychotherapy, group therapy of children and adults and group dynamics are among his professional interests and specialties. He is in private practice.

HENRY I. SCHNEER, M.D.

Associate professor of psychiatry, Department of Psychiatry, State University of New York, Downstate Medical Center, Dr. Schneer is co-editor of "Adolescents: A Psychoanalytic Approach To Problems and Therapy". He is in private practice.

Dr. Schneer teaches case seminars in "The Psychotherapy of Adolescents" to psychiatrists training to be psychoanalysts. He is director of the Division of Child and Adolescent Psychiatry at the Downstate Medical Center. His professional memberships include: fellow, American Psychiatric Association; diplomate, American Board of Psychiatry and Neurology and member, American Psychoanalytic Association.

S. R. SLAVSON

Consultant in group psychotherapy, Mr. Slavson is the founder and first president of the American Group Psychotherapy Association, founder and editor (1950-1960) of the International Journal of Group Psychotherapy, and co-president of the International Council of Group Psychotherapy.

Author of numerous contributions to professional journals and chapters in books, Mr. Slavson wrote "Introduction To Group Psychotherapy", "Analytic Group Psychotherapy", "Child-Centered Group Guidance of Parents", "The Practice of Group Therapy", "The Fields of Group Psychotherapy", among others. His latest book is "A Textbook in Analytic Group Psychotherapy."

Formerly on the faculty of New York University, Yeshiva University and Springfield College, Mr. Slavson's current work includes being director of the Evaluation Project in Group Psychotherapy for the Treatment of Delinquency, Children's Village, Dobbs Ferry, New York.

OTTO E. SPERLING, M.D.

Clinical associate professor of Psychiatry, Department of Psychiatry, State University of New York, Downstate Medical Center, Dr. Sperling is consultant in psychiatry at Hillside Hospital, Queens, New York, consultant in neuropsychiatry at the Jewish Hospital of Brooklyn and consultant in psychiatry at the Veterans Hospital, Northport, New York.

Vice-president of The Psychoanalytic Association of New York, he is a training analyst and supervisor of the Division of Psychoanalytic Education, State University of New York, Downstate Medical Center. His professional memberships include: fellow, American Academy of Child Psychiatry; fellow, American Psychiatric Association; member, American Psychoanalytic Association; member, New York Psychoanalytic Association, and member, American Psychosomatic Society.

Dr. Sperling, who is in private practice, is the author of many articles in scientific journals.

HYMAN SPOTNITZ, M.D.

Fellow of the American Psychiatric Association, Dr. Spotnitz is the author of "The Couch and the Circle", and many published papers on psychoanalytic psychiatry, group psycho-therapy and neurology. He is in private practice.

His professional memberships include: fellow, American Association for the Advancement of Science; fellow, American Orthopsychiatric Association; fellow, American Group Psychotherapy Association; fellow, New York Academy of Medicine; fellow, New York Academy of Sciences and fellow, American Society of Psychoanalytic Physicians.

Former consultant psychiatrist to the Jewish Board of Guardians, New York, Dr. Spotnitz is interested in research in the psychotherapy of severe psychiatric disorders. He is a member of the American Medical Association, the Association for Research in Nervous and Mental Diseases, the American Psychosomatic Society, the Neurological Society and the New York Society for Clinical Psychiatry.

CORNELIA B. WILBUR, M.D.

Clinical director, Falkirk Hospital, Central Valley, New York, Dr. Wilbur is a member of the Research Committee of the Society of Medical Psychoanalysts who have recently published the results of nine years of research on male homosexuality under the title, "Homosexuality, A Psychoanalytic Study of Male Homosexuals". She is in private practice.

A vice-president of the National Association of Private Psychiatric Hospitals, Dr. Wilbur was graduated from the University of Michigan College of Medicine and received her psychoanalytic training in New York City. She has long been interested in the care of the mentally ill, and has served as an officer on committees of various psychiatric and psychoanalytic societies as well as an advisor to the Joint Legislative Committee on Health Insurance of the New York State Legislature.

An explosively realistic novel of cruelty, rebellion, and death.

STOCKADE

By JACK PEARL

75133 / 75¢

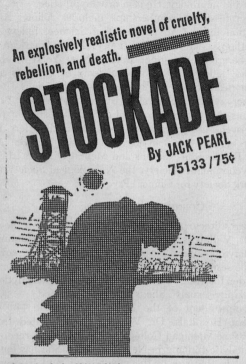

Other books by JACK PEARL:

ROBIN AND THE 7 HOODS.............50033/50¢
THE YELLOW ROLLS-ROYCE..........50143/50¢
OUR MAN FLINT............................50243/50¢

If your bookseller does not have these titles, you may order them by sending retail price, plus 10¢ for mailing and handling to: MAIL SERVICE DEPARTMENT, Pocket Books, Inc., 1 W. 39th St., New York, N. Y. 10018. Not responsible for orders containing cash. Please send check or money order.

Published by POCKET BOOKS, INC.